MRS. RUGGIERI

Life Skills Health

PEARSON

AGS Globe

Shoreview, MN

Photo credits for this textbook can be found on page 555.

The publisher wishes to thank the following educators for their helpful comments during the review process for *Life Skills Health*. Their assistance has been invaluable.

Heidi Ann Coe, SELPA Program Specialist, Morongo Unified School District, 29 Palms, CA; **Susan G. Helman,** Special Education Teacher, Alma High School, Alma, MI; **Alva Jones, Ed.S.,** Educational Consultant, Evans, GA; **Russell Laya,** Special Education Teacher, Roy Miller High School, Corpus Christi, TX; **Deik Maxwell, M.S., M.A.,** Department Chair of Special Education, R. Rex Parris High School, Palmdale, CA; **Brenda P. Seigler,** ESE Teacher, Mandarin High School, Jacksonville, FL

Publisher's Project Staff

Vice President of Curriculum and Publisher: Sari Follansbee, Ed. D.; Director of Curriculum Development: Teri Mathews; Managing Editor: Julie Maas; Senior Editor: Jody Peterson; Development Assistant: Bev Johnson; Director of Creative Services: Nancy Condon; Senior Designer: Diane McCarty; Project Coordinator/Designer: Jen Willman; Purchasing Agent: Mary Kaye Kuzma; Product Manager–Curriculum: Brian Holl

ISBN 0-7854-4133-6

A 0 9 8 7 6 5 4 3

PEARSON
AGS Globe

1-800-328-2560
www.agsglobe.com

Contents

How to Use This Book: A Study Guide

Welcome to the study of health. Everyone wants to have good health and wellness. Studying health helps us learn ways to promote wellness. It helps us identify causes of health problems and ways to prevent them.

As you read this book, you will learn about promoting emotional, physical, and social health.

How to Study

◆ Plan a regular time to study.

◆ Study in a quiet place with good lighting where you will not be distracted.

◆ Gather all the books, pencils, and paper you need to complete your assignments.

◆ Decide on a goal. For example: "I will finish reading and taking notes on Chapter 1, Lesson 1, by 8:00."

◆ Take a 5- to 10-minute break every hour to keep alert.

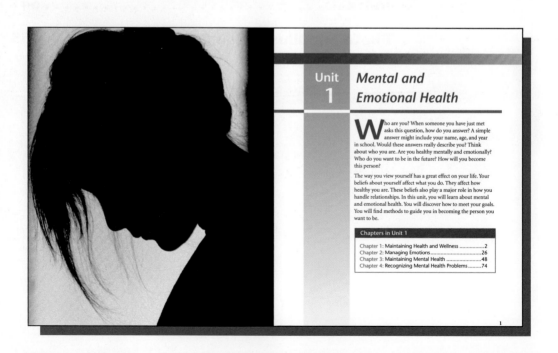

Before Beginning Each Unit

◆ Read the title and the opening text.
◆ Study the photograph. What does it say to you about health?
◆ Read the titles of the chapters in the unit.
◆ Look at the headings of the lessons and paragraphs to help you locate main ideas.
◆ Read the chapter and unit summaries to help you identify key issues.

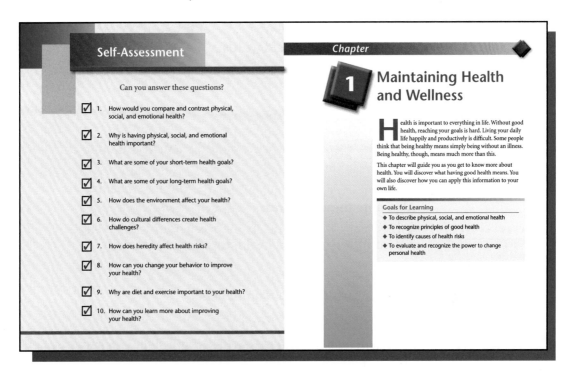

Self-Assessment

Can you answer these questions?

☑ 1. How would you compare and contrast physical, social, and emotional health?

☑ 2. Why is having physical, social, and emotional health important?

☑ 3. What are some of your short-term health goals?

☑ 4. What are some of your long-term health goals?

☑ 5. How does the environment affect your health?

☑ 6. How do cultural differences create health challenges?

☑ 7. How does heredity affect health risks?

☑ 8. How can you change your behavior to improve your health?

☑ 9. Why are diet and exercise important to your health?

☑ 10. How can you learn more about improving your health?

Chapter

1 Maintaining Health and Wellness

Health is important to everything in life. Without good health, reaching your goals is hard. Living your daily life happily and productively is difficult. Some people think that being healthy means simply being without an illness. Being healthy, though, means much more than this.

This chapter will guide you as you get to know more about health. You will discover what having good health means. You will also discover how you can apply this information to your own life.

Goals for Learning

◆ To describe physical, social, and emotional health
◆ To recognize principles of good health
◆ To identify causes of health risks
◆ To evaluate and recognize the power to change personal health

Before Beginning Each Chapter

◆ Read the chapter title.
◆ Take the Self-Assessment to rate your knowledge of that health topic.
◆ Study the goals for learning. The chapter review and tests will ask questions related to these goals.

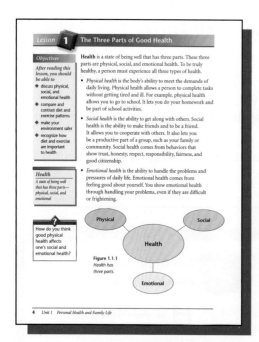

Before Beginning Each Lesson

Read the lesson title and restate it in the form of a question. For example:

Read: Lesson 1 The Three Parts of Good Health
Write: What are the three parts of good health?

Look over the entire lesson, noting:

◆ objectives ◆ text organization
◆ figures ◆ questions in the margins
◆ tables ◆ lesson review
◆ bold words

Also note these features:

Health in Your Life — A description of how a health topic applies to you

Health at Work — A health career and its requirements

Decide for Yourself — A topic that allows you to practice health skills you have learned

Health Myth — A correction of a false statement that many people think is true

Link to — A subject such as math or literature related to the chapter topic

Technology and Society — A technological advance related to the chapter topic

An exercise on researching and writing about a health topic

 Note: A short fact or tip about health, fitness, or nutrition

 Application Question: A question linking the text and your life

 A widespread real-life health problem and its possible solutions

As You Read the Lesson

◆ Read the lesson headings. The subheads are questions.
◆ Read the paragraphs that follow to answer the question.
◆ Before moving on to the next heading, see if you can answer the question. If you cannot, reread the section to look for the answers.

Using the Bold Words

Wellness
An active state of health

Knowing the meaning of all the boxed words in the left column will help you understand what you read. These words appear in **bold** type the first time they appear in the text and are defined in the paragraph.

Wellness is an active state of health.

All of the words in the left column are also defined in the Glossary.

Wellness (wel´ nis) An active state of health (p. 9)

Taking Notes

Taking notes during class and as you read this book is helpful.

◆ Use headings to label the main sections of your notes.

◆ Summarize the important information, such as main ideas and supporting details.

◆ Use short phrases.

◆ Use your own words to describe, explain, or define things.

◆ Try taking notes using a three-column format. Use the first column to write headings or vocabulary words. Use the middle column to write the main information. Use the last column to draw diagrams, write questions, record homework assignments, or for other purposes.

◆ Right after taking notes, review them to fill in possible gaps.

Vocabulary	Definition	Additional information
Health	A state of being that has three parts	The three parts of health are physical, social, and emotional

Preparing for Tests

The Summaries and Reviews for lessons, chapters, and units can help you prepare to take tests.

◆ Read the summaries from your text to make sure you understand the chapter's and unit's main ideas.

◆ Make up a sample test of items you think may be on the test. You may want to do this with a classmate and share your questions.

◆ Review your notes and test yourself on words and key ideas.

◆ Practice writing about some of the main ideas from the chapter or unit.

◆ Answer the questions under Vocabulary Review.

◆ Answer the questions under Concept Review.

◆ Write what you think about the questions under Critical Thinking.

Using the Test-Taking Tip

Read the Test-Taking Tip with each Chapter Review of the text.

 Test-Taking Tip After you have completed a test, reread each question and answer. Ask yourself: Have I answered the question completely?

Using Graphic Organizers

A graphic organizer is a way to show information visually. It can help you see how ideas are related to each other. A graphic organizer can help you study for a test or organize information before you write. Here are some examples.

Concept Map

A concept map includes a main idea and related concepts. Each concept is written in a circle or box. The organization of concepts in the map shows how they are related.

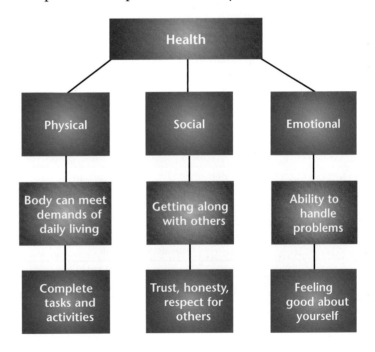

Flowchart

A flowchart can be used to show the steps in a process. Flowcharts can be vertical or horizontal. Each step is shown in order in a box. Arrows connect the boxes to show how to get from one step to the next.

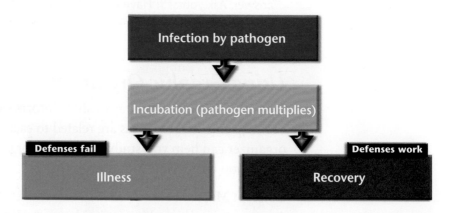

Column Chart

A column chart or a table is a good way to record information and organize it into groups or categories. Each column has a heading. Under each heading, you can write details, questions, and other information. You can also use a column chart to take notes.

Genetic Disorders and Their Causes		
Disorder	Description	Cause
Hemophilia	Blood does not clot, or clump, normally	Recessive abnormal gene
Dwarfism	Long bones do not develop properly	Dominant abnormal gene
Cystic fibrosis	Abnormally thick mucus, constant respiratory infections	Two recessive genes
Sickle cell disease	Abnormally shaped red blood cells, weakness, irregular heart action	Two recessive genes

Venn Diagram

A Venn diagram is used to compare and contrast two ideas or objects. A Venn diagram has two circles of equal size that partially overlap. The circles represent the two ideas or objects being compared. Information about each idea or object is written in the circles. Things that the ideas or objects have in common are found where the circles intersect.

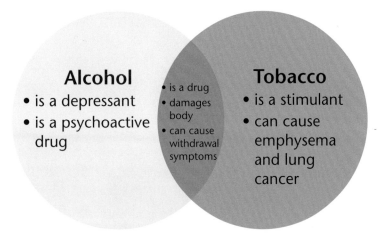

Graph

A graph is used to make comparisons and identify patterns among data. Graphs come in many forms such as line graphs, bar graphs, and circle graphs.

The Leading Causes of Death

Mental and Emotional Health

Who are you? When someone you have just met asks this question, how do you answer? A simple answer might include your name, age, and year in school. Would these answers really describe you? Think about who you are. Are you healthy mentally and emotionally? Who do you want to be in the future? How will you become this person?

The way you view yourself has a great effect on your life. Your beliefs about yourself affect what you do. They affect how healthy you are. These beliefs also play a major role in how you handle relationships. In this unit, you will learn about mental and emotional health. You will discover how to meet your goals. You will find methods to guide you in becoming the person you want to be.

Self-Assessment

Can you answer these questions?

☑ 1. How would you compare and contrast physical, social, and emotional health?

☑ 2. Why is having physical, social, and emotional health important?

☑ 3. What are some of your short-term health goals?

☑ 4. What are some of your long-term health goals?

☑ 5. How does the environment affect your health?

☑ 6. How do cultural differences create health challenges?

☑ 7. How does heredity affect health risks?

☑ 8. How can you change your behavior to improve your health?

☑ 9. Why are diet and exercise important to your health?

☑ 10. How can you learn more about improving your health?

1 Maintaining Health and Wellness

Health is important to everything in life. Without good health, reaching your goals is hard. Living your daily life happily and productively is difficult. Some people think that being healthy means simply being without an illness. Being healthy, though, means much more than this.

This chapter will guide you as you get to know more about health. You will discover what having good health means. You will also discover how you can apply this information to your own life.

Goals for Learning

◆ To describe physical, social, and emotional health

◆ To recognize principles of good health

◆ To identify causes of health risks

◆ To evaluate and recognize the power to change personal health

Health

A state of being well that has three parts—physical, social, and emotional

?

How do you think good physical health affects one's social and emotional health?

Health is a state of being well that has three parts. These three parts are physical, social, and emotional health. To be truly healthy, a person must experience all three types of health.

• *Physical health* is the body's ability to meet the demands of daily living. Physical health allows a person to complete tasks without getting tired and ill. For example, physical health allows you to go to school. It lets you do your homework and be part of school activities.

• *Social health* is the ability to get along with others. Social health is the ability to make friends and to be a friend. It allows you to cooperate with others. It also lets you be a productive part of a group, such as your family or community. Social health comes from behaviors that show trust, honesty, respect, responsibility, fairness, and good citizenship.

• *Emotional health* is the ability to handle the problems and pressures of daily life. Emotional health comes from feeling good about yourself. You show emotional health through handling your problems, even if they are difficult or frightening.

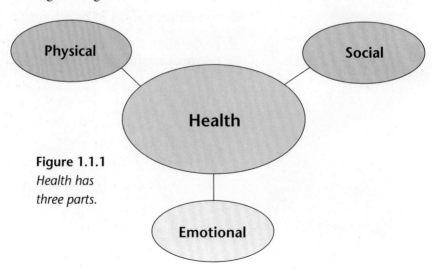

Figure 1.1.1
Health has three parts.

Exercise and healthy eating go hand in hand. Making healthy food choices gives you energy to exercise. Exercising releases chemicals in your brain that reduce appetite and make you feel happy. Then you are less likely to overeat. Overeating can make you feel tired. Because you're not overeating, you have more energy to exercise. What a positive circle!

The physical, social, and emotional parts of health all work together. If one part gets weak, the other parts may weaken, too. For example, you might have trouble getting along with others if you are sick. In a similar way, problems you may have can affect how you feel physically. For example, you may feel extra tired when you have stress at home or at school. You may notice you are more likely to get upset when you are worried about something.

Health in Your Life

Your Environment

Your environment, or surroundings, can affect your health. You can have a big effect on the things around you, like air, land, water, plants, and animals. Copy the list on the right. Use it to improve your community's environment. Add to it as you learn more about ways to make your environment safer.

On a sheet of paper, write the answers to the following questions. Use complete sentences.

1. How can your family members help you apply these ideas?

2. How can you influence your community to make environmental changes?

3. Why should you add to your list?

- Do not leave water in containers outside your home. Standing water creates a breeding ground for mosquitoes. Mosquitoes can give people diseases.

- Do not use lead-based paint. Young children can eat paint chips and be poisoned.

- Store gasoline for your lawn mower in safe, approved containers. Gasoline in unsafe containers can cause fire dangers.

- Do not smoke. Smoking creates health risks for you and those around you.

- Do not dump used motor oil into sewers, lakes, or streams. It can kill wildlife and leave behind harmful chemicals.

Lesson 1 Review On a sheet of paper, write the answers to the following questions. Use complete sentences.

1. What is health?

2. What are the three types of health required for someone to be truly healthy?

3. Which type of health includes making friends?

4. **Critical Thinking** Which type of health includes the ability to handle the breakup of a relationship?

5. **Critical Thinking** Which type of health allows a person to exercise regularly?

Decide for Yourself

As you set your own health goals, think about choices that work well for others. Ask yourself why their food and exercise choices work well for them. Then think about whether these choices would work for you—and why or why not. Developing healthy eating patterns should be part of your lifestyle. You should make healthy food choices every day.

Remember that exercise and healthy eating are important for many reasons.

Interest in losing or gaining weight is only one of them. You will learn about many more reasons while reading this chapter and later chapters in the book.

On a sheet of paper, write the answers to the following questions. Use complete sentences.

1. Compare the eating patterns and exercise habits of the two students below. Which student do you think is living a healthier lifestyle? Explain your answer.

2. After you read the rest of the chapter, come back to this page. Has your answer to question 1 changed or remained the same?

Inez	Ahmed
eats three meals each day	eats three meals each day
eats no snacks	eats two fruit snacks each day
runs two fast miles once a week	walks five blocks four times a week

Disease

A condition that harms or stops the normal working of the body

How Is Good Health Achieved?

It is important to take action to achieve good health. Taking the right steps will offer many benefits. You can reach good physical, social, and emotional health, as well as prevent **disease.** Disease is a condition that harms or stops the normal working of the body.

Achieving good health is like playing a musical instrument well. It requires the practice of basic principles. For example, to achieve physical health, you must apply good judgment and self-control in diet and exercise. Then you can give your body the food, activity, rest, and other care it needs. To achieve social health, you need to practice making and keeping good friends. To achieve emotional health, you need to practice handling your feelings in acceptable ways.

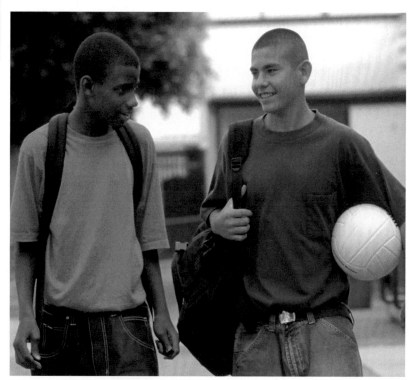

Figure 1.2.1 *To be socially healthy, you need good friendships.*

There is no "right" amount of water everyone needs daily. Needs can differ for reasons such as illness, environment, and exercise level. A good rule is to drink eight 8-ounce glasses daily. Drink more in hot weather or if you are exercising hard. What if you don't like to drink water? You might be able to substitute other fluids. Ask your health care professional for suggestions.

How Can You Stay Healthy?

You can control many ways of achieving and maintaining good health. By practicing healthy behaviors, you can help increase the quality and length of your life. What are some of these healthy behaviors?

Eight Basic Steps to Staying Healthy

1. Exercise three to five times during the week.

2. Eat three balanced, healthy meals each day, including breakfast.

3. Choose to eat healthy snacks, such as fruits, vegetables, and low-fat yogurt.

4. Drink enough water every day.

5. Maintain a healthy weight for your height and age.

6. Sleep at least eight hours each night.

7. Do not smoke, drink **alcohol,** or use other **drugs** your health care professional has not recommended.

8. Seek medical and dental care and advice from qualified health care professionals.

All of these behaviors can help you prevent health problems and maintain good health.

Figure 1.2.2 *Exercise three to five times during the week to stay healthy.*

What Is Wellness?

Wellness is an active state of health. To achieve wellness, a person moves toward balancing physical, social, and emotional health. The Wellness Scale shows how to chart a person's level of wellness. At the far right of the scale, the chart shows an excellent state of physical, social, and emotional health. The middle indicates average health. At the far left, the chart indicates very poor health and even death.

Wellness Scale

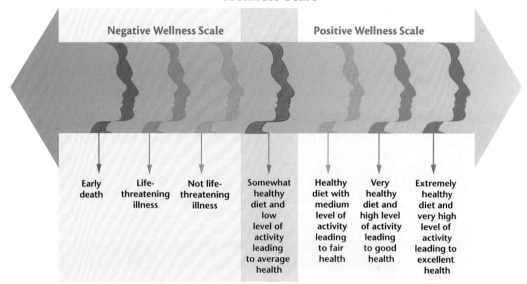

| Early death | Life-threatening illness | Not life-threatening illness | Somewhat healthy diet and low level of activity leading to average health | Healthy diet with medium level of activity leading to fair health | Very healthy diet and high level of activity leading to good health | Extremely healthy diet and very high level of activity leading to excellent health |

Figure 1.2.3 *The Wellness Scale*

As you read on, you will learn even more about achieving good health and wellness. As you read, consider your own health. Think about how it relates to the three parts of health. Where do you stand on the Wellness Scale? Then identify ways you can achieve and maintain good health. Develop ideas to help others do the same.

Health Myth

Myth: People should not eat carbohydrates.

Fact: People need carbohydrates. Healthy carbohydrates are an important part of a balanced diet. They give you energy. Some foods that contain carbohydrates are healthier than others. For example, sugar is not as healthy as oatmeal or whole-grain pasta.

Word Bank _____

behaviors

illness

wellness

Lesson 2 Review On a sheet of paper, write the word from the Word Bank that best completes each sentence.

1. Improving and balancing physical, social, and emotional health helps a person achieve _____.

2. Taking steps to achieve good physical, social, and emotional health helps you prevent _____.

3. Practicing healthy _____ helps you live a longer and better life.

On a sheet of paper, write the answers to the following questions. Use complete sentences.

4. **Critical Thinking** Suppose a student plays basketball six days a week. Is the student getting enough exercise to stay healthy? Explain your answer.

5. **Critical Thinking** Juanita is getting ready to go to soccer practice. She is choosing her snack. Name two foods that would be good choices. Name two foods that would not be good choices. Explain your answers.

❀ ❀

Technology and Society

What is a healthy weight for you? How much should you exercise? Web sites are waiting with answers. Use an Internet search engine. Sites ending in *.gov, .edu,* or *.org* are usually the most trustworthy. Evaluate information carefully. Enter terms such as *weight range, exercise,* or *physical exercise.* Be sure to discuss personal needs with your health care professional before making major changes. Remember, everyone's health needs are different.

After reading this lesson, you should be able to

◆ understand what a health risk is

◆ identify causes of health risks related to heredity and environment

◆ recognize causes of health risks related to culture and behavior

◆ develop the power to make changes that will improve health

Health risk

An action or a condition that may contribute to injury or disease

Heredity

Passage of physical characteristics from parents to children

Physical environment

The area around a person

What Is a Health Risk?

A **health risk** is an action or a condition that may contribute to injury or disease. Some causes of these risks include:

• heredity

• environment, both physical and social

• culture

• behavior, including drug use and sexual activity

How Does Heredity Cause Risk?

Heredity is the passage of physical characteristics from parents to children. Heredity can be a cause of health risks. It can make a person more likely to get certain diseases. It can make a person unable to fight a disease. For example, some people are born with a likelihood they will get heart disease. They cannot change their heredity. They can, though, change their lifestyle to make becoming ill less likely.

How Does Environment Cause Risk?

Environment can also create health risks. The **physical environment,** or the area around a person, can hold a number of risks. The physical environment includes air, water, land, plants, animals, and buildings. How might the physical environment cause a health risk? A young child might live in a home that has been painted with lead-based paint. The child might eat small bits of paint that have chipped off the walls. The lead could poison the child and cause serious illness or death.

Other environmental health risks also exist. For example, a nonsmoker might get lung disease from breathing in another person's cigarette smoke. Still another environmental health risk can come from poor air quality caused by harmful substances that factories release into the air.

Social environment

Community resources such as access to doctors, hospitals, family counseling, and after-school programs

The **social environment** is made up of community resources. A poor social environment can cause health risks. For example, people might not have safe neighborhoods or access to healthy food. Finding jobs that pay a fair wage might be difficult. Some communities do not offer good health care or other important social services. People who are ill may not have enough money to pay a doctor. If the community does not offer health care to people who cannot pay for it, this is a health risk.

Risks in the social environment can be lowered. Community education and attention to the needs of all people can help. Community leaders can work together with police officers to make a neighborhood safer. Elected officials and doctors can help communities set up neighborhood clinics that provide health care.

Research and Write

Research an environmental challenge in your community. Think about the quality of air, water, and land as you research. E-mail city council members or other elected local officials for additional information. Then write a letter to your local newspaper. Suggest ways to help your community deal with the challenge.

▼◀▲▼◀▲▼◀▲▼◀▲▼◀▲▼◀▲▼◀▲▼◀▲▼◀▲▼◀▲▼◀▲▼◀▲▼◀▲▼◀▲▼

Health at Work

Environmental Protection Specialist

The Environmental Protection Agency (EPA) is a government agency that works to protect human health and the environment. Environmental protection specialists work for the EPA. They check the quality and safety of water, air, land, and other environmental features. The specialists work to make sure that environmental laws and procedures are being followed.

The EPA requires at least a four-year college degree of most of its environmental protection specialist jobs. A postgraduate degree, or education after college, is necessary for some positions.

How Does Culture Cause Risk?

A **culture** is made up of the beliefs, way of living, and language of a group of people. People's culture can affect how they receive, understand, and use health information. Imagine you have recently moved to another country and are ill. You go to the doctor, but the doctor does not speak your language. You try to tell the doctor what is wrong. She might not understand what you are trying to explain. She might give you information written in a language you do not understand.

Additional problems may arise when sick people cannot understand where to go to get health care. Even if they know where to go, they might have problems inside the health care office. Perhaps they cannot speak or read the language on the signs in the office. They might become scared or **frustrated,** or blocked from getting what they want. They might leave the office before getting the care they need. This causes a health risk to them. It can also cause a risk to others who might catch their untreated illness.

Suppose a health care provider's belief system and way of doing things differ from the patient's. What if a health care provider does not understand what is often done and what is never done in a specific culture? These situations can cause risks. Even the differences in facial expressions and other **nonverbal,** or unspoken, communication can cause risks. For example, in Bulgaria, nodding the head up and down means "no." Shaking the head from side to side means "yes."

Here are some ways cultural risks can be decreased:

- Communities can offer health care providers who speak the languages and understand the cultures of the people they serve.

- Directions and information can be printed in more than one language.

- Information can be made available in many ways. Possible ways to communicate information include TV, radio, newspapers, Web sites, and bulletin boards at community centers, sports arenas, schools, and churches.

What Are the Causes of Behavioral Risks?

You know you cannot change your heredity. You may not be able to change every risk in your environment. Still, you can make changes to improve your health and the health of others. You can do this through understanding the causes of behavioral risks. Then you can change the action that causes the risks. You can greatly decrease your risks by living a healthy lifestyle.

Examples of Behavioral Risks

- making poor food choices

- using poisonous substances carelessly

- riding without a seat belt

- failing to observe safety rules in the home

- failing to observe safety rules during sports activities

- engaging in unsafe sexual activity

- using **tobacco** (smoking or chewing), alcohol, and other drugs not advised by your health care professional

- having a **sedentary** lifestyle, a lifestyle including little or no exercise, which can cause sadness, weight gain, and an inability to fight disease

You have learned a great deal about different types of health risks. Read on to learn more about the causes of behavioral risks.

Alcohol

Alcohol is a drug which affects every major system in the body. Drinking alcohol can cause dizziness and poor driving ability. Alcohol use also can cause problems with the senses and memory. Some dangers of long-term alcohol use include disease and damage to body parts such as the heart, liver, stomach, colon, and mouth.

Secondhand smoke

Smoke from a cigarette or cigar someone else is smoking

Deteriorate

Wear away a little bit at a time

Abstain

Choose not to use or do something

Impair

Have a negative effect on

Tobacco

Tobacco use also has harmful effects. It can increase heart rate and blood pressure to very dangerous levels. Tobacco use causes a buildup of material in the blood vessels or lungs. This buildup can result in life-threatening diseases. Smoking also can cause serious coughing and diseases that interfere with breathing.

Smokers do not cause damage only to themselves. Nonsmokers can be injured through **secondhand smoke,** smoke from a cigarette or cigar someone else is smoking. Secondhand smoke can give a nonsmoker the same kinds of health problems the smoker has.

Other Drugs

Taking drugs that have not been advised by your health care professional can cause many serious health problems. Using the wrong drugs can even lead to death. Drugs can cause heartbeat and breathing to speed up or slow down. They can cause body temperature to rise or fall. They can cause body organs to **deteriorate,** or wear away a little bit at a time. Drugs can cause people to feel confusion and panic. This can lead people to make unhealthy decisions. Some drugs also can cause dependence. A person using the drugs may not be able to stop.

Never take a drug that has been prescribed for someone else. Even legal, over-the-counter drugs can cause serious health effects if taken in large amounts or used incorrectly.

You will learn more about the effects of alcohol, tobacco, and other drugs in Chapters 14 and 15.

Failure to Abstain

Failure to **abstain** from, or choose not to have, a sexual relationship can result in unexpected pregnancy. This can have serious effects on the mother, father, their families, and the child. Failure to abstain can also result in diseases.

Using alcohol or other drugs can **impair,** or have a negative effect on, a person's judgment. Alcohol or other drugs might cause a person to do something dangerous. The person's judgment is impaired.

?

Why is it dangerous to take a drug that has been prescribed for someone else?

Failure to Observe Safety Rules in the Home

Specific actions you take or do not take in the home also can cause health risks. Keep your home in good repair. For example, fix loose carpet on stairs. Clean up spills right away. Do not use something inappropriate, such as boxes, in place of a ladder. Make sure appliances are correctly wired and electrical outlets are not overloaded.

Clean chimneys and place screens in front of fireplaces when fires are burning. Keep fire extinguishers handy and install smoke detectors and carbon monoxide detectors. These examples represent only a small number of ways to observe safety rules and ways to be safer.

Lesson 3 Review On a sheet of paper, write the letter of the answer that best completes each sentence.

1. Alcohol is a drug that affects the brain and _____.
   A speeds up heart rate
   B increases blood pressure
   C solves emotional problems
   D slows down the central nervous system

2. The physical environment includes all of the following EXCEPT _____.
   A animals   C language
   B air   D land

3. A sedentary lifestyle is a lifestyle with little _____.
   A exercise   C risk
   B food   D water

On a sheet of paper, write the answers to the following questions. Use complete sentences.

4. **Critical Thinking** What is nonverbal communication? Provide two examples.

5. **Critical Thinking** What is a health risk you have seen in your home or someone else's home? What solutions can you offer?

Objectives

After reading this lesson, you should be able to

◆ distinguish between long-term and short-term goals

◆ develop health literacy

◆ solve health problems and change behaviors

◆ evaluate your own health

You have learned there are risks to health. You know you can control some, but not all, of the causes of these risks. What if you cannot control a cause? You still have the power to make choices that will lessen the risks. You can set goals and change your behaviors by using many "tools." These tools include awareness, knowledge, decision making, and application of skills. Making positive decisions and setting goals promote good health throughout your life.

How Do You Set Goals?

As you think about promoting good health, think about your short-term and long-term goals. A short-term goal is one you can reasonably accomplish quickly. For example, you can choose to eat healthy foods and to exercise regularly during upcoming weeks. A long-term goal is one you accomplish over a long period of time. For example, you can plan to arrive at your desired weight within the upcoming year.

Setting goals is important. It gives you a positive direction. When you set goals, you figure out what you want to accomplish. Then you can figure out how to move forward to reach the goals. When you set goals, you can develop daily steps to take toward a healthy lifestyle. You can control your life and work to make yourself healthy and happy.

Health Myth

Myth: You should choose just one kind of exercise and stick with it.

Fact: You are likely to get bored with only one kind of exercise. Then you might stop exercising completely. Also, a variety of exercises will benefit a variety of muscles.

Health literacy

Gathering, understanding, and using information to improve health results

How do you decide which goals to set? How do you decide which decisions to make to help you reach those goals? You learn all you can about a healthy lifestyle. You work actively toward **health literacy.** You work to gather and understand information. Then you use the information to improve your health. You can use the information to develop skills for making good decisions and solving problems. This helps you begin to work toward your goals.

How Do You Change Behaviors?

Gaining Awareness
Being aware means paying attention to the signals your mind and body send you. Do you feel tired all the time? Does your stomach often hurt? Are you constantly sad? These are all signals that deserve your attention. You can work toward solving the problems these signals point out. You have the power to make decisions that will help you feel healthier.

Gaining Knowledge
You can use your power to learn more about health. Health literacy will guide you in this direction. You can read information in books, in magazines, and online. You can watch DVDs and use CDs that provide health information. You can also ask teachers, family members, and health care professionals for information.

How Do You Make Decisions and Solve Problems?

After you gain awareness and knowledge, you are ready to make decisions. You will consider all you have learned as you move forward. Through thinking about decisions, you will gain skills that can help you in the future.

Applying Skills
You will learn how best to deal with your symptoms based on what you have been told and how you have made your decision. You can apply these same skills in the future to help you gain knowledge and make decisions about your health. Read on to see how one student made decisions to solve a problem.

Lou felt sad all the time. He had no energy. His clothes were starting to fit tightly. He became aware he had a health problem when he listened to the signals his mind and body were sending him. Lou followed a five-step process. He solved his problem and made a decision about what to do to feel better.

1. **Define the problem.** Lou thought about his tired feelings, sadness, and tight clothes. He asked, "Why is this a problem? How did the problem start? How long have I had the problem?" He did not blame himself. He did not blame anybody else. He just looked for answers to his questions.

   Lou collected as much information as he could. He gained knowledge through reading information online and in his health book at school. He learned that his diet was not healthy. He also learned that he was not getting enough exercise.

2. **Come up with possible solutions.** Lou knew from information he had gathered that he needed to eat healthier foods. He needed more exercise. He asked a doctor at his community center about the best way to move forward. The doctor suggested several different meal plans. The doctor also suggested many kinds of exercise for Lou to try.

3. **Consider the consequences of each solution.** Lou thought about each meal plan the doctor had suggested. One would include a great deal of preparation time at home, time Lou did not have. He knew he probably would not follow that meal plan. He decided to try a meal plan that would require less preparation time. One kind of exercise the doctor had suggested was swimming. Lou knew the weather would become cold soon. The community pool would close, so he probably would not continue that exercise. He chose to do an exercise program at home instead.

4. **Put your plan into action.** Lou thought about how to make his solution work. He knew he would have to plan his meals and cut out unhealthy snacks. He knew he would have to set aside exercise time at least three days a week. He made his plans and put them into action.

5. **Evaluate the outcome.** After eating healthier foods and exercising, Lou found he was not feeling sad anymore. He had more energy. His clothes were fitting better. He found, though, that he was growing bored with his exercise routine. He was afraid he would not continue it, so he explored other types of exercise.

Consider your own health as you use the Health Assessment Chart on the next page to uncover valuable information. The chart will help you assess your own health and wellness. It will help you rate behaviors and choices that affect your health. The chart also will guide you in making choices to maintain or change behaviors.

Link to ➤➤➤

Biology

Exercise causes many positive changes in your body. It makes your heart beat at a healthy higher rate. This higher rate strengthens your heart. Then your circulation, the flow of blood through your body, is better. The blood more efficiently delivers substances your body needs throughout your body. Then you have more energy, and you are less likely to become ill.

HEALTH ASSESSMENT CHART

Directions: Create three columns on a sheet of paper. Copy the titles from the columns below. Write the numbers as they appear in the columns. Then read each statement. If it is mostly true for you, write *yes* next to its number. If it is mostly false for you, write *no*.

Answer honestly to learn more about yourself. The results are your own, and you do not need to share them.

Follow instructions at the bottom of each column to find your score for the type of health. Then add all three scores to check your overall health.

Overall Health Score
30–36 = excellent health
25–29 = above average health
20–24 = average health
19 or below = below average health

PHYSICAL HEALTH

1. I eat a balanced diet made up of different foods every day.
2. I avoid unhealthy snacks.
3. I do not use tobacco or alcohol. I do not take drugs unless my health care professional has advised me to take them.
4. I get at least 8 hours of sleep a night.
5. I rarely feel tired or run down.
6. I exercise energetically, getting my heart to beat quickly, at least three times a week.
7. I work to develop muscle tone at least three times a week, using resistance exercises and weight lifting.
8. I do stretches at least three times a week to make me more flexible.
9. I try different kinds of exercise.
10. I relax at least 10 minutes a day.
11. I get medical and dental checkups at least twice a year.

Score one point for each *yes* answer.
10–11 = excellent physical health
8–9 = good, but physical health could use improvement
6–7 = physical health could use quite a bit of improvement
5 or lower = physical health needs a great deal of improvement

SOCIAL HEALTH

1. I meet people and make friends often.
2. I have at least one close friend.
3. I can say no to my friends if they want me to do something I do not want to do.
4. I balance having my way with allowing others to have theirs.
5. I respect the right of others not to be like me.
6. I work cooperatively with others.
7. If I have a problem with others, I face it. I try to work through the problem with them.
8. I am comfortable communicating with most adults.
9. I am comfortable talking with most young men and women my own age.
10. I practice good citizenship.
11. I am fair and trustworthy when dealing with others.

Score one point for each *yes* answer.
10–11 = excellent social health
8–9 = good, but social health could use improvement
6–7 = social health could use quite a bit of improvement
5 or lower = social health needs a great deal of improvement

EMOTIONAL HEALTH

1. I try to accept my feelings of love, fear, anger, and sadness.
2. I can tell when I feel as though I am under pressure.
3. I try to find ways to deal with pressure and control my reaction to it.
4. I try to have a positive outlook.
5. I ask for help when I need it.
6. I can discuss problems with my friends and family members.
7. I can accept compliments.
8. I give compliments.
9. I can accept and use constructive comments.
10. I take responsibility for my actions.
11. I am honest with myself and others.

Score one point for each *yes* answer.
10–11 = excellent emotional health
8–9 = good, but emotional health could use some improvement
6–7 = emotional health could use quite a bit of improvement
5 or lower = emotional health needs a great deal of improvement

Lesson 4 Review On a sheet of paper, write the answers to the following questions. Use complete sentences.

1. What are the five steps for solving a problem and making a decision?

2. What is health literacy?

3. What are three tools for changing behaviors?

4. **Critical Thinking** Name one of your short-term goals and one of your long-term goals.

5. **Critical Thinking** Why is it important to evaluate the outcome of a decision?

Link to ➤➤➤

Language Arts

Keeping a daily journal of the food you eat and your exercise can help you achieve health goals. (You may be surprised by the end of a week to see what you have actually eaten!) When you list the foods you are eating and the exercise you have done, be sure to include your feelings while you eat—happy, sad, nervous, or scared. Your journal can help you recognize patterns and choose behaviors to continue or discontinue.

Chapter 1 SUMMARY

- People need good health to accomplish the things they need and like to do.

- Being healthy means much more than just not being ill.

- A person must have physical health, social health, and emotional health to be truly healthy.

- People should take basic steps to prevent disease and stay healthy.

- A health risk can cause disease. Many health risks relate to heredity, the environment, and behavior.

- The physical environment includes air, water, land, plants, animals, and buildings. Cigarette smoke is an example of an environmental health risk.

- The social environment is made up of community resources. Lack of health care for those who cannot pay creates a risk in the social environment.

- Cultural risks occur when health information is not received, understood, or used properly. Risks can be decreased when health care providers understand languages and cultures of community members.

- Behavioral risks relate to action or inaction. You have the power to control behavioral risks.

- You can set short-term and long-term goals as you make health decisions.

Vocabulary		
abstain, 15	health, 4	physical environment, 11
alcohol, 8	health literacy, 18	secondhand smoke, 15
culture, 13	health risk, 11	sedentary, 14
deteriorate, 15	heredity, 11	social environment, 12
disease, 7	impair, 15	tobacco, 14
drug, 8	nonverbal, 13	wellness, 9
frustrate, 13		

Chapter 1 REVIEW

Word Bank

abstain

culture

deteriorate

health literacy

health risk

heredity

impair

nonverbal

physical environment

secondhand smoke

sedentary

social environment

wellness

Vocabulary Review

On a sheet of paper, write the word or phrase from the Word Bank that best completes each sentence.

1. The _____ is the area around a person.

2. Another name for an active state of health is _____.

3. The passage of physical characteristics from parents to children is _____.

4. An unspoken answer is _____.

5. A(n) _____ lifestyle includes little or no exercise.

6. To _____ is to wear away a little bit at a time.

7. Smoke from a cigarette someone else is smoking is _____.

8. The _____ is made up of community resources.

9. To _____ is to choose not to use or do something.

10. To have a negative effect is to _____.

11. A(n) _____ is made up of the beliefs, way of living, and language of a group of people.

12. Gathering, understanding, and using information to improve your health results in _____.

13. A(n) _____ is an action or condition that may contribute to injury or disease.

Concept Review

On a sheet of paper, write the letter of the answer that best completes each sentence.

14. The state of being healthy includes all of these parts EXCEPT _____ health.

A social   **C** physical

B medical   **D** emotional

15. The first step in changing behaviors is _____.

A applying skills   **C** making decisions

B gaining knowledge   **D** gaining awareness

16. A good example of physical health is _____.

A having energy for sports

B getting along with others

C handling daily pressures

D being a good friend

17. A _____ goal can be accomplished quickly.

A long-term   **C** short-term

B physical   **D** complex

Critical Thinking

On a sheet of paper, write the answers to the following questions. Use complete sentences.

18. What is an example of good physical health? social health? emotional health?

19. Name three types of health risks and their causes.

20. What changes in behavior would you like to make to become a healthier person? Explain your answer.

Test-Taking Tip Read test questions carefully to identify those that require more than one answer.

Self-Assessment

Can you answer these questions?

☑ 1. What is emotional health?

☑ 2. What kinds of needs do people have?

☑ 3. In what way do people show their needs?

☑ 4. How does your body respond to stress?

☑ 5. What life events cause stress?

☑ 6. How is fear linked to stress?

☑ 7. What are some common responses to anger?

☑ 8. What can you do to handle stress?

☑ 9. Why is paying attention to emotional signals important?

☑ 10. What suggestions for coping with stress would you give a friend?

2 Managing Emotions

Being healthy involves both the body and the mind. If you are excited about something, that feeling can affect your body in a positive way. If you are worried about something, that too can affect your body. Your mind affects your body.

We also know that the opposite is true—the body affects the mind. For example, if you are well rested, you are usually able to think clearly. However, if you are tired or feel ill, you may not be able to think as clearly.

In this chapter, you will learn about keeping your mind and body healthy by understanding emotions and stress. You will also learn about common needs that people have and how these needs affect your emotions.

Goals for Learning

◆ To explain the purpose of emotions and how they happen

◆ To describe five different levels of basic human needs

◆ To list three ways mental health affects physical health

◆ To create a stress management plan

The same experience can cause different people to react, or respond, in different ways. This happens because every human being has **emotions,** or feelings. Emotions are a person's individual **reactions** to an experience. A reaction is a response. Your emotions are a special part of who you are.

Emotions can be difficult to understand. Emotions start with thoughts. When you think about something, you may feel a certain way about it. Your thinking triggers an emotion. This emotion may then cause your body to react. It may cause a physical change. For example, if you think about going to a party, you may feel excited when it is time to leave. Then your heart may beat faster. Your thoughts about people and events trigger the emotions that cause physical changes in your body.

What Do Emotions Do?

Emotions are natural. They serve a purpose. Emotions signal reactions to events and experiences. They let you know when something is right, as well as when things are wrong. Learning about your feelings can help you understand yourself better.

People's emotions show up in the way the people look, act, and sound. You often can tell how people feel by how loudly and forcefully they speak. **Body language,** or the way people move and hold their heads, arms, and legs, also gives clues about how people feel.

All people have basic needs, including emotional needs. Understanding these needs can help you understand yourself and your emotions.

Body language plays an important role in classrooms and other settings. You show interest in a teacher or speaker by pointing your body toward that person.

What Basic Needs Do People Have?

Abraham Maslow studied what humans need. He observed that people have five basic needs. They are physical, safety, belonging, **esteem,** and self-actualization needs. Maslow put the needs in a **hierarchy,** or order, beginning with the most basic needs. Physical needs are at the bottom of the hierarchy. Safety needs come next, and so on. Maslow's hierarchy of needs appears in Figure 2.1.1.

Esteem

Value or worth; how one sees oneself or others

Hierarchy

Order from most to least important

Figure 2.1.1 *Maslow's hierarchy of needs*

Maslow said that most people spend their lives working on the first three needs. Each day, you work to meet the needs on the first three levels. Then you can work on meeting the next higher level of needs. For example, a person must first satisfy the physical need to eat—that need is basic to staying alive. Once that need is met, a person can satisfy the need to find a safe place to live. Later, that person can satisfy the need to be with others and to belong to groups. As you read these explanations of needs, think about where you are in the hierarchy.

Friendship
Love based on choices

Attachment
Emotional bond or tie to others

Family love
Love based on attachment and support

Romantic love
Strong physical and emotional attraction between two people

Physical Needs

Physical needs are everything necessary to stay alive—water, food, and oxygen. Regularly eating the right foods meets many of your physical needs.

Safety Needs

Safety needs are protection needs. That means protecting yourself from danger and from the conditions around you. Being sheltered from harm meets your basic safety needs.

Belonging Needs

There are two kinds of belonging—belonging in a place and belonging with people. Belonging in a place helps you feel secure and meet other needs such as safety. This may be in your home, school, town, or country.

Needing to belong with people leads you to form **friendships** or join groups. Friendships, or love based on choices, help you feel healthy and secure. A relationship based on need is called an **attachment,** which is an emotional bond or tie to others.

People experience different kinds of love in their need to belong with people. **Family love** is based on attachment and support. Family members often feel safe when they are in contact with one another and support one another.

You are born into your family, but you can choose your friends. You usually choose friends because you have common interests and goals. The more similar you are to someone, the easier it is to be friends. You can have many friends. Usually, however, you have only a few friends to whom you feel especially close.

Romantic love is a strong physical and emotional attraction between two people. When it is part of belonging, romantic love is based on need. Two people may feel they are in love because they want to be together and are unhappy when they are apart.

Esteem Needs

If you are able to meet your needs for survival, safety, and belonging, you then seek esteem. Esteem is the value or worth you place on yourself or others. People need two kinds of esteem—the esteem of others and **self-esteem,** or how you feel about yourself. You feel the esteem of others when family members express their love for you. You feel it when friends tell you that you have done a good job. Another word for self-esteem is self-confidence.

Self-esteem, or self-respect, is your sense of being valuable and worthwhile. Feeling happy and content is usually part of high self-esteem. Feeling unimportant and unsatisfied is usually part of low self-esteem. Your **self-concept,** or your ideas about who you are, determines your self-esteem. Good self-concept usually leads to high self-esteem. Poor self-concept usually leads to low self-esteem. Anything that affects your self-concept can influence your self-esteem. Your self-concept and self-esteem continue to develop throughout life.

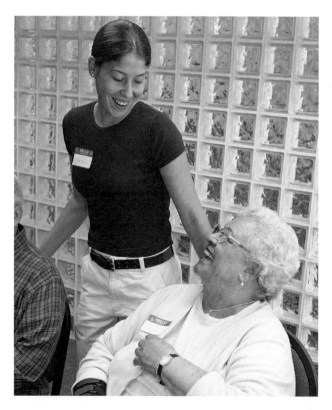

Figure 2.1.2

Volunteering to help others is a way to meet belonging needs of both the volunteer and the person being helped.

Self-Actualization Needs

If you are able to satisfy all the other needs, you can begin to work on **self-actualization.** Self-actualization means achieving your possibilities. People who have satisfied their physical, safety, belonging, and esteem needs are able to become self-actualized. They can go beyond themselves to give to others. For example, you might feel good about yourself when you spend time volunteering at a hospital.

Decide for Yourself

A bully is someone who tries to hurt someone else to gain power. Bullies often have low self-esteem and try to make themselves feel better by picking on others. Bullying can take many forms. Physical bullying includes physically harming someone. Emotional bullying includes spreading rumors or ignoring someone on purpose. Verbal bullying is name-calling or making fun of someone. Racist and sexual bullying involve offensive words and actions. Cyber bullying includes the use of technology such as cell phones or computers to threaten or send hurtful messages. Here are some ways you can deal with bullying behavior:

- Remember that the bully is at fault, not you. No one deserves to be bullied.

- Do not use physical force to stop a bully. This only encourages a physical response from the bully.

- Ignore the bully and walk away. A bully looks for a reaction. Do not provide one.

- In times when walking away is not possible, compliment the bully. This will buy you some time to walk away.

- Talk about what happened with a trusted adult who can help.

- Join positive groups. Stay with friends who treat others with respect. Be sure you treat others with respect.

- Work with your student council and school leaders to stop bullying at your school.

On a sheet of paper, write the answers to the following questions. Use complete sentences.

1. How might bullying harm a person's self-esteem?

2. Why do most bullies pick on others?

3. Make a plan that shows how you can work with others to stop bullying at your school.

Guilt
A feeling of having done something wrong

How Do Needs Lead to Different Emotions?

Emotions help you realize what you need. For example, if you often feel frightened, your need for safety is not being met. Your feelings or emotions are closely connected to your needs. Sometimes you may feel unpleasant emotions such as **guilt** or shame. Guilt is the feeling of having done something wrong. Shame is an emotion coming from a strong sense of guilt, embarrassment, or unworthiness. If you make a mistake in front of friends, you may feel shame or embarrassment. Your need to belong is what leads to your feeling of embarrassment. While people have the same needs, they may have different ways of showing those needs. For example, you may wear a certain style of clothing to feel you belong. Another person may behave in a certain way to feel secure or socially accepted. You both have a need to belong, but you each show that need in a different way.

Lesson 1 Review On a sheet of paper, write the letter of the answer that best completes each sentence.

1. Emotions start with _____.
  A actions   **C** body language
  B thoughts   **D** guilt

2. Self-actualization means _____.
  A meeting physical needs **C** achieving possibilities
  B setting goals   **D** feeling unimportant

3. According to Maslow, the type of need people try for when their physical and safety needs are met is

_____.
  A self-actualization   **C** belonging
  B esteem   **D** love

On a sheet of paper, write the answers to the following questions. Use complete sentences.

4. Critical Thinking How can your words and body language affect your relationships with others?

5. Critical Thinking What are two ways a person can satisfy his or her need for self-actualization?

Stress

A state of physical or emotional pressure

Stress response

Automatic physical reactions to stress

Some people overeat during times of stress. Others eat too little. Eating healthy foods like whole grains, fruits, and vegetables regularly will help your body handle stress better.

Emotions begin with thoughts. Emotions may cause physical changes or reactions. When basic needs are threatened, people experience **stress.** Stress is a state of physical or emotional pressure. It is a reaction to anything that places demands on the body or mind to which people must adapt. Understanding how stress affects your mind and your body is important.

Stress is normal, and it can be either good or bad. For example, if you are excited about a project and do a good job on it, you benefit from good stress. Happy events such as graduations, dates, and weddings can all be sources of good stress. Good stress helps people to accomplish goals and to change. Usually we hear about bad stress because its effects are harmful. Examples of bad stress are family problems or the death of a loved one. Bad stress can interfere with healthy living.

How Do People React to Stress?

When you face stress, you try to find out what is wrong and whether it is dangerous. For example, if your teacher seems unhappy and says she wants to talk with you, you may feel stressful. You think you may hear bad news. First, ask yourself what might be wrong and if it could be serious. Then decide what your reactions will be.

Most of your reactions may be automatic and physical. You may feel worried and notice that your heart is beating faster. This is called the **stress response.** The stress response affects your body in ways you may not be able to control. Your heart beats faster, you sweat, and your breathing quickens. These are automatic physical reactions to stress. Other examples are blushing, gasping in surprise, and crying out. Stronger reactions to stress are headaches, stomach pain, sleeping problems, and nervous feelings.

Exercise is a good way to relieve stress. Take a walk, dance to your favorite music, or work out at a gym or health club. Not only will you feel better physically, you will have a sense of emotional well-being.

A person's response to stress often takes one of two forms: fight or flight. When something threatens or angers you, you may feel an impulse to fight it. If you fight, you attack what threatens you. Fighting may simply be using words to stand up for what you believe. The other response is to flee. If you flee, you leave the situation, but nothing changes. The fight-or-flight impulse is natural and happens without your thinking about it.

You can also react to stress by thinking about what to do. For example, if you enter a dark room and hear a noise, you may react by jumping back. Your body becomes calmer after your first reaction. You may then decide to turn on a light to see what is making the noise. You find the noise is nothing to fear. What prompted the stress was imagined, and you were able to overcome it. Overcoming the stress helps you feel more at ease.

Relating to peers and adults in positive ways helps you avoid stress. Avoid negative comments when talking with others. Carefully choose your words during a disagreement. Make good risk decisions. For example, avoid high-risk behaviors such as drug use. Taking charge of your mental and physical health will help you manage stress and promote your emotional maturity. By doing so, you become a good role model and help promote positive health behaviors among your peers.

Technology and Society

In biofeedback, electronic sensors are placed on a person's head or muscles. Computers then track and measure muscle activity. By learning to use positive thoughts, people can learn to manage pain and stress.

Biofeedback is used to treat migraine headaches, sleeplessness, hyperactivity, attention deficit disorders, and chemical dependency. Athletes use biofeedback to control anxiety before games and sporting events.

What Physical Reactions Does Stress Cause?

When you interpret something as a threat, your thought processes trigger your brain into action. Your brain triggers your body to fight or flight. Your brain also sends a chemical message to the body system that controls bodily processes. The chemicals go directly into your bloodstream. Some chemical messages cause faster breathing, sweating, and a rush of blood to your arms, legs, and head. Other chemical messages from your brain strengthen your muscles for endurance in case the stress lasts a long time.

Normally, physical reactions to stress help you resist it. The chemicals that your body produces help you react quickly. They help you remain alert while you choose the best way to respond to the threat. While good stress can have a positive effect on your body, bad stress can have a harmful effect.

What Life Events Cause Stress?

A number of events can cause stress. Table 2.1.1 lists a few events that commonly cause stress for teens.

Table 2.1.1 Common Stressful Life Events for Teens	
Death of a parent	An outstanding personal achievement
A visible deformity	Acceptance to college
Parents' divorce or separation	Being a senior in high school
Involvement with alcohol or other drugs	A change in acceptance by peers
Death of a brother or sister	A change in parents' financial status
Pressure of getting good grades	Start of dating

Lesson 2 Review On a sheet of paper, write the letter of the answer that best completes each sentence.

1. The three automatic physical reactions to stress are _____.

   A blood rushing, muscle strengthening, and faster breathing

   B blood rushing, muscle weakening, and faster breathing

   C blood slowing, muscle strengthening, and slowed breathing

   D blood slowing, muscle strengthening, and fast breathing

2. An example of good stress is _____.

   A a fight with a friend

   B getting a bad grade

   C getting a promotion

   D changing schools

3. Bad stress affects your body _____.

   A positively

   B negatively

   C very little

   D the same way good stress does

On a sheet of paper, write the answers to the following questions. Use complete sentences.

4. **Critical Thinking** How can you avoid stress when relating to peers and adults?

5. **Critical Thinking** What is the fight-or-flight response?

Link to ➤➤➤

Biology

When embarrassed or nervous, do you blush? Blushing is a reddening of the face caused by nerves that widen blood vessels. More blood flows and causes the skin to look red. Some people also blush in their ears, neck, and chest. Some people blush easier than others do. Blushing can cause a feeling of heat as the blood flows through the vessels under the skin.

Objectives

After reading this lesson, you should be able to

◆ understand which emotions are related to stress

◆ create a plan to manage stress

◆ identify three ways to relieve stress

Fear

A strong feeling of fright; awareness of danger

Well-being

State of being physically and emotionally healthy

Anxiety

A feeling of uneasiness or fearful concern

Several emotions are related to stress. Understanding these emotions and how the body reacts to some of them is helpful.

Which Emotions Are Linked to Stress?

The emotions most commonly linked to stress are fear, anxiety, anger, grief, and relief.

Fear

You feel **fear** when something important to your survival and **well-being** is threatened. Well-being is the state of being physically and emotionally healthy. Fear is a strong feeling of fright or awareness of danger. It causes you to want to escape. For example, you would feel fear if a car turned in front of you just as you crossed a street. Anything that might cause you physical or emotional pain can cause fear.

Your body reacts to fear. You may notice muscle tightness, especially in your legs. Your hands may shake nervously. You may bite your fingernails or feel like crying. To deal with fear, you can try to change the situation causing the fear or you can talk about the fear. Talking with a trusted person is a healthy way to deal with fear.

Anxiety

An emotion related to fear is **anxiety,** a feeling of uneasiness or fearful concern. For example, when you are nervous about a test, you may feel anxious. You do not really feel fear, because the test cannot hurt you, but you may worry about getting a low grade. Anxiety is very unpleasant. The best way to deal with anxiety is to identify its source and take effective action. For example, if you are anxious about giving a speech, you can practice it. If you feel well prepared, you will be more relaxed and self-confident when giving your speech.

Anger

Strong feeling of
displeasure

Aggression

Any action that intends
harm to someone

Anger

Anger is a strong feeling of displeasure. Everyone feels angry at times. Strong anger, however, can lead to the desire to attack or be aggressive. **Aggression** is any action that intends harm to someone. Frustration, or a feeling of being blocked from something you want, often causes aggression. You might push someone who blocks your way. You might hit the vending machine that keeps your money. Aggression is a common impulse, but it is not an effective response to frustration. Aggression is likely to cause more problems than it solves.

When you are angry, you have a complaint about someone or something. The best way to express your anger is to say why you are angry and what you want to happen. You can do that without accusing or blaming another person by using "I" messages. For example, you could try saying, "I feel hurt when you tease me," instead of, "You hurt me when you tease me." Sometimes this alone solves the problem. Talking about your complaint is a more successful way to handle anger than aggression is.

Uncontrolled anger keeps you from thinking through your decisions clearly. Working out a solution and talking about feelings helps manage anger. Staying calm is another way to control anger. Self-talk also helps. For example, you can calm your body by telling yourself, "Stay calm. Relax. Stay in control." Taking deep breaths and breathing in and out slowly relaxes your muscles. You can redirect the anger by doing something physical such as taking a walk, exercising, or dancing to music. All of these actions can help you think more clearly and consider what to do when you feel angry.

Research and Write

All children experience anger. For example, they may fight over a toy or yell at each other. Talk to preschool and elementary school teachers about positive ways to help children cope with their anger. Develop a creative booklet to show children what you learned. Share your booklet with an area preschool or elementary class, or share it with a child care center.

Grief

Term	Definition

Grief
A feeling of sorrow; feelings after a loss

Depression
A state of deep sadness

Relief
A light, pleasant feeling after something painful or distressing is gone

Grief

Loss is a common source of stress that you cannot fight or escape. You experience loss when a relationship breaks up, a good friend moves away, or someone dies. The feelings you experience after a loss are part of **grief,** or sorrow. Grief can be a mixture of several emotions, including fear, anger, anxiety, and guilt.

Every culture expresses grief. However, each culture deals with grief in its own way. Traditions direct how long people mourn the death of an individual. Different cultures have different rules for what they wear or how they act following someone's death. Respecting the way people from different cultures deal with grief is important.

Grief is a natural healing process. Usually a person goes through these reactions to grief:

- Denial—pretending a loss has not occurred
- Anger—feeling angry about the loss
- Bargaining—wishing for a second chance
- **Depression**—feeling deep sadness
- Acceptance—accepting something over which you had no control

Each reaction to grief can take a long time. The length of time is different for each person. Each person may go through the reactions in any order or may go back and forth among them. Talking about the painful emotions felt from the loss helps. Depression is the most common of these reactions. A depressed person sometimes needs professional help.

Relief

Relief is the light, pleasant feeling you experience when stress is gone. Sometimes, stress returns. Then you only feel relief for a little while. You may be nervous, because you know the stress can return. For example, you feel relief because your math test was delayed until tomorrow. But the relief does not last long, because you still have to take the test. Learning to deal with stress brings relief that lasts. Relief is an emotion you can work to achieve.

Cope

To deal with or overcome problems and difficulties

How Can Stressful Emotions Be Handled?

All emotions are normal. Emotions are neither good nor bad. Your mental health depends on how you handle an emotion. Pay attention to emotional signals and take positive action. Recognize what you do best and be willing to ask for help when you need it. If you need help with your homework, for example, ask a friend, parent, or teacher.

Being direct works best. Dropping hints or hoping others will guess what you need or how you feel usually does not work. Expressing your thoughts and feelings in an open and honest way helps improve communication between you and others. It also helps reduce problems that might arise from misunderstandings.

You can do a great deal to help yourself and others stay emotionally healthy, especially at school. Understand and follow school rules. Participate in your school's efforts to promote healthy living through your actions and words. Encourage others to live healthy lives.

What Are Some Ways to Relieve Stress?

To **cope** is to find a way to overcome stress or other problems. Coping with a situation relieves the stress for a while and brings relief. You will always have to deal with problems and emergencies. Coping with one threat will not solve all your problems. However, it can reduce the number of your daily problems. When an emotion signals a need, the healthiest response is to cope.

Link to ➤➤➤

Social Studies

Different cultures and religions deal with death in different ways. In the Jewish faith, a person's body is buried in a wooden coffin within 24 hours of death. Mourning takes place for seven days afterward. Among Buddhists, bodies are burned until they become ash on the day of the funeral. The urn holding a person's ashes is honored for 35 days before burial. Among Muslims, the dead are wrapped in a plain cloth and buried in a raised grave soon after death.

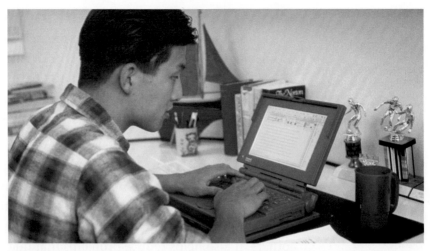

Figure 2.3.1 *Studying is a way to handle school-related stress and improve your outlook for the future.*

You can do three things to cope with a problem:

1. Identify what causes the problem.

2. Decide on a way to solve the problem.

3. Carry out your plan as a way to cope.

What is something positive you have learned from a success? What is something positive you have learned from a failure?

Coping helps you feel better and relieves anxiety. For example, you might feel anxious about finding a job. To cope with the problem, plan ways to get help—check the newspaper or online job ads and ask trusted adults for suggestions. Set a plan and act on it. Your chance for success in finding a job is better because you are able to cope with the problem.

When you solve a problem successfully, you relieve stress. Learning to cope with one problem may help you deal with other problems. You can learn from your successes as well as your mistakes.

Experience and time also help relieve stress. Often when people try something new, they find it stressful. The more you do things and gain experience, the less stress you will associate with those things. For example, a first date can be stressful. The more you date an individual or a variety of people, the more experience you have in dating. While the first date with a new person may still be stressful, the stress may be less powerful with experience.

C *Calm down*

O *Outline options*

P *Pick a plan*

E *Evaluate your plan*

?

How do you think planning ahead helps you relieve the stress of homework assignments?

Here are some other actions that can relieve stress:

- Pay attention to your emotional signals.

- Identify what you need—make sure your needs are reasonable.

- Take responsibility for meeting your needs.

- Ask respectfully for what you need.

- Get the rest of what you need honestly and fairly.

- Respect others, even when they may do or say things that are difficult for you to understand or accept.

- Seek help through talking with trusted individuals.

- Use positive self-talk—keep an "I can" attitude.

- Engage in physical activity.

- Set personal goals for maintaining a healthy body.

- Plan ahead.

▼ ◢ ▲ ▼ ◢ ▲ ▼ ◢ ▲ ▼ ◢ ▲ ▼ ◢ ▲ ▼ ◢ ▲ ▼ ◢ ▲ ▼ ◢ ▲ ▼ ◢ ▲ ▼ ◢ ▲ ▼ ◢ ▲ ▼ ◢ ▲ ▼ ◢ ▲ ▼ ◢ ▲ ▼ ◢ ▲ ▼

Health at Work

Mental Health Specialist

Do you think of yourself as caring and trustworthy? Then why not become a mental health specialist? Mental health specialists give emotional support and assistance to individuals and families. They help people work through marriage, family, or job-related problems. Some mental health specialists work just with infants and their families. They help new parents work through the changes that come with having a baby. They also assist families in getting help for any mental health or physical problems the new baby may have. Mental health specialists must have a college degree in social work, psychology, or a related field. Infant mental health specialists often have training in speech and language therapy, physical therapy, nursing, or child welfare. Being a mental health specialist can be a very rewarding career.

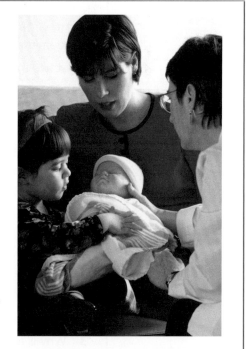

Word Bank

coping
grief
relief

Lesson 3 Review On a sheet of paper, write the word from the Word Bank that best matches each description.

1. Feeling you might have after a loss

2. Dealing with or overcoming problems

3. A feeling after stress is gone

On a sheet of paper, write the answers to the following questions. Use complete sentences.

4. Critical Thinking What can you do at school to help yourself and others stay emotionally healthy?

5. Critical Thinking How does coping help relieve stress?

Health in Your Life

Stress Management Plan

Everyone experiences stress. Finding a way to manage stress will help you lead a healthy life. One effective way to manage stress is to have a stress management plan. Making a stress management plan will help you recognize the things in your life that cause stress. It will help you plan how you will manage that stress. Here is how you can have an effective stress management plan:

- List five things that create the most stress for you.
- Write one way you can avoid stress.
- List five things that happen to your body when you feel stress.
- Write one idea for what you will do when your body shows signs of stress.
- List five things that you can do to make you feel more relaxed.
- Put your plan into action!

On a sheet of paper, write the answers to the following questions. Use complete sentences.

1. How will a stress management plan help you?

2. Why is identifying what causes you stress important?

3. Why is relaxation important?

Chapter 2   S U M M A R Y

- Emotions begin with thoughts and may cause physical changes or reactions.

- Five basic human needs are physical, safety, belonging, esteem, and self-actualization needs.

- Physical and safety needs are the most basic needs.

- The two kinds of belonging needs are belonging in a place and belonging with people.

- Esteem needs involve the esteem of others and self-esteem, which your self-concept determines.

- Self-actualization needs involve achieving your possibilities and going beyond yourself to give to others.

- While people have the same needs, they may have different ways of showing those needs.

- Stress is a natural mental and physical reaction to anything that requires you to adapt.

- Your brain triggers physical reactions to stress. It sends chemical messages into your bloodstream that may cause faster breathing, blushing, sweating and other physical reactions.

- Anger can lead to aggression. The best way to handle anger is to talk about it.

- Emotions that are often linked to stress are fear, anxiety, anger, grief, and relief.

- All emotions are normal. How you handle emotions is important to your mental health.

- Coping with stress involves thinking through a problem, deciding how to solve the problem, and carrying out your decision.

Vocabulary

aggression, 39	esteem, 29	relief, 40
anger, 39	family love, 30	romantic love, 30
anxiety, 38	fear, 38	self-actualization, 32
attachment, 30	friendship, 30	self-concept, 31
body language, 28	grief, 40	self-esteem, 31
cope, 41	guilt, 33	stress, 34
depression, 40	hierarchy, 29	stress response, 34
emotion, 28	reaction, 28	well-being, 38

Chapter 2 REVIEW

Word Bank

aggression
anger
attachment
cope
depression
emotions
friendship
grief
hierarchy
relief
self-esteem
stress
stress response

Vocabulary Review

On a sheet of paper, write the word or phrase from the Word Bank that best completes each sentence.

1. Individual reactions to experiences are _____.

2. A relationship based on need is called a(n) _____.

3. Maslow identified a(n) _____ of needs.

4. Self-concept determines _____.

5. A state of physical or emotional pressure is _____.

6. Blushing is an example of a physical _____.

7. Love based on choices is _____.

8. A state of deep sadness is _____.

9. Feelings most often linked to stress are fear, anxiety, _____, grief, and relief.

10. Anger can lead to _____, which is any action intended to harm someone.

11. Another word for deep sorrow is _____.

12. Finding positive ways to _____ with stress helps relieve anxiety.

13. A light, pleasant feeling that comes after stress is gone is _____.

Concept Review

On a sheet of paper, write the letter of the answer that best completes each sentence.

14. When you are sheltered from harm, your _____ need is being satisfied.

   A belonging   C self-actualization
   B safety   D physical

15. People experience _____ when their basic
needs are threatened.

    A relief   **C** grief

    B aggression   **D** stress

16. Fear is a common response when a person's
_____ is threatened.

    A well-being   **C** anger

    B anxiety   **D** grief

17. Coping with stress includes identifying the problem,
deciding how to solve the problem, and _____.

    A gaining relief

    B carrying out the plan

    C thinking through the issue

    D solving another problem

Critical Thinking

On a sheet of paper, write the answers to the following
questions. Use complete sentences.

18. How can stress be both good and bad?

19. Why do you think coping with stress and other emotions is
important to your physical and mental health?

20. What could you do to help a friend who feels sad and
upset?

Test-Taking Tip If you know you will have to define certain terms on a test,
write each term on one side of a card. Write its definition on the
other side. Use the cards to test yourself, or work with a partner
and test each other.

Self-Assessment

Can you answer these questions?

☑ 1. How would you describe yourself?

☑ 2. What early experiences have influenced your personality?

☑ 3. What is social esteem?

☑ 4. What actions can you take to maintain and improve your social health?

☑ 5. What are some of your values and beliefs?

☑ 6. How do you manage your impulses?

☑ 7. What are healthy ways to cope with emotional challenges?

☑ 8. How can you solve problems through compromise?

☑ 9. How are communication skills important to your well-being?

☑ 10. How are citizenship skills important to your well-being?

3 Maintaining Mental Health

Many things can affect your mental and emotional health. Your personal well-being has many sources. Learning about yourself can make a difference in your emotional well-being. It also can make a difference in how you look at things and in the quality of your relationships.

In this chapter, you will learn what affects mental health. You will learn about the characteristics, or qualities, of mentally healthy people and healthy relationships. You will also learn some ways that you can improve and maintain good mental and emotional health.

Goals for Learning

◆ To describe well-being and ways to promote it

◆ To identify ways to reach and maintain good emotional health

◆ To explain the characteristics of healthy relationships

◆ To describe ways to accept yourself and others

Objectives

After reading this lesson, you should be able to

◆ explain how personality develops

◆ identify influences on self-concept

◆ describe how the different areas of well-being work together

◆ promote physical, emotional, social, and personal well-being

Personality

All of one's behavioral, mental, and emotional characteristics

Temperament

A person's emotional makeup

How can a person who gets teased a lot develop a good self-concept?

What kind of person are you? Friendly, helpful, cooperative? Grouchy, fearful, selfish? You may at different times be all of these things. Your thoughts, feelings, and behaviors form your **personality.** As you grow older, your personality will change. This is because your thoughts and behaviors will change as a result of your experiences and opportunities.

How Does Personality Develop?

When you were a baby, your personality had not yet developed. However, you did have a certain temperament. **Temperament** is your emotional makeup. A baby's temperament appears soon after birth. As children grow, they develop new thoughts and feelings. They learn new behaviors. Their temperament remains the same, but they begin to develop their personality.

Early experiences may influence a child's personality. For example, a baby needs close contact with a caregiver to feel secure. If that need is met, the baby is content. Whether this need is met as a baby may influence how that person relates to others later.

What Influences Your Self-Concept?

Several factors influence self-concept. One is your own natural positive esteem. Another is what other people tell you about yourself. Suppose your music teacher says you have a good sense of rhythm. Part of your self-concept is that you have musical talent. The actions of others also help shape self-concept. Suppose team captains want to choose you for every game. You might think of yourself as a good athlete.

The messages you get from others are called social messages. These messages may not always match your self-concept. For example, you may think of yourself as shy and not interesting. Your friends, however, may think you are quiet and sincere. They say you have a good sense of humor. In this case, you may decide to change your belief about yourself.

Social esteem

How others value a person

Sometimes, you will not want to change a belief about yourself. Suppose you believe you are good at baseball, but you drop the ball during a game. Your classmate tells you that you are not a good player. You made four other good plays, so you decide not to change your belief.

Social messages play a part in forming your self-concept. They reflect your **social esteem,** or how others value you. If others have a good opinion of you it is more likely you will have high self-esteem. Unfortunately, this also works the other way. If others do not seem to value you, it is more likely you will have low self-esteem.

Figure 3.1.1 *Images in the media are an important influence on self-concept.*

One important influence on self-concept is media such as TV and magazines. Many advertisements show people who are beautiful, talented, muscular, or just the right size. If you compare yourself to the people in these ads, you might feel that you do not measure up. This can lead to a negative self-concept. You can promote, or support, a positive self-concept by not comparing yourself to the people you see in the ads. Focus on your positive qualities. Remember that you are special and unique, or one of a kind.

What Is Well-Being?

Well-being is feeling happy, healthy, and content. Well-being involves balancing many different needs and behaviors. If you feel healthy and content, then many areas of your well-being are working together. These include your physical, emotional, social, and personal well-being.

Link to >>>

Biology

The brain contains chemicals that carry messages between it and other parts of your body. These chemicals are present at birth and influence temperament. Brain chemicals can affect whether you tend to be irritable or calm.

Physical well-being is your body's ability to meet the demands of daily living. You are physically healthy and free from pain and illness.

Emotional well-being is your ability to handle problems and stress in daily life. You look at life in a positive way and are in control of your emotions.

Social well-being is your ability to get along well with others. You can successfully work, play, and talk with others many times every day. Social well-being promotes healthy relationships.

Your sense of personal well-being depends on whether you are satisfied with your values and beliefs. Your values and beliefs increase your well-being if they are right for you and respectful of others. Your system of beliefs can guide you when you feel confused. It can help you make good decisions.

Health in Your Life

Create Your Own Support System

An important part of mental health is asking others for support. You might have a problem you cannot solve on your own. You might feel down. Talking to someone helps you see things more clearly. Make a list of people you can contact for these times. Write down the names, phone numbers, and e-mail addresses of your closest friends. Include other trusted adult family members and maybe your school counselor or the school nurse.

In turn, be a health advocate for your friends by supporting their health. You can support your friends' health by offering to listen when they need to talk. Make sure your friends have your contact information. Let them know you are there for them.

On a sheet of paper, write the answers to the following questions. Use complete sentences.

1. How can talking to people help you have good mental health?

2. Why is it a good idea to have a list of names ready when you need support?

3. Think about a time you needed support but did not ask for it. How do you think talking might have helped?

How Are the Forms of Well-Being Related?

Your overall well-being depends on how all these areas of well-being work together. For example, when you are physically healthy, you can handle emotional challenges better. A good mental attitude can promote physical health. Problems in one area of well-being can affect another area. For example, you may feel depressed if you do not feel well physically. You may not want to be with others if you are worried about something.

What Actions Promote Your Well-Being?

You can promote your well-being when you pay attention to how its different parts work together. Problems in one area may cause problems in another. The key to mental health is to support all four areas of your well-being. You do this by practicing healthy behaviors in all four areas.

Physical well-being means eating right, resting, and exercising. If you do become ill, knowing what to do can help you get well faster. For example, when you know that rest helps you get over the flu, you may sleep more.

For your emotional well-being, you need to learn how to handle stress. Many times, physical activity helps to relieve stress. This can be as simple as taking a walk. Understanding and dealing with your different emotions will also help relieve your stress.

To promote your social well-being, you can improve your understanding of others. You can learn about what others need. Some social skills that you can learn are:

- communication skills—listen, ask questions, be honest in what you say, and pay attention when others speak

- friendship skills—be a friend, ask others for advice, show respect and loyalty, and keep promises and confidences

- citizenship skills—follow the rules of society, respect others, do your part, and volunteer to help

Research and Write

What you choose as entertainment can help you have good mental health. It also can have negative health effects. Work in small groups to research healthy forms of entertainment. Then prepare posters with messages about healthy forms of entertainment. Aim the messages at people who are your age. Display the posters in the cafeteria, gym, or hallway.

For your personal well-being, you need to decide what your values and beliefs are. You need to figure out what is important to you and act in a way that is true to your beliefs. Is it right to help a friend? Is it right to copy answers on a test? Is it right to stay up too late and oversleep the next day? You face many similar questions and choices every day. Your sense of personal well-being can help you find the answers.

Working on all these areas of well-being helps promote your mental health. Maintaining your mental health can be difficult. Sometimes, you will be more successful than other times. However, maintaining your mental health is important to your overall well-being.

Lesson 1 Review On a sheet of paper, write the answers to the following questions. Use complete sentences.

1. What is one important early influence on personality development?

2. What are the four areas of well-being?

3. What are some skills that promote social well-being?

4. **Critical Thinking** Think of a positive social message that someone has given you recently. The person could be a classmate, teacher, or family member. How did that message affect your self-concept?

5. **Critical Thinking** A student is depressed because her best friend moved away. How might her depression affect her social health?

Objectives

After reading this lesson, you should be able to

◆ describe how to maintain healthy relationships

◆ explain how to set and reach goals

◆ use problem-solving skills to settle conflicts

◆ identify healthy ways of thinking

Emotional well-being is an ongoing process rather than an unchanging state of mind. Everyone has occasional setbacks and problems. Emotionally healthy people learn to solve problems and adjust to their world. People can learn abilities and behaviors to make themselves emotionally healthy.

How Can a Person Learn and Change?

People learn most things through experience. They change their behavior when they discover a better way to act.

When you make a mistake, you may feel upset or embarrassed. You can overcome this feeling by reminding yourself that everyone makes mistakes. You can also analyze, or figure out, what you learned from your mistake. Then you can decide to act differently next time.

Health Myth

Myth: Conflicts in relationships are not normal.

Fact: Conflicts are common and natural because people have different wants and needs. They see things in different ways. You cannot avoid conflict. What you can do is deal with conflict in a peaceful way. The skills you learn now to solve conflicts will help you the rest of your life.

How Can Relationships Be Maintained?

Problems in relationships are common. After all, people do not always want the same things or see things the same way. Emotionally healthy people learn how to communicate well with others. They usually can balance their own wishes with those of others. They learn to get along. When they have problems with others, they work through the problems. They pay attention to the needs of friends and family members.

Relationships change as you mature, or grow older. When you were young, you depended completely on others for love, care, and survival. As you mature, you form ties to other people. Emotionally healthy people value these ties. At the same time, they think for themselves. For example, you may ask your friends for advice about an important decision. You do that because you value their opinions.

In the end, however, you must decide for yourself what is right for you. Emotionally healthy people can form bonds with others and still follow their own belief system.

The Importance of Goals

Realistic

Practical or reasonable

Pessimism

Tending to expect the worst possible outcome

Optimism

Tending to expect the best possible outcome

For good emotional health, you need to set **realistic,** or reasonable, goals. Realistic goals are balanced between **pessimism** and unrealistic **optimism.** Pessimism is tending to expect the worst possible outcome. If you feel pessimistic about a goal, you may give up without trying. Optimism is tending to expect the best possible outcome. If your goal is too optimistic, you may not be able to reach it.

Decide for Yourself

Following the steps in this sequence chart can help you set and reach goals.

Setting Goals

Write down your goal.

↓

List the steps you need to reach your goal.

↓

Set up a time line for completing each step.

↓

Identify any problems that might get in your way.

↓

Check your progress as you work toward your goal.

On a sheet of paper, write the answers to the following questions. Use complete sentences.

1. List a goal you would like to achieve.
2. Go through the "Setting Goals" steps, using your specific goal.

Compromise

*Agree by giving in
a little*

Rational

Realistic or reasonable

Impulse

*The urge to react before
taking time to think*

How Can Conflicts Be Solved?

Conflicts happen for many reasons. Suppose you argue with a friend about how to raise money for your school. You think your plan is best. Your friend disagrees. You both become frustrated, or upset. Frustration is a common feeling when you are kept from reaching a goal. Emotionally healthy people find a way to solve conflicts. One way is to **compromise.** Both sides agree to give in a little. In that way, no one "loses." Another way to solve a conflict is to look at other choices. You and your friend could find out about other ways to raise money. Then you can work together to decide which way is best.

Rational thinking is important in solving problems. Something rational is realistic or reasonable. For example, imagine you want to buy a new music system. Your parents think it costs more than you can afford. You have to think rationally. Do you have enough money, or can you earn the amount you need? If you borrow the money, will you be able to pay it back? After careful thought, you may decide that your plan can work. Or you may decide that the item is too expensive to buy.

How Can Emotions Be Managed?

Remember that emotions signal needs. However, these signals are not always adjusted to the correct "volume." For example, when you are tired, you may react too strongly, or overreact, to a situation. If you were rested, you might react with more control.

Everyone has **impulses.** An impulse is the urge to react before taking time to think. For example, if someone bumps into you, your impulse may be to bump that person back. Emotional health depends on being able to think about the consequences and learning to control your impulses. Consider what might happen if you react a certain way. In this example, you can predict that if you followed through with your impulse and bumped the person back, you might get into an argument or even a fight. You think about it and realize that the person did not bump you on purpose, and you let it go. You have thought about the consequence and controlled your impulse.

What Are Some Healthy Ways of Thinking?

Most actions and emotions begin with thoughts. For example, if you think someone has insulted you, you may feel angry. If you believe the person did not mean to insult you, you may not feel angry. Emotionally healthy people think in ways that help them adjust and reach their goals. They have four helpful thinking styles—realistic optimism, meaningful values, coping, and healthy explanations.

Realistic Optimism

Realistic means practical. When emotionally healthy people think with realistic optimism, they:

- set and work toward goals that are challenging but reachable

- recognize what can and cannot be controlled in their life

- have faith in themselves and hope that events will work out for the best

Meaningful Values

Emotionally healthy people make sure their actions are based on their values. They look on **disadvantages** as challenges to be overcome. A disadvantage is a condition or situation that makes reaching a goal harder. Emotionally healthy people:

- develop values that become part of them and guide their thinking and behavior

- reflect on their own feelings and thoughts instead of worrying about how others might judge them

- face and overcome disadvantages

- find meaning in their work or actions

Coping

People respond, or react, in two ways to stress—avoidance or coping. Sometimes, avoidance is the best response. For example, you should get away from someone who tries to harm you. Most often, however, avoidance does not remove the stress.

If you avoid a problem, you may develop **symptoms** of illness. A symptom is a bodily reaction that signals an illness or a physical problem. For example, you may feel anxious about a long assignment. You could avoid the feeling by playing video games and trying to forget about it. You will probably still continue to feel anxious. You may even develop other symptoms, such as a headache or an upset stomach. Coping deals with and removes stress and anxiety.

Emotionally healthy people cope by:

- learning from experiences, mistakes, and successes

- knowing when to change behaviors that are not working

- asking for help from family members, school counselors, or other trusted adults

- trying again after a failure

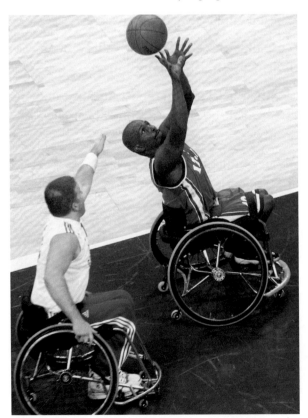

Figure 3.2.1 *People can overcome disadvantages.*

Healthy Explanations

Sometimes a loss or a disappointment can result in stress. **Resilient** people tend to bounce back or recover easily from misfortune or hardship. How do they do it? Resilient people have a positive way of looking at things. They cope by talking to friends and family. They often find that volunteering in their communities and giving back to others less fortunate is helpful. Resilient people believe they have some control over their lives. They accept that they cannot control everything.

Emotionally healthy people use a positive thinking style to explain events. You may wonder why unpleasant events occur. The answers you come up with can influence the quality of your life. For example, a student receives a poor grade on a test. He could react by thinking "This isn't fair! Why is it happening to me?" A more positive reaction would be "That was a hard test! I think I can do better next time."

Emotionally healthy people who have positive attitudes cope by:

- looking on the positive side

- talking to friends, family, or trusted adults

- helping someone else or volunteering in the community

- letting go of the worries about things they cannot change

Lesson 2 Review On a sheet of paper, write the word or phrase in parentheses that best completes each sentence.

1. A person who usually expects the best possible outcome is showing (optimism, pessimism, compromise).

2. People who base their behavior on their values are showing the thinking style called (meaningful values, healthy explanations, coping).

3. One way to solve a conflict is through (avoidance, compromise, pessimism).

On a sheet of paper, write the answers to the following questions. Use complete sentences.

4. **Critical Thinking** A student gets kicked off the soccer team because she did not pass her English class. How might she use coping skills to deal with what happened?

5. **Critical Thinking** Suppose you trip over someone's foot in the hall as you're going to your next class. Your impulse is to react angrily because you think the person tripped you on purpose. What might you do to manage your anger?

Everyone has a need to belong to a group. The most common way people meet that need is to form and maintain close relationships. Some relationships, such as those with family members, are chosen for you. You choose other relationships, such as friendships. Healthy relationships can help make your life happier.

What Makes a Relationship Healthy?

A healthy, close relationship has these characteristics:

• emotional attachment

• mutual, or common, dependence between partners

• satisfaction of both partners' needs

The needs that a close relationship satisfies include **intimate** communication and the need to **nurture.** Something intimate is very personal or private. Intimate communication is being able to confide in someone you trust. To nurture means to help someone or something grow or develop.

What Is the Basis of Friendships?

The most common close relationship is friendship. Most friendships are based on something people have in common. You make friends because you share interests and activities. You can more easily plan time doing things with someone who enjoys what you do. You might also share similar backgrounds with your friends. You might share the same values and goals. Sharing common values and goals can strengthen your self-concept and lift your self-esteem.

How Can Relationships Be Maintained?

As close as two people may be, they are still individuals with separate lives and experiences. Staying friends can be difficult when one or both of you grow and change.

Since everyone changes throughout life, you must work at maintaining relationships. One action you can take is to keep communicating with each other. Writing or talking can help you avoid misunderstandings. Both will help you keep learning about each other. Another action you can take is to show an interest in your friend's new hobbies or activities. In turn, you can share your own new hobbies or activities with your friend.

Self-acceptance helps maintain a strong, healthy relationship. When you accept yourself, accepting others is easier. You do not feel threatened by others' differences. Healthy relationships allow people to be themselves. Suppose you are interested in photography, but your friends are not. If your relationships are healthy, your friends will respect your need to spend time on your hobby by yourself. Relationships that limit people are unhealthy. Relationships in which people are asked to go against their belief systems also are unhealthy. Suppose a friend dislikes you because you will not go along with something. That is an unhealthy relationship.

Figure 3.3.1 *Sharing your interests with friends helps maintain relationships.*

What Makes Communication Successful?

Communication is a basic part of relationships. You must be able to clearly state your beliefs, opinions, and feelings. Good communication skills strengthen relationships and reduce conflicts. They bring you closer to friends and family. Communication can mean talking, writing, touching, listening, smiling, and even knowing when to be silent.

Every communication has a sender and a receiver. The sender sends a message to the receiver with a specific purpose or intent.

Communication is effective, or successful, when the sender's intent matches the effect on the receiver. Suppose you want to compliment your friend. If she feels good because of the words you say, your communication was effective.

Successful communication includes three basic skills: speaking, listening, and body language. Body language, or **nonverbal communication,** is using your body to send messages. Examples of body language are arm or head movements, looking away from the speaker, nodding your head, and frowning.

To communicate effectively:

- Think about what you want to say before you say it.

- Speak as clearly as possible.

- Avoid statements that put down the other person.

- Use "I" messages. "I" messages clearly state how you feel. "I" messages help other people understand how their behavior affects you. They are different from "you" messages, which tend to make other people feel angry, hurt, or embarrassed. Suppose a friend is often late for the movies. A "you" message would be "You're always late! Can't you get anywhere on time?" This message might make your friend angry. An "I" message would be "I like seeing the beginning of a movie and when you're late, I miss it." This message would tell your friend that it is important to you to be on time.

To listen effectively:

- Avoid interrupting the speaker.

- Give the speaker your attention. Do not fidget or look away.

- Focus on what the speaker is saying. Do not think about what you are going to say next. You might miss something important.

※ ※ ※ ※ ※ ※ ※ ※ ※ ※ ※

Technology and Society

About 75 percent of teens use the Internet regularly. In spite of fears that teens online might avoid communicating with people, the opposite is true. Teens use e-mail and instant messaging to stay in touch with friends and family. Most also spend at least the same amount of time with people as they did before.

- Repeat in your own words what the speaker said. By doing this, you make sure you understand the speaker's intended message. You might start by saying "What you mean is" or "What I'm hearing is."

To use nonverbal communication effectively:

- Make sure your body language matches the message you intend. Suppose you tell a friend that you are happy to see him. You frown and your arms are crossed. Your body language shows the opposite of what you are saying.

- Pay attention to your tone of voice. If you use positive words with a negative or insincere tone, your friend may feel insulted instead of complimented.

What Makes Communication Unsuccessful?

Ineffective, or unsuccessful, communication has three possible sources. They are twisted sending, twisted receiving, and poor communication conditions. Twisted sending can be poor word choices or not knowing what to say. It can mean your body language is sending the opposite message from your words. Twisted receiving usually results from poor listening. Suppose you think you know what the teacher is going to say. You may pretend to listen while your attention is elsewhere. Later, you realize that you have no idea what the teacher really said.

Poor communication conditions may include noise, interruptions, and lack of time. For example, suppose your friend's cell phone rings while you are talking with her. She answers the call, and you lose your train of thought. You forget what you were going to tell her.

Research and Write

In small groups, research other communication skills. You might survey people to gather their favorite tips. Then write and perform a skit in which you show effective communication skills. Make sure you use nonverbal communication to help get your message across.

How Does Self-Esteem Affect Relationships?

Relationships meet some, but not all, needs. Expecting too much from a friend or partner is easy. Romantic fairy tales and movies make people hope another person can make them happy. The truth is that happiness comes from your own thoughts, feelings, and actions. Likewise, other people should not depend on you for their happiness.

Relationships are healthy when both people have high self-esteem. People who accept themselves and have meaningful goals are better able to give affection to others. You promote healthy relationships when you learn about and appreciate yourself. Continue to develop your interests and improve your skills. The more you like yourself, the healthier your relationships will be.

Lesson 3 Review On a sheet of paper, write the answers to the following questions. Use complete sentences.

1. What is the basis of most friendships?

2. What are two things you can do to maintain a relationship?

3. What three things can make communication unsuccessful?

4. **Critical Thinking** A friend said she would call you. You are upset that she did not. What "I" message would express your feelings?

5. **Critical Thinking** A friend says, "My girlfriend makes me very happy." Can that be true? Explain your answer.

Link to ➤➤➤

Culture

Nonverbal communication does not always mean the same things in all cultures. For example, in some cultures, looking someone in the eye is disrespectful. Smiling may mean the person is really angry. Touching a stranger may be considered rude. Learning how people from other cultures communicate can help you avoid conflicts.

Objectives

After reading this lesson, you should be able to

◆ explain what self-awareness and social comparison are

◆ describe how you can improve your self-acceptance

◆ describe how self-acceptance improves relationships

◆ identify ways to accept yourself

Self-awareness

Understanding oneself as an individual

Social comparison

Observing other people to determine how to behave

You can perform better when you accept and feel good about yourself. Your mind will work better, too. Your relationships will be healthier. Improving your self-acceptance and relationships with others can support your mental health. Two things that can help you improve your self-acceptance are **self-awareness** and **social comparison.**

What Is Self-Awareness?

Self-awareness is understanding yourself as an individual. You understand your feelings and goals from moment to moment. For example, what are you feeling right now as you read this book? You may be comfortable, or you may be tired and unable to concentrate. If you are not comfortable, you may decide to find a better place to study. Being self-aware will help you make a good choice and will increase your chances for success.

Self-awareness also means understanding how you feel about things. How do you feel about your abilities, appearance, and behavior? What are your goals? The more you understand yourself, the better you can understand others.

What Is Social Comparison?

Social comparison is observing other people to help you decide how to behave. You can use social comparison to improve your self-acceptance. Suppose you are taking a new computer class and do not know what to do. You notice other students ask permission before using the computers. You copy their behavior and in that way learn for yourself.

How Does Self-Acceptance Improve Relationships?

As you accept yourself more, others will be more comfortable with you. Spending time with people who have poor self-acceptance can be uncomfortable. They may constantly put themselves down. You may try to help them see themselves differently, but they may not accept your help.

Prejudice

Negative, or unfavorable, opinions formed about something or someone without enough experience or knowledge

Discriminate

Treat differently on the basis of something other than individual worth

What is one thing teenagers can do to stop prejudice?

People who feel good about themselves do not expect others to build them up or entertain them. People who accept themselves are more likely to accept individual differences, get to know a variety of people, and give and accept help.

Accept Individual Differences

By nature, people are different from one another. Some differences are easy to see, such as skin color, gender, and height. Some differences are not visible, such as thoughts and feelings. For example, some people are born with a more sensitive temperament than others. Some people have different personal beliefs than do others. Everyone has different talents and abilities.

Unfortunately, people may form negative, or unfavorable, opinions about someone who is different from themselves. This is called **prejudice.** They may not even know this person but may still dislike him or her. Prejudiced people tend to **discriminate** against others who are different from themselves. They treat others differently on the basis of something other than individual worth. Prejudice creates unhealthy situations. Suppose you learn that people you have never met dislike you. You are different from them in some way. You, in turn, may find it hard to like these people because you believe they are being unfair. This cycle becomes difficult to break. Prejudice can destroy the fairness, honesty, and goodwill of a school and community.

Link to ➤➤➤

Language Arts

Tony Morrison's novel *The Bluest Eye* focuses on two African American girls from different families. One girl is abused and feels ugly for being black. She believes that she can be happy only if she becomes white. She prays for blue eyes. Her sadness makes her ill. The other girl likes the way she looks. Her self-acceptance helps her stay healthy.

You can learn to value differences in people. You can do this by truly getting to know a person. Differences in people add richness to your relationships. Suppose you get to know someone from another country. You may find you are developing new tastes in food and music. You may come to appreciate and respect different points of view.

Get to Know a Variety of People

You can overcome prejudices when you get to know members of different groups. Working together toward a common goal is a way to learn cooperation. Through this, you discover how you are alike. You begin to have **empathy** with one another. You recognize and understand other people's feelings. Close relationships are healthiest when they are based on empathy.

Here are some other ways you can get to know a variety of people:

- Get to know a person of the opposite sex as a friend rather than as a possible date.

- Meet people from different cultural backgrounds or religions through common interests such as music or sports.

- Establish relationships with older adults—grandparents, family friends, or others. They can offer practical advice for problem solving and decision making based on their experiences.

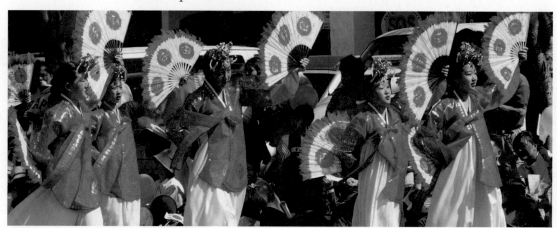

Figure 3.4.1 *One way to overcome prejudices is by learning about people from different cultural backgrounds.*

Give and Accept Help

Social support

Help for those you care about

Friends help you do things, solve problems, and deal with hard times. Help for those you care about is called **social support.** To improve your relationships with others, you can learn how to give and accept social support. This is also another way to improve your emotional health.

When a friend is in need, you may empathize and want to help. Suppose your best friend has had a painful loss. However, your friend may not be willing to ask you for help. You can still do many things to support your friend. You can take notes in a class your friend had to miss. You can offer to take care of a pet or run an errand. It is best to offer something particular. For example, you might ask "Can I help by taking care of your younger brother for you today?"

Sometimes, you are the one to accept social support when you need help. Needing help is not a sign of weakness or failure. Everyone needs help at times. When you let others give you social support, your friendships grow stronger.

▼◀▲▼◀▲▼◀▲▼◀▲▼◀▲▼◀▲▼◀▲▼◀▲▼◀▲▼◀▲▼◀▲▼◀▲▼◀▲▼◀▲▼◀▲▼◀▲▼◀▲▼

Health at Work

High School Counselor

High school counselors help students handle problems. They also help students develop realistic school and career goals. They advise students about college majors and technical schools. They help provide students with life skills that will improve their personal and social health. Counselors are trained to help students deal with personal problems. For example, they help students avoid drug use and learn how to solve conflicts. Counselors are dedicated to their jobs and deal with problems every day. A master's degree in counseling is usually required. All states require school counselors to be certified in counseling.

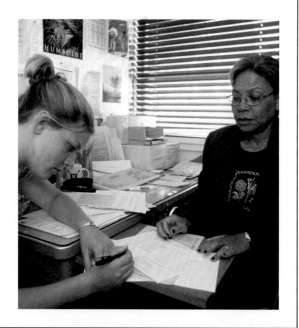

Lesson 4 Review On a sheet of paper, write the letter of the answer that best completes each sentence.

1. When you observe other people to decide how to behave, you are practicing _____.
    A empathy   **C** social comparison
    B prejudice   **D** social support

2. A person who discriminates against others is likely to _____.
    A feel empathy for others
    B have poor self-acceptance
    C have different abilities from others
    D have a high degree of self-acceptance

3. Self-accepting people _____.
    A make friends only with people who are like them
    B get to know older adults, such as grandparents
    C refuse social support to show how tough they are
    D look only to themselves to decide how to behave

On a sheet of paper, write the answers to the following questions. Use complete sentences.

4. **Critical Thinking** A friend has missed several days of school because of illness. What are two things you could do to show your friend social support?

5. **Critical Thinking** Describe one form of prejudice you have observed at your school. Suppose you could talk with the people who are prejudiced. What would you say to them?

Chapter 3   S U M M A R Y

- Personality development is affected by temperament, meaningful relationships formed early in life, and self-concept.

- What other people tell you about yourself and how they act toward you help shape your self-concept. The media also help form your self-concept.

- The areas of well-being are physical, social, emotional, and personal well-being. The four areas of well-being balance and influence one another.

- You can promote your well-being by staying healthy and learning how to handle stress. You can also promote your well-being by improving your understanding of others and forming beliefs and values.

- Emotional well-being is an ongoing process that you work on throughout your life.

- Characteristics of emotional health include the ability to learn and change through experiences, balancing personal needs with the needs of others, setting and reaching goals, solving conflicts rationally, controlling impulses, and thinking in healthy ways.

- Healthy relationships involve emotional attachment, mutual dependence, and satisfaction of both partners.

- Maintaining healthy relationships involves successful communication and good self-esteem.

- You can become more emotionally healthy by improving your self-acceptance through self-awareness and social comparison.

- Self-acceptance helps you improve relationships with others. You can learn about and value differences among people.

Vocabulary

compromise, 57	nurture, 61	resilient, 59
disadvantage, 58	optimism, 56	self-awareness, 66
discriminate, 67	personality, 50	social comparison, 66
empathy, 68	pessimism, 56	social support, 69
impulse, 57	prejudice, 67	social esteem, 51
intimate, 61	rational, 57	symptom, 59
nonverbal communication, 63	realistic, 56	temperament, 50

Chapter 3   R E V I E W

Word Bank

compromise

discriminate

empathy

impulses

intimate

nonverbal
   communication

optimism

prejudice

rational

resilient

social comparison

social esteem

symptom

temperament

Vocabulary Review

On a sheet of paper, write the word or phrase from the Word Bank that best completes each sentence.

1. A person's emotional makeup is the person's _____.

2. The way others value you is your _____.

3. Realistic goals are balanced between pessimism and unrealistic _____.

4. When people work out a solution to a problem by giving in a little, they _____.

5. Solving problems requires _____ thinking.

6. Emotionally healthy people learn to control their _____.

7. A(n) _____ may develop if a person avoids dealing with a difficult situation.

8. People who are _____ bounce back from disappointments.

9. Being able to confide in someone you trust is the basis of _____ communication.

10. Shaking your head and smiling are examples of _____.

11. Observing others to determine how to behave is called _____.

12. A negative opinion formed without enough experience or knowledge is _____.

13. Prejudiced people tend to _____ against people who are different from themselves.

14. Trying to identify and understand other people's feelings is _____.

Concept Review

On a sheet of paper, write the letter of the answer that best completes each sentence.

15. The factor that has the most influence on a child's personality development is _____.

   A beliefs   **C** values

   B temperament   **D** well-being

16. An example of how two different forms of well-being affect each other is _____.

   A eating healthful foods gives a person energy

   B good communication skills help a person be a friend

   C having many friends helps a person handle stress

   D strong values guide a person in making decisions

17. The difference between coping and avoidance as a way to deal with stress is that _____.

   A coping deals with stress, while avoidance does not

   B coping is more likely to lead to symptoms of illness

   C avoidance is more likely to get rid of the source of stress

   D avoidance means asking for help from friends or family

Critical Thinking

On a sheet of paper, write the answers to the following questions. Use complete sentences.

18. What can you do to teach someone to be less prejudiced?

19. Are you better at sending or receiving communications? How can you become better at either sending or receiving?

20. Is it healthy to feel that you must control everything in a relationship? Explain your answer.

Self-Assessment

Can you answer these questions?

☑ 1. What does having good mental health mean?

☑ 2. What are self-defeating behaviors?

☑ 3. What defense mechanisms do you use?

☑ 4. Why are dysfunctional relationships unhealthy?

☑ 5. What is a substance abuse disorder?

☑ 6. How can anxiety disorders be treated?

☑ 7. What is a phobia?

☑ 8. How many people suffer from clinical depression?

☑ 9. Are teens at risk for suicide?

☑ 10. How serious is an eating disorder?

4 Recognizing Mental Health Problems

Have you ever heard someone called "crazy"? What did you think that meant? Have you wondered about the difference between mentally healthy and unhealthy behavior? Mental health covers a wide range of behaviors. The most helpful sign of mental health is how well a person gets along in his or her world. Everyone has difficulties at times. While calling someone "crazy" is never OK, a person whose behavior is often unhealthy may have mental health problems. The person may even have a mental disorder. Most mental health problems and disorders can be treated successfully.

In this chapter, you will learn about some of the symptoms of poor mental health and some self-defeating behaviors. You will learn about mental disorders and what can be done for them. You will learn some ways to improve your emotional well-being.

Goals for Learning

◆ To identify some characteristics of poor mental health

◆ To explain self-defeating behaviors

◆ To identify substance abuse disorders, anxiety disorders, affective disorders, and thought disorders, and how these disorders are treated

◆ To describe three kinds of eating disorders

A person is usually neither completely mentally healthy nor completely mentally ill. Mentally healthy people may have problems, make mistakes, and behave in self-defeating ways. People with mental health problems still do many things well. The difference has to do with patterns of behavior that are either normal or **abnormal.** Abnormal means not usual.

How Do Behaviors Indicate Mental Health?

A **psychologist** is someone who studies mental and behavioral characteristics. Most psychologists evaluate mental health by determining the level of normal behavior. If a person has many abnormal behaviors, that person may not be mentally healthy. The more abnormal a behavior or thinking pattern is, the greater the possible risk of mental illness.

Psychologists define normal and abnormal behavior in many ways. One way is to judge how well a person adjusts to life's changes. People who meet their basic needs and personal goals show a normal pattern of behavior. They get along independently and maintain personal relationships. People who have difficulty getting along with others or who depend too much on others show abnormal behavior patterns. People whom failure easily defeats also show behavior that is considered abnormal.

Abnormal

Unusual or different from normal

Psychologist

A person who studies mental and behavioral characteristics

Self-defeating behavior

An action that blocks a person's efforts to reach goals

What is an adjustment you have made recently?

What Are Self-Defeating Behaviors?

Self-defeating behaviors block a person from reaching his or her own goals. For example, suppose you want to try out for the swim team. You know you must practice and increase your speed. The day before tryouts, you practice for a long time. Then you decide to practice even more that evening. You end up being tired and do not perform well at tryouts the next day. The decision to practice too much was self-defeating. It actually blocked you from reaching your goal.

Defense mechanism

A mental device one uses to protect oneself

Dysfunctional

Harmed or unhealthy

Repression

A refusal to think about something that upsets you

Denial

A refusal to believe or accept something negative or threatening

Projection

Assuming that another person has one's own attitudes, feelings, or purposes

Displacement

Shifting an emotion from its real object to a safer or more immediate one

Sometimes self-defeating behavior is a sign of poor mental health. Such behavior can take many different forms. Two common forms of self-defeating behavior are **defense mechanisms** and **dysfunctional** relationships. A defense mechanism is a mental device that people use to protect themselves. A dysfunctional relationship is harmed in some way, or unhealthy.

Defense Mechanisms

People use various defense mechanisms to hide from their problems instead of solving them. The most common defense mechanisms are **repression, denial, projection, and displacement.**

- Repression is a refusal to think about something that upsets you. For example, you may "forget" about a dental appointment that you don't want to go to.

- Denial is a refusal to believe or accept something negative or threatening. For example, an older person you know is very ill, but you do not believe that the person might die.

- Projection is assuming that someone has the same attitudes, feelings, or purposes as you. For example, if you are angry with your brother, you may project your anger on him. You might say "What are you so mad about?"

- Displacement is shifting an emotion from its real object to a safer one. For example, your supervisor made you stay late to fix a problem at work. You are angry but afraid to say anything to the supervisor. When your mother calls, you yell at her for asking a simple question. You displaced your anger from its real object to a safer one.

You can probably identify many examples of these defense mechanisms in your own and others' behavior. Using defense mechanisms is often normal, but using them too much leads to self-defeating behavior.

Writing down your thoughts and feelings can help you deal with them. You can write letters that you do not mail. You can also write stories about something that has happened.

You can watch your use of defense mechanisms by reviewing your behavior. For example, if you often "forget" important or unpleasant events, you may be using repression too much. If you often say "This isn't serious" when talking about difficulties, you may be overusing denial. Realizing that you use these defense mechanisms is the first step toward changing your behavior.

Dysfunctional Relationships

In many dysfunctional relationships, people meet each other's needs in what turn out to be destructive ways. A common form of dysfunction in a relationship is poor communication. For example, you are worried about something but refuse to confide in a close friend about it. Your friend cannot offer help or understand what is wrong. If you continue to refuse help, others may feel pushed away and may withdraw from you. Unfortunately, you may be cutting yourself off from others' support when you need it most.

Health at Work

Resident Assistant

Resident assistants work with residents in mental health settings, hospitals, and nursing homes. When residents need help, assistants answer the call. They may check a resident's temperature, blood pressure, pulse, and breathing rate. Sometimes they bathe residents or give massages. Resident assistants help people who must stay in bed or a wheelchair. They deliver and serve meals and help residents eat when necessary. They socialize with residents, make them comfortable, and lift their spirits. Sometimes resident assistants are called nurses' aides or nurse assistants. Training varies from on-the-job training to formal training programs. The training programs may take several weeks or more to complete.

Give "I" messages respectfully and kindly to maintain communication in relationships.

Link to ➤➤➤

Language Arts
Journaling is one way to deal with emotional problems. By writing your thoughts and feelings down, and connecting them with the events in your life, you can gain valuable insights. Some artists and famous people have published their journals. These expressions about their lives are part of their craft.

You can avoid this self-defeating pattern of shutting out other people. You do this by identifying the people you trust. When you are troubled, you can talk with these people about your feelings. A helpful hint is to start your sentences with "I" messages. For example, "I feel nervous" or "I worry that you'll get upset with me." Starting a statement with "I" makes it easier for others to understand and respond to you.

Figure 4.1.1 *When you are angry, you may project your anger on the person you are angry with.*

When you have problems, you may make heavy demands on a friend or family member. You may want the person to reassure you or spend time with you. If you do this too often, the other person may become worn out and refuse to help you. Expecting another person to make you happy is unreasonable. People who love you will give you help, but only you can be responsible for your happiness.

If you feel you make too many demands on friends or family members, you can work on changing your behavior. You can try to help yourself. By learning to take care of yourself, you can become more independent. You can also become less demanding and can improve your mental health.

Lesson 1 Review On a sheet of paper, write the answers to the following questions. Use complete sentences.

1. What is one way to decide if a person is mentally healthy?

2. What are self-defeating behaviors?

3. What are four defense mechanisms?

4. **Critical Thinking** Give an example of a dysfunctional relationship.

5. **Critical Thinking** What is an example of an "I" message?

Objectives

After reading this lesson, you should be able to

◆ explain what substance abuse and anxiety disorders are

◆ describe the symptoms of clinical depression

◆ explain thought disorders

◆ describe three eating disorders

Substance abuse disorder

An unhealthy dependence on alcohol or other drugs

Addicted

Unable to stop using alcohol or another drug

Anxiety disorder

A mental problem that makes normal life difficult because of intense anxiety

Panic attack

A feeling of terror that comes without warning and includes symptoms of chest pain, rapid heartbeat, sweating, shaking, or shortness of breath

While many mental health problems are not considered serious, some are quite serious. The more you know about the most common mental disorders, the less frightening they may seem. A disorder is a sickness or a disease. More knowledge can also help you promote your own and others' mental health.

What Are Substance Abuse Disorders?

A **substance abuse disorder** is an unhealthy dependence on alcohol or other drugs. Most substance abuse begins as a defensive behavior pattern. For example, a person may drink alcohol because he thinks he will feel less shy and self-conscious. Someone else may use another drug because it helps her feel happy and confident. Alcohol and other drugs never solve the real problem. Since the problem still exists, the user must rely on the drug more and more. Many substances are habit forming. You can become **addicted** to alcohol and certain other drugs. That means you cannot stop using the drug.

What Are Anxiety Disorders?

Anxiety is a feeling of uneasiness or fearful concern. All people have anxiety at some time. An **anxiety disorder** is a mental problem that makes normal life difficult because of intense anxiety. An extreme symptom of an anxiety disorder is a **panic attack.** A panic attack is a feeling of terror that comes without warning. Its symptoms include chest pain, rapid heartbeat, sweating, shaking, or shortness of breath. It can be triggered by a particular place or situation or may result from increasing stress.

There are different types of anxiety disorders. One is social anxiety disorder. This disorder makes people intensely afraid of situations where they might be embarrassed. These are usually social situations. People with social anxiety disorder may sweat heavily, blush, tremble, and have heart palpitations. They also may become confused.

Phobia

Excessive fear of an object or a specific situation

Affective disorder

A mental problem in which a person has disturbed or uncontrolled emotions

Clinical depression

An affective disorder involving long-lasting, intense sadness

Suicide

The act of killing oneself

Bipolar disorder

An affective disorder involving an uncontrolled shift from feeling too much energetic emotion to feeling very depressed

Research and Write

There are other types of anxiety disorders than the ones discussed in this lesson. Research these other types and write an article that explains them.

Another type of anxiety disorder is a **phobia.** A phobia is an excessive fear of an object or a specific situation. An example is claustrophobia. This is a fear of small spaces. People with claustrophobia will have difficulty doing ordinary things such as riding in elevators.

What Are Affective Disorders?

An **affective disorder** is a mental disorder in which a person has disturbed or uncontrolled emotions. The most common affective disorder is **clinical depression.**

Many people have mild depression. For example, you may feel depressed if you break up with someone. For most people, the level of depression is related to the loss. If it is not a serious loss, you will feel better and go back to normal activities quickly.

Clinical depression is a long-lasting, intense sadness. It comes from a change in brain chemistry. That means it has a physical cause.

People with clinical depression have trouble handling normal activities. They may not eat and might lose weight. They often have trouble sleeping, or they may want to sleep all day. They find it difficult to concentrate and have poor performance in school. Clinically depressed people cannot take pleasure in activities they used to enjoy. They feel worthless and guilty. They have low energy levels and withdraw from other people.

In any given 1-year period, almost 10 percent of Americans have clinical depression. In its most dangerous extremes, clinical depression may lead an individual to attempt **suicide,** or the act of killing oneself. Depression affects many teens. Suicide is the third leading cause of death among 15- to 24-year-olds.

Another example of an affective disorder is **bipolar disorder.** This disorder causes people to experience a wide shift in feeling. Their behavior changes from one extreme of overly energetic emotion to the other extreme of serious depression.

What Are Thought Disorders?

A **thought disorder** is the most serious kind of mental disorder. Symptoms of thought disorders are twisted or false ideas and beliefs. An example of a twisted idea is a **hallucination,** which is an idea about an unreal object or event. For example, a person who has hallucinations might see things that do not exist. An example of a twisted or false belief is a **delusion.** A person who has delusions might falsely believe that he or she is an entirely different person.

The combination of twisted ideas and false beliefs keeps a person with thought disorders out of touch with reality. This loss of touch with reality may range from mild to severe. A person with thought disorders may have only a few unrealistic ideas or may seem to live in a dream world. The person may say things that make no sense and may do things that seem very odd. The behavior can be frightening and dangerous. This is the type of mental illness most people think of when they say someone is "crazy."

Thought disorder

A mental problem in which a person has twisted or false ideas and beliefs

Hallucination

A twisted idea about an unreal object or event

Delusion

A false belief

Research and Write

A part of diagnosing depression is asking questions. Research the questions that doctors ask patients who might be depressed. Create an informational brochure that includes these questions.

Link to ➤ ➤ ➤

Geography

Scientists have found that seasonal affective disorder (SAD) affects about five million Americans. This condition causes depression, difficulty sleeping, and energy loss. Less daylight during winter months causes SAD. Northern areas of the United States have more cases of SAD than southern areas. Alaska has the highest rate, at 20 percent. Florida's rate of 1.4 percent is the lowest. Decreased daylight seems to reduce the amount of an important chemical in some people's brains. Recent tests show that treatment with light can restore the chemical. People sit in front of a light box for 30 minutes a day. When they do, they find their SAD symptoms are greatly reduced.

What Are Eating Disorders?

Eating disorders are attempts to cope with psychological problems through eating habits. People falsely believe that they do not look good and have to change their appearance. This focus on appearance may lead to an eating disorder. An eating disorder can be a way of avoiding the pain of regular life. Every feeling and struggle can be like a war between the individual and food. Eating disorders are serious. They can affect females and males. They severely challenge physical health. People can die from eating disorders. Look at Table 4.2.1 below to learn about three eating disorders.

Disorder	Description	Characteristics	Consequences
Anorexia	Emotional problem characterized by severe weight loss	• Extreme dieting, food rituals, not eating • Compulsive exercising • Frequent weighing • Intense fear of becoming fat	• Malnutrition • Menstruation stops • Lowered metabolic rate • Poor temperature regulation • Heart problems • Death
Bulimia	Emotional problem involving bingeing (eating large amounts of food in a short time) followed by purging (ridding one's body of the food) or severe dieting	• Fear or inability to stop eating • Vomiting or use of laxatives • Secretly storing up food • Extreme concentration on appearance • Feeling of being out of control • Depression	• Enlarged or ruptured stomach • Eroded tooth enamel • Pneumonia from inhaling vomit • Behavioral problems • Psychological problems • Danger of substance abuse
Binge Eating	Emotional problem involving bingeing but no purging	• Continually snacking • Large meals and frequent snacks while bingeing • Great feelings of guilt and shame for feeling out of control • Inability to stop eating during binges	• Obesity (condition of being extremely overweight) • Heart disease • Diabetes • Some kinds of cancer • Reduced life span

Table 4.2.1 *Eating disorders*

Lesson 2 Review On a sheet of paper, write the word from the Word Bank that best completes each sentence.

1. A person with _____ anxiety disorder may tremble, sweat, or have heart palpitations.

2. An extreme fear of an object is a(n) _____.

3. An inability to stop drinking alcohol is a(n) _____.

On a sheet of paper, write the answers to the following questions. Use complete sentences.

4. Critical Thinking Suppose a person has clinical depression. Will he or she be able to reach a challenging goal? Explain your answer.

5. Critical Thinking Name three eating disorders and describe how they are alike and how they are different.

❋❋❋❋❋❋❋❋❋❋❋❋❋❋❋❋❋❋❋❋❋❋❋❋❋❋❋❋❋❋❋❋❋❋❋

Technology and Society

The Internet has opened new avenues for people with mental disorders. Here are some things available online:

- **Information.** The Internet lists many sites for people with mental disorders. Some offer information. Others describe support groups, their work, and how to get in touch with them.

- **Communication.** Online magazines and newsletters are written by, for, and about people with mental disorders.

- **Community.** People with mental disorders can use online chat rooms and bulletin boards. They can share experiences and concerns. In online forums, experts speak on related topics and answer questions from online audiences.

Objectives

After reading this lesson, you should be able to

◆ explain how mental disorders are treated

◆ describe psychotherapy

◆ describe behavior modification

Psychotherapy

Psychological treatment for mental or emotional disorders

Behavior modification

Form of psychotherapy that teaches a person to replace a less effective behavior pattern with a more effective one

Cognitive therapy

Form of psychotherapy that teaches a person to replace destructive thoughts with positive ones

Trained mental health professionals are the best people to treat mental disorders. Symptoms of mental health problems can be relieved so the person is better able to live well. Many disorders can be cured, or people can learn to cope with them.

How Are Substance Abuse Disorders Treated?

People who abuse substances can get help. How well they respond to treatment depends on their determination to get well and regain control. They must decide never to use the drug again. The most important step is admitting a problem exists. For this reason, most treatment programs begin with self-awareness and admitting the need for help. Treatment may involve individual counseling, behavior change programs, or support groups.

How Are Anxiety Disorders Treated?

Anxiety disorders are really many different kinds of problems. Some are physical and some are psychological. Physical problems can be treated with medicine that a physician orders. Medicine can reduce the symptoms long enough for the person to learn how to prevent further problems. Psychological problems can be treated with **psychotherapy,** including behavior modification. Psychotherapy is psychological treatment for mental or emotional disorders. Counseling is a type of psychotherapy. People talk over their problems with a therapist or counselor. The counselor or therapist listens more than he or she talks. **Behavior modification** is another form of psychotherapy. It teaches a person to replace less effective behavior patterns with more effective ones. For example, through behavior modification, a person can learn to relax and avoid panic by using deep breathing. **Cognitive therapy** is also a way of treating anxiety disorders. In this type of therapy, people are taught to replace destructive thoughts with positive ones.

How Are Affective Disorders Treated?

Depression is an affective disorder. One way to deal with or prevent mild depression is to become involved in a goal-directed activity. Working to reach a reasonable goal helps set a new direction. The depressed person gains a sense of involvement in life and of being busy. Some examples are caring for a pet or taking up a hobby such as painting, photography, or writing stories. Physical activity also helps to relieve mild depression.

Clinical depression can be treated with help from professionals. Medical help includes medicines that work to bring the brain chemistry back to normal. Treatment also includes psychotherapy to help people see their problems and change their behavior patterns.

As with clinical depression, bipolar disorder requires professional help for treatment.

Health in Your Life

Advertising of Medications

Many people have suffered from clinical depression or an anxiety disorder without being diagnosed. They have not gotten help. In recent years, advertising for antidepressant and anti-anxiety medicines has helped with this. Ads for these medicines have appeared on TV, in magazines and newspapers, on billboards, and on the Internet.

By telling what a medicine is for, the ads explain to people what clinical depression or anxiety disorders are. Possible negative side effects of a medicine are quickly described at the end of TV commercials or in small print in ads. The person watching can then go to a doctor for diagnosis and treatment.

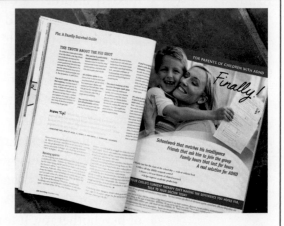

On a sheet of paper, write the answers to the following questions. Use complete sentences.

1. What is an advantage of advertising medicines?

2. What is a disadvantage of advertising medicines?

?

Should mentally ill people be allowed to have jobs and live by themselves?

How Are Thought Disorders Treated?

Only mental health professionals can treat thought disorders. Some medicines can reduce the symptoms, but there is no cure yet for thought disorders. Most individuals with thought disorders respond to treatment. Their symptoms may become fewer or may completely disappear. Some people do not respond to treatment and continue to have symptoms throughout their lives.

How Are Eating Disorders Treated?

People with eating disorders require professional help for treatment. People who have eating disorders often resist professional help. If you know someone who may have an eating disorder, encourage the person to get help. Let the person know you care about his or her well-being. Encourage the person to talk about his or her feelings. You can be a good role model by not criticizing your own body or appearance.

How Does Society Deal with Mental Illness?

Society has gradually changed the way it treats people who are mentally ill. Few people today believe that a person can catch mental illness from someone else. Yet, society still has great difficulty accepting mental illness without fear. People tend to fear what they do not understand. Other people's prejudices against mental illness can influence attitudes. For example, a person might find it hard to befriend someone whom others think is "sick" or "crazy."

Fortunately, developments in psychology and medicine have helped change attitudes toward people who are mentally ill. Almost everyone knows or is related to someone who has had psychological problems. For most of these problems, people can get help that will lessen or solve these problems.

Lesson 3 Review On a sheet of paper, write the word or phrase in parentheses that best completes each sentence.

1. Many treatment programs for substance abuse disorders begin with the person admitting the need for (confidence, help, willpower).

2. People who replace destructive thoughts with positive ones are using (cognitive therapy, defense mechanisms, hallucinations).

3. Mild depression can be relieved with (clinical depression, guilt, physical activity).

On a sheet of paper, write the answers to the following questions. Use complete sentences.

4. **Critical Thinking** An alcohol addict decides to drink alcohol only on weekends. Is this a good plan for treating this substance abuse disorder? Explain your answer.

5. **Critical Thinking** Why do people with thought disorders need treatment from mental health professionals?

Decide for Yourself

What kinds of messages about your body have you received from popular culture and the media? Popular culture glorifies thinness. All kinds of media—newspapers, magazines, billboards, movies, and TV—show only thin models and actors.

Every person's body is different. Suppose we all ate exactly the same thing and exercised the same way for a year. We still would not all look alike.

Here are some things to remember:

- Media images and messages rarely reflect reality.

- Ads have one purpose: to convince you to buy something.

- Ads often create an emotional experience. They show you what the advertiser thinks you want to see.

On a sheet of paper, write the answers to the following questions. Use complete sentences.

1. How much influence do you think popular culture and the media have on mental disorders? Explain your answer.

2. We would not all look alike even if we ate exactly the same thing and exercised exactly the same way. Why do you think this is true?

Chapter 4 SUMMARY

■ Mental health includes a broad range of behaviors.

■ Normal or abnormal behavior is best judged by how well a person adjusts to meeting basic needs and goals.

■ Patterns of self-defeating behaviors may indicate abnormal behavior.

■ Two common self-defeating behavior patterns are defense mechanisms and dysfunctional relationships.

■ Defense mechanisms are mental devices people use to protect themselves.

■ People with severe emotional problems may need professional help.

■ Substance abuse disorders involve a dependence on alcohol and other drugs.

■ A phobia, or irrational fear of an object or situation, is one kind of anxiety disorder.

■ One kind of affective disorder is clinical depression.

■ Thought disorders, the most serious kind of mental disorder, involve twisted thoughts and false beliefs.

■ Eating disorders are a type of mental problem involving overemphasis on appearance to avoid the pain of regular life.

■ Society's attitudes toward mental illness have changed, but some people still fear it.

■ Substance abuse disorders can be treated if an individual with the disorder is determined to get well.

■ Anxiety disorders can be treated with medication and psychotherapy.

■ People who are clinically depressed require help from professionals to get better.

Vocabulary

abnormal, 76

addicted, 80

affective disorder, 81

anxiety disorder, 80

behavior modification, 85

bipolar disorder, 81

clinical depression, 81

cognitive therapy, 85

defense mechanism, 77

delusion, 82

denial, 77

displacement, 77

dysfunctional, 77

eating disorder, 83

hallucination, 82

panic attack, 80

phobia, 81

projection, 77

psychologist, 76

psychotherapy, 85

repression, 77

self-defeating behavior, 76

substance abuse disorder, 80

suicide, 81

thought disorder, 82

Chapter 4 REVIEW

Word Bank

affective disorder

anxiety disorder

defense mechanisms

dysfunctional

eating disorder

hallucination

phobia

psychologist

repression

self-defeating behavior

substance abuse disorder

suicide

thought disorder

Vocabulary Review

On a sheet of paper, write the word or phrase from the Word Bank that best completes each sentence.

1. A(n) _____ is someone who studies mental and behavioral characteristics.

2. An irrational fear of an object is a(n) _____.

3. A(n) _____ blocks a person's efforts to reach goals.

4. Mental devices people use to protect themselves are _____.

5. A(n) _____ relationship is one that works in an unhealthy way.

6. A(n) _____ is an unhealthy dependence on alcohol and other drugs.

7. A panic attack is a symptom of a(n) _____.

8. Clinical depression is one kind of _____.

9. Symptoms of a(n) _____ are twisted ideas or false beliefs.

10. Extreme clinical depression may lead to _____.

11. A twisted idea about an unreal object or event is a(n) _____.

12. The refusal to think about something upsetting is _____.

13. A(n) _____ is an attempt to cope with psychological problems through eating habits.

Concept Review

On a sheet of paper, write the answers to the following questions. Use complete sentences.

14. How do most psychologists evaluate mental health?

15. What are two forms of self-defeating behavior?

16. Why are some relationships dysfunctional?

17. What is clinical depression and how is it treated?

18. What are two consequences of eating disorders?

Critical Thinking

On a sheet of paper, write the answers to the following questions. Use complete sentences.

19. Do you feel anxiety when you have to give a speech? How could you handle the anxiety?

20. If you believe a friend is feeling depressed, what could you do to help?

Test-Taking Tip Avoid waiting until the night before a test to study. Plan your study time so you can get a good night's sleep the night before a test.

The World Health Organization

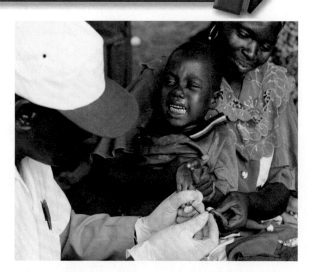

As part of the United Nations, the World Health Organization (WHO) identifies health issues around the world. The WHO represents 192 countries. All of these countries work together to fight disease and to work on other health issues. Some programs that the WHO supports address the health needs of specific countries. Other programs address worldwide heath issues. Each program responds to an immediate health crisis. The WHO works to stop the spread of AIDS. It also brings health care workers to regions in need and provides medicine to the poorest regions of the world. The following is an example of one of the WHO's many programs.

Niger

Niger is a country between Algeria, Chad, and Nigeria in Africa. It has a population of about 11.6 million people. More than 60 percent of its people live on less than one dollar a day. Most people do not live beyond the age of 44. More than 80 percent of the people cannot read. In 2004, a huge number of grasshoppers and a lack of rain totally destroyed the year's crop in many regions. About 3.6 million people, including nearly 200,000 children, were left without enough food.

People did not have safe drinking water. These poor living conditions resulted in widespread diseases.

A team of experts from the WHO arrived in Niger to study the problem. They worked with Niger's leaders. The WHO asked members of the United Nations for $1.3 million to help the people of Niger get medicine and food. The project in Niger was part of the WHO's efforts in many African countries to improve health.

On a sheet of paper, write the answers to the following questions. Use complete sentences.

1. Why is the WHO important?

2. How does the WHO bring countries together?

3. What do you think is the biggest challenge for the WHO?

- People need good health to accomplish the things they need and like to do.

- A person must have physical health, social health, and emotional health to be truly healthy.

- A health risk can cause disease. Many health risks relate to heredity, the environment, and behavior.

- You can set short-term and long-term goals as you make health decisions.

- Emotions begin with thoughts and may cause physical changes or reactions.

- Five basic human needs are physical, safety, belonging, esteem, and self-actualization needs.

- Stress is a mental and physical reaction to anything that requires you to change.

- Coping with stress involves thinking through a problem, deciding how to solve the problem, and carrying out your decision.

- All emotions are normal. How you handle emotions is important to your mental health.

- Personality development is affected by temperament, meaningful relationships formed early in life, and self-concept.

- Maintaining your emotional well-being is an ongoing process that you work on throughout your life.

- Characteristics of emotional health include the ability to learn and change through experiences and balancing personal needs with the needs of others. They also include setting and reaching goals, solving conflicts rationally, controlling impulses, and thinking in healthy ways.

- Healthy relationships involve emotional attachment, mutual dependence, and the satisfaction of both partners.

- Normal or abnormal behavior is best judged by how well a person adjusts to meeting basic needs and goals.

- Substance abuse disorders involve a dependence on alcohol and other drugs. This type of disorder can be treated if the individual is determined to get well.

- One kind of affective disorder is clinical depression. People who are clinically depressed require help from professionals to get better.

- Society's attitudes toward mental illness have changed, but some people still fear it.

Unit 1   R E V I E W

Word Bank

bipolar disorder

defense
  mechanism

depression

phobia

physical
  environment

prejudice

sedentary

self-esteem

social comparison

stress

symptom

wellness

Vocabulary Review

On a sheet of paper, write the word or phrase from the Word Bank that best completes each sentence.

1. People who do not get much physical activity have a(n) _____ lifestyle.

2. The value that you place on yourself is your _____.

3. A bodily reaction that signals an illness or a physical problem is a(n) _____.

4. The extreme fear of an object or a specific situation is a(n) _____.

5. The area around you, including the air, land, and buildings, is your _____.

6. Learning about proper behavior by watching other people is _____.

7. Balancing physical, social, and emotional health is a way to achieve _____.

8. If one's feelings shift uncontrollably from energetic emotions to serious depression, the person may have _____.

9. Having a negative opinion about a group of people before even meeting them is a form of _____.

10. A mental device that people use to hide from their problems is a(n) _____.

11. A common reaction to grief is a state of deep sadness called _____.

12. People must change in response to physical or emotional pressure, and this reaction is _____.

Concept Review

On a sheet of paper, write the letter of the answer that best completes each sentence.

13. Heredity, environment, culture, and behavior all can be causes for _____.

   A biofeedback   **C** secondhand smoke

   B community resources   **D** health risks

14. Abraham Maslow's list of human needs includes physical, safety, _____, esteem, and self-actualization needs.

   A belonging   **C** hierarchy

   B fight-or-flight   **D** aggression

15. One way that people can solve a conflict is by agreeing to _____.

   A discriminate   **C** have delusions

   B compromise   **D** use body language

16. Anorexia and bulimia are types of _____.

   A hallucinations   **C** eating disorders

   B clinical depression   **D** panic attacks

Critical Thinking

On a sheet of paper, write the answers to the following questions. Use complete sentences.

17. What are some negative effects of choosing to smoke cigarettes?

18. What are the characteristics of a person who meets his or her self-actualization needs?

19. Why is empathy an important part of a close relationship?

20. What is a self-defeating behavior? How can it be avoided?

MY FAMILY TREE

Katherine — Peter

Charles — Helen

Doris — John

Glen — Rosetta

Gary — Karin — Peter — Barbara

Jeffrey — Heather

Samuel

Unit 2

Personal Health and Family Life

What do you think of when you hear the word *family*? Research shows that today's families are often made up differently than families of the past. Still, many things about the family have remained the same. It is within the family group that you learn to relate to others. You learn to care for other people.

What does it mean to be healthy? Decisions you make every day determine your physical, social, and mental well-being. This unit provides information about how your body systems are related to one another. What else will you learn through this unit? You will discover how the parts of the body affect the whole. You will find information about the life cycle—from reproduction and birth through old age. You will learn about different family systems and family relationships.

Chapters in Unit 2

Self-Assessment

Can you answer these questions?

- ☑ 1. Why is exercising important?

- ☑ 2. How do muscles and bones work together?

- ☑ 3. How does the nervous system work with the other body systems?

- ☑ 4. How do sense organs give information to the brain?

- ☑ 5. How does the endocrine system work with the other body systems?

- ☑ 6. What does the respiratory system do for the rest of the body?

- ☑ 7. How do the respiratory and circulatory systems work together?

- ☑ 8. What happens to food after you eat it?

- ☑ 9. How does the body rid itself of liquid waste?

- ☑ 10. How does the skin protect the body?

Identifying Human Body Systems

Your body is amazing. All your body systems work together as one unit to keep you in good health. When your body systems stay within limits, your body is in a state of balance. For example, your body temperature should not to be too high or too low. Your body systems always work together to stay in balance.

This chapter will tell you about your body's systems and how they work together. You will learn about the skeletal and muscular systems. Then you will learn about the nervous system, the sense organs, and the endocrine system. Next, you will learn about the respiratory and circulatory systems and the digestive and excretory systems. Finally, you will learn about the body's protective covering—the skin, hair, and nails.

Goals for Learning

- ◆ To describe the purpose of the muscular and skeletal systems
- ◆ To explain the parts of the nervous system and how information comes through the sense organs
- ◆ To explain how the endocrine glands work with the nervous system
- ◆ To describe respiration and how the body circulates blood
- ◆ To explain the digestive and excretory systems
- ◆ To describe the purpose and structure of the skin, hair, and nails

Nutrient

A part of food that helps the body function and grow

Two body systems that work together closely are the skeletal and muscular systems. The skeletal system is your body's system of connected bones, or your skeleton. It provides the frame for your body and protects your organs. The muscular system allows your body to move.

Figure A.1 in Appendix A shows the skeletal system. Figure A.2 in Appendix A shows the muscular system.

What Is the Purpose of Bones?

Your body has more than 200 bones. Your bones provide your body's structure. They also protect your organs, store important minerals, and produce certain blood cells.

Bones are living material. They are made of cells, the basic structure of life. Each cell has its own job to do. Cells that do the same job form tissues. Bone cells make up bone tissue. Because bones are living tissue, they need **nutrients,** just as other parts of your body do. A nutrient is a part of food that helps the body function and grow properly. You get nutrients from the food you eat. Your blood carries the nutrients to your bones.

The size of the bones in your body ranges from large to very small. There are four basic kinds of bones: long, short, flat, and irregular. Long bones are in arms and legs. Short bones are in such places as wrists and ankles. Flat bones are in such places as the ribs. Irregular bones are in such places as fingers and toes.

How Are Bones Joined?

Long bones have larger ends that form a joint with another bone. Joints allow for several kinds of movement. For example, the joint that has the greatest range of motion is the ball-and-socket joint. You have a ball-and-socket joint in each of your hips and shoulders. This joint allows you to move your arms and legs forward and backward. It also allows your legs and arms to move from side to side and in a circle.

Your knee joint is a hinge joint. It is similar to a hinge on a door. You can bend your leg back at the knee, but you can't bend it forward after you straighten it again. Pivot joints are in your elbows and between your head and spinal column. They move in the same way hinge joints do but also can rotate.

Tough bands of tissue called **ligaments** hold joints together. Ligaments are stretchy. They move easily.

Long bones are somewhat hard on the outside. Inside, however, is a soft substance called **marrow.** Bone marrow forms blood. Bone marrow makes both red blood cells and white blood cells. As these cells become worn-out or damaged, the marrow replaces them. You will learn about blood cells in Lesson 4.

How Do the Muscular and Skeletal Systems Work Together?

Joints allow your body's skeletal frame to move. However, all body movements also depend on muscles. Your body has about 600 muscles, which do many things. They move your bones, pump blood, and carry nutrients. They also move air in and out of your lungs.

A muscle is made up of fibers grouped together. When muscles **contract,** or shorten, they produce movement. Muscles hold your skeleton in place, and they also produce body heat. They act on messages they receive from your body's nervous system. You will learn about the nervous system in Lesson 2.

Link to ▷▷▷

Social Studies

Very old bones can show us how some people died long ago. Here is one example. Herculaneum was a Roman city destroyed when Mount Vesuvius erupted in 79 B.C. Modern scientists discovered bodies in beachside storerooms there. First, scientists thought the people had died because they could not breathe. Later tests on the bones proved the people had died immediately from the heat. The bones showed that people had not curled up or moved in pain. They did not have time to react.

Tendon

A strong set of fibers joining muscle to bone or muscle to muscle

How can you keep your cardiac muscles healthy?

It is important to warm up muscles before you exercise. Warming up helps oxygen and blood flow better through your body. It prepares your heart for exercise, and it keeps you from hurting yourself. Cooling down after exercise is also important. Cooling down slows your heart rate and stretches your muscles while they are warm.

Your body has three basic types of muscles—smooth, skeletal, and cardiac. Smooth muscles are involuntary. They work even though you don't think about making them work. Some smooth muscles are in the walls of your stomach and of your blood vessels. They move food, waste, and blood through your body.

Skeletal muscles are voluntary muscles. You control them. You decide what they will do. For example, if you decide to stand, walk, jump, or run, your voluntary muscles move. They react to your decision. Skeletal muscles are connected to the skeletal system. Tough tissues called **tendons** usually attach skeletal muscles to bones. A tendon is a strong set of fibers joining muscle to bone or muscle to muscle.

Cardiac muscles are in the walls of your heart. They contract regularly to pump blood throughout your body. Cardiac muscles are similar to smooth muscles because they are involuntary.

Figure 5.1.1 *Muscles make it possible for you to play basketball.*

How Do Muscles Work?

Muscles work by contracting and relaxing. When a muscle contracts, it pulls on a tendon. The tendon acts on the bone to produce a movement. Some muscles work in pairs. When one contracts, the other one relaxes. You can feel this happening when you bend your arm at the elbow. The muscle on the top of the upper arm contracts. At the same time, the muscle on the bottom of the upper arm relaxes. When you extend your arm, the opposite happens.

What Is Muscle Tone?

Some muscles never relax completely. They are somewhat contracted all the time. This is because of muscle tone. When you are in good health, a constant flow of messages runs from your nerves to your muscles. This helps you keep good muscle tone. Exercise and healthy eating are important for good muscle tone.

Word Bank
cardiac
joints
marrow

Lesson 1 Review On a sheet of paper, write the word from the Word Bank that best completes each sentence.

1. The soft inside part of a bone is called _____.

2. Your body's skeletal frame can move because of your _____.

3. The three basic types of muscles in your body are smooth, skeletal, and _____.

On a sheet of paper, write the answers to the following questions. Use complete sentences.

4. **Critical Thinking** What would happen if you had no bones? Explain your answer.

5. **Critical Thinking** How are voluntary and involuntary muscles different?

Cerebrum

The part of the brain that lets a person read, think, and remember

The nervous system is the body's communication network. It sends messages throughout your body. Figure A.3 in Appendix A shows the nervous system. The nervous system has two parts—the central nervous system and the peripheral nervous system. The central nervous system is made up of the brain and the spinal cord.

How Does the Brain Control the Body?

Your brain receives messages from your nerves and sends messages through the nerves to all parts of your body. Your brain is like a computer and a chemical factory combined. It can process and store information. It produces and uses chemicals to send signals. The brain has three main parts that work together to control your body. Figure 5.2.1 shows the parts of the brain.

The **cerebrum** is the part of the brain that lets a person read, think, and remember. It is the largest part of the brain. The cerebrum is divided into two halves. The right half controls the movement on the left side of your body. It also is the site for artistic skills and instinctive thinking. Instinctive thinking relates to actions that happen instantly without your thinking about them. The left half controls the movement on the right side of your body. It is the site for math and language skills and logical, or sensible, thinking.

Figure 5.2.1 *Parts of the brain*

Cerebrum

Cerebellum

Brain Stem

Medulla

Why is wearing a helmet important when riding a bike?

The other two parts of your brain are much smaller than your cerebrum. They are the **cerebellum** and **brain stem.** The cerebellum lies between the cerebrum and brain stem. Your cerebellum controls balance and helps coordinate muscular activities such as walking. The brain stem connects the cerebrum to the spinal cord.

One part of the brain stem—the **medulla**—controls the body's automatic activities. These include breathing, digesting food, circulating blood, swallowing, coughing, and sneezing.

How Does the Spinal Cord Assist the Brain?

The **spinal cord** is a major pathway your brain uses to send messages to your body. Your spinal cord is a large batch of long nerve cells wound together. It connects to your brain stem and extends to the lower part of your back. The **spinal column** is made up of a series of small bones. These bones surround and protect your spinal cord.

The nerves that make up the spinal cord send and receive messages. These nerves receive messages from the brain and send them to other sets of nerves.

What Does the Peripheral Nervous System Do?

The **peripheral nervous system** is a network of peripheral nerves. They carry messages between your brain and spinal cord and the rest of your body. *Peripheral* means "located away from the center."

One part of the peripheral nervous system helps control your body's automatic activities. It helps your body do what it must to remain stable, or under control. It also helps your body act in an emergency. For example, suppose you are in a dangerous situation and need to run fast. The peripheral nervous system signals your body to speed up your breathing and heartbeat so you can act on the signal to run. This happens in the body's stress response. Afterward, the peripheral nervous system slows the workings of your body and returns your body to normal.

Reflex

Automatic response

Cornea

Part of the eye that light passes through

Pupil

Dark center part of the eye that adjusts to let in the correct amount of light

A special part of your peripheral nervous system controls your **reflexes.** Reflexes are automatic responses to something such as heat or pain. For example, when you touch something hot, you jerk your hand away without thinking. Your nerves have sent a message to the muscles in your hand. A person cannot stop reflex actions from happening.

How Do the Sense Organs Work?

Nerves throughout your body carry messages to your brain. Your brain receives messages and then sends signals to other parts of your body. When messages come from outside your body, your sense organs receive them. The sense organs are your eyes, ears, tongue, nose, and skin.

The Sense of Sight

Your eye is your organ of sight. Look at Figure 5.2.2 to see the parts of the eye. How does the eye work? First, light enters the eye through the **cornea.** The cornea sends the light to the **pupil,** the dark center of the eye. The pupil can adjust its size. It gets smaller in bright light and larger in dim light. This causes the pupil to let the right amount of light into the eye.

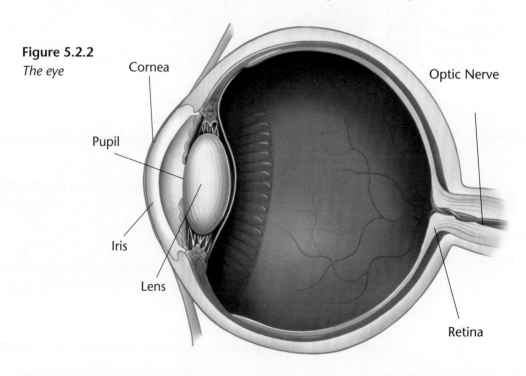

Figure 5.2.2
The eye

Cornea

Optic Nerve

Pupil

Iris

Lens

Retina

Lens

The soft, clear tissue behind the pupil

Retina

Part of the eye that sends information about light

Optic nerve

Part of the eye that sends information to the brain

Iris

Colored part of the eye around the pupil

Behind your pupil is the soft, clear tissue called the **lens.** The lens helps direct the light energy onto the **retina.** The retina contains special cells that send the light information to the **optic nerve.** This is the nerve that sends the information to the brain. Then the brain changes the light information into understandable pictures. This entire process happens faster than you can blink.

Another part of your eye is the **iris.** The iris is the colored part surrounding the pupil that gives your eye its color.

Health Myth

Myth: Reading in dim light is bad for your eyes.

Fact: Reading without enough light may be hard for you. Even so, reading in dim light will not cause any part of the eye to wear out. You will not harm your eyes by reading in dim light.

▼◀▲▼◀▲▼◀▲▼◀▲▼◀▲▼◀▲▼◀▲▼◀▲▼◀▲▼◀▲▼◀▲▼◀▲▼

Health at Work

Optician

Many workers help people care for their eyes. Opticians help people who need eyeglasses or contact lenses. What does an optician do? First, an ophthalmologist or optometrist writes a prescription for eyeglasses.

The optician helps the patient choose a pair of frames. Then the optician uses the prescription to make lenses that fit into the frames. Afterward, the optician makes sure the eyeglasses fit the patient. The optician can also make contact lenses for a patient. Patients can learn from an optician how to take care of their glasses and contact lenses.

This career requires a high school diploma and a great deal of on-the-job training. Many community colleges offer formal training for students interested in becoming opticians. Some states require opticians to have special licenses.

The Sense of Hearing

You may not notice that the air vibrates, or shakes, when a sound is made. Your ears, however, do notice. Figure 5.2.3 shows the parts of the ear. Your outer ear picks up air vibrations and sends them through the ear canal to your **eardrum.** Your eardrum is a thin piece of tissue stretched across the ear canal. When your eardrum receives the vibrations, it also vibrates.

Eardrum vibrations cause three small bones in the middle ear to vibrate. These bones—the hammer, anvil, and stirrup—pass the vibrations to a snail-like organ in the inner ear. There, tiny cells transfer the vibrations to your **auditory nerve.** The auditory nerve is the part of the ear that sends information to your brain. Your brain interprets the message and tells you what kind of sound you have heard. All of this happens in the time it takes for the sound to be made.

Figure 5.2.3
The ear

Hammer

Anvil

Stirrup

Inner Ear

Outer Ear

Eardrum

Ear Canal

Middle Ear

Auditory Nerve

Link to ➤➤➤

Arts

Scientists have learned that music vibrations act as triggers through the ears to the brain. Vibrations trigger different groups of brain cells. Different feelings result from setting off different cell groups. This is why some music can make you feel sad and some can make you feel happy.

The Senses of Smell and Taste

Both your tongue and your nose contain **receptor cells,** or cells that receive information. The receptor cells in your nose send messages through nerves. These nerves include the olfactory nerve. Your olfactory nerve is connected to your brain. Your nose can pick up thousands of different odors.

Your tongue, however, can recognize only four kinds of taste. The four tastes are sweet, salty, sour, and bitter. Different **taste buds** are receptors for each kind of taste. The taste buds send messages to your brain through your nerves. The taste buds are located on different parts of your tongue. They tell you how something tastes. Different parts of your tongue can recognize each of the four tastes.

The Sense of Touch

Your skin, your sense organ for touch, is your body's largest organ. Sense receptors all over your skin receive different sensations. You have receptors for touch, pressure, pain, heat, and cold. Your sense receptors send messages through the nerves to your spinal cord and brain. This is how you determine whether something is hot, cold, rough, or smooth. Your fingertips and lips are the most sensitive parts of your body because they have the greatest number of sense receptors.

Lesson 2 Review On a sheet of paper, write the answers to the following questions. Use complete sentences.

1. Which half of the cerebrum controls artistic skills?

2. What is the main job of the peripheral nervous system?

3. What is a reflex?

4. **Critical Thinking** What might happen if the pupil of your eye could not change size?

5. **Critical Thinking** Why is being able to feel heat and pain important?

Receptor cell

Cell that receives information

Taste bud

Receptor on the tongue that recognizes tastes

Gland

A group of cells or an organ that produces a substance and sends it into the body

Hormone

A chemical messenger that helps control how body parts do their jobs

Metabolism

Rate at which cells produce energy

What Does the Endocrine System Do?

The endocrine system is made up of **glands.** A gland is a group of cells or an organ that produces a special substance and sends it into the body. Figure 5.3.1 shows these glands. Endocrine glands produce **hormones** and send them directly into the bloodstream. Hormones are chemical messengers that help control the working of different body systems.

How Do Glands Affect the Body's Growth?

One of the endocrine glands is the pituitary gland. It is a small gland at the base of the brain. The pituitary gland produces several hormones. One of these is a growth hormone. Too much or too little of this hormone can affect a person's body size. For example, too much growth hormone can make bones unusually long. The person becomes much taller than average.

What Does the Thyroid Gland Do?

Another endocrine gland is the thyroid gland. It is located in the neck. The hormone it produces affects all tissues. Each cell in your body turns food into energy. The rate at which cells produce energy is called **metabolism.** The cells depend on the thyroid to change food into energy. Too much of the hormone can cause a person to have too much energy. This signals high metabolism. Too little of the hormone may result in low metabolism.

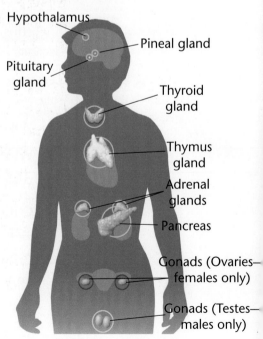

Hypothalamus
Pineal gland
Pituitary gland
Thyroid gland
Thymus gland
Adrenal glands
Pancreas
Gonads (Ovaries— females only)
Gonads (Testes— males only)

Figure 5.3.1 *The endocrine system*

Adrenal gland

Part of the endocrine system that releases several hormones

Adrenaline

Hormone released into the bloodstream that causes the heart to beat faster and blood pressure to rise in an emergency

Sleep affects all the functions of your body. Lack of sleep can cause you to feel sad and make concentrating hard. When you do not get enough sleep, smaller amounts of growth hormone are released, affecting growth. These are only a few of the many possible effects of lack of sleep.

This causes a person to feel tired. The pituitary gland produces a hormone that causes the thyroid to act.

What Do the Adrenal Glands Do?

The system also contains two **adrenal glands,** located on top of each kidney. These glands produce a mixture of hormones that affect the working of many body systems. These hormones help the body keep the proper water balance. One adrenal hormone helps a person deal with stress.

The adrenal gland also produces a hormone called **adrenaline.** Adrenaline causes your heart to beat faster and blood pressure to rise. It is released into the blood in greater amounts when a person feels fear or faces an emergency.

Lesson 3 Review On a sheet of paper, write the letter of the answer that best completes each sentence.

1. The pituitary gland mainly affects _____.
   A taste   **C** vision
   B thought   **D** growth

2. The adrenal glands help a person deal with _____.
   A hearing   **C** smell
   B stress   **D** balance

3. Cells depend on the thyroid to change food into

_____.
   A energy   **C** hormones
   B cell   **D** liquids

On a sheet of paper, write the answers to the following questions. Use complete sentences.

4. Critical Thinking Suppose that a person's adrenal glands are not producing enough adrenaline. What might happen to the person in an emergency?

5. Critical Thinking Suppose that a person's thyroid gland is not producing enough hormone. What are two possible effects?

Objectives

After reading this lesson, you should be able to

◆ explain why the body needs blood

◆ recognize how the respiratory and circulatory systems work together

◆ understand how the body takes in and processes oxygen

Platelet

Small part in the blood that helps with clotting

Carbon dioxide

A gas that is breathed out of the lungs

Clotting

Sticking together to form a plug and stop a wound from bleeding

Pulse

Regular beat of the heart

All systems in your body work together. You know that all systems depend on your nervous system. They also depend on your circulatory and respiratory systems. The circulatory system includes the heart, and three kinds of blood vessels. It is your body's transportation system. Figure A.4 in Appendix A shows the circulatory system.

Why Does the Body Need Blood?

The circulatory system moves blood through the body. Blood carries food and oxygen to every cell. Cells use the food and oxygen to do their work. The blood also carries waste products away from the cells.

Blood is made up of red blood cells, white blood cells, and **platelets.** Red blood cells carry oxygen to all parts of your body. They also remove **carbon dioxide,** a gas, from these parts. White blood cells work to keep your body healthy by fighting disease and germs. Usually, your body has fewer white blood cells than red blood cells. However, white blood cells increase when your body is fighting germs. Platelets are the smallest parts in blood. They prevent the body from losing blood through a wound by **clotting,** or sticking together to form a plug. Clotting stops bleeding.

How Does Blood Move Through the Body?

The heart pumps blood to all parts of your body. Your heart has been beating every minute since you were born, and even before that. In fact, your heart beats about 72 times a minute. This regular beat is your **pulse.**

Your heart is in the left side of your chest. It has four chambers—two on the left side and two on the right. Blood from all parts of your body flows into the right side of your heart. This blood contains carbon dioxide. The blood must get rid of the carbon dioxide through the lungs. The right side of your heart pumps the blood to the lungs, where you breathe out the carbon dioxide.

Research and Write

Research the ways that smoking is dangerous to your circulatory and respiratory systems. Check the American Heart Association and American Lung Association Web sites. Then talk to someone in your community who provides health care. Make a fact sheet to share with your classmates. Provide warnings about the dangers of smoking to all body systems.

In your lungs, blood gets rid of carbon dioxide and picks up oxygen. Then the blood travels to the left side of your heart. From there, your heart pumps blood to all parts of your body to get oxygen to the cells.

Blood vessels distribute blood, or send it, throughout your body. You have three kinds of blood vessels—**arteries, capillaries,** and **veins.** Arteries are the largest blood vessels and carry blood away from your heart. They have thick, three-layered walls. Arteries branch into smaller vessels. These small branches regulate, or control, the flow of blood into the capillaries.

Capillaries are the smallest blood vessels. Capillaries connect arteries and veins. They have thin walls. These walls allow nutrients and oxygen to pass from the blood to the body cells. Capillaries also pick up waste products from the cells.

When blood leaves the capillaries, it travels to veins. Veins carry the blood back to your heart. Veins that receive blood from capillaries are small. They become larger, though, as they come closer to your heart. This passage of the blood throughout your body happens quickly. It takes about one minute for blood to travel through your whole body.

What Is Blood Pressure?

Blood pressure is the force of blood on the walls of blood vessels. Pressure is created as your heart pumps blood to all parts of your body. Your body needs to keep a certain level of blood pressure. Many things affect blood pressure, including age, tobacco use, diet, exercise, and heredity.

How Do the Respiratory and Circulatory Systems Work Together?

The circulatory system carries blood to all areas of your body. That blood carries oxygen to the cells. The cells need oxygen to break up nutrients in the cells. Energy is released from the nutrients. Then the respiratory system gets the oxygen into your body. It also gets rid of carbon dioxide, a waste product. Together, the respiratory and circulatory systems give all your cells the oxygen they need to survive.

Respiration is breathing in oxygen and breathing out carbon dioxide. The respiratory system is a system of tubes and organs that allows you to breathe. You need to breathe about 20 times every minute. Figure 5.4.1 shows the respiratory system.

How Does the Body Take in Oxygen?

When you breathe, you take in air through your nose or mouth. The air flows down through a long tube called the **trachea,** or windpipe. The trachea divides into two branches called **bronchi,** or breathing tubes. Each one leads into one of the lungs—the major breathing organs. In the lungs, each of the bronchi divides. Then it divides again to form a network of tubes called **bronchioles.**

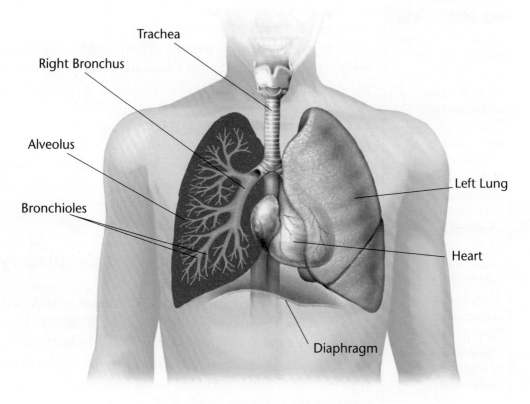

Figure 5.4.1 *The respiratory system*

Alveolus

Air sac with thin walls (plural is alveoli)

Diaphragm

Band of muscle tissue beneath the respiratory organs

Chest cavity

Part of the body that includes ribs and muscles that surround the heart and lungs

Inhale

Breathe in

Exhale

Breathe out

At the end of each bronchiole is a cluster of air sacs with thin walls. These are called **alveoli.** You have about 300 million alveoli in your lungs. The alveoli are covered with a network of capillaries. The thin walls of the alveoli and capillaries allow the gases to change places. That is, the oxygen goes in, and the carbon dioxide comes out.

Your lungs need help from your **diaphragm** and **chest cavity.** The diaphragm is a band of muscle tissue beneath your respiratory organs. Your chest cavity includes ribs and muscles that surround your heart and lungs. When you **inhale,** or breathe in, your rib muscles and diaphragm contract. This enlarges your chest cavity and allows air to rush in. When you **exhale,** or breathe out, your rib muscles and diaphragm expand. This forces the air out.

Lesson 4 Review On a sheet of paper, write the answers to the following questions. Use complete sentences.

1. What do white blood cells do?

2. What are the three kinds of blood vessels?

3. What happens to rib muscles and the diaphragm when you inhale and hold your breath?

4. **Critical Thinking** Why is clotting important?

5. **Critical Thinking** Why is blood pressure important?

✿ ✿

Technology and Society

A treadmill can be good for more than just exercise. An electrocardiograph (EKG) treadmill can tell how well the heart is working. Special sensors hooked up to a patient's body send information to a computer. Treadmill speed and level are increased and decreased. A doctor reads the information to determine whether the patient is at risk of heart problems.

Digestion

Breaking down food into smaller parts and changing it to a form that cells can use

Saliva

A liquid in the mouth

Enzyme

Special chemical that breaks down food

Your body needs food for energy, growth, and repair. Your body must break down food into substances that cells can use. Breaking down food into smaller parts and changing it to a form that cells can use is called **digestion.** The digestive system is the system that breaks down food for your body's use. Figure 5.5.1 shows the digestive organs.

How Does the Digestive System Break Down Food?

When your mouth waters at the sight, smell, or thought of food, it produces **saliva.** Saliva is a liquid in your mouth. It contains an **enzyme,** a special chemical that breaks down food. Enzymes are in all your digestive organs. When you take a bite of an apple, your tongue pushes the food around. Your teeth help you chew the food into small pieces. The food mixes with saliva. The enzyme in saliva begins to break down the food.

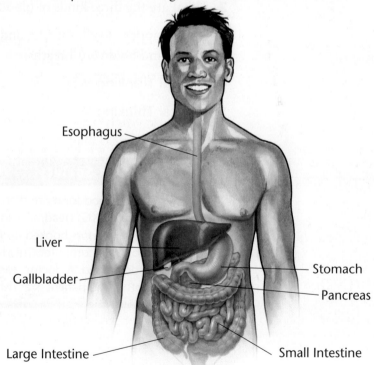

Esophagus

Liver

Gallbladder

Stomach

Pancreas

Large Intestine

Small Intestine

Figure 5.5.1 *The digestive system*

Esophagus

Long tube that connects the mouth and the stomach

Small intestine

A curled-up tube just below the stomach where most of the breakdown of food takes place

Villus

Fingerlike bulge that absorbs food after it has been broken down into chemicals (plural is villi)

Liver

A large organ that produces bile

Gallbladder

Digestive organ attached to the liver that stores bile

Bile

Liquid in the liver that breaks down fats

Pancreas

A gland that produces insulin and enzymes

Insulin

Hormone produced in the pancreas that helps cells use sugar

Large intestine

Tube connected to the small intestine

Food next enters your **esophagus,** a long tube that connects your mouth and your stomach. Muscles in the walls of your esophagus push the food along to your stomach. Your stomach walls give off juices containing enzymes that break down food more. Your stomach also breaks down food through twisting and churning it. Food stays in your stomach for 3 to 4 hours. During that time, the enzymes change solid food into partly liquid form.

From your stomach, food enters the **small intestine.** The small intestine is a curled-up tube just below your stomach. Most of the breakdown of food into chemicals takes place in your small intestine. The small intestine is lined with millions of tiny, fingerlike bulges called **villi.** Villi absorb the food that has been broken down into chemicals. Villi contain tiny blood vessels that are connected to the rest of your bloodstream. The chemicals from the broken-down food enter your blood vessels in the villi. Your bloodstream then sends the chemicals to all parts of your body.

Your **liver** and **gallbladder** are also digestive organs. Your liver is a large organ that produces **bile.** This liquid breaks down fats, such as butter. Your gallbladder is a small pouch attached to the liver. The gallbladder stores bile. When bile is needed for digestion, it is pushed into the small intestine.

Your **pancreas** also helps in digestion. This gland produces a hormone called **insulin,** which helps cells use sugar. Your pancreas also gives off enzymes that break down foods. Most food moves through your small intestine in 1 to 4 hours. Some foods are digested very quickly.

How Does the Body Get Rid of Solid Waste?

Anything that the villi do not absorb in the small intestine moves on to the **large intestine.** The large intestine is a tube connected to the small intestine. It helps your body by gathering and removing waste materials that are left over after digestion. Through its walls, the large intestine absorbs water and nutrients from the waste material.

Feces

Solid waste material remaining in the large intestine after digestion

Rectum

Lower part of the large intestine

Anus

Opening through which solid waste leaves the body

Excretory system

System that allows the body to eliminate liquid and solid waste

Kidney

Organ in the excretory system where urine forms

The solid material left in the large intestine is called **feces.** Feces are stored in the **rectum,** or lower part of the large intestine. Feces leave the body through an opening called the **anus.**

How Does the Body Get Rid of Liquid Waste?

Your body is good at using nutrients it needs. It can also eliminate, or get rid of, the rest. The **excretory system** allows the body to eliminate liquid and solid waste. Figure 5.5.2 shows the excretory system. This system removes water and salts through your sweat glands.

The excretory system also takes waste products out of your blood. The main excretory organs that do this are your two **kidneys.** The kidneys are on either side of your spine in your lower back. The kidneys take waste products out of your blood. Then they return water and minerals to your blood.

Research and Write

Doctors sometimes perform organ transplants. That is, they take one person's organ and put it in another person's body. With a partner, research the challenges these doctors face. Then write a short article to explain the challenges. Look for ideas to help make organ transplants work better.

Figure 5.5.2 *The excretory system*

Ureter

Tube through which urine passes from a kidney to the urinary bladder

Urinary bladder

Bag that stores urine

Urine

Liquid waste product formed in the kidneys

Urethra

Tube through which urine passes out of the body

As your blood supplies nutrients to your cells, the cells form waste products. These wastes flow through cell walls into your bloodstream. When blood circulates through your kidneys, wastes are strained out. The blood then travels back to your heart through your veins.

Waste products move out of your kidneys through tubes called **ureters** to your **urinary bladder.** This bag can stretch to hold this liquid waste, which is called **urine.** Urine passes out of your body through the **urethra.**

Lesson 5 Review On a sheet of paper, write the answers to the following questions. Use complete sentences.

1. What happens when your mouth waters?

2. What is the esophagus?

3. What do enzymes do to solid food?

4. **Critical Thinking** Why are villi important?

5. **Critical Thinking** What do you think would happen if the kidneys stopped working properly?

Decide for Yourself

Tanya's best friend came to her with a problem. The friend often felt faint and shaky. She wanted to eat strange foods sometimes. Other times, she couldn't eat at all. Her toes had started feeling numb. "I haven't told anyone," she said. "I feel so awful today. I just can't make it to soccer practice. Please cover for me. Tell them I couldn't come. Don't tell them why. I don't want to get kicked off the team."

Tanya knew her friend's mom had diabetes, which meant that her body did not have the right amount of insulin. Tanya thought her friend might have diabetes, too. Her friend needed to see a doctor.

Her friend had begged Tanya not to say anything to anybody. Tanya didn't want her friend to get kicked off the team.

On a sheet of paper, write the answers to the following questions. Use complete sentences.

1. What are Tanya's possible choices in this situation?

2. Tanya's friend is afraid she will be kicked off the soccer team. Why else might she be scared to admit she is sick?

3. Which choice do you think Tanya should make?

Objectives

After reading this lesson, you should be able to

◆ describe the structure of the skin

◆ explain how skin protects the body

◆ understand the structure of hair and nails

Skin is the body's largest organ. It is part of a system that covers and protects your entire body. The skin is one of your sense organs and is also part of the excretory system. It is a separate system that includes your sweat glands, hair, and nails.

What Is the Structure of the Skin?

Figure 5.6.1 shows that the skin is made up of three layers. The **epidermis** is the outer layer of skin. The lower part of the epidermis makes new cells that are pushed toward the skin's surface. The layer on the top of the epidermis is made up of dead cells. The dead cells flake off as the new ones take their place.

The **dermis** is the inner layer of skin that is made up of living cells. Nerves and blood vessels are in the dermis. Oil glands in the dermis help keep your hair and skin from cracking.

Epidermis

Outer layer of skin

Dermis

Inner layer of skin made up of living cells

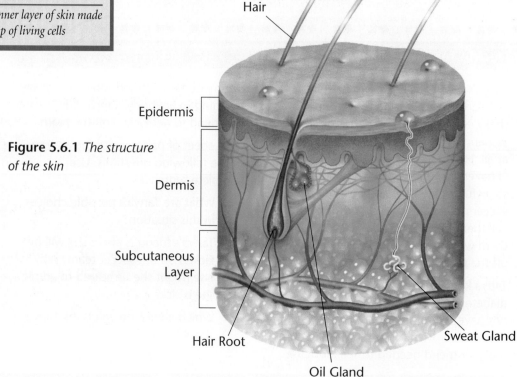

Hair

Epidermis

Figure 5.6.1 *The structure of the skin*

Dermis

Subcutaneous Layer

Hair Root

Oil Gland

Sweat Gland

Below the dermis is the **subcutaneous layer**—the deepest layer of skin. It is made up mostly of fatty tissue. The tissue protects your body from heat and cold. This layer also protects your body from injury.

How Does the Skin Protect the Body?

Skin protects your body in many ways. First, your skin prevents most **bacteria** from entering your body. Bacteria are tiny germs that cause disease.

Skin also helps control your body's temperature. The epidermis has tiny openings called **pores.** Pores are connected to the sweat glands.

Your body gets rid of **perspiration,** or sweat, through sweat glands. Perspiration helps to cool your body.

The dermis helps protect your skin through cells that produce **melanin.** Melanin is the substance that gives skin its color. When you are in the sun, your skin produces more melanin. This shields the skin from the sun's harmful rays. The increase in melanin makes skin look tanned. Freckles are actually small spots of melanin.

What Is the Structure of the Hair and Nails?

Hair and nails are two other parts of your body's protective covering. The roots of hair are made up of living cells and grow out of the dermis. A hair root grows out of a small pocket in the dermis that holds the root.

Hair is like the skin in that new cells are pushed up to replace the old cells. The hair on your head and body is made up of dead cells.

Nails are also dead cells. Nails grow out of the skin's epidermis. They contain a type of protein called **keratin,** which makes nails hard. Your nails protect the soft ends of your fingers and toes.

Lesson 6 Review On a sheet of paper, write the word in parentheses that best completes each sentence.

1. Sweat (glands, pores, cells) help the body remove water and salt.

2. The skin has (two, three, four) layers.

3. Skin protects the body from (bacteria, perspiration, melanin).

On a sheet of paper, write the answers to the following questions. Use complete sentences.

4. **Critical Thinking** What would happen if the dead cells of the epidermis did not flake off as new cells were formed?

5. **Critical Thinking** Suppose that someone's pores were blocked and sweat could not escape. What would happen?

Health in Your Life

Skin Protection

Protecting your skin is important. Sunburn is painful. It can also lead to illnesses, such as skin cancer, when you get older. To keep your skin safe, use a sunscreen with a sun protection factor (SPF) of at least 15. You may need to reapply the sunscreen later because it wears off. Check the bottle for instructions.

It is a good idea to use sunscreen on your face every day. Protect all of your skin when you plan to be out in the sun. Be sure to use a waterproof sunscreen so it will not wear off or wash off.

The sun's rays can burn you through the water of a pool or lake. On a cloudy day, the sun is still shining, and it can burn you. Using sunscreen is an important protection.

On a sheet of paper, write the answers to the following questions. Use complete sentences.

1. Why is sun protection important?

2. Why is using sunscreen on your face every day a good idea?

3. Why should people swimming outdoors wear sunscreen?

Chapter 5 S U M M A R Y

- The body systems are the skeletal and muscular systems, the nervous system, the endocrine system, the circulatory and respiratory systems, the digestive and excretory systems, and skin.

- The sense organs receive messages from outside your body and send them to the brain. The sense organs are eyes, ears, tongue, nose, and skin.

Vocabulary

adrenal gland, 111	esophagus, 117	perspiration, 121
adrenaline, 111	excretory system, 118	platelet, 112
alveolus, 115	exhale, 115	pore, 121
anus, 118	feces, 118	pulse, 112
artery, 113	gallbladder, 117	pupil, 106
auditory nerve, 108	gland, 110	receptor cell, 109
bacteria, 121	hormone, 110	rectum, 118
bile, 117	inhale, 115	reflex, 106
blood pressure, 113	insulin, 117	respiration, 114
brain stem, 105	iris, 107	retina, 107
bronchus, 114	keratin, 121	saliva, 116
bronchiole, 114	kidney, 118	small intestine, 117
capillary, 113	large intestine, 117	spinal column, 105
carbon dioxide, 112	lens, 107	spinal cord, 105
cerebellum, 105	ligament, 101	subcutaneous layer, 121
cerebrum, 104	liver, 117	taste bud, 109
chest cavity, 115	marrow, 101	tendon, 102
clotting, 112	medulla, 105	trachea, 114
contract, 101	melanin, 121	ureter, 119
cornea, 106	metabolism, 110	urethra, 119
dermis, 120	nutrient, 100	urinary bladder, 119
diaphragm, 115	optic nerve, 107	urine, 119
digestion, 116	pancreas, 117	vein, 113
eardrum, 108	peripheral nervous system, 105	villus, 117
enzyme, 116		
epidermis, 120		

Word Bank

arteries

auditory nerve

bile

blood pressure

dermis

hormones

ligament

medulla

melanin

pupil

reflexes

small intestine

spinal cord

vein

Vocabulary Review

On a sheet of paper, write the word or phrase from the Word Bank that best completes each sentence.

1. The substance that gives skin its color is _____.

2. A vessel that carries blood back to the heart is a(n) _____.

3. The liquid in the liver that breaks down fats is _____.

4. The central nervous system is made up of the brain and the _____.

5. One part of the brain stem, the _____, controls automatic activities such as breathing.

6. Automatic responses to heat or pain are _____.

7. The _____ in the middle of the eye adjusts its size to let in the right amount of light.

8. The ear picks up vibrations that are transferred to the _____.

9. The endocrine system includes glands that produce _____, which control how the body does its jobs.

10. Blood is carried away from the heart by _____.

11. The tough band of tissue that holds joints together or keeps organs in place is a(n) _____.

12. The force of blood on the walls of the blood vessels is _____.

13. The _____ is where most of the breakdown of food into chemicals takes place.

14. The inner layer of the skin made up of living cells is the _____.

Concept Review

On a sheet of paper, write the letter of the answer that best completes each sentence.

15. All of these are types of muscles EXCEPT

_____.

    A smooth   **C** skeletal

    B cardiac   **D** auditory

16. The body makes nutrients from _____.

    A hair   **C** hormones

    B food   **D** bones

17. The air you breathe travels to your lungs through your

_____.

    A pancreas   **C** trachea

    B kidneys   **D** cornea

Critical Thinking

On a sheet of paper, write the answers to the following questions. Use complete sentences.

18. Why are healthy food and exercise important to all body systems?

19. Do you think one system of the body is more important than the others? Explain your answer.

20. What do you think is most amazing about how the human body works? Explain your answer.

Test-Taking Tip   Read and follow each set of directions carefully.

Self-Assessment

Can you answer these questions?

☑ 1. What is hygiene?

☑ 2. What are three ways to keep your eyes healthy?

☑ 3. What effect does loud music have on your hearing?

☑ 4. What are two basic rules for healthy skin?

☑ 5. What is most important for healthy hair, nails, and teeth?

☑ 6. What are three benefits of exercising?

☑ 7. What is the difference between aerobic and isometric exercise?

☑ 8. What is a personal health plan?

☑ 9. Why is a cooldown a necessary part of exercising?

☑ 10. Why are rest and sleep important parts of personal health?

6 Maintaining Personal Hygiene and Fitness

Taking care of yourself helps you feel healthier. Taking care of yourself has other benefits, as well. It can help you look better and feel better about yourself. Taking care of your eyes, ears, skin, hair, nails, and teeth shows you value yourself. Exercising and getting enough sleep are other ways you value yourself.

In this chapter, you will learn about ways to take care of yourself and stay healthy. You will also learn about the importance of exercise, fitness, and rest to your health. You will learn how these actions are important to your social and emotional well-being. Finally, you will have the opportunity to create a fitness plan for yourself.

Goals for Learning

- ◆ To explain the purpose of basic hygiene
- ◆ To describe ways to protect eyes, ears, skin, hair, nails, and teeth
- ◆ To identify the benefits and parts of a regular exercise program
- ◆ To create a personal fitness plan
- ◆ To explain why your body needs rest and sleep

Hygiene

Practices that promote cleanliness and good health

Hygiene refers to things you do to promote cleanliness and good health. Taking care of your eyes, ears, skin, hair, nails, and teeth are part of hygiene. These are all important parts of your body, so taking care of them is important. Good hygiene habits can have a positive effect on your personal health and your personal and work-related relationships.

How Can You Take Care of Your Eyes and Sight?

Your body protects your eyes and sight in many ways. The hard bones of your skull surround your eyes. Your eyelids, eyebrows, and eyelashes keep dirt, sweat, and direct light out of your eyes. Blinking protects your eyes from dirt and direct light. Tears wash away tiny objects and help get rid of harmful germs that may get into your eye.

To protect your eyes, avoid touching them with dirty hands. Keep sharp objects away from your eyes. Avoid being in bright sunlight for long periods. If you wear contact lenses, follow instructions for cleaning and wearing them. Wear safety glasses, goggles, or a helmet to shield your eyes from glare, damaging light, chemicals, dirt, and sports injuries. Wear sunglasses in the sun but not indoors.

Table 6.1.1 lists some common vision problems.

Table 6.1.1 Some Vision Problems	
Farsightedness	Difficulty seeing close objects
Nearsightedness	Difficulty seeing distant objects
Astigmatism	Blurred vision caused by an uneven shape of the cornea or lens
Strabismus	Crossed eyes; the eye muscles do not work together; one or both eyes turn inward or outward
Color blindness	Inherited lack of ability to see certain colors; usually occurs in males

Infection

A sickness caused by a germ in the body

Allergy

A bad reaction of the body to a food or to something in the air

You need regular eye exams by an eye doctor to check for eye and vision problems. You know your vision is fine if you can see a sharp, clear picture. If your vision is not fine, your eye doctor can write an order for lenses to correct the problem.

How Can You Take Care of Your Ears and Hearing?

Your skull protects the most delicate parts of your ears. The wax in your outer ears keeps dirt from going into other parts of your ears. A certain amount of wax in your ears is normal. Sometimes, the wax may build up so you don't hear well. If that happens, a doctor or nurse can remove the wax.

The most common reason for hearing loss is loud noise. If you are around loud noise a lot, you may be at risk for hearing loss. The loss usually happens gradually and without pain. Sometimes, it can happen instantly from a single extremely loud noise. You can almost always avoid noises that cause hearing loss.

Other things that can cause hearing loss are **infection,** heredity, **allergies,** too much wax, or a wound. Infection is a sickness caused by a germ in your body. An allergy is a bad reaction of your body to a food or to something in the air.

A hearing test shows how well you hear. If a hearing test or an ear exam show you have hearing or ear problems, a doctor can tell you what to do.

Protect your hearing and your ears by avoiding loud noise and music. Wear earplugs or earmuffs when you are near loud noise. Clean your ears only with a damp washcloth on your fingertip—never with a cotton swab. Avoid putting objects in your ears. Swim only in clean water and dry your ears after swimming. Wear a head guard or helmet when playing contact sports such as football or rugby.

Link to ➤➤➤

Biology

Some hearing and vision problems can begin as early as your 30s. A person's eardrums may become thicker, making sounds less clear. Some older people may need a hearing aid. Changes in the shape of the eye can reduce how sharply a person sees things. Many older people need to wear glasses or contacts. Driving at night may also become harder.

Deodorant

A product that covers body odor

Antiperspirant

A product that helps control perspiration by closing the pores

Acne

Clogged skin pores that cause pimples and blackheads

Pimple

An inflamed swelling of the skin

Risk factors are things that may be able to harm your health. How can knowing about risk factors help you stay in good health?

How Can You Protect Your Skin?

The first rule of good skin care is to keep your skin clean. The best way to keep your skin clean is to wash with soap and water. How often you need to wash depends on your skin type and how active you are.

You may think perspiration has an odor, but it doesn't. Odor results when perspiration mixes with bacteria on your skin. A **deodorant** is a product that can cover up the odor. An **antiperspirant** is a product that helps control perspiration by closing your pores. Neither product, however, removes odor-causing bacteria. Washing with soap and water reduces body odor by removing bacteria.

The second basic rule for skin care is to protect your skin from wind, cold, and sun. Strong wind and cold weather can cause your skin's outer layer to lose moisture quickly. Your skin can crack and split, or become chapped. Staying out too long in the sun can hurt your eyes and give you sunburn. It can wrinkle your skin and cause skin disease. Damage from the sun builds up over the years. It cannot be reversed. The chance of getting sunburned rises when you are skiing or at the beach. This is because the sun's rays bounce off snow, sand, and water. It is possible to get sunburned even on cloudy days.

Here are some other ways you can protect your skin. In windy, cold weather, dress warmly and cover your face and hands. Use a cream or lotion to keep in your skin's natural moisture. Use a sunscreen to protect your skin. A sunscreen with a sun protection factor (SPF) of 15 or more gives the best protection.

How Can You Take Care of Skin Problems?

Acne is the most common skin problem for teens. Acne occurs when pores, the tiny openings in the skin, get clogged. The amount of hormones in your body increases when you are a teen. These hormones cause oil glands to make more oil and may plug up your pores. Then you may get **pimples,** whiteheads, or blackheads. A pimple is an inflamed swelling of the skin. A whitehead forms when oil becomes trapped in a pore. A blackhead is an oil plug that darkens when the air hits it.

Athlete's foot

Itching or cracked skin between the toes

Fungus

An organism that grows in damp places

Health Myth

Myth: People who sweat a lot while exercising are not fit.

Fact: People who are fit sweat more than those who do not exercise regularly. As you exercise, your body sends blood to the surface of your skin. If you exercise regularly, this happens faster than it does in someone who does not exercise regularly. When the blood reaches the surface of your skin, you give off heat. Your sweat glands then make more sweat to cool you off.

There are many oil glands in your face, neck, and back. Acne usually affects these areas. Acne has no cure, but you can reduce the problem by doing the following:

- Wash with soap and water every morning and evening. If your face is very oily, wash it once more during the day.

- Wash right after exercise to remove sweat and bacteria that can clog your pores. Use a clean washcloth every day. Bacteria grow quickly on a damp washcloth.

- Shampoo your hair often to limit acne on your forehead, neck, and shoulders.

- Eat well-balanced meals and get plenty of rest and exercise.

- Limit time in the sun and avoid tanning booths and sunlamps. Tanning booths damage skin in the same way the sun does.

- Avoid oil-based creams and lotions.

- Do not squeeze or pick pimples and blackheads. This can cause infection or leave a scar on your skin.

- Visit a skin doctor if you have very bad acne.

Athlete's foot is itching or cracked skin between the toes. A **fungus** causes it. A fungus is an organism that grows in damp places, such as a locker room. To keep from getting athlete's foot, keep your feet dry. Avoid walking barefoot in locker rooms or showers. Mild athlete's foot can be treated with a special foot powder or ointment found in drugstores. Severe cases of athlete's foot are treated with prescription medication.

Technology and Society

Lasers can create strong beams of light. Unlike a lightbulb, a laser creates a beam of light that does not spread out. This light can be focused to a small point. Doctors use lasers to close up blood vessels and break up kidney stones. Lasers can help remove scars, whiten teeth, and correct vision problems. Lasers are used in eye surgery to change the eyeball's shape and improve vision.

How Can You Take Care of Your Hair and Nails?

Shampooing and brushing your hair get rid of dirt and help spread the oils that make your hair shiny and soft. To protect your hair, do not overuse blow dryers and curling irons. Too much heat can damage your hair.

Some **dandruff,** or flaking from your scalp, is normal. Your scalp is skin. It sheds dead cells just as the rest of your skin does. Special shampoos can control dandruff. Check with a doctor if you have a lot of dandruff.

For good nail care, you can do two things regularly: (1) Keep your nails clean, especially underneath. (2) Cut your nails evenly and file ragged edges.

How Can You Take Care of Your Teeth?

Your teeth play a part in how you feel about yourself and how others think of you. When your teeth are clean and healthy, you can smile with confidence. A bright smile with clean, strong teeth is one of the first things people notice. With proper care, teeth can last a lifetime. You should brush your teeth at least twice a day for 3 to 4 minutes each time. You should also floss at least once a day. Use toothpaste with fluoride, a chemical that helps prevent tooth decay, or use a fluoride rinse. Have regular dental checkups and cleanings. Avoid eating too many sweets. Wear a mouth guard if you play contact sports. Do not chew on hard objects such as pens, pencils, and hard candies.

You should also take care of your gums to avoid gum disease. Gum disease can damage your teeth. The first stage of gum disease is **gingivitis.** Signs of gingivitis are red, swollen gums. The gums may bleed and be painful. Proper brushing and flossing and a healthy diet can prevent gingivitis.

Word Bank

allergies

blinking

sunscreen

Lesson 1 Review On a sheet of paper, write the word from the Word Bank that best completes each sentence.

1. You can keep dirt out of your eyes by _____.

2. Hearing loss can be caused by _____.

3. To protect your skin from sunburn, use _____.

On a sheet of paper, write the answers to the following questions. Use complete sentences.

4. Critical Thinking Why is getting regular medical and dental checkups important?

5. Critical Thinking How can taking care of your hair, skin, and teeth improve your self-concept?

Health in Your Life

Noise and Your Hearing

Loud noise can cause hearing loss over time. Strength, or intensity, of sound is measured in decibels (dB). Here are the decibel levels for some common sounds:

Normal breathing	10 dB
Whisper	30 dB
Normal conversation	60 dB
Truck traffic	90 dB
Rock concert	120 dB
Jet engine at takeoff	140 dB

Decibel levels higher than 85 can cause hearing loss. You can protect your hearing from harmful noise levels. Be aware of the noise levels around you. Keep the volume at safe levels on CD players, computers, radios, and TVs.

On a sheet of paper, write the answers to the following questions. Use complete sentences.

1. What are some places where loud noise can cause hearing loss?

2. What can you do to protect your hearing from loud noises?

3. In what way are loud noises a risk factor for good lifelong health?

Objectives

After reading this lesson, you should be able to

◆ identify four benefits of exercise

◆ explain the different purposes of exercise

◆ describe how to determine your pulse rate

◆ explain the purpose of warm-up and cooldown activities

Endurance
____
The ability to stay with an activity for a long time

Flexibility
____
The ability to twist, turn, bend, and stretch easily

Resistance
____
The pushing back of something

You are physically fit when your body can meet the demands of daily living. That means having enough energy to do all the things you want to do. Physical fitness is a key part of your overall good health. It affects your emotional, social, and physical well-being.

What Are Three Parts of Health-Related Fitness?

Three parts of health-related fitness are heart and lung **endurance, flexibility,** and muscular fitness. Endurance is the ability to stay with an activity for a long time. Heart and lung endurance is the fitness of your heart, blood vessels, and lungs. It means that your heart and blood vessels are easily able to move oxygen through your blood to your lungs. Your energy depends mainly on your body being able to take in and use oxygen. To do this, you need a strong heart, clear lungs, and blood vessels free of fat buildup.

Flexibility is the ability to twist, turn, bend, and stretch easily. Flexibility helps keep your muscles from pulling and straining. It also increases the range of motion in your joints.

Muscular fitness is the strength and endurance of your body's muscles. Muscular strength is the amount of force that your muscles put out against **resistance,** or the pushing back of something. Muscular endurance allows you to lift, push, and pull objects without your muscles getting too tired.

How Does Exercise Help You?

Regular exercise can improve your health-related fitness. It increases your heart and lung endurance. It firms and strengthens your muscles. It improves your flexibility. Exercise gives you more energy. It helps you feel better and look better.

Calorie

A unit that measures the amount of energy in food

Aerobic exercise

Activity that raises your heart rate

Anaerobic exercise

Activity that quickly uses up oxygen in your body

Isometric exercise

Activity that builds muscle strength by using tension

Isotonic exercise

Activity that builds muscle strength by using weights and repeated movements

Isokinetic exercise

Activity that builds muscle strength by using resistance

Exercise does not have to be hard to be good for you. Cleaning the house and gardening have been shown to be as helpful as biking and walking.

Exercise also can reduce your chances of getting sick. For example, regular exercise reduces the risk of heart disease. Regular exercise can shorten the time needed to get well if you do become sick.

Another reason to exercise is weight control. Exercise burns up extra **calories.** A calorie is a measure of the amount of energy in food. Besides burning up extra calories, exercise speeds up the rate at which your body burns calories.

Finally, exercise helps you reduce anxiety and get rid of stress. Exercise can be fun and is a good way to make friends.

What Is the Purpose of Exercise?

Different types of exercise have different purposes. Look at Table 6.2.1 to see five types of exercise and their purpose. Exercise is one of the best ways of keeping your mind and body healthy.

Table 6.2.1 Types of Exercise		
Exercise Type	**Purpose**	**Examples**
Aerobic exercise (steady, continuous activity)	Helps heart and lungs work better by raising the heart rate	Walking, running, bicycling, cross-country skiing, swimming
Anaerobic exercise (short spurts of activity)	Improves how the body works when it is working the hardest by quickly using up oxygen	Sprinting, tennis
Isometric exercise	Builds muscle strength by tensing muscles	Pushing against a wall
Isotonic exercise	Builds muscle strength using weights	Any body movement, push-ups, pull-ups
Isokinetic exercise	Builds muscle strength by using resistance	Workout with machines that control force of pushing and pulling

What Are the Parts of an Exercise Program?

A good exercise workout includes these five parts:

- a warm-up period

- an aerobic exercise to improve heart and lung endurance

- exercise to improve muscular fitness

- exercise to improve flexibility

- a cooldown period

Warm-Up

Always begin your exercise workout with a 5-minute warm-up. Warming up makes more blood flow to your muscles. It allows your heart rate to rise gradually. You can get hurt if you push your body into hard exercise too fast. You can warm up by walking and doing stretching exercises.

Exercises to Improve Heart and Lung Endurance

Your heart rate is the number of times your heart beats in a minute. Your **maximum heart rate** is your heart rate when you exercise as hard, fast, and long as you can.

Pulse rate is another term for heart rate. To determine your pulse rate, do the following:

- Place two fingers of your right hand on the side of your neck just below your jawbone.

- You can also place two fingers of your right hand on the inside of your left wrist. CAUTION: Do not take your pulse with your thumb, because it has its own pulse.

- To locate your pulse, feel the thump against your fingers.

- Count each thump as one heartbeat.

- Use a watch with a second hand to count the number of heartbeats in 10 seconds.

- Multiply this number by 6 to get your heart rate for 1 minute.

- The number of thumps each minute is your pulse rate.

Although maximum heart rate is different for everyone, it should be about 220 minus your age. For example, if you are 16, your maximum heart rate should be about 204 beats in a minute.

To find out how long you should exercise to improve your heart and lung endurance, do this test:

1. Figure out your maximum heart rate by subtracting your age from 220.

2. Do an aerobic exercise for at least 10 minutes.

3. Immediately after you stop exercising, take your pulse for 10 seconds.

4. Multiply this number by 6 to get your exercising pulse rate per minute.

5. Divide your exercising pulse rate by your maximum heart rate.

6. Multiply the result by 100 to determine the percent of maximum heart rate used.

7. Look at Table 6.2.2 to find the number of minutes of exercise you need to do three times a week.

Here is an example for a 15-year-old with a pulse rate per minute of 123 after walking briskly for 10 minutes:

$220 - 15 = 205$
$123 \div 205 = 0.60$
$0.60 \times 100 = 60$ percent

This person must walk at this pace for 30 to 37 minutes three times a week to improve heart and lung endurance.

Table 6.2.2 Pulse Rate and Exercise Times	
If your maximum pulse rate is:	You can exercise three times a week for:
50 percent	45–52 minutes
55 percent	37–45 minutes
60 percent	30–37 minutes
65 percent	25–30 minutes
70 percent	20–25 minutes
75 percent	15–20 minutes

Research and Write

You can find lots of information on the Internet about health. What is something about health that interests you? Choose something about health to research. Write a report and prepare an online presentation showing what you learned.

If you want to lower your exercising pulse rate, slow down. If you want to raise it, pick up your pace. How hard or how fast should you exercise? Do not push yourself past the point of being able to talk to someone next to you.

When you exercise to improve heart and lung endurance, you need to do two things:

1. Run, swim, bicycle, walk, or exercise at a steady pace without stopping. Sports such as baseball and softball are not aerobic, because the activity is not steady.

2. At least three times a week, exercise at a level that is 50 to 75 percent of your maximum heart rate for the number of minutes shown in Table 6.2.2 on page 137.

Exercises to Improve Muscular Fitness

To improve muscular fitness, you must use resistance. Your muscles need to overcome some sort of resistance to become stronger. Exercises such as push-ups, sit-ups, and pull-ups improve muscle strength and endurance. Weight lifting and isometric exercises also improve muscular fitness.

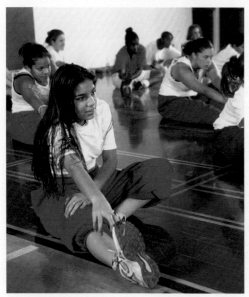

Figure 6.2.1 *End your workout with a cooldown.*

Exercises to Improve Flexibility

Slow stretching exercises can improve your flexibility. Stretching makes your muscles relax and lengthen. Slow, gradual movements are best for building flexibility. Avoid movements that are fast and bouncy. These make your muscles tighten instead of relax.

Cooldown

End your workout with a cooldown. Your body needs a chance to slow down gradually. If you stop suddenly, you could become light-headed or even faint. Your blood flow needs time to adjust itself. To cool down, continue to exercise but at a slower pace. Also, stretch to improve your flexibility. A cooldown should take about 5 minutes.

?

Why do some
people avoid
exercising?

Lesson 2 Review On a sheet of paper, write the word from the Word Bank that best completes each sentence.

1. Sprinting and other short spurts of activity are examples of _____ exercise.

2. Lifting weights, doing push-ups, and other muscle-building activities are examples of _____ exercise.

3. Swimming, running, walking, or some other activity that improves the health of your heart and lungs is _____ exercise.

On a sheet of paper, write the answers to the following questions. Use complete sentences.

4. **Critical Thinking** Why should an exercise program include all five parts of a good program?

5. **Critical Thinking** How can regular exercise improve your health?

Link to ➤➤➤

Arts

Ballet dancers leap and turn across the stage. Many of the moves in ballet can help people who play sports. Many athletes study parts of ballet to improve how they move. The moves taught in ballet can be used in sports such as baseball, basketball, ice-skating, and football.

Objectives

After reading this lesson, you should be able to

- describe the parts of a good fitness plan
- explain how rest and sleep are important to fitness
- explain how fitness can be a part of your life

A personal fitness plan includes eating well, exercising, and getting enough rest and sleep. The first step in any fitness plan is eating the right foods. You need foods that provide a good balance of nutrients and calories.

Exercising should be a part of your day. It will strengthen your muscles and burn extra calories. Table 6.3.1 shows the number of calories burned for different types of activities.

Talk to your doctor before you start a fitness plan. Make sure there are no limits on the type of activities you can include in your plan. You might want to ask a friend to be a part of your fitness plan. Exercising is always fun to do with a friend.

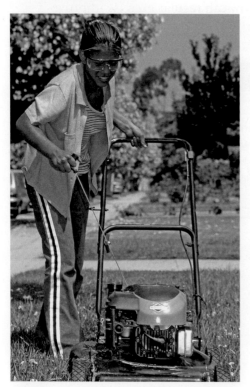

Figure 6.3.1 *Jobs such as lawn mowing can be good exercise.*

Table 6.3.1 Calories Burned for a Person Weighing 150 Pounds	
Activity	**Calories**
Jogging	675 per hour
Soccer	468 per hour
Dancing	370 per hour
Yoga	360 per hour
Brisk walk	297 per hour
Golf (using no golf cart)	240 per hour
Sitting	81 per hour
Watching TV	72 per hour
Sleeping	45 per hour
Mowing lawn	240 per hour

Here are a few things to remember as you think about your fitness plan:

- Choose activities that you enjoy.

- Drink lots of water before, during, and after you exercise.

- If you miss a day of exercise, plan for a makeup day. Do not double your exercise time to make up for a lost day.

- Start slowly. Do not overdo it.

- Wear comfortable clothes and shoes.

What Are the Steps of a Fitness Plan?

To make a fitness plan that will work for you, follow these steps.

Step 1 Determine your current fitness level. How much do you exercise? What kinds of exercise do you get? Do you eat a variety of healthy foods?

Step 2 Set realistic goals. Do you want to lose weight or gain weight? Do you want to increase your heart and lung health? What activities will you add to your current exercise level?

Step 3 Find resources to help you meet your goals. Where will you work out? What kinds of equipment will you need? Will you have friends or family members supporting you?

Step 4 Get started. After you start exercising, pay attention to your body. Are you feeling dizzy or short of breath? Do your muscles hurt too much? You can always talk with your healthcare professional about how to change your plan to better suit your body.

Step 5 Keep a record. Keep track of what you did to meet your goals daily or weekly. What exercises did you do? How many minutes did you exercise?

Decide for Yourself

Before you start on a personal fitness plan, you should do two things. First, decide what your fitness needs are. Next, decide how much time each day you can give to your fitness plan. Then follow these steps in making your personal fitness plan. Remember that eating healthy foods is part of any fitness plan. Be sure to include grains, vegetables, fruits, milk, meat, or beans every day.

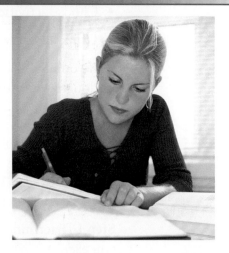

Step 1 Establish a starting point of your fitness level. Write down the answers to these questions:

- How fit is my body? Choose *not at all fit, somewhat fit,* or *very fit.*

- How flexible am I? Choose *not at all flexible, somewhat flexible,* or *very flexible.*

- How much exercise can I do now at one time? Choose *less than 15 minutes, 15–30 minutes,* or *more than 30 minutes.*

Step 2 Design a written program for yourself based on goals you can actually meet. Write down the answers to these questions:

- Do I just want to lose weight?

- Do I want to increase my endurance and flexibility?

- What activities will be a part of my plan?

- How will my fitness plan fit into my life?

- When will I look at how well I am doing?

Step 3 Get what you need. For example, does your school or community have a fitness center? Do you have the right kinds of workout clothes and shoes?

Step 4 Get started. Listen to your body. Pay attention to signs that you are doing too much, such as shortness of breath, dizziness, or feeling sick to your stomach. Make a list of these signs. Share this list with your doctor before you go on with your fitness plan. Be flexible. Change your fitness plan to match what your body can handle.

Step 5 Every week, figure out how you are doing. Are you sticking to your plan? Do you need to change your activities? How much time do you spend on them? Do you feel more fit? Keep a record of how well you do.

On a sheet of paper, write the answers to the following questions. Use complete sentences.

1. How can a personal fitness plan improve your physical health?

2. How can a personal fitness plan improve your social health?

3. How can a personal fitness plan improve your emotional health?

Why Are Rest and Sleep Important to Fitness?

Rest is basic to the body's well-being. When you are tired, your body cannot work right. You have a harder time paying attention and often feel more stressed. Your body also is at greater risk of disease and injury when you are tired. Sleep and rest are necessary to feel better and to stay healthy.

Most teens need at least 8 hours of sleep each night. Depending on your level of activity, you might need more rest. Rest does not always have to mean sleep. Relaxing or reducing your level of activity are good ways to rest during the day.

Health Myth

Myth: No pain, no gain!

Fact: Being sore after first exercising is common. However, you should not feel pain during or after exercise. If you do, it may mean you are doing something wrong. You may be pushing yourself too hard. You do not need to have pain to improve your muscle strength or endurance. If you continue to exercise when you feel pain, you could injure yourself.

Health at Work

Fitness Instructor

If you like helping others stay fit, you might think about becoming a fitness instructor. Many companies have health and wellness programs. Fitness instructors work with companies to design health programs for their workers. They show workers the correct way to exercise. Fitness instructors also explain how the right exercises help the body. They may work with doctors and physical therapists to help workers get over medical problems. You must have at least a college degree to be a fitness instructor.

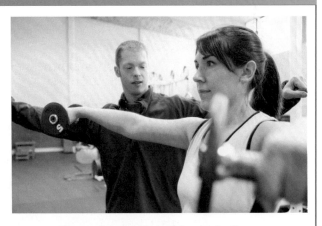

The training you receive is similar to the training for physical therapists, physical education teachers, or recreation specialists.

Lesson 3 Review On a sheet of paper, write the letter of the answer that best completes each sentence.

1. You should decide about _____ before you start a personal fitness plan.
   A school sports
   B a friend's plan
   C your fitness needs
   D local fitness centers

2. Every personal fitness plan should include _____.
   A the use of fitness machines and classes
   B a look at how well you are doing
   C jogging, running, or walking
   D isokinetic exercise

3. Rest and sleep are important for _____.
   A maximum heart rate
   B nutrition
   C well-being
   D calorie intake

On a sheet of paper, write the answers to the following questions. Use complete sentences.

4. **Critical Thinking** Why is eating healthy foods an important part of a personal fitness plan?

5. **Critical Thinking** Why is exercising an important part of a personal fitness plan?

Chapter 6   S U M M A R Y

■ Hygiene refers to things you do to have good health. It means taking care of your eyes, ears, skin, hair, nails, and teeth.

■ Your body protects your eyes and sight with bones, eyebrows and eyelashes, blinking, and tears. You can protect your eyes in several ways, including having regular eye checkups.

■ Your skull protects your ears, and wax keeps dirt out of them. You can protect your ears by avoiding loud sounds and by keeping objects out of them.

■ Loud noise is the most common reason for hearing loss. You can almost always avoid hearing loss.

■ The two basic rules of good skin care are to keep your skin clean and to avoid strong winds, cold, and sun.

■ You can take care of your teeth by brushing after meals, flossing daily, and having regular dental checkups.

■ Physical fitness is your body's ability to meet the demands of daily life.

■ Three parts of health-related fitness are heart and lung endurance, flexibility, and muscular fitness.

■ Regular exercise increases energy, lowers the chances of getting sick, helps control weight, reduces anxiety, and helps get rid of stress.

■ Some types of exercise are aerobic, anaerobic, isometric, isotonic, and isokinetic exercise.

■ A good exercise program includes a warm-up activity, aerobic activity, exercises to improve muscular fitness and flexibility, and a cooldown activity.

■ Lifelong health includes a personal fitness plan that sets reasonable goals.

■ Rest and sleep are basic to fitness. The body does not work right without enough sleep.

Vocabulary

acne, 130	dandruff, 132	infection, 129
aerobic exercise, 135	deodorant, 130	isokinetic exercise, 135
allergy, 129	endurance, 134	isometric exercise, 135
anaerobic exercise, 135	flexibility, 134	isotonic exercise, 135
antiperspirant, 130	fungus, 131	maximum heart rate, 136
athlete's foot, 131	gingivitis, 132	pimple, 130
calorie, 135	hygiene, 128	resistance, 134

Maintaining Personal Hygiene and Fitness   Chapter 6   **145**

Chapter 6 REVIEW

Word Bank

acne

allergy

athlete's foot

calorie

dandruff

deodorant

endurance

flexibility

fungus

infection

maximum heart
rate

pimple

resistance

Vocabulary Review

On a sheet of paper, write the word or phrase from the Word Bank that best completes each sentence.

1. Using _____ each morning will cover body odor.

2. You can find your _____ after you exercise as hard, fast, and long as you can.

3. A(n) _____ is an inflamed swelling on the skin.

4. A measure of the amount of energy in food is a(n) _____.

5. Some causes of hearing loss are _____ and heredity.

6. A(n) _____ is a bad reaction of the body to a food or to something in the air.

7. Clogged skin pores cause _____.

8. A(n) _____ can cause athlete's foot.

9. The pushing back of something is _____.

10. You can buy shampoos that will prevent _____ on your scalp.

11. People with heart and lung _____ can easily move oxygen through the blood to the lungs.

12. Being able to bend and stretch easily shows you have good _____.

13. If the skin between your toes is itching, you might have _____.

Concept Review

On a sheet of paper, write the letter of the answer that best completes each sentence.

14. One way to protect your ears is to _____.

    A wear earplugs when there is loud noise

    B clean them daily with a cotton swab

    C keep them wet after swimming

    D avoid head guards

15. One thing you can do to take care of your teeth is to _____.

    A avoid fluoride   **C** not eat too many sweets

    B chew on hard objects   **D** eat mostly soft foods

16. A good reason to exercise regularly is that it _____.

    A makes you less flexible   **C** gets you out in the fresh air

    B improves your hearing   **D** helps control your weight

17. Your body needs sleep to _____.

    A work right   **C** improve lung endurance

    B lose weight   **D** get rid of body odor

Critical Thinking

On a sheet of paper, write the answers to the following questions. Use complete sentences.

18. How can you help others understand the risk factors that might affect the health of your eyes and ears?

19. What goals can you set for yourself to stay healthy for the rest of your life?

20. Why do you think physical fitness needs to be lifelong?

Test-Taking Tip When taking a test where you must write your answer, read the question twice to make sure you understand what is being asked.

Self-Assessment

Can you answer these questions?

- [x] 1. What are the eight stages of life?

- [x] 2. What are the early stages of human development?

- [x] 3. What are some of the changes that occur during puberty?

- [x] 4. How does the hormone testosterone affect males during puberty?

- [x] 5. How do hormones affect females during puberty?

- [x] 6. How can a woman tell if she is pregnant?

- [x] 7. How do a human embryo and fetus develop?

- [x] 8. What are some healthy behaviors for pregnant women?

- [x] 9. How did you inherit traits, or qualities, from your parents?

- [x] 10. Why is the history of your family's health important to your own health?

Chapter

7 The Life Cycle and Human Development

People pass through many stages during their lifetime. When you were younger, your life was very different. You have grown, developed, and moved through many stages since you were born. Even before you were born, you passed through many stages. At one time, your body was just one tiny cell. One of life's most remarkable events is how that cell developed into the person you are today.

In this chapter, you will learn about the stages in the life cycle. You will learn about the physical changes that happen during your teen years. You will learn how new life forms and develops and what happens during childbirth. Finally, you will learn about how families pass characteristics, or qualities, from parents to their children.

Goals for Learning

◆ To identify the stages in the life cycle

◆ To explain the changes that take place as young people mature into adults

◆ To describe the male and female reproductive systems

◆ To describe how new life forms and develops

◆ To describe the process of birth

◆ To explain the importance of prenatal care

◆ To explain how characteristics are passed from parents to their children

Objectives

After reading this lesson, you should be able to

◆ identify and describe the eight stages of life
◆ describe changes that occur during puberty
◆ recognize and accept differences in body types

Many years ago, Doctor Erik Erikson determined that people usually go through eight life stages. Erikson's ideas are called a model of social and psychological development.

Erikson believed that a person could overcome an unpleasant experience in one stage by being successful in a later stage. Look at the overview of these stages in Table 7.1.1 as you read. Keep in mind that different people progress through different stages of the life cycle at different rates.

What Are the Early Stages of Development?

The first stage is from birth to 12 months. If the basic needs of infants are met during this time, they learn to trust. Infants who are not well cared for may learn to mistrust others.

Table 7.1.1 Stages of Social and Psychological Development			
Stage	Ages	Psychological Task	Description of Task
1	0–1	Trust and mistrust	Baby whose needs are met by caretaker develops a sense of trust in others.
2	2–3	Independence and doubt	Older baby tries to learn independence and self-confidence.
3	4–6	Enterprise and guilt	Young child learns to start his or her own activities.
4	7–12	Ability and inability	Child tries to develop skill in physical, mental, and social areas.
5	13–19	Identity and role confusion	Adolescent tries out several roles and forms a connected, single identity.
6	20–40	Closeness and loneliness	Young adult tries to form close, permanent relationships and to make career commitments.
7	41–64	Caring for children and self-absorption	Middle-aged person tries to contribute to the world through family relationships, work productivity, and artistry.
8	65 on	Meaning and purpose and despair	Older person thinks back on life, experiencing satisfaction or disappointment.

During the second stage, from 2 to 3 years, children begin to do things on their own. They begin to depend less on others. If they are not allowed to learn some independence, they may start to doubt their abilities or feel shame.

Children between ages 4 and 6 are in the third stage of development. Here they learn to explore their world within safe limits. They begin to ask "Why?" They begin to use their imagination. They initiate, or begin, activities instead of simply following someone else. If children are encouraged at this time, they begin to feel able to do things. If not, they may develop feelings of guilt.

Children usually enter the fourth stage between ages 7 and 12. This is when they begin to make things. This is called having a sense of industry. If children hear positive comments about their efforts, they feel good about their abilities. If they are scolded or told negative comments, they may feel **inferior.** Children who feel inferior think they are not as good as others or as good as they should be.

What Happens from Adolescence to Early Adulthood?

The fifth stage begins at **adolescence,** the years from ages 13 to 19. This is when many young people are trying to discover things about themselves. They are asking themselves questions such as "Who am I?" and "What do I believe in?" At this stage, teens are involved with many groups of people the same age, or peer groups. They sometimes think about themselves as others do. They are trying to figure out their own identity— a sense of who they are. They try to determine their needs, abilities, and values.

If a person had trouble with any of the earlier stages of development, that person may have difficulty dealing with the fifth stage. If they have feelings of mistrust, guilt, or being inferior, they may become confused about their role in life. **Role confusion** is being unclear about one's sense of identity.

You may be concerned about the changes that happen to you during adolescence. Talking with your parents or other trusted adults can help. Use effective communication skills. Listen without interrupting. If you are embarrassed, be honest. Keep in mind that adults went through puberty at one time. They understand what you are going through.

The sixth stage is early adulthood. This stage usually includes ages 20 to 40. This is often the point in life when people leave their parents' home. They decide how they feel about a close relationship with another person. Again, if they have had problems during earlier stages, this time can be difficult. People who do not feel good about forming close relationships may feel isolated, or alone.

What Are the Later Stages of Development?

The seventh stage represents middle adulthood. During this stage, adults often turn their attention to their families. They also may help others outside the family. If they do not, they may become too concerned with their personal needs. This is called being self-absorbed. Self-absorbed people may have a difficult time finding satisfaction in life.

The eighth stage is older adulthood. This last stage of life is a time when people look back and think about what they have achieved. If they feel good about what they have done, they experience a sense of completeness. If not, they may feel depressed. Older adults also are at higher risk for diseases and disorders. As a person gets older, the body's immune system does not work as well as it once did. The immune system protects against diseases. Older adults may get the flu more easily, for example. Aging also causes changes in the senses. Parts of the ear and eye weaken or break down. As a result, many older adults have hearing or vision problems.

What Changes Occur During Puberty?

The beginning of adolescence is called **puberty.** Puberty is the time in life when children begin to develop into adults and are able to have children. Puberty begins at different ages for different people. Girls may begin puberty at ages 8 to 13. Boys may begin puberty at ages 10 to 15. During puberty, the body changes size and shape. These changes are called growth spurts. They occur at different rates and at different times for each person.

Sometimes adolescents worry if they have not reached puberty at the same time as their peers. Others are embarrassed because they feel awkward. During a growth spurt, for example, hands and feet often grow first. Until the arms and legs catch up, a person may feel clumsy. It is normal for adolescents to have different body types and different rates of growth. You can promote your self-esteem and that of others by accepting these differences. You can focus on strengths and abilities rather than differences.

Health in Your Life

Good Health Habits in Adolescence

Each stage of life is important. Yet the fifth stage, or adolescence, has some special challenges. As teens become more independent, they may take more risks. For example, they may decide to use alcohol or other drugs. An adolescent's brain is not fully developed. Alcohol damages a part of the brain that is still growing. It can cause memory and learning problems.

Drinking alcohol is a behavior to avoid. Other behaviors are healthy and help your body develop properly. During adolescence, your body is growing and changing. You need at least 8 hours of sleep each night. Sleep helps you grow and handle stress better. Exercise and good eating habits also help your body develop. You need at least 60 minutes of activity every day. This helps you keep a healthy weight and build muscles and bones.

You can be a spokesperson for good health habits during adolescence. Write a public service announcement (PSA) that encourages your classmates to practice healthy behaviors.

On a sheet of paper, write the answers to the following questions. Use complete sentences.

1. Teens who practice healthy behaviors are more likely to continue them when they are adults. Why do you think this is true?

2. What is a healthy behavior that you are not practicing now? How can you make it a daily habit?

3. As you gain independence, you also become more responsible. What is one way you can show you are responsible for your health?

Reproductive organ

Organ in the body that allows humans to mature sexually and to have children

Genitals

Reproductive, or sex, organs

Secondary sex characteristic

Feature that signals the beginning of adulthood

The endocrine system includes glands that produce hormones. The pituitary gland produces hormones that signal many changes during puberty. Some hormones control the amount and timing of growth. Some hormones control the development of the **reproductive organs.** Reproductive organs allow humans to grow up, develop sexually, and have children.

Hormones signal changes in both males and females. Oil and sweat glands become more active. Hair begins to grow in other areas of the body and around the **genitals,** or sex organs. Hormones also signal the body to develop **secondary sex characteristics,** or features that signal the beginning of adulthood. Males develop hair on their faces, their voices change, and their shoulders broaden. Females develop breasts, wider hips, and a narrower waist.

Decide for Yourself

During adolescence, you start thinking about what you want to do with your life. You are making the change from your role as a child to your role as an adult. Here is an example of how one teen set a goal for a career after high school.

1. **Write down your goal.** The teen wants to work with children in a day care setting.

2. **List the steps needed to reach your goal.** Step 1 is to find out the type of degree needed. Step 2 is to identify several schools that offer the degree and the cost of each. Step 3 is to look at ways to pay for school. Step 4 is to apply to study at one or more schools.

3. **Set up a timeline for completing each step.** The teen wants to be ready to start college right after high school graduation.

4. **Identify any problems that might get in your way.** The teen gets a part-time job now to save money for school.

5. **Check your progress as you work toward your goal.** The teen realizes that more time is needed to find out about loans. The teen changes the timeline for Step 3.

On a sheet of paper, write the answers to the following items. Use complete sentences.

1. List a goal you would like to achieve.

2. Go through numbers 2, 3, 4, and 5 above, using your specific goal.

Testosterone

Male sex hormone

Estrogen

Female sex hormone

Progesterone

Female sex hormone

Three hormones signal the body's reproductive system to develop during puberty. These are **testosterone, estrogen,** and **progesterone.** Testosterone is the hormone that signals the development of secondary sex characteristics in males. Estrogen and progesterone control reproductive development in females.

Lesson 1 Review On a sheet of paper, write the answers to the following questions. Use complete sentences.

1. What might cause a child to feel inferior?

2. What health problems might an older adult have?

3. What three hormones signal the body's reproductive system to develop?

4. **Critical Thinking** During the fifth stage of development, why is it important for teens to choose peers who share their values?

5. **Critical Thinking** What would you tell a friend who is upset because he is shorter than the other boys in your class?

Health at Work

Medical Technologist

Medical technologists work in hospitals and laboratories. They are like detectives, because they observe and discover things. They collect samples for medical tests. They test for drug levels and chemicals in the blood. They look for germs that cause disease. They check for cells that are not normal that might show health problems. Medical technologists usually need a college degree. They take courses in chemistry, biology, math, and statistics. Technologists must have good judgment and be able to work under pressure. They must pay close attention to detail and be good at problem solving. A medical technician usually has a 2-year degree. Technicians perform simpler tasks and work for a technologist. Most states require both technologists and technicians to be licensed or registered.

Reproduction

The process through which two human beings produce a child

Testes

Two glands in males that produce sperm cells

Sperm

Male sex cells produced by the testes

The ability to reproduce is one of the most amazing things about the body. **Reproduction** is the process through which two human beings produce a child. The reproductive system is the only body system that differs between males and females.

What Changes Occur in Males During Puberty?

At puberty, the male hormone testosterone begins to be released into a young man's body. Testosterone is produced in the **testes,** the two main glands in the male reproductive system. Figure 7.2.1 shows the male reproductive system. Another function of the testes is to make **sperm,** or male sex cells. Beginning at puberty, the testes make more than 200 million sperm cells every day. Males are usually able to produce sperm from puberty throughout the rest of their life.

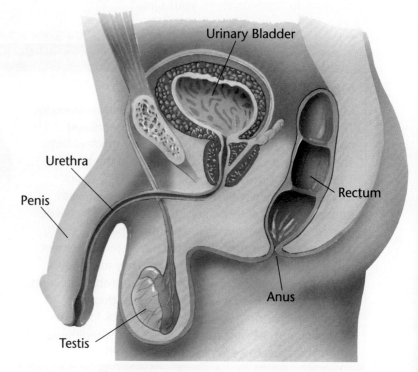

Figure 7.2.1 *The male reproductive system*

Ovaries

Two organs in females that produce egg cells

Ovulation

The release of a mature egg cell

Conceive

To become pregnant

Fallopian tube

Passage through which mature egg cells pass from the ovaries to the uterus

Uterus

Female organ that holds a growing baby

Vagina

Canal connecting the uterus to the outside of a female's body

What Changes Occur in Females During Puberty?

When girls reach puberty, hormones begin to act on the **ovaries.** Ovaries are the two organs in a woman's body that produce egg cells. Females are born with more than one million egg cells already present in the body. Hormones cause the egg cells to mature. As they mature, the ovaries release egg cells. This is called **ovulation.** Once a woman begins to ovulate, she is able to **conceive,** or to become pregnant. Each ovary usually releases one egg every other month. Figure 7.2.2 shows the female reproductive system and part of the excretory system.

The released egg then travels into one of the two **fallopian tubes.** The egg cell moves in these tubes to the **uterus.** The uterus is an organ where an egg will grow into a baby if it is joined by a sperm. Otherwise, the egg cell leaves the body through the **vagina,** a canal that leads to the outside of a female's body.

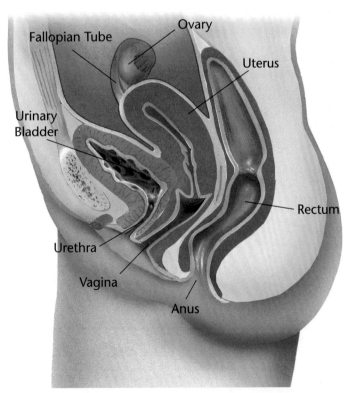

Figure 7.2.2 *The female reproductive system*

Menstrual cycle

The monthly cycle of changes in a female's reproductive system

Menstruation

The process in females during which blood tissue leaves the lining of the uterus

The process of releasing an egg is one step in a monthly cycle in women. This process is called the **menstrual cycle.** When the ovary releases an egg cell, the lining of the uterus begins to thicken with blood tissue. If the egg is to become a baby, it attaches to the wall of the uterus. It stays there for 9 months to grow. The blood tissue is the source of nutrients, or food, for a developing baby. Figure 7.2.3 shows the menstrual cycle. FSH and LH are hormones that play important roles in the menstrual cycle.

If the egg does not attach to the wall of the uterus, it leaves the body through the vagina. The blood tissue is not needed. It leaves the body during **menstruation,** a process that takes 4 to 6 days.

The entire menstrual cycle is usually about 28 days long. When one cycle ends, the next cycle begins. The menstrual cycle repeats itself until a woman is between 45 and 55 years old. Then the body produces less and less estrogen and progesterone, and the menstrual cycle stops.

Figure 7.2.3 *The menstrual cycle*

How Does New Life Form?

Once males and females reach puberty, they are able to reproduce. **Sexual intercourse** is the insertion of the **penis** into the vagina. This allows the male sperm and a female egg cell to join together to form a new life.

During intercourse, sperm pass from the testes through tubes that lead to the penis. The penis is the male reproductive organ. It has many small blood vessels. When these vessels fill with blood, the male has an **erection.** That means the penis becomes hard and larger. During this time, sperm can travel through the penis to enter the female body through the vagina.

During intercourse, millions of sperm are released into the female. If the female is in the right stage of the menstrual cycle, an egg may become **fertilized,** or joined by the sperm. If not, the sperm cells die and leave the female's body. Only one sperm cell is needed to fertilize the female's egg cell. If the sperm and egg unite, the woman becomes **pregnant,** or carries a developing baby.

Lesson 2 Review On a sheet of paper, write the word or phrase in parentheses that best completes each sentence.

1. The male hormone is _____ (estrogen, progesterone, testosterone).

2. Males produce _____ (testes, sperm, egg cells) from puberty throughout adult life.

3. The organs that produce eggs are the _____ (ovaries, testes, fallopian tubes).

On a sheet of paper, write the answers to the following questions. Use complete sentences.

4. **Critical Thinking** Explain how egg cells and sperm are different in the numbers that are produced and when they are produced.

5. **Critical Thinking** Suppose a classmate says that menstruation is about 28 days long. What is wrong with this statement?

Sexual intercourse

Insertion of the penis into the vagina

Penis

Male reproductive organ

Erection

Condition in which the penis becomes hard and larger

Fertilize

An egg cell and a sperm join together

Pregnant

Carrying a developing baby in the female body

Health Myth

Myth: All girls start menstruating around age 12.

Fact: The average age is around 12. However, every girl is different. It is normal for a girl to start as young as age 8 or as old as age 16.

Gestation

The period of development in the uterus from the time the egg is fertilized until birth; pregnancy

Ultrasound

The use of sound waves to show pictures of what is inside the body

As you learned in Lesson 2, when an egg cell and sperm join, the egg becomes fertilized. This begins the process called pregnancy, or **gestation.** Gestation lasts about 9 months in humans. This is the period of time needed to allow the fertilized egg to grow and develop.

How Does a Woman Know She Is Pregnant?

There are several signs of pregnancy. A woman may feel sick or very tired. Her breasts may feel sore. She has probably missed a menstrual cycle, because menstruation stops during pregnancy.

If a woman believes she might be pregnant, she should see a doctor. A blood test at a doctor's office can check for pregnancy as early as 6 to 8 days after ovulation. Some urine tests can tell in as little as 6 days after the egg is fertilized. Both tests look for a certain hormone that is released only during pregnancy. A doctor can determine whether a woman is pregnant in three ways: (1) The doctor can hear the fetus's heartbeat. (2) The fetus shows signs of movement. (3) An **ultrasound** picture shows a developing baby. Ultrasound is the use of sound waves to show what is inside the body. See Figure 7.3.1.

Figure 7.3.1 *This ultrasound picture shows a baby developing in the uterus.*

Prenatal care

Health care during a
pregnancy

*Fetal alcohol
syndrome*

A condition caused by
drinking alcohol during
pregnancy

Women can
test at home for
pregnancy by using
kits they buy at a
drugstore. Most
home tests give the
right information
if done correctly.
If a result tells the
woman she is not
pregnant, she
should repeat the
test in a few days.
If a woman thinks
she is pregnant
but the test keeps
telling her she is
not, she should see
a doctor.

What Is Prenatal Care?

Prenatal care is health care during a pregnancy. A pregnant woman needs to take special care of her body. She needs to see a doctor many times during the pregnancy. The doctor can tell her about health behaviors that will help her take care of herself and her unborn baby. Here are some ways a woman can take good care of herself and her unborn baby:

- Take a multivitamin that has folic acid. This vitamin helps prevent certain birth defects. A pregnant woman should not take any other drugs or medicines unless a doctor tells her to.

- Eat healthy foods, such as fruits, vegetables, and whole grains.

- Exercise regularly, but only the type and length of time the doctor recommends.

- Get regular checkups. Women who do not have health insurance usually can go to a public health clinic in their community.

Smoking, drinking alcohol, and using other drugs can harm the developing baby. Smoking tobacco can cause a baby to be born too early. The baby might weigh too little at birth. The baby might develop a disease of the lungs called asthma. A baby whose mother drinks alcohol might develop **fetal alcohol syndrome** (FAS). FAS causes unusual facial features, damage to the nervous system, and growth problems. Children who have FAS may have trouble learning and may have other birth defects. Other drugs also can harm the developing baby.

Link to ➤➤➤

Environmental Science

Lead is a mineral that used to be common in paint and gasoline. It also is found in some drinking water and soil. Lead that enters a pregnant woman's body is harmful to the developing baby. It can cause mental slowness, hearing problems, and kidney damage. Pregnant women should avoid breathing lead dust and drinking water from pipes that contain lead.

For example, cocaine can cause early birth. Children whose mothers smoked marijuana during pregnancy may have trouble concentrating.

Substances in the environment also can harm an unborn baby. Pregnant women should avoid chemicals such as paint thinners and products that kill insects. They should read the labels on household products. Most dangerous products have pregnancy warnings.

What Happens as the Fertilized Egg Grows?

The tiny fertilized egg takes about 4 days to travel from the fallopian tube to the uterus. While it travels, its cells divide many times. It becomes a ball of cells that plants itself in the lining of the uterus. This process, called **implantation,** happens about 6 to 8 days after fertilization. Figure 7.3.2 shows the steps from ovulation to implantation.

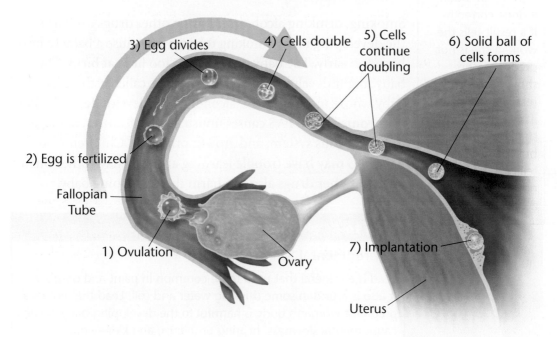

Figure 7.3.2 *Journey of a fertilized egg from ovulation through implantation*

Embryo

Fertilized egg after implantation

Placenta

An organ lining the uterus that surrounds the embryo or fetus

Umbilical cord

Structure that joins the embryo or fetus with the placenta

Trimester

A period of 3 months

Fetus

Unborn baby from 8 weeks after fertilization until birth

Link to ➤➤➤

Social Studies

Through history, most women have had their babies at home without a doctor. Today, 99 percent of babies in the United States are born in a hospital. There, mother and child are more likely to remain healthy. Ultrasound and other tests can check for problems. Doctors and nurses are there to help.

The uterus is normally small enough to fit into the palm of your hand. As the tiny cells grow, the uterus expands to hold the fully developed baby. At this time, the fertilized egg becomes an **embryo.** An embryo is about the size of the dot on the letter *i.*

A special organ called the **placenta** develops from the embryo along the lining of the uterus. The placenta surrounds the embryo. The **umbilical cord** joins the embryo with the placenta. The cord carries nutrients to the embryo and removes its wastes. The cord also carries anything else the mother eats or drinks.

A special fluid protects the embryo in the uterus. The embryo floats in this liquid, which protects the embryo against temperature changes and injury.

How Does the Embryo Develop?

Figure 7.3.3 on the next page shows the major events that usually occur during each month of pregnancy. The 9 months of pregnancy are divided into three **trimesters.** Each trimester is 3 months long. After 8 weeks, or about 2 months, all the vital organs have started to develop. By this time, the embryo is called a **fetus.** The fetus continues to develop during the rest of the gestation period. At the end of this time, the fetus is considered full term and is ready to be born.

❋ ❋

Technology and Society

An ultrasound picture helps the health of the baby in many ways. The doctor can tell whether the baby has health problems. Sometimes these can be corrected before the baby is born. Ultrasound also can tell how far along the pregnancy is. The doctor can try to prevent labor, or childbirth, if the baby is not yet fully developed.

9 weeks

11 weeks

15 weeks

36 weeks

Changes During Pregnancy		
Trimester/ Month	Embryo/Fetus	Mother
First Trimester First Month	Embryo ¼ inch long, heart is obvious; eyes, nose, and brain appear; arms and legs are small bumps	Menstruation stops; breasts are tender; fatigue; frequent urination; positive pregnancy test
Second Month	Embryo 1 inch long; head quite large; fingers, toes appear; nervous system and brain coordinate body functions; mouth opens and closes	Possible nausea and vomiting lasting into third or fourth month
Third Month	Embryo becomes a fetus; 4 inches long; weighs about 1 ounce	Breasts possibly swollen; thickened waist; uterus well rounded
Second Trimester Fourth Month	Fetus 6 inches long; weighs 3½ ounces; sex may be determined; body covered with soft hair	Breasts may discharge liquid; uterus wall more stretched; larger midsection
Fifth Month	Fetus 9½ inches long; weighs 10 ounces; skin less transparent	Feels stronger fetal movements; uterus higher; breasts not much larger; midpoint of pregnancy
Sixth Month	Fetus 12 inches long; weighs 1½ pounds; eyebrows, eyelashes showing; sucks thumb; hiccups; if born at this time, usually dies	Uterus increases in size; fetal movements may feel sharp
Third Trimester Seventh Month	Fetus 14 inches long; weighs 2½ pounds; covered with a greasy substance to protect it; responsive to sound and taste; if born at this time, moves actively, cries weakly; if born, can live with expert care	Still feels fetal movements; size of uterus increases; weight gain continues
Eighth Month	Fetus 15½ inches long; weighs 3½ pounds; hair on head; skin red and wrinkled; if born, can survive with proper care	Gains some additional weight; uterus extends; fetal movements continue
Ninth Month	Fetus 18 inches long; weighs 5½ pounds; gestation period ends; body fat makes figure more round, less wrinkled in face	Top of uterus nears breastbone; possible frequent urination because of pressure on bladder; possible difficulty in walking

Figure 7.3.3 *Events in pregnancy. The drawings from top to bottom show the development of the fetus at 9, 11, 15, and 36 weeks.*

What Happens During Childbirth?

Childbirth has three stages. Figure 7.3.4 shows the second stage. The process of birth begins with labor pains that happen when the uterus tightens, or contracts. These contractions begin to pull open the **cervix.** The cervix is the narrow outer end of the uterus. The cervix has been closed to hold the growing baby inside the uterus. The cervix must open, or dilate, to a diameter of about 4 inches.

Dilation of the cervix is the first stage of birth. It lasts an average of 7 to 15 hours. During this time, the woman feels labor pains that happen more often as the contractions continue. The protective placenta around the fetus breaks, and fluid flows out of the woman's body.

When the cervix is dilated, the second stage begins. During this stage, the baby is pushed out, usually head first, from the uterus. The baby is then able to breathe on its own. The second stage of birth usually takes from 15 to 60 minutes.

The third stage is called the afterbirth. At this time, the uterus contracts to release the placenta, which leaves the woman's body. This stage usually lasts just a few minutes.

There are different types of childbirth. The process just described is vaginal childbirth. **Cesarean childbirth** is the delivery of a baby through a cut in the abdomen and uterus. A cesarean may be done for many reasons. For example, labor may be lasting too long. The baby's head may be too large to pass through the birth canal. Cesarean births make up about one-fourth of all childbirths in the United States.

Cervix
Narrow outer end of the uterus

Cesarean childbirth
The delivery of a baby through a cut in the abdomen and uterus

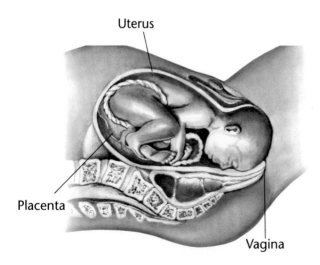

Uterus

Placenta

Vagina

Figure 7.3.4 *A baby leaves the uterus through the vagina.*

What Is Perinatal Care?

Perinatal care is care of the baby around the time of birth and through the first month. Here are ways to provide good perinatal care:

- Keep all appointments with the baby's doctor.

- Place the baby on his or her back to sleep on a firm mattress. This helps to prevent crib death, or sudden infant death syndrome (SIDS).

- Consider breast-feeding the baby for at least the first few months. Breast milk is the perfect food for babies. It is easier to digest than cow's milk or baby formula. It helps protect babies from diseases.

- Do not allow anyone to smoke around the baby.

How Do the Woman's Body and Mind Adjust After Childbirth?

The new life has begun, and it is usually a happy, exciting time for the new parents. The woman's body must adjust after birth. It may take several months to return to normal. Women may have emotional ups and downs as a result of changing hormone levels. Sometimes, women have **postpartum** depression, which can happen any time within the first year after giving birth. It can last from a few weeks to several months. If it lasts longer or is severe, a woman may need to ask her doctor for help.

Lesson 3 Review On a sheet of paper, write the answers to the following questions. Use complete sentences.

1. How long is gestation in humans?

2. What happens to the fertilized egg during the first 4 days?

3. When is an embryo called a fetus?

4. **Critical Thinking** Suppose a woman thinks she is pregnant, but the home test results are negative. Why is it important for the woman to find out for sure?

5. **Critical Thinking** Suppose a woman drinks alcohol while pregnant. How does the alcohol affect the baby?

Heredity is important because it explains why many children look much like their parents. Heredity also influences our health.

What Is Genetics?

Genetics is the science that studies heredity. Heredity is possible because of tiny structures called **chromosomes.** Every cell in the human body has 46 chromosomes, except sperm and egg cells. These cells have only 23 chromosomes each. When a sperm and an egg unite, the fertilized egg cell receives 23 chromosomes from each parent. The fertilized cell then contains 46 chromosomes. As the cell divides, each chromosome copies itself for a total of 92 chromosomes. When the cell divides into two cells, each cell receives 46 chromosomes. This process in the cells continues throughout life.

Each chromosome is made up of thousands of **genes.** Genes contain chemical codes that determine a person's **traits,** or characteristics. Traits of each parent are passed to the children. Genes determine your hair, eye, and skin color, and even the tone of your voice. Genes can also be the cause of diseases passed from parents to children.

What Determines Gender?

Two of the 46 chromosomes in a fertilized egg cell determine the **gender,** or sex, of the baby. Females have two copies of an X chromosome. Males have one X and one Y chromosome. Each egg cell has an X chromosome. Each sperm cell has either an X or a Y chromosome. When the two cells join, the chromosome in the sperm determines the sex of the baby. X + X results in a girl. X + Y results in a boy. Look at the following example.

Objectives

After reading this lesson, you should be able to

- explain how genes are passed from parents to children
- describe how traits are determined
- identify some genetic disorders

Genetics

The science that deals with heredity and inherited characteristics

Chromosome

Tiny structure in cells that contains hereditary information

Gene

A tiny structure in chromosomes that controls the transfer of traits from parents to children

Trait

Quality

Gender

The condition of being male or female; sex

Figure 7.4.1 *Example of chromosome combinations*

How Are Traits Determined?

The chromosomes from each parent determine the traits of a child. All the chromosomes from the mother line up with the chromosomes from the father. The genes for each trait are next to each other in pairs. One or more gene pairs control a trait. In most pairs of genes, one is **dominant,** or has the most control. That gene determines which trait a child will inherit. The other gene is called **recessive,** or hidden. That gene does not determine the trait. For example, suppose the genes a girl received from her father were for dark hair. The genes from the mother were for blond hair. The genes for dark hair are dominant, so the daughter has dark hair. To have blond hair, she would have to receive a gene for blond hair from both parents.

The Y chromosome is shorter than the X chromosome. The Y chromosome does not have as many genes. Sometimes this can result in health problems for the male. With fewer genes, the male may not have a dominant gene to link with the X chromosome. A male could receive a gene for an inherited disease that could be a recessive gene. Without the dominant gene to link to it, that trait then appears in the male. The gene and the trait it produces are called **sex-linked,** because the sex chromosome carries the gene.

One example of a sex-linked trait is red-green color blindness. A person with this condition cannot tell the difference between these two colors. Color blindness rarely affects females.

What Are Genetic Disorders?

Genetic disorders are diseases caused by unusual genes or chromosomes. These genes or chromosomes are abnormal. They are passed from parents to their children. Table 7.4.1 lists some genetic disorders and their causes. Parents with a family history of a genetic disorder may ask for help from a **genetic counselor.** This health care professional can perform tests and advise parents about the chances of passing on a genetic disorder. If the risk is great, the couple may choose not to have children. They may decide to adopt children instead.

Which of your traits do you think were passed from your father? from your mother?

Table 7.4.1 Genetic Disorders and Their Causes		
Disorder	**Description**	**Cause**
Hemophilia	Blood does not clot, or clump, normally	Recessive abnormal gene
Dwarfism	Long bones do not develop properly	Dominant abnormal gene
Cystic fibrosis	Abnormally thick mucus, constant respiratory infections	Two recessive genes
Sickle cell disease	Abnormally shaped red blood cells, weakness, irregular heart action	Two recessive genes
Down syndrome	Mental slowness, slanting eyes, broad skull, broad hands, short fingers	Extra chromosome
Spina bifida	Open spine	Many causes
Cleft palate	Roof of the mouth does not grow together during development	Many causes

Cancer

A harmful growth that destroys healthy cells

How Is Genetics Important to Health?

Genes cause many health traits that tend to run in families. That is why doctors ask about family health histories. For example, genes influence your risk of getting **cancer.** Cancer is a harmful growth in the body that destroys healthy cells. Suppose you know that several family members had or have cancer. This does not mean that you will necessarily develop cancer. You can practice healthy behaviors that decrease your chances of developing cancer. You can eat healthy foods, keep a normal weight, exercise, and avoid smoking.

Health Myth

Myth: Genetics is important only to people planning to have children.

Fact: Genes influence many health conditions. Your family's health background can help your doctor predict your risk of certain diseases, such as cancer. Your doctor may do more tests to check for those diseases. He or she may advise you on health behaviors or give you medicine to decrease your risk of getting the disease.

Lesson 4 Review On a sheet of paper, write the letter of the answer that best completes each sentence.

1. The number of chromosomes in a fertilized egg cell is
   _____.

   A 2   **C** 46
   B 23   **D** 92

2. In most pairs of genes, the gene that determines which trait a child will inherit is_____.
   A normal   **C** recessive
   B dominant   **D** sex-linked

3. A person who inherits a health trait such as high blood pressure _____.
   A can help keep the condition from developing
   B probably has a sex-linked disorder
   C has two recessive genes for the trait
   D will always develop high blood pressure

On a sheet of paper, write the answers to the following questions. Use complete sentences.

4. **Critical Thinking** Could a scientist tell if a person was male or female by examining a skin cell? Explain your answer.

5. **Critical Thinking** Suppose a woman has high blood pressure. One of her sons develops high blood pressure. The other does not. Besides a healthy lifestyle, what might be another reason the other son does not have high blood pressure?

- Adolescence is a time of many changes. Puberty is the time when children become adults and are able to have children.

- Three hormones signal the body's reproductive system to develop during puberty. They are testosterone for males, and estrogen and progesterone for females.

- The male produces sperm cells, and the female produces egg cells. If these two cells join during sexual intercourse, they form a new life.

- If the egg cell is fertilized, it begins to grow and divide. The uterus expands to hold the growing embryo or fetus. Gestation is about 9 months.

- The three stages of childbirth are the dilation of the cervix, the pushing out of the baby, and the afterbirth.

- Genetics is the science that studies heredity, or the passing of traits from parents to children.

Vocabulary

adolescence, 151

cancer, 169

cervix, 165

cesarean childbirth, 165

chromosome, 167

conceive, 157

dominant, 168

embryo, 163

erection, 159

estrogen, 155

fallopian tube, 157

fertilize, 159

fetal alcohol syndrome, 161

fetus, 163

gender, 167

gene, 167

genetic counselor, 168

genetic disorder, 168

genetics, 167

genitals, 154

gestation, 160

implantation, 162

inferior, 151

menstrual cycle, 158

menstruation, 158

ovaries, 157

ovulation, 157

penis, 159

perinatal care, 166

placenta, 163

postpartum, 166

pregnant, 159

prenatal care, 161

progesterone, 155

puberty, 152

recessive, 168

reproduction, 156

reproductive organ, 154

role confusion, 151

secondary sex characteristic, 154

sex-linked, 168

sexual intercourse, 159

sperm, 156

testes, 156

testosterone, 155

trait, 167

trimester, 163

ultrasound, 160

umbilical cord, 163

uterus, 157

vagina, 157

Word Bank

cervix
embryo
fertilization
gender
genetics
gestation
ovulation
pregnant
prenatal care
puberty
recessive
testosterone
ultrasound
umbilical cord

Vocabulary Review

On a sheet of paper, write the word or phrase from the Word Bank that best completes each sentence.

1. Adolescents are able to have children when they reach _____.

2. The hormone that signals the development of secondary sex characteristics in males is _____.

3. The release of a mature egg cell every month is _____.

4. When an egg cell joins with a sperm cell, _____ has taken place.

5. If a sperm cell and an egg cell unite, a woman becomes _____.

6. Pregnancy, or _____, usually lasts 9 months.

7. The use of sound waves to show a picture of something inside the body is _____.

8. After implantation, a fertilized egg is called a(n) _____.

9. The _____ joins the embryo or fetus with the placenta.

10. Labor pains that pull open the _____ are called contractions.

11. The science that deals with heredity is _____.

12. Part of _____ is seeing a doctor many times during a pregnancy.

13. A trait that is hidden is _____.

14. The _____ of a child is determined by the chromosome that comes from the male.

Concept Review

On a sheet of paper, write the letter of the answer that best completes each sentence.

15. It is important for children to make things to _____.

   A avoid being self-absorbed

   B determine their identity

   C feel they have ability

   D reflect on their achievements

16. A woman can tell for sure whether she is pregnant if _____.

   A a doctor hears the fetus's heartbeat

   B a home pregnancy test is done

   C her breasts are large and sore

   D she always feels sick and tired

17. A fertilized egg cell attaches itself to the wall of the _____.

   A cervix   **B** ovary   **C** uterus   **D** vagina

Critical Thinking

On a sheet of paper, write the answers to the following questions. Use complete sentences.

18. Someday, you may have children. Which of your physical traits would you want your children to have? Explain your answer.

19. What are two goals you plan to reach as an adult to help you feel good about your achievements?

20. It takes only one sperm cell to fertilize an egg. Why do you think the body produces so many sperm?

Test-Taking Tip Study for a test in short sessions rather than in one long session.

Self-Assessment

Can you answer these questions?

- [x] 1. How does dating fit into a family's life cycle?

- [x] 2. For what reasons do couples marry?

- [x] 3. What are some signs of a healthy marriage?

- [x] 4. How does life change when a person becomes a parent?

- [x] 5. What are parents responsible for?

- [x] 6. What are some different ways children learn from parents?

- [x] 7. What are some different kinds of families?

- [x] 8. What are some signs of a healthy family?

- [x] 9. What are some problems that families face?

- [x] 10. Where can families get help if they have problems?

The Family

Most people belong to a family and depend on the support they get from their family. There are many different types of families.

In this chapter, you will learn about the family life cycle. You will learn how new families are formed when people marry. You will learn about being a parent and what kinds of things parents are responsible for. You will also learn about several different kinds of families and what makes a family healthy. Finally, you will learn about problems families have and where to get help with these problems.

Goals for Learning

◆ To explain the place of dating and marriage in the family life cycle

◆ To identify some signs of a healthy marriage

◆ To describe what a parent is and what parents are responsible for

◆ To identify several different kinds of families

◆ To describe some signs of a healthy family

◆ To identify where families can get help for problems

Objectives

After reading this lesson, you should be able to

◆ discuss some of the difficult parts of dating

◆ explore abstinence as a choice

◆ describe some healthy reasons for marrying

◆ look at the difference between a healthy marriage and an unhealthy one

Socializing

Getting together with others during free time

Just as a person has a life cycle, a family also has a life cycle. The family life cycle usually includes events such as marriage and the birth of children.

A new family life cycle begins when two people decide to marry. Deciding to get married is one of the most important choices you will make in your life. Many events lead up to getting married and starting a new family.

What Is Socializing?

Throughout your life, you have grown physically and socially. During adolescence, from ages 12 through 19, you grow into an adult and are usually ready to experience many new things. You are ready to meet and spend time with many different people. You are forming ideas about yourself and are ready to form ideas about others.

Socializing is getting together with others to enjoy free-time activities. Socializing includes learning about many male and female friends. By socializing, you learn what you like and dislike about others. You learn more about yourself and the kind of future you hope to have.

One part of socializing is dating. Usually, when you date, you pair up with another person and go out as a couple. Dating is a good way to get to know other people of the opposite sex better. You learn about other people by doing things together. You learn about interests you have in common. For example, you might learn that you both enjoy bike riding. You also learn about interests that are different from your own. You may enjoy seeing movies, while others would rather go dancing. Dating can be a good experience. Going out in groups can also be a positive experience. Going out in groups gives you the chance to get to know other people without the stress that a one-to-one date can cause.

If two people enjoy being with each other, they may decide to date only each other. This can help you become closer and learn more about each other. However, when you date only one person, you give up the chance to get to know other people.

Two people who date usually have affection for each other. Even early in a relationship, there are many appropriate ways to express this affection. Physically, you might hold hands, hug, and kiss. You can also show affection by paying close attention to another person. Or you can give small gifts or write letters.

What Are Some Difficult Parts of Dating?

Having a healthy dating relationship means agreeing on certain things. Both people should talk openly about their feelings and values. Sometimes, it can be difficult for two people to agree.

One of the most important parts of all relationships is communication. When you communicate successfully, you express your thoughts and feelings openly and honestly. Talking openly and honestly helps you understand each other. It keeps mix-ups and fights from happening. While it can be hard to express your feelings or thoughts, this is an important part of a relationship. Carefully listening to another person is also an important part of communication.

Figure 8.1.1 *Couples should talk about who pays for things they do together.*

Another part of dating is deciding who pays for things you do together. Couples should talk this over. They may decide that one person always pays for the date. They may decide to take turns paying, or to "go dutch," with each person paying his or her own way.

Something else to think and talk about is your physical relationship. A healthy relationship is based on many things. Sometimes, relationships are based mainly on physical attraction. This attraction may cause you to begin a sexual relationship. If this happens too early in a relationship, you may have big problems. Some problems include diseases and unexpected pregnancy. Beginning a sexual relationship too early can lead to one person losing respect for the other. It can keep you from getting to know each other in other ways.

Many dating couples choose **abstinence.** Abstinence is the choice not to have a sexual relationship. It allows you to get to know each other in many ways before you begin a sexual relationship. It allows you time to become more grown up, to make better decisions, and to avoid problems. It allows you time to find other ways to be close, such as sharing deep personal thoughts and feelings. Abstinence is the best way to keep from getting pregnant or catching a disease.

Sometimes, a person does not want to have sex but is talked into it on a date. Staying away from places or not doing things that often lead to sex can make abstaining easier. Using alcohol and other drugs, for example, can make you think you have changed your mind. Someone may try to talk you into having sex. Sometimes, friends want you to have sex to fit in. These are all wrong reasons to have sex. You should never feel as if you should have sex. Having sex when you do not really want to do so lowers your self-esteem.

Sometimes, a part of dating is breaking up. You may decide the person you are dating is not right for you after all. Or the person you are dating decides you are not right for him or her. Sometimes, the decision to break up is hard. You may think of it as a loss and be sad. If you feel depressed, look for support from your friends and family.

Why Do People Marry?

Getting married is a step people may take after dating. Where dating helps you get to know a person, getting married means a **commitment,** or a promise, to that person. This commitment involves promising to support your partner and to care for your partner if he or she gets sick. It also means being a friend to your partner.

Health Myth

Myth: If a couple really loves each other, they will not have problems.

Fact: All couples have problems. With care and communication, almost all problems can be worked out.

There are many healthy and unhealthy reasons to get married. Some healthy reasons include loving a person and wanting to have a family with that person. If two people understand themselves and each other, they have a good chance for a healthy life together. Being married can help them be happy and satisfied with their lives.

Being married is usually good for couples. Many married people live longer than single people. They have better health and usually have more money. Marriage partners can be best friends. They enjoy talking with each other and working together on their home and family. They enjoy making a social life together with other friends and family members. Getting along well and staying together as partners takes work but is usually worth the effort. Dividing up chores and having good communication help a couple stay together.

Unhealthy reasons for getting married include doing it because other people want you to get married. Some people get married because they are trying to avoid an unhappy home life or loneliness. They think if they get married, their problems will be solved.

Sometimes, people decide to marry because of an unexpected pregnancy. This usually puts a strain on the couple from the start. The decision to have children is an extremely important one. The couple can best make it when they are ready to be responsible for another human being. If a couple has a baby accidentally, they may not be ready for the huge responsibility.

When Do People Marry?

In the past, people often got married when they were quite young. This is changing for many reasons. One reason is that people live longer now. They do not need to marry young. Also, people have found that they need more education to get the jobs they want. They spend more time in school or in training and wait to get married. Some people wait to marry because they want to earn enough money to support themselves and their families.

Today, the average age at which men in the United States marry is 27. For women, the average age is 25. Studies show that if a couple is older when they marry, they will have a longer life together. For example, 75 percent of all teenagers who get married end up getting a **divorce.** Divorce is the legal end of a marriage.

Some people choose not to get married. Some people choose a career or close friendships over married life. This does not mean that their lives are less happy or emotionally healthy.

What Are Some Signs of a Healthy Marriage?

Many studies have been done on things that usually lead to happy married life. No one answer is sure to work. Here are some things that are important:

- agreeing on money matters

- having shared interests

- knowing each other well before getting married

- accepting and supporting each other

- agreeing about having children and about how to rear children

- having common goals

- sharing jobs around the house

- having family backgrounds that are somewhat alike

- having good relationships with parents

At some time or another, good and bad things affect a marriage. Moving to a new home or a new job is exciting, but both are stressful. Losing a job or getting sick can be hard. Couples who support each other are better able to cope with these changes.

A happy marriage usually needs more than just love. Couples have to be able to communicate, trust each other, and agree on many things. Couples should encourage each other. They should take a **collaborative** approach to life. This means they approach life as a team. They have to be willing to work out problems.

Some common problems include handling money, getting along with relatives, and raising children. Some couples have trouble working out a fair way to divide household jobs. Some may not agree about how often to have sex. However, married people are likely to have more sex than single people. Also, married people are more likely to enjoy sex both physically and emotionally.

Marriages are happier when the two people know and understand themselves. Then they are better able to understand their partner and to have a stronger relationship.

Lesson 1 Review On a sheet of paper, write the letter of the answer that best completes each sentence.

1. Having sex when you do not want to do so _____ your self-esteem.
   A lowers
   B increases
   C does not harm
   D maintains

2. The best way to keep from getting pregnant is _____.
   A divorce
   B abstinence
   C dating
   D marriage

3. About _____ percent of teenage marriages end in divorce.
   A 33
   B 50
   C 66
   D 75

On a sheet of paper, write the answers to the following questions. Use complete sentences.

4. Critical Thinking What are some healthy reasons for getting married?

5. Critical Thinking What signs might show you that a marriage is healthy?

Objectives

After reading this lesson, you should be able to

◆ describe what a parent is responsible for

◆ identify four different kinds of families

◆ describe signs of a healthy family

Why is it usually harder for teens to be parents than it is for adults?

A major event in the family life cycle is having children. Deciding to have children is an important one and can be healthy or unhealthy.

Why Do Couples Decide to Have a Baby?

When couples purposely decide to make their family larger, they are likely to feel good about what they decided. Sometimes, couples have a baby for other reasons. They may be talked into it by friends or parents. They may want to pass on the family name. Some couples have children because they believe it will make their marriage stronger. Often, the opposite happens. If a marriage already has problems, the stress of having a baby can make the problems worse.

Some couples have a baby that they did not plan to have. This also causes stress because being a parent means being responsible for many things.

Technology and Society

About 10 percent of U.S. couples face infertility. Infertility is a condition in which a woman cannot get pregnant. Couples can be infertile because of physical problems in either the man or the woman. One way to treat infertility is assisted reproduction, in which doctors try to help couples overcome infertility.

First, fertility drugs are often used. Doctors may be able to fix a problem in the man or woman with surgery. Another option is to collect eggs from the woman. Sperm is collected from the man. The sperm fertilizes the egg in a laboratory. Then the fertilized eggs are placed in the woman. In 2003, more than 40,000 babies were born in the United States through assisted reproduction. However, assisted reproduction is very expensive. It also can be hard on the couple physically and emotionally.

What Are Parents Responsible For?

Parents are responsible for the health, safety, and well-being of their children. When you have a baby, your life changes. There are many jobs that you must do, many times a day, every day. Babies need to be fed, held, and have their diapers changed often. Someone must always be in the home when a baby is present. Babies often cry in the middle of the night and must be comforted and fed. Babies sometimes cry for no reason you can see. This is extremely stressful. Spending time with children reduces the time you have to spend with your partner. You also must pay the costs of having a child, including food, clothing, and medical care. It is important for you to talk to your partner to work out plans to take care of the child.

You need to learn parenting skills. You may want to go to classes or read books or articles on child care. You need to learn how to take care of the physical health of your child. You also need to learn how to help your child grow emotionally. You need to help and encourage your children to begin to do things for themselves.

You need to set fair limits for your child. Children should learn at an early age that they must follow certain rules. If children break the rules, you need to present a **consequence.** A consequence is what happens as a result of something else. For example, if a child does something wrong, the consequence may be to sit alone for a few minutes. Using a consequence is one way to **discipline** children. Discipline is a way to teach children how to behave correctly. Discipline should be fair and never cause harm.

Finally, you are an important teacher for your children. Children learn from you in many ways. They may learn from stories you read or tell them. They learn life skills. Children also learn by watching you. They copy the things you do. You must set a good example so your children can learn healthy behaviors.

When a couple decides to have a child and be responsible for it, they form what is called a **nuclear family.** This is one of many different types of families.

What Are Some Family Types?

The most common type of family today is a family with only two people—a couple without children. The second most common type is the nuclear family—parents and children.

Another family type is the **blended family.** In this family, one or both parents have been married or in a relationship before. When children from an earlier marriage or relationship live with the new couple, they become a blended family.

In a **single-parent family,** just one adult raises the children. This family type often results from a divorce or the death of a partner. Sometimes, the adult has never married. Mothers are most often the head of these families. Sometimes, the father, a grandparent, an aunt, or an uncle heads a single-parent family.

Decide for Yourself

When you have children, you must decide who is going to take care of them. When both parents have jobs, someone must take care of the children while the parents are at work. Many parents must use day care centers. However, this can be expensive. For many families, the three biggest expenses they have are housing, food, and child care. Most families spend about one-fourth of what they do make on child care. Many families cannot afford it.

National and state governments provide some help to families. However, neither have much money to spend. Both levels of government spend more than they take in. Because of this, many families find themselves on waiting lists for help.

Many states have made it harder to qualify. Some states have decided to give out less money for help.

On a sheet of paper, write the answers to the following questions. Use complete sentences.

1. About how much money does a family with little money spend on child care?

2. Why do families who need child care help end up on waiting lists?

3. Do you think the government should spend more money on child care? Explain your answer.

A fourth family type is the **extended family.** An extended family is a nuclear family plus other relatives, such as grandparents, aunts, uncles, and cousins. Grandparents often support a family by babysitting, helping with household chores, or giving money. Extended families can be valuable support systems.

Families may form and change in other ways. For example, when children are adopted, they become part of an **adoptive family.** Some same-sex couples have adopted children. Other children may join a **foster family** for a while. A foster family is one that cares for children who are in need of short-term parenting from people other than their birth parents.

Sometimes, children have two families. The parent who is responsible for children after a divorce is the **custodial parent.** In blended and some single-parent families, children live with the custodial parent. They may spend time with the noncustodial parent in another home. This is true when parents have joint **custody** of children. Both parents are responsible for raising and caring for their children.

Any of these types of families can be healthy or unhealthy. What is important is how the family members work together.

How Is the Family Changing?

Family life is changing. Many families are smaller today than they were many years ago. Parents may decide to have fewer children because of the cost or because of their jobs. They may believe that they can provide a healthy home for only two rather than four or five children.

Many families want or need extra money. To help support the family, both parents work. This may be hard in some ways. For example, with both parents working outside the home, deciding how to divide the household chores may be harder for them. Also, many parents must leave their children in day care centers while the parents work.

The number of single-parent families is increasing in the United States. A single-parent family may have a harder time because only one adult is responsible for the family.

Research and Write

Use the Internet to find Web sites with information to support parents who have jobs. Write some helpful hints for parents who are struggling to balance working and raising a family.

No matter what type of family you live in, you must talk about and work out problems for all the relationships to be healthy.

Research and Write

Research family life in ancient Rome. Find out about food, houses, and jobs in ancient Rome. What would a teenager have done on a normal day in ancient Rome? Make a poster that shows the differences in families then and now.

How must family members work together to make a family healthy?

What Are the Signs of a Healthy Family?

Any family can be healthy or unhealthy. In a healthy family, members value, encourage, and trust one another. All family members help with the household chores. A good thing about doing chores is that you feel better about yourself. When you do more than you are told to do, you learn to be self-disciplined and dependable. This raises your self-esteem. Also, you know that you are helping and supporting your family. Healthy families also play together.

Two people who have studied families are Nick Stinnet and John DeFrain. They found that healthy families have these qualities:

- Commitment—Family members support and encourage one another.

- Appreciation—Family members appreciate one another.

- Communication—Everyone talks with and listens to everyone else.

- Time—Family members spend time together either working or having fun.

- Beliefs—Family members use their common beliefs to give them strength and purpose.

- Coping ability—Everyone is better able to handle problems because they get help and support from one another.

Lesson 2 Review On a sheet of paper, write the answers to the following questions. Use complete sentences.

1. Name two ways parents are responsible for their children.

2. What are four types of families?

3. What is a blended family?

4. **Critical Thinking** Describe three characteristics of healthy families.

5. **Critical Thinking** Of all the things that parents are responsible for, which do you think would be hardest? Explain your answer.

Objectives

After reading this lesson, you should be able to

◆ describe how separation and divorce can affect a family

◆ explain how aging can affect a family

◆ describe how illness and death can affect a family

◆ explain how abuse can affect a family

◆ explore ways for a troubled family to get help

Separation

A couple's agreement, or a court decision made for the couple, to stop living together

Families change for many reasons. Some changes are hard for families, such as divorce, illness, and death. However, troubled families can get help.

How Do Separation and Divorce Affect a Family?

Sometimes, when a couple decides they cannot live together, they separate. **Separation** may be an agreement between the two people, or it may be a court decision. During the separation, couples usually think about their marriage. They decide if they can make things better. If they believe they cannot, they may decide to divorce.

Separation and divorce can be hard for children. They may worry or feel depressed. They miss the parent who is gone or feel they are losing a parent. They may believe that they caused their parents' problems, but children are almost never the cause.

Children may feel sad if one parent tries to blame the other parent. Children should not be put in the middle of the adults' problems. A child cannot solve this kind of problem. Parents have a responsibility to work on their conflicts without blaming their children.

How Does Aging Affect a Family?

People are living longer than ever before. Many older people want to live on their own. Sometimes, however, an older person in a family may have special needs. For example, as people age, they may have a hard time getting around. They may need to use a cane, a walker, or a wheelchair. They may have vision or hearing loss or get sick more often. Sometimes, older adults begin to lose their memory. They become confused and cannot remember simple things. They may have a harder time taking care of their basic needs. They may have to give up driving.

Since family members do not automatically know what you are thinking or feeling, you are responsible for telling them.

Sometimes these age-related problems cause changes in a family. A home may have to be adapted to meet the needs of an older adult. Some family members may need to spend more time taking care of an older adult. A grandparent may need to live with a family if he or she needs more support.

A parent who takes care of a grandparent has less time to take care of his or her own needs. This parent also has less time to spend with children and less energy to help with their problems. When an older person comes to live with a family, everyone in the family has to adjust. Sometimes, all members must take on more chores. Everyone needs to be patient and considerate. Having an older person come to live with a family can be a positive experience. The family gets ideas from another point of view. Older people often have a lot of wisdom to share. Being with an older person is helpful to children, because it gives them another adult to learn to relate to.

How Do Illness and Death Affect a Family?

When a family member gets sick, other members must adjust. They may have to help by doing more chores. They may have to give more support or get support from others. If an adult is sick for a long time, he or she may not be able to work. That may mean less money coming in and high medical bills.

Another difficult change is when someone in the family dies. For most people, a sudden death is harder to deal with than one that is expected. It is often easier to accept the death of someone who has been sick for a long time. When a young person dies suddenly, that death may be especially hard to accept. When anyone dies, each person deals with it in his or her own way. However, everyone goes through the five stages of grief—denial, anger, bargaining, depression, and acceptance. Everyone gets through these stages at their own speed and in their own order. Sometimes people repeat stages.

As with other changes, family members adjust to their loss in time. They may look for support from others or talk with one another about their grief.

How Does Abuse Affect a Family?

Problems such as illness and death cannot be avoided. However, **violence** is a problem that can be avoided. Violence is actions or words that hurt people. It can destroy relationships and cause physical and emotional pain. Violence should never be accepted in a family.

Violence in families has many causes. Sometimes, members become angry and hit others. People who use alcohol or other drugs may become violent. Violence can also result from stress or be a learned behavior.

Abuse is a form of violence. Many kinds of abuse can affect families and be a serious problem. Both children and adults can be abused. Abuse can be physical or emotional. Physical abuse can be so bad that it results in bruises, broken bones, or even death. Emotional abuse also causes many problems. Most often, people do not show signs of emotional abuse on the outside, such as cuts and bruises. Harsh words and threats, however, can affect a person on the inside for a lifetime. People who are emotionally abused are often depressed and afraid, avoid others, and have low self-esteem.

Abuse is usually not just a one-time thing. It happens over and over. A child who is abused often is afraid to ask for help. The abuser may threaten the child. The child believes that something even worse will happen if he or she tries to get help.

Another form of abuse is **neglect,** or failure to take care of a person's basic needs. It may include leaving a young child alone for long periods at a time. It may mean the adult does not provide food, clothing, or a safe place to live. A child who is neglected may become ill or die.

Sexual abuse is any sexual contact that is forced on someone. Sexual abuse includes unwanted touching and talk as well as forcing a child to have sex. This kind of abuse affects many children and teens. Sexually abusing any child is illegal. It should be reported to someone such as a teacher, a counselor, or a police officer.

Violence

Actions or words that hurt people

Abuse

Physical or emotional mistreatment; actions that harm someone

Neglect

Failure to take care of a person's basic needs; regular lack of care

Sexual abuse

Any sexual contact that is forced on a person, including unwanted talk and touching

Domestic violence

Violence that happens mostly at home

Marriage counselor

A person trained in helping couples work on their relationship with each other

Link to ➤➤➤

Arts

The 1998 film *Good Will Hunting* tells about Will, a young man who works as a university janitor. A professor discovers that Will is a math genius. He wants to work with Will, who has been a victim of abuse. Will can work with the professor only if he has counseling. With the help of a psychologist, Will learns about himself. Then Will has to choose. Should he stay in the same job he is used to, or should he try to do something in which he can use his abilities?

Some people who are abused physically, emotionally, or sexually may not seek help. They may be afraid to report it. Some people try to hide abuse because they feel shame, even though it is never their fault.

Sometimes, older people are abused or neglected. In an unhealthy marriage, one partner may hurt or abuse the other. This is called **domestic violence,** because it happens mostly at home. People can get seriously hurt and die from domestic violence.

With any abuse, the people who get hurt, the abusers, and the other family members need to get professional help. People who are abused need to know that the abuse is not their fault. They did not in any way deserve, ask for, or encourage the abuse. The abused person is not wrong. The abuser's behavior is wrong in all cases.

How Can a Troubled Family Find Help?

Problems in a family can affect the health of each member. Sometimes, families need help. Dealing with a problem is better than trying to avoid it. For example, a teenager may run away to avoid a problem. That usually causes more problems. Some problems are so serious that people may even try to kill themselves.

Family members can do several things to get help. Children can talk to teachers or school counselors. Families can go to special counseling centers at little or no cost. People at these centers give advice about dealing with the problem. The counselors help families figure out how to avoid these same problems in the future.

A couple whose marriage is in trouble can talk with a **marriage counselor.** Marriage counselors are trained to help couples improve or save their marriage.

Family counselors work with problems in families. They talk with family members and offer suggestions to help solve these problems.

Many communities have several kinds of support groups. These are groups of people who share a common problem and offer one another encouragement in dealing with it. Many support groups help people who have had a death in the family. Other support groups help people deal with alcohol or other drug problems.

Health in Your Life

Family Belief Systems

Although people may not realize it, all families have specific ideas that guide how they behave. These ideas are about how family members are expected to behave, what the family sees as being important, and the things they believe to be true. These ideas are handed down in families from generation to generation. Figuring out these ideas is important so that family members can change their behavior if needed. Generally, when adolescents are having problems, they are either acting upon or questioning these ideas.

For example, many parents have strong feelings about education. They expect that their child will do well in school and go to college. A teen who is questioning his or her family's ideas might fail in school or skip classes. A counselor would have to uncover the family's ideas about education to help the family solve this problem.

In some families, abusing others may be part of how that family has always dealt with anger. An abusive parent may somehow believe that this is how parents should behave. For example, a great-grandfather abused his son, who abused his son, who abuses his son. This is how abuse is passed down through families.

To find out what ideas the family has, a counselor listens to the stories family members tell. The counselor looks at how the stories are told and pays attention to how family members describe one another. The counselor asks questions about how the family members act and react toward one another. Sometimes, the counselor encourages family members to change. Other times, the problem may be in school or in peer relationships.

On a sheet of paper, write the answers to the following questions. Use complete sentences.

1. What makes up the ideas that families believe in?

2. Is the family always the reason a teen has problems? Explain your answer.

3. Name one idea that is part of your family's group of ideas.

If you are experiencing any form of abuse, get help. Talk with a trusted adult, such as a teacher, school counselor, or police officer.

Support groups can sometimes be found by looking in the phone book. Many groups advertise in the newspaper or appear in the newspaper's calendar section. They can also be found by searching the Internet. School counselors can recommend support groups. Finding help for a problem in your school, community, or home will help you feel better. It will also help you stay happier and healthier.

Lesson 3 Review On a sheet of paper, write the word or phrase in parentheses that best completes each sentence.

1. When there is a divorce, children may feel (worried, happy, content).

2. A parent who has to care for a grandparent has (less time and energy, more time and energy, less time but more energy) for his or her children.

3. When parents fail to take care of a child, they are guilty of (violence, sexual abuse, neglect).

On a sheet of paper, write the answers to the following questions. Use complete sentences.

4. **Critical Thinking** If you had a problem in your family, where would you go for help? Explain your answer.

5. **Critical Thinking** If a grandparent came to live with your family, what adjustments would you have to make?

Health at Work

Adolescent Counselor

Many teens face problems such as alcohol and other drug abuse, eating disorders, depression, violence, and AIDS. Adolescent counselors help teens with these problems. They may also be asked to find safe places for runaway and homeless teens. Sometimes, adolescent counselors can help teens prepare for jobs. Adolescent counselors must be able to understand how teenagers feel. They must be able to form good relationships with young people. Requirements are a master's degree and a state license or certification.

- Socializing and dating may lead to marriage. A new family life cycle begins when two people get married.

- Dating couples must agree on their physical or sexual relationship. A sexual relationship can lead to an unexpected pregnancy or a disease.

- Often couples who are dating decide to stop dating. This can leave a person feeling unhappy or depressed.

- Most people in the United States marry at some time. People get married for both healthy and unhealthy reasons.

- Coming from the same background, being educated, and having good jobs usually lead to healthy marriages.

- People have a baby for both healthy and unhealthy reasons.

- Parents are responsible for the health, safety, and well-being of their children.

- Parents need to learn certain skills to help their children grow physically and emotionally. They must set rules and provide discipline.

- There are several types of families. These are nuclear, blended, single-parent, extended, adoptive, and foster families.

- Any type of family may be healthy or unhealthy.

- Separation, divorce, aging, illness, and death can affect families.

- Abuse may be physical or emotional. It may be directed at children or adults. Violence and abuse should never be accepted in a family.

- Married couples and families with problems can get help.

Vocabulary

abstinence, 178	custody, 185	neglect, 189
abuse, 189	discipline, 183	nuclear family, 184
adoptive family, 185	divorce, 180	separation, 187
blended family, 184	domestic violence, 190	sexual abuse, 189
collaborative, 180	extended family, 185	single-parent family, 184
commitment, 178	foster family, 185	socializing, 176
consequence, 183	marriage counselor, 190	violence, 189
custodial parent, 185		

Chapter 8   R E V I E W

Word Bank

- abstinence
- abuse
- collaborative
- consequence
- divorce
- domestic violence
- emotional abuse
- extended family
- foster family
- marriage counselor
- neglect
- nuclear family
- sexual abuse
- single-parent family

Vocabulary Review

On a sheet of paper, write the word or phrase from the Word Bank that best completes each sentence.

1. Avoiding a sexual relationship, or _____, will help you avoid an unexpected pregnancy.

2. Parents need to set fair rules and provide a(n) _____ if children break the rules.

3. A married couple living with their own children is a(n) _____.

4. One adult raising children alone is a(n) _____ family.

5. Treating someone badly, either physically or emotionally, is _____.

6. A(n) _____ helps married couples work out their problems.

7. Couples who choose not to live together after separating may choose to get a(n) _____.

8. A family that works together as a team is using a(n) _____ approach to life.

9. A nuclear family, plus aunts, uncles, and grandparents, is a(n) _____.

10. Saying mean and hurtful things to children is _____.

11. Failing to care for a child's basic needs is _____.

12. Unwanted touching and talk are part of _____.

13. Violence that takes place in the home is _____.

14. A(n) _____ cares for children who are in need of short-term parenting.

Concept Review

On a sheet of paper, write the letter of the answer that best completes each sentence.

15. One sign of an unhealthy marriage is _____.

   A companionship   **C** lack of appreciation

   B communication   **D** working together

16. One way families are changing is that people _____.

   A are getting married younger

   B are waiting to get married so that they can get more education

   C are working less after they get married

   D have stopped earning money to support the family

17. Having a baby always adds _____ to a marriage.

   A ease   **C** discipline

   B strength   **D** stress

Critical Thinking

On a sheet of paper, write the answers to the following questions. Use complete sentences.

18. Age-related problems can be hard for older adults. How could you help an older adult?

19. Why is it better for a family to solve problems than to avoid them? Explain your answer.

20. What signs of a healthy marriage are most important to you? Explain your answer.

Test-Taking Tip Before you begin a test, look it over quickly to see how much time you may need for each section. Try to set aside enough time to complete each section.

Overpopulation and Health

Every year, the world's population grows by about 76 million people. Currently, world population is more than 6.3 billion. This growth is faster in some places than in others. Population is growing six times faster in developing nations than it is in the nations of Europe, North America, Oceania, and Japan.

More than 500 million people around the world do not have enough clean water to drink. This leads to diseases such as cholera, typhoid fever, and dysentery. The more the population grows, the less land and water there are for everyone. Also, higher populations put heavier strains on food supplies and health care systems.

About 8 million children die every year from malnutrition or other diseases caused by not getting enough food. Clearly, overpopulation has negative effects on health.

On a sheet of paper, write the answers to the following questions. Use complete sentences.

1. Why do you think the population grows faster in developing nations than it does in the nations of Europe and North America?

2. How does population growth put a strain on health care systems?

3. What are some ways to solve the serious problem of malnutrition around the world?

- The bones in the skeletal system give your body its shape and protect your organs.

- The muscular system allows your body to move. The body has smooth, skeletal, and cardiac muscles.

- The central nervous system controls your body's activities. It includes your brain and spinal cord.

- The circulatory system includes your blood, heart, and three kinds of blood vessels. Blood carries food and oxygen to every cell. Your heart pumps blood throughout your body.

- The respiratory system allows you to breathe in oxygen and breathe out carbon dioxide. Cells need oxygen to break up nutrients.

- Good hygiene means taking care of your eyes, ears, skin, hair, nails, and teeth.

- Physical fitness is your body's ability to meet the demands of daily life.

- Three parts of health-related fitness are heart and lung endurance, flexibility, and muscular fitness.

- Regular exercise improves fitness, increases energy, lowers the chances of getting sick, helps control weight, reduces anxiety, and reduces stress.

- Three hormones signal the body's reproductive system to develop during puberty. They are testosterone for males, and estrogen and progesterone for females.

- In the reproductive system, the male produces sperm cells, and the female produces egg cells. If these two cells join during sexual intercourse, they form a new life.

- The female's ovaries release egg cells in a monthly cycle. If the egg cell is not fertilized, it passes out of the body.

- If the egg cell is fertilized, it begins to grow and divide, and it plants itself in the uterus. The uterus expands to hold the growing embryo or fetus.

- Genetics is the science that studies heredity, or the passing of traits from parents to children.

- There are several types of families. These are nuclear, blended, single-parent, extended, adoptive, and foster families.

- Some qualities of healthy families are commitment, appreciation, communication, common beliefs, and being able to cope. Healthy families spend time together.

- Abuse may be physical or emotional. People who suffer any kind of violence or abuse need to get help.

Unit 2 R E V I E W

Word Bank

abstinence

chromosome

domestic violence

endurance

epidermis

estrogen

hygiene

iris

metabolism

socializing

tendon

uterus

Vocabulary Review

On a sheet of paper, write the word or phrase from the Word Bank that best completes each sentence.

1. The part of an eye that gives an eye its color is the _____.

2. One of the hormones that control reproductive development in females is _____.

3. Getting together with people during your free time is _____.

4. Protecting and caring for your ears and hearing are important parts of _____.

5. The female organ where an egg grows into a baby is the _____.

6. One form of abuse that sometimes takes place between family members is _____.

7. A strong set of fibers joining muscle to bone or muscle to muscle is a(n) _____.

8. When two people choose _____, they are choosing not to have a sexual relationship.

9. The outer layer of skin is the _____.

10. A tiny structure inside a cell that contains hereditary information is a(n) _____.

11. The ability to keep doing a physical activity for a long time is _____.

12. Cells in the human body produce energy at a rate that is called a person's _____.

Concept Review

On a sheet of paper, write the letter of the answer that best completes each sentence.

13. The three parts of blood are red blood cells, white blood cells, and _____.

  A platelets   **C** ligaments

  B bronchioles   **D** villi

14. Exercise that builds muscle strength by using resistance from a machine is _____.

  A aerobic   **C** isometric

  B anaerobic   **D** isokinetic

15. A male is usually able to produce sperm from puberty through _____.

  A adolescence   **C** about age 60

  B early adulthood   **D** the rest of his life

16. An extended family includes _____.

  A only adopted children

  B parents, children, and other relatives, such as grandparents

  C one or two parents who have been married before

  D just one adult who raises the children

Critical Thinking

On a sheet of paper, write the answers to the following questions. Use complete sentences.

17. Why are a person's reflexes important? Explain your answer.

18. Why is it dangerous to begin exercising without doing a warm-up first?

19. What is the difference between a dominant gene and a recessive gene? Explain your answer.

20. What are the qualities of a healthy family? How is a healthy relationship with a relative similar to a healthy relationship with a friend?

Unit 3

Nutrition

Did you have breakfast this morning? Eating breakfast is important. Students who do not eat breakfast usually score lower on tests than those who have had a healthy morning meal. Consider food as fuel for your body. Think about how a radio sounds when the batteries are low. Without food, your body fades like music on a radio when its batteries are low.

People are becoming more concerned about the importance of eating properly. A poor diet can play a major role in causing heart attacks. It can also be one of the reasons for strokes and some types of cancer. Even with serious health warnings, many people still choose unhealthy diets. In this unit, you will learn how to make healthy food choices.

Chapters in Unit 3

Self-Assessment

Can you answer these questions?

- ☑ 1   Which food groups are the healthiest?

- ☑ 2.   What is an example of a healthy meal menu?

- ☑ 3.   Which foods contain saturated fat?

- ☑ 4.   Why is it important to clean utensils, dishes, and your hands before eating?

- ☑ 5.   How can you read and understand a nutrition label?

- ☑ 6.   Which foods have natural sugar and fiber in them?

- ☑ 7.   How much sugar is in a soft drink?

- ☑ 8.   Why is protein important to your diet?

- ☑ 9.   What foods give you calcium to strengthen your bones?

- ☑ 10. What is the connection between your diet and your health?

The Role of Diet in Health

Food is fuel. Food provides the nutrients your body's systems need to work right. Deciding which foods to eat is important. Good food choices help you stay healthy. Poor food choices can have a bad effect on your life. Eating too much or not enough food can also have a bad effect on your health. The food you eat not only affects your health. It can also affect the quality of your life.

In this chapter, you will learn what a healthy diet is. You will discover how health guidelines can help you choose a healthy diet. You will learn about the nutrients your body needs. You will also learn about special dietary needs and how diet relates to health problems.

Goals for Learning

◆ To describe how healthy eating affects the body

◆ To explain how food provides calories and nutrients

◆ To study the importance of the six essential nutrient classes and name which foods contain them

◆ To name special dietary needs

◆ To understand how diet can affect health

Food Guide Pyramid

A chart that helps you decide how much and what kinds of food to eat

The word *diet* does not mean just a way of losing or gaining weight. A diet is made up of the foods you eat and drink. Diet can affect the way you look, feel, and perform. A well-balanced diet gives you a healthy appearance. It makes your hair shine and helps keep your skin clear. It gives you energy to do everything you need or want to do. Eating healthy food also adds to your emotional health. It gives you energy to deal with stress. Your diet affects your general health. Clearly, choosing healthy food to eat is important to your overall health.

Look at Tables C.2 and C.3 in Appendix C in this book. Gather information about what you should weigh based on your age and how tall you are. Your doctor or school nurse can help you learn about healthy ways to maintain or change your weight. A healthy diet and exercise are both important for maintaining or changing your weight.

What Is a Healthy Diet?

A healthy diet includes different kinds of foods. The U.S. government has set up guidelines to help people choose a healthy diet. These guidelines are listed here.

Dietary Guidelines

• Eat lots of different kinds of foods.

• Balance the food you eat with physical activity.

• Choose a diet with plenty of grains, vegetables, and fruits.

• Choose a diet low in fat, saturated fat, and cholesterol.

• Choose a diet low in sugar.

• Choose a diet low in salt and sodium.

The Food Guide Pyramid

The government developed the **Food Guide Pyramid** (see Figure 9.1.1 on page 205). It is a chart that helps you decide how much and what kinds of food to eat. It groups foods according to the number of servings you should eat each day.

The six bands on the pyramid represent five food groups plus oils. The five groups are grains, vegetables, fruits, milk, and meat and beans. The wider food group bands, such as grains, show that you should eat more of these foods than of foods in narrower bands. The narrow yellow band stands for oils. It shows that you should eat very few fats and oils.

Notice that each food group band of the pyramid is wider at the base than at the top. The wide base stands for foods that are low in fats and added sugars. People should choose more of these foods. The narrow tops of the bands stand for foods with more fats and added sugars. People should eat fewer of these foods. However, the more you exercise, the more you can choose foods that are higher in fat. The person climbing the steps of the pyramid reminds people of the importance of exercise.

Figure 9.1.1 *The Food Guide Pyramid.*   *Source: U.S. Department of Agriculture*

The chart that goes along with the Food Guide Pyramid (see Figure 9.1.2 below) gives details about the pyramid. The chart lists some of the foods to choose in each food-group band. It gives information about how much of each food to eat each day. Information about finding a balance between food and physical activity is also in the chart. Facts about how to choose and limit fats, sugars, and salt are also listed.

How Does Food Provide What Your Body Needs?

Food contains nutrients. Nutrients the body gets from food are called **essential nutrients.** Essential nutrients are chemicals in foods that the body cannot make. Scientists have discovered about 50 of these nutrients. They are divided into six essential nutrient classes you will read about in Lessons 2 and 3. These nutrient classes are carbohydrates, fats, proteins, vitamins, minerals, and water. No one food contains all the nutrients your body needs. A healthy diet must include different kinds of foods. Some food sources for the six essential nutrient classes can be found in Table B.1 of Appendix B.

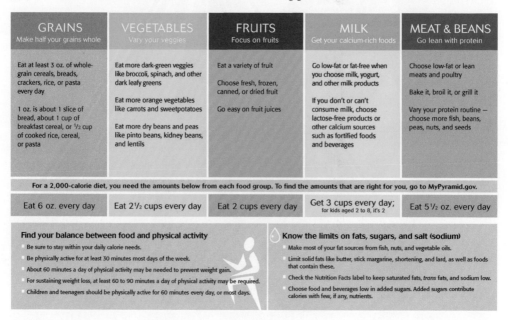

GRAINS Make half your grains whole	VEGETABLES Vary your veggies	FRUITS Focus on fruits	MILK Get your calcium-rich foods	MEAT & BEANS Go lean with protein
Eat at least 3 oz. of whole-grain cereals, breads, crackers, rice, or pasta every day. 1 oz. is about 1 slice of bread, about 1 cup of breakfast cereal, or ½ cup of cooked rice, cereal, or pasta	Eat more dark-green veggies like broccoli, spinach, and other dark leafy greens. Eat more orange vegetables like carrots and sweetpotatoes. Eat more dry beans and peas like pinto beans, kidney beans, and lentils	Eat a variety of fruit. Choose fresh, frozen, canned, or dried fruit. Go easy on fruit juices	Go low-fat or fat-free when you choose milk, yogurt, and other milk products. If you don't or can't consume milk, choose lactose-free products or other calcium sources such as fortified foods and beverages	Choose low-fat or lean meats and poultry. Bake it, broil it, or grill it. Vary your protein routine — choose more fish, beans, peas, nuts, and seeds

For a 2,000-calorie diet, you need the amounts below from each food group. To find the amounts that are right for you, go to MyPyramid.gov.

Eat 6 oz. every day	Eat 2½ cups every day	Eat 2 cups every day	Get 3 cups every day; for kids aged 2 to 8, it's 2	Eat 5½ oz. every day

Find your balance between food and physical activity
- Be sure to stay within your daily calorie needs.
- Be physically active for at least 30 minutes most days of the week.
- About 60 minutes a day of physical activity may be needed to prevent weight gain.
- For sustaining weight loss, at least 60 to 90 minutes a day of physical activity may be required.
- Children and teenagers should be physically active for 60 minutes every day, or most days.

Know the limits on fats, sugars, and salt (sodium)
- Make most of your fat sources from fish, nuts, and vegetable oils.
- Limit solid fats like butter, stick margarine, shortening, and lard, as well as foods that contain these.
- Check the Nutrition Facts label to keep saturated fats, *trans* fats, and sodium low.
- Choose food and beverages low in added sugars. Added sugars contribute calories with few, if any, nutrients.

Figure 9.1.2 *Chart for the Food Guide Pyramid. Source: U.S. Department of Agriculture*

Foods vary in the amount of calories and nutrients they contain. Some foods are high in calories but low in nutrients. For example, a teaspoon of sugar has about 16 calories. A teaspoon of green beans has about 1 calorie. Green beans have more nutrients and fewer calories than sugar has. This is important for two reasons. First, your body needs nutrients to stay healthy. Second, it is important to know which foods contain the most nutrients. Your body also needs a specific number of calories. Foods that are good sources of nutrients but are low in calories are **nutrient-dense.** A healthy diet includes many nutrient-dense foods.

Food provides the calories and nutrients your body needs. A calorie is a unit that measures the amount of energy in food. Your body uses the calories for heat, movement, growth, and repair. What should you think about to figure out how many calories you need each day? Whether you are a male or female, how fast you grow, and how active you are all play a role. Here's one example. A person who is tall, muscular, and active needs more calories than a small, inactive person.

Look at serving size when reading nutrition labels. A label may show only 100 calories and 8 grams of fat. This information is for just one serving. A package may contain more than one serving. What if you eat all the food in the package? You will have to multiply the fat and calories by the number of servings you eat.

Link to ➤➤➤

Math

All the information you need about the Food Guide Pyramid is on the United States Department of Agriculture's (USDA's) Web site *(www.MyPyramid.gov)*. You can go to this site to create a healthy eating plan just for you. Under "My Pyramid Plan," you can type in your age, sex, and physical activity level. Then the site gives you the amounts and kinds of foods you should eat each day.

How Can You Plan a Healthy Diet?

Use the Food Guide Pyramid as your guide to plan a healthy diet. You will be able to make healthy choices that include plenty of different kinds of foods. The pyramid can help you plan your diet. It shows the six food groups and how many servings you need each day. Table 9.1.1 shows sample food plans for 13-year-olds who are physically active 30 to 60 minutes a day in addition to their normal routines.

Table 9.1.1		
Sample Daily Food Plans for Moderately Active 13-Year-Olds		
Food Group	Females	Males
Grains	6 ounces	7 ounces
Vegetables	2.5 cups	3 cups
Fruits	2 cups	2 cups
Milk	3 cups	3 cups
Meat and beans	5.5 ounces	6 ounces
Oils	6 teaspoons	6 teaspoons
Other fats and sugars	No more than 265 calories	No more than 290 calories

Go to the USDA Food Pyramid Web site (www.MyPyramid.gov) and enter your information. Use your results to plan what you will eat for the next week. The Web site also offers a meal tracking worksheet you can print out to help you plan what you will eat. At the end of each day, check to see how many of the planned foods you actually ate.

Word Bank

essential nutrients

Food Guide
  Pyramid

nutrient-dense

Lesson 1 Review On a sheet of paper, write the phrase from the Word Bank that best completes each sentence.

1. Foods that are a good source of nutrients and are low in calories can be described as _____.

2. The _____ is a way to plan how much and what kind of food to eat.

3. Food provides calories and _____ for your energy needs.

On a sheet of paper, write the answers to the following questions. Use complete sentences.

4. **Critical Thinking** What would happen if you ate the number of calories of someone who is much taller and more active than you are?

5. **Critical Thinking** Suppose you are planning your meals for the day. Which should you have more of—brown rice or cheese? Explain your answer.

Objectives

After reading this lesson, you should be able to

◆ compare carbohydrates, fats, and protein

◆ state the difference between simple and complex carbohydrates

◆ understand how the body uses carbohydrates, fats, and protein

Carbohydrate

Chemical in foods that provides starches and sugars

Fat

Stored energy

Protein

A material in food needed for growth and repair of body tissues

Complex carbohydrate

Carbohydrate that contains fiber; the best source of dietary carbohydrates

Simple carbohydrate

A sugar the body uses for quick energy

Your diet must provide your body with six essential nutrients. The nutrients that provide energy in the form of calories are **carbohydrates, fats,** and **protein.** Carbohydrates are starches and sugars that come mainly from plant food. Fats are stored energy. Protein helps build muscle and repair all body tissues. Carbohydrates, fats, and protein are all nutrients your body needs. Not enough or too much of these nutrients may result in health problems. Eating the right amount of many foods gives your body the nutrients it needs. This creates a healthy, balanced diet.

What Are Carbohydrates?

Carbohydrates give your body much of the energy it needs each day. There are two kinds of carbohydrates—complex and simple. **Complex carbohydrates** are found in foods such as potatoes, pasta, and bread. Table 9.2.1 shows examples of foods with high amounts of complex carbohydrates. Most of your calories should come from complex carbohydrates. **Simple carbohydrates** are found in sugar, fruits, jelly, and syrup. Many carbonated beverages contain simple carbohydrates.

Technology and Society

Learning what your body mass index (BMI) is can help you decide if you have health risks related to your weight. Web sites can help you find your BMI. Use a safe, reliable site from a government or school agency. Enter the search term *body mass index.* You will not need to enter your name or contact information. As you learned earlier, sites that end in *.gov, .edu,* or *.org* are usually the most reliable.

Complex carbohydrates are important to the body. They are the best source of carbohydrates to eat. Foods with complex carbohydrates make you feel satisfied and full. They also contain other nutrients that add **fiber** to your diet. Fiber is not a nutrient, but it is important in helping move food through your digestive system. It is a coarse material in fruits, vegetables, and grains. Table B.2 in Appendix B lists the fiber content of specific foods. Studies show that some types of fiber in the diet help protect against certain health risks.

Simple carbohydrates, or sugars, have many different names. For example, **sucrose** is table sugar. **Fructose** is the natural sugar found in fruit. **Lactose** is the natural sugar found in milk.

Your body uses sugar for quick energy. Your body easily digests sugar and it enters your bloodstream quickly. However, the energy boost you get from sugar wears off quickly. You then feel tired. This is because sugar has no other nutrients.

Sugars found in foods are either **added sugar** or **natural sugar.** Natural sugar is already present in a food as the food grows in nature. It is not added when it goes to the factory or store.

Table 9.2.1 Foods High in Complex Carbohydrates			
	Total Carbohydrates (grams)	Simple Carbohydrates (grams)	Complex Carbohydrates (grams)
Bread, 1 slice	13	1	12
Corn flakes cereal, 1 ounce (low sugar)	24	2	22
Pasta or rice, $\frac{1}{2}$ cup (cooked)	20	0	20
Beans, 1 cup (cooked)	40	0	40
Potatoes, corn, or peas, 1 cup	30	6	24
Carrots or beets, 1 cup	12	6	6
Broccoli, 1 cup (cut up)	7	0	7

Eating fruit is usually healthier than drinking fruit juice. You will feel satisfied longer if you eat the fruit, because it has more fiber. Fruit has lots of fiber. Most of the fiber is lost when the juice is squeezed out of fruit. Also, many fruit juices contain added sugars.

Added sugar is put into a food at the factory or plant where it is made. For example, an apple contains the natural sugar fructose. The sugar is part of the apple as it grows. A candy bar contains added sugar. The sugar is put into the candy bar when it is being made. Some foods with added sugar have little or no nutrients. For example, a 12-ounce can of sweetened cola contains 9 teaspoons of sugar. It contains few nutrients. Too much added sugar in your diet can cause health problems.

Many foods that are a source of sugar also have other nutrients. Fruits, vegetables, and bread have carbohydrates that give you enough sugar for your body.

How Does Your Body Use Carbohydrates?

Carbohydrates are a mixture of chemicals. Your body changes carbohydrates into **glucose,** the main sugar in blood. Glucose moves through your body to give your cells fuel for energy. Extra glucose is stored in your liver and muscle tissue as **glycogen,** or starch. When your body needs more glucose, it changes the glycogen back into glucose. Glucose is the main nutrient your brain needs to help you think clearly and pay attention to what you are doing.

What happens when you eat too many carbohydrates and do not get enough physical activity? You do not use all of the sugar and starch that the carbohydrates give you. Then your body stores the extra sugar and starch as fat.

What Are Fats?

Like carbohydrates, fats give your body energy, but fats are stored energy. Fats are part of all body cells. They help protect your internal organs from temperature changes. They protect your body if you bump into or are hit by anything and are part of what protects your nerves.

Fats in your diet are broken down in your body into **fatty acids.** These are either saturated or unsaturated. Examples of foods that have a lot of **saturated fat** are butter, meat, ice cream, and chocolate. Eating too much fat can lead to health problems.

Cholesterol

A waxy, fatlike material in your body cells that helps with certain body functions

Blood cholesterol

Cholesterol in the bloodstream

Dietary cholesterol

Cholesterol found in some foods

Unsaturated fat

Material in food from vegetable and fish oils that helps lower cholesterol

Eating too many saturated fats can cause you to have too much **cholesterol.** Cholesterol is a waxy, fatlike material that is important in making hormones. It also helps digestion. This good kind of cholesterol, **blood cholesterol,** is carried in your bloodstream. But some cholesterol can build up in blood vessels and clog them. Then your blood cannot flow freely. If this happens, you could have serious health problems.

Another kind of cholesterol, **dietary cholesterol,** is found in some foods. One way to lessen your chances of having high blood cholesterol is to stay away from foods that have a lot of saturated fats. Instead, eat foods containing **unsaturated fats.** For example, you can eat less red meat and more fish. Fish contains unsaturated fat. You can also use vegetable oils instead of animal fats and butter. You can drink skim milk instead of whole milk.

Fats are important to your body. However, too many fats can lead to a greater chance of getting some diseases, such as clogged arteries. Eating too many fats can also cause you to gain weight. Table C.1 in Appendix C shows some exercises to do to keep your body weight at a good level.

What Is Protein?

Protein helps build muscle and repair all your body tissues. It is part of every cell in your body. Your muscles, bones, blood, and skin all contain protein. Since cells are always being replaced, your body needs protein throughout your life. Carbohydrates, fats, and proteins are all sources of energy. When does your body use protein as an energy source? This happens only when it does not get enough calories from carbohydrates and fats.

Research and Write

Why might people in a poorer community find it hard to eat healthy foods? Work with a partner to discover the answer. Visit a library and gather information from newspapers, magazines, and the Internet. Then write an editorial to your local newspaper. Explain ways that people might overcome this problem and suggest ways in which a poorer community might get more healthy foods to eat.

Amino acid

A small chemical unit that makes up protein

Essential amino acid

An amino acid the body cannot make by itself but that can be obtained from food

Why is not skipping meals important?

Proteins are made up of chains of building blocks called **amino acids.** There are many kinds of amino acids. Your body is able to make many proteins. It is unable to make nine proteins called **essential amino acids.** You must get these amino acids from your diet. Your body can make new proteins from these nine essential amino acids.

The foods that include all nine essential amino acids are fish, meat, eggs, milk, and poultry. Some foods provide only a few of the essential amino acids. These are plant foods such as grains, seeds, peas, and beans. Combining certain foods can provide all nine amino acids. Two such combinations are peanut butter and wheat bread or macaroni and cheese.

As with other nutrients, your body needs only a specific amount of protein. If it gets more than it needs, protein becomes a source of extra calories. Foods give you different levels of nutrients. A food high in protein may also be high in fat. For example, eggs are a good source of protein. They also have a lot of fat. It is important to choose foods with protein carefully. Do not eat more than your body needs.

Decide for Yourself

You just got home from school. Dinner will not be until 7:30. What kind of snack should you eat? Consider time, taste, cost, nutrition, and your goals for a healthy diet. Here is a recipe you might try.

Baked Apples

4 apples
1 teaspoon brown sugar (optional)
2 cups unsweetened apple juice
1 teaspoon allspice or ground cloves
1 teaspoon cinnamon

Preheat oven to 350°F. Use a knife or apple corer to remove the core of each apple. Place the apples in a baking dish. Add apple juice so the liquid covers halfway up the apples. Bake for 40 to 50 minutes.

Remove apples. Drain juice into a small saucepan. Add cinnamon, allspice or cloves, and brown sugar. Boil liquid until it turns syrupy. Pour over apples. Serve warm.

Yield: 4 servings
Per Serving: 126 calories, 4 g fiber, 1 g fat, 0 mg cholesterol

On a sheet of paper, write the answers to the following questions. Use complete sentences.

1. What should you consider when deciding what to eat?

2. Why are baked apples a healthy snack?

3. What are three other healthy snacks you could suggest to someone?

Lesson 2 Review On a sheet of paper, write the answers to the following questions. Use complete sentences.

1. How does glucose help your body?

2. What are two foods that have saturated fat and two that have unsaturated fat?

3. What are essential amino acids?

4. **Critical Thinking** What might happen if you did not eat any fat? Explain your answer.

5. **Critical Thinking** How can you use the Food Guide Pyramid to plan your meals?

Objectives

After reading this lesson, you should be able to

◆ explain why vitamins, minerals, and water are important

◆ recognize the healthiest way to prepare vegetables

◆ identify ways in which you can get different types of vitamins

◆ understand where to find calcium

Vitamin

A material needed in small amounts for growth and activity

Mineral

A natural material needed for fluid balance, digestion, and other bodily functions

Carbohydrates, fats, and proteins are three essential nutrients that give your body energy. The other three essential nutrients are **vitamins, minerals,** and water. A vitamin is a material your body needs. Minerals are materials formed in the earth. Vitamins, minerals, and water do not give you energy. They help your body change food into energy. Your body needs smaller amounts of vitamins and minerals than it does carbohydrates, fats, and protein. Your body also needs enough water to replace the amount it loses every day.

Why Are Vitamins Important?

Your body needs vitamins so you can grow and stay healthy. Table 9.3.1 shows why you need certain vitamins and where you can get them.

When you cook, your food loses a number of vitamins. For example, the B vitamins and vitamin C dissolve in water. What happens when you cook vegetables that contain these vitamins? Many of the vitamins mix with the water. When you pour off the water, you lose the vitamins. To keep this from happening, use only a small amount of water to cook vegetables. Also, do not cook them too long. You get more vitamins from uncooked vegetables than from cooked vegetables. To stay healthy, you should eat foods with vitamins every day. Your body does not store vitamins from one day to the next.

Vitamins A, D, E, and K dissolve in fat. These vitamins can build up and be stored in your body's fatty tissues. These vitamins are found in meat, milk, eggs, and other foods.

As with other nutrients, vitamins help keep your body healthy. It is possible, however, to have too many vitamins. Extra vitamins such as vitamins A and E can be bad for your body. Some people can harm their bodies by taking too many vitamin supplements, or pills. You need vitamins in small amounts. If you eat healthy foods, you are probably able to get all the vitamins you need from your diet.

Why Are Minerals Important?

Your body needs small amounts of many minerals to stay healthy. Minerals are needed to help you digest your food and keep your bodily fluids balanced.

One important mineral is **calcium.** Calcium is found in dairy products and green leafy vegetables. It is important for controlling how parts of your body behave and for keeping your bones and teeth strong. Another important mineral is **phosphorus,** which mixes with calcium to keep your bones firm. Phosphorus is found in peas, beans, milk, meat, and other foods. Your body needs larger amounts of calcium and phosphorus than of other minerals.

Table 9.3.1 Essential Vitamins		
Vitamin	**Purpose**	**Sources**
Vitamin A	Helps skin, hair, eyes, lining of nose and throat	Milk, egg yolk, beef liver, carrots, sweet potatoes, yellow squash, spinach, other greens
B Vitamins: Niacin	Protects skin and nerves, aids digestion	Beef, chicken, turkey, liver, whole wheat, milk, cereals, mushrooms
Thiamin	Protects nervous system, aids appetite and digestion	Pork, sunflower seeds, whole grains, cereal, green beans, peanuts, liver
Riboflavin	Increases resistance to infection, prevents eye problems	Milk, milk products, pork, liver, eggs, breads, rolls, crackers, green leafy vegetables
Vitamin C	Helps form bones and teeth, increase iron absorption, resist infection and stress	Tomatoes, most citrus fruits, kiwis, potatoes, fruit juices, green pepper
Vitamin D	Helps form strong bones and teeth	Fish oils, milk, sunlight
Vitamin E	Helps maintain cell health, has possible role in reproduction	Vegetable oils, margarine, peaches
Vitamin K	Aids in blood clotting	Green leafy vegetables, soybeans, bran, peas, green beans, liver

Sodium

Mineral that controls fluids in the body

?

What are crash diets? Why are they dangerous?

Health Myth

Myth: You should take as many vitamins as you can.

Fact: Taking more than the suggested dose of vitamins can have serious health effects. Some problems from taking too many vitamins are bone pain, itching, and involuntary movements of the muscles.

Your body uses only small amounts of the mineral iron. Iron is found in liver, beef, dried fruits, whole-grain foods, and green leafy vegetables.

Sodium is another mineral used in small amounts. It is necessary for controlling the amount of fluids in your body. You need only a small amount of sodium in your diet. Too much sodium may give you high blood pressure. Sodium is found in table salt and many other foods. You probably do not have to add salt to your foods.

Minerals cannot be stored in the body. It is important to get enough minerals every day to keep your body working as it should. A balanced diet includes all the minerals your body needs.

Why Is Water Important?

Water helps each cell in your body do its work. About 65 percent of your body's weight is water. Water carries nutrients, hormones, and waste products to and from the cells in your body. It helps you digest and use the food you eat. Water also helps control your body's temperature.

Water does not contain calories, but it is an important nutrient. Each day, your body loses about eight glasses' worth of water. This is why you should drink at least eight 8-ounce glasses of water every day. You can drink plain water or get water in soups and juices and other healthy drinks.

Research and Write

Do some research to learn more about nutrition labels. Visit a grocery store and use the Internet to learn about the information shown on these labels. Make a set of posters to teach people in your community about healthy eating. Show large nutrition labels on the posters. Explain what each part of the label means. Then explain which parts of the labels show healthy choices.

Avoiding Germs

There is more to good health than a healthy diet. You also need to keep your hands clean and free of germs. Your hands pick up germs throughout the day. If you do not wash your hands before you touch your food, the germs get on your food, and you are eating the germs!

Wash your hands thoroughly. Use soap and warm water, not hot or cold. Use soap on both sides of your hands. Wash your wrists and the areas between your fingers. Do not forget to get soap under your fingernails. Wash for about 30 seconds. To measure 30 seconds, slowly count to 10 three times. Then rinse your hands well.

You may not have the chance or time to wash your hands before lunch at school. There is a solution. You can carry a small bottle of hand sanitizer. It does not require water or soap. You can easily carry it in your pocket, lunch bag, purse, or backpack.

On a sheet of paper, write the answers to the following questions. Use complete sentences.

1. Where can you wash your hands at school before eating breakfast or lunch? Describe a way in which you can remind yourself to wash your hands before eating at school.

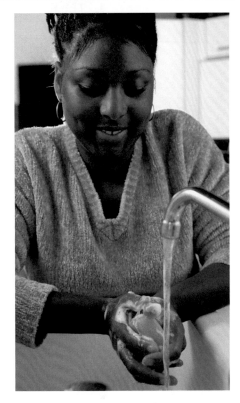

2. Why is it important for waiters and waitresses to wash their hands when they are working?

3. Name two jobs in which employees not only wash their hands frequently but also wear disposable rubber gloves. Explain why these employees wear and throw away several pairs of rubber gloves throughout the day.

Lesson 3 Review On a sheet of paper, write the letter of the answer that best completes each sentence.

1. The healthiest way to prepare vegetables is to
   _____.

   A reheat them over high heat
   B boil them in a lot of water
   C bake them in a hot oven
   D cook them in a little water

2. A good source of calcium is _____.
   A milk   **C** water
   B oil   **D** cola

3. Calcium and phosphorus are examples of _____.
   A fluids   **C** minerals
   B vitamins   **D** vegetables

On a sheet of paper, write the answers to the following questions. Use complete sentences.

4. **Critical Thinking** What might happen if your body does not get enough calcium and phosphorus?

5. **Critical Thinking** What might happen to your body temperature if you do not drink water for a long time?

Link to ➤➤➤

Social Studies

Fresh vegetables and orange or grapefruit juice are good sources of vitamin C. What happens when a person does not get vitamin C for a long time? He or she might get sick with scurvy. Scurvy is a disease that affects the skin, gums, teeth, and bones. A person can die from scurvy. Scurvy was a big problem for sailors during the 1700s and 1800s. They could not keep fresh vegetables on their ships when they were gone for a long time. Later, people realized that eating fruits such as lemons and limes could prevent scurvy.

The Food Guide Pyramid gives general guidelines to follow so people can choose a healthy diet. You must adjust your diet to meet your own needs. For example, you must know how many calories you need each day. This is based on your size, your activity level, and whether you are male or female. You also must know which foods give you the nutrients you need. As you get older, your calorie needs will change.

What Special Dietary Needs Do Teenagers Have?

Because you are still growing and changing, you need large quantities of calories, calcium, and iron. Since boys are usually larger and grow more than girls do, they need more calories.

Calcium is an important mineral in a teenager's diet. You need calcium for bone growth. If your diet does not contain enough calcium, your body takes calcium from your bones. Over time, if your body keeps taking the calcium from your bones, it can cause them to break easily. The best sources of calcium are milk, yogurt, and cheese (see Table B.3 in Appendix B). Your body is able to absorb calcium from dairy products because they contain vitamin D.

Iron is important for getting oxygen into your blood and cells. It is found in liver and other meats, dried fruits, and whole-grain foods. It is also found in green leafy vegetables. Foods with vitamin C in them help your body absorb iron. For example, a meal with meat and potatoes is a healthy choice. It provides iron and vitamin C to help your body absorb the iron. If you are a teenage girl, you need more iron to make blood cells to replace the ones you lose during menstruation.

What Special Dietary Needs Do Athletes Have?

If you play sports, you need more calories. The extra calories give you the extra energy you need. What if you play sports and eat a balanced diet? Studies show that you do not need extra protein, vitamins, or minerals.

If you play sports, you should eat at least 3 hours before your game or race. That way, your stomach has time to digest the food. Your meal should be low in fat and easy to digest. It should include three glasses of water or another drink. You need to replace the water you lose when you sweat before, during, and after your game or race.

Over the years, athletes have tried many different diets to try to improve how they play. Sometimes, these diets can be harmful. It is safest for people who play sports to eat a healthy, balanced diet. If you play sports, make sure you get enough calories every day.

How Is Diet Important in Weight Control?

Eating foods with too many calories can cause you to gain weight. Not getting enough calories can cause you to lose weight. A healthy diet with the right amount of physical activity can help you maintain a healthy weight.

If you want to make a big change in your weight, talk to a health care professional first. Some plans can be unhealthy and cause other problems. A healthy and balanced diet is the best way to keep a healthy weight.

How Does a Poor Diet Affect Health?

If your diet lacks the six essential nutrients, you may have **malnutrition.** Malnutrition comes from a diet that lacks one or more of the essential nutrients. Some people eat enough food but still do not get enough nutrients.

Some signs of malnutrition are tiredness, frequent headaches, stomachaches, or depression. Malnutrition may lead to serious health problems such as softened bones.

Another problem that comes from a poor diet is a **deficiency.** A deficiency is a lack of something. For example, people without enough iron in their diet may have an iron deficiency. Deficiencies may lead to more serious health problems. These include damage to the nervous system or heart. You can keep from getting malnutrition and deficiencies by eating a balanced diet.

How Are Diet and Disease Related?

Several diseases are linked to diet. If your diet is unhealthy, your risk is greater for some diseases. These include high blood pressure, heart disease, and cancer. For example, a person may have too much salt in his or her diet. The extra salt makes the body hold extra fluid. This affects the blood vessels and can cause higher blood pressure.

Health at Work

Nutrition Technician

Hospitals and retirement homes need workers who know about nutrition. Nutrition technicians follow guidelines to prepare and serve meals to patients. Nutrition technicians change recipes based on specific needs of patients. Some record keeping is also required. An additional duty might be keeping track of what supplies are on hand and what supplies are needed.

Nutrition technicians can be supervisors. A supervisor manages and trains other kitchen workers. A supervisor might also create work schedules.

A nutrition technician needs a high school diploma. A college degree is generally not needed.

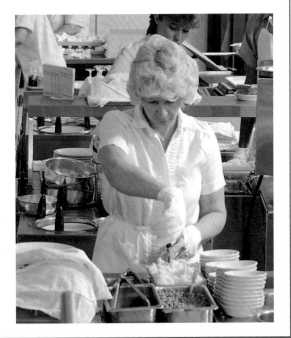

Your body systems need the different nutrients that specific foods give you. If your diet does not include these foods, your systems may not work well. As a result, you may get a disease. You can also have too many of some nutrients, including salt, sugar, and fat. This condition also may cause you health problems.

A healthy diet cannot keep you from getting every disease. A healthy diet can often lower your chances of getting sick. Nutrition is one thing you can control.

Lesson 4 Review On a sheet of paper, write the word or phrase in parentheses that best completes each sentence.

1. Teenage boys usually need more (water, calories, iron) than girls need.

2. Teenagers usually need more (salt, calcium, iron) in their diets for bone growth.

3. Too much sodium in your diet can lead to (deficiency, high blood pressure, depression).

On a sheet of paper, write the answers to the following questions. Use complete sentences.

4. **Critical Thinking** Name three reasons you should talk to a health care professional before you make plans to change your weight.

5. **Critical Thinking** Person A eats mostly candy bars, grilled cheese sandwiches, and soft drinks. Person B eats mostly fish, vegetables, and yogurt. Which person is more likely to get sick? Explain your answer.

Chapter 9 SUMMARY

- The U.S. government's Food Guide Pyramid shows how much and what kinds of foods to eat.

- Your body needs six types of essential nutrients. Carbohydrates, fats, and protein give your body energy. Vitamins, minerals, and water help your body change food into energy.

- Carbohydrates are starches and sugars that provide much of your energy.

- Fats are stored energy. Fats protect your organs and nerves. Too many saturated fats can lead to high levels of cholesterol in your blood. Some kinds of cholesterol can clog your blood vessels.

- Protein builds muscle and repairs tissue. Animal products and some plants give you protein.

- Your body needs vitamins in small amounts for normal growth and activity.

- Minerals are important in small amounts for fluid balance and digestion. Calcium, phosphorus, and iron are especially important minerals.

- Water carries nutrients, hormones, and waste products to and from your body's cells.

- Teenagers have special dietary needs, including more calcium and iron.

- A healthy diet is an important tool in weight control.

- Some diseases are linked to diet. A healthy diet can lower your chances of getting some diseases.

Vocabulary

added sugar, 211	essential nutrient, 206	mineral, 216
amino acid, 214	fat, 210	natural sugar, 211
blood cholesterol, 213	fatty acid, 212	nutrient-dense, 207
calcium, 217	fiber, 211	phosphorus, 217
carbohydrate, 210	Food Guide Pyramid, 204	protein, 210
cholesterol, 213		saturated fat, 212
complex carbohydrate, 210	fructose, 211	simple carbohydrate, 210
deficiency, 223	glucose, 212	sodium, 218
dietary cholesterol, 213	glycogen, 212	sucrose, 211
essential amino acid, 214	lactose, 211	unsaturated fat, 213
	malnutrition, 222	vitamin, 216

Word Bank

amino acids

calcium

carbohydrates

cholesterol

deficiency

fiber

glucose

lactose

malnutrition

protein

saturated fat

sodium

unsaturated fat

vitamins

Vocabulary Review

On a sheet of paper, write the word or phrase from the Word Bank that best completes each sentence.

1. If you lack something, you are said to have a(n) _____.

2. The kind of fat that comes from vegetable and fish oils is _____.

3. Potatoes, pasta, and bread are good sources of _____.

4. Carbohydrates are broken down into blood sugar, or _____.

5. The natural sugar that is found in milk is _____.

6. A mineral found in table salt is _____.

7. Muscles, bones, blood, and skin all contain _____.

8. The body needs nine _____ that are the building blocks of protein.

9. Water soaks up some _____, which means you may lose their health value.

10. An important mineral found in dairy products is _____.

11. The kind of fat that comes from animal products is _____.

12. If you eat too much fat, you can get a buildup of _____, which can clog your blood vessels.

13. The coarse material found in food that helps in digestion is called _____.

14. A condition you might get if your diet lacks some or all nutrients is called _____.

Concept Review

On a sheet of paper, write the letter of the answer that best completes each sentence.

15. All of these foods give you complex carbohydrates EXCEPT_____.

    A bread   **C** pasta

    B soft drinks   **D** rice

16. Extra sugar and starch in your body is _____.

    A turned into fat

    B used for energy

    C passed out as waste

    D stored to repair body tissues

17. Calcium is a _____.

    A fat   **C** carbohydrate

    B vitamin   **D** mineral

Critical Thinking

On a sheet of paper, write the answers to the following questions. Use complete sentences.

18. What are four foods you would choose to make a balanced dinner? Explain your reasoning.

19. How could you change your own diet to make it healthier?

20. Imagine you are a health care worker. How does the advice you would give a teenaged athlete differ from the advice you would give a teenager with an average activity level?

Test-Taking Tip Always read directions more than once. Underline words that tell how many examples or items you must provide.

Self-Assessment

Can you answer these questions?

1. ☑ What is a healthy eating pattern?

2. ☑ Why do you choose the kinds of foods you eat?

3. ☑ How can stress affect food choices?

4. ☑ How can advertising affect food choices?

5. ☑ How can fads affect diet?

6. ☑ How has the fast-food industry affected the American diet?

7. ☑ What does the government do to make sure food is safe?

8. ☑ What information is found on a food label?

9. ☑ How do you read a food label?

10. ☑ Why is knowing about food additives important?

10 Choosing Healthy Foods

Food is an important part of life. For most people, mealtimes are times to talk with family members or friends. Social events often include food. Many things affect the food choices you make. Realizing why you choose the foods you do is important. Developing an eating pattern that will help you keep eating healthy foods is also important.

In this chapter, you will learn about healthy eating patterns. You will also learn about how advertising and the fast-food industry affect how you eat. You will find out what is done to make sure foods are safe. Finally, you will learn about reading food labels and about things that are added to foods.

Goals for Learning

◆ To identify healthy eating patterns

◆ To describe what influences food choices

◆ To describe how government agencies make sure food is safe

◆ To explain how to read food labels in order to make healthy food choices

◆ To understand how things that are added to foods may change them

Your lifestyle affects your diet. Sometimes a busy lifestyle results in a poor diet. Knowing more about what affects the foods you choose can help you improve your diet.

How Does Your Eating Pattern Affect Your Life?

People usually have a set time for when they eat. For example, their normal lunchtime may be noon. Eating at a set time is helpful. It gives your body food for energy at regular times each day. Sitting down to a balanced meal each morning, midday, and evening will help you set a healthy eating pattern.

Sometimes, following a healthy eating pattern is difficult. Today, many people try to fit mealtimes into very busy lives. People may not have time to prepare and eat meals at home. They may rely on fast-food restaurants or have high-calorie snacks. Some people may skip breakfast or other meals.

Setting a healthy eating pattern is important. For example, eating a good breakfast every morning helps give you the energy you need for the day. In some ways, breakfast is more important than an evening meal. You are usually more active in the earlier part of the day. You use up more calories and energy during that time, so you need a nutritious breakfast. In the evening, you may be less active and need fewer calories. So the evening meal could be smaller. Breakfast foods should include complex carbohydrates to give your body the energy it needs. Avoid foods high in sugar. They give you an energy burst that your body uses up quickly and then leaves you feeling tired.

Snacks can be a part of a healthy diet, as long as they do not take the place of regular meals. Nutritious snacks can add protein, vitamins, and minerals to your diet. For example, you can add vitamin C by eating fruit. You can add vitamin A by eating carrots or green peppers. Avoid high-calorie foods such as candy and cookies. Also, avoid late-night snacking, which can disturb your sleep and cause you to gain weight.

Association

Something that reminds a person of something else

Exercise can affect your eating patterns. It is best not to eat 2 to 3 hours before you exercise. During exercise, blood is sent to your working muscles instead of to your intestines. Eating before exercise can cause you to have cramps and feel sick. A slow walk right after you eat, however, should not bother you.

What Affects Your Food Choices?

Many things affect the foods you choose to eat. These may include where you live, the time of year, your religion, or your cultural background. For example, if you live close to a body of water, you are more likely to eat fish and other seafood. Some foods are in season only at certain times during the year. For example, you may find fresh strawberries at the grocery store during June but not during December.

Cultural background or religion often affect your food choices. Some cultural groups include more rice, beans, or spicy foods in their diets than others do. Some religions have rules about foods, such as not eating certain kinds of meat. Eating foods that are common to other cultures can enrich your diet and be fun to try.

Several other things can affect what you choose to eat. The cost of food can affect what you buy. Checking prices and knowing the nutritional value of food will help you get the best food for the best price. Your family and friends can also influence your food choices. For example, you may have dinner at a friend's house and discover a food that you have never tried before.

Association also influences what you choose to eat. Association means that the food reminds you of something else. You may strongly like or strongly dislike certain foods because of association. For example, you may enjoy toasted marshmallows because they remind you of a picnic that you enjoyed with friends. You may dislike marshmallows because you once got sick eating them.

If you think about why a certain food is a part of your diet, you may decide to make some changes. For example, you may choose to skip the high-sugar cereal at breakfast and have whole-grain toast instead.

Figure 10.1.1 *How much you can afford to spend affects what you buy.*

Link to >>>

Social Studies

North Americans get 10 times as many heart attacks as do people who live in Greenland or Japan. People who live in places such as these eat more fish than North Americans do. Many North Americans eat a great deal of meat. Meat has cholesterol that can clog blood vessels. The oils in fish contain cholesterol that helps blood flow quickly. Many nutrition experts suggest eating fish at least twice a week.

Think about a time when you felt stress. How did the stress affect your eating patterns?

At times, making healthy food choices may be difficult, such as at a party where only high-calorie and high-fat foods are offered. Keep in mind the nutritional value of food. Choose foods that are the best for your health. You might make suggestions to people planning parties or other events about healthy food to serve.

How Does Stress Affect Eating Patterns?

Stress often affects the food you choose to eat. If you feel a great deal of mental stress, you may forget about your diet. You may not realize that during times of stress you are using more energy and need more nutrients. You may ignore your feelings of hunger and may not eat enough. By not getting the nutrients you need, you may have even greater physical stress.

Stress can sometimes cause you to eat too much. When you are stressed, you may choose foods that have too much sugar or salt. Remember that a healthy diet and exercise may help cut down the effects of stress. When you are stressed, choose foods that are high in vitamins, minerals, and protein. Good food choices would be nuts, orange juice, or bananas. Stay away from coffee, tea, cola, chocolate, and other foods that have a lot of caffeine. The caffeine can make you feel more nervous and make sleeping difficult. Choosing food wisely is a good way to help manage your stress.

Lesson 1 Review On a sheet of paper, write the answers to the following questions. Use complete sentences.

1. What is a healthy eating pattern?

2. What are four factors that affect your food choices?

3. What effect can stress have on healthy eating patterns?

4. **Critical Thinking** What are three strategies you can use to avoid a diet of unhealthy foods?

5. **Critical Thinking** What can you do to improve your eating patterns?

Media

Ways people can communicate information: TV, Web sites, newspapers, radio, magazines, and so on

Product

Item for sale made by someone or something

Advertise

Communicate to draw attention to a product

The **media** can have a big effect on what people do. The media is made up of the many ways we communicate information: TV, Web sites, newspapers, radio, magazines, and so on. Companies that make **products,** or items to be sold, use the media to reach people who may buy the products. Understanding how the media influences your food choices will help you make better ones.

How Does Advertising Affect the Food You Choose?

Many foods and drinks are **advertised** in the media. Advertising is communicating to draw attention to a product. The idea is to make the product appealing to people so they will buy it.

Food products are advertised often. Many times, people choose foods simply because they have heard about them. Food companies spend large amounts of money to encourage people to buy their products.

Some phrases companies use to try to get you to buy their food products are explained below.

- *New product*—Packages may include the words *new* or *improved.* Advertisers use these words to interest you in something that may be a little different or easier to use. Sometimes, the product may be almost the same, but the packaging is designed to look new.

- *Old-fashioned*—Some products say the food is prepared as it was many years ago. Adults may associate certain foods with happy memories from childhood. They may buy a food because it reminds them of a relative or an old friend. For example, a company may say its mashed potatoes are "just like Grandma used to make."

- *Expensive and the best*—These advertisements make people feel that the more something costs, the more they should want it. Usually, products advertised as "the best" cost more. For example, advertisers say their mustard "may cost a little bit more, but it's worth it."

- *Inexpensive and a good deal*—Some companies try to convince people they are getting the most for their money. Buyers must look at the price and number of servings to figure out if this is true.

- *Quick and easy to prepare*—These advertisements try to interest people who have little time to prepare meals. Most often, the meals are heated in a microwave oven. Technology and busy lifestyles have made a demand for many new food products that are simple to make.

- *Contains no cholesterol*—People may buy a product simply because it says that the product has no cholesterol. For example, an ad for peanut butter may state "This product has no cholesterol." Yet, no peanut butter contains cholesterol. This is because peanuts come from plants, and cholesterol is found only in animal products.

- *Fat free or low carb*—Many food packages use terms that appeal to people who are following a certain kind of diet. People who want to avoid fat may buy products that are advertised as fat free. People who carefully count carbohydrates may buy products that are advertised as being low in carbohydrates or "carbs." A product may be low in carbohydrates and fat but high in calories.

- *Organic foods*—Food products must meet government standards before they can be called **organic foods.** The word *organic* also means *natural.* Yet not all products called "natural" are organic. Some advertisers would like people to think that natural and organic foods are the same in every case. However, foods advertised as "natural" do not have to meet the same government standards as foods labeled "organic."

Companies use all these ways to encourage you to buy products. You must look closely at the foods you buy to be sure you are choosing foods that are nutritious and priced fairly.

How Does the Fast-Food Industry Affect Your Diet?

Today, many people want food that is fast and easy to prepare and eat. Almost one-third of all children in the United States eat fast food at some point each day. Studies have shown that fast-food companies target much of their advertisements at children. Children who watch TV ads for fast food are more likely to ask for fast food. Fast-food ads also have a strong effect on adults.

Fast foods have been linked to the growth in weight problems in America. Many fast foods are high in fat. Your body needs a certain amount of fat for growth and good health. Fat also provides energy for your body in the form of calories. However, taking in too much fat is unhealthy. Fat should make up only 30 percent of your total daily calories. A fast-food burger can contain many of your daily calorie needs. Half or more of those calories in the burger can come in the form of fat.

Health in Your Life

A Look at Food Advertising

Today, many foods are advertised as *light, low fat, nonfat, low calorie,* or *fat free.* The use of these terms is regulated by the FDA. Words in ads and on food labels are written to get you to choose a certain food. Many people think these foods will help them stay healthy.

Some fast-food restaurants advertise reduced-fat menu items, such as salads and low-fat sandwiches. Yet foods that are low in fat can still be less healthy because they are high in sugar. Many fast-food restaurants have information on the nutritional value of their menu items.

Request this information from the restaurant's manager, or find it on the Internet. Then you can decide if you should eat the food.

On a sheet of paper, write the answers to the following questions. Use complete sentences.

1. Why do advertisers of food use the words they do?

2. In what way can fast food be part of a healthy eating pattern?

3. What are three strategies you can use to make sure you have a healthy eating pattern?

Trans fat

Type of fat from processed vegetable oil

Daily Values (DV)

Section of a nutrition label that provides information about the percentage of nutrients in a product

Health Myth

Myth: Eating fatty foods makes you overweight.

Fact: Your body changes the fat you eat into calories that give you energy. Fat has twice as many calories as carbohydrates or protein. If you eat a lot of fat, you are eating a lot of calories. A little bit of fat should be a part of your daily diet. However, if you eat too much fat, you will gain weight.

Many of the foods you eat contain fat. Saturated fat is found in meat, poultry, milk, butter, eggs, and palm oil. Unsaturated fat is found in vegetables, nuts, seafood, and certain oils such as olive oil. Another kind of fat, called **trans fat,** is made from processed vegetable oil. Trans fat is added to food to lengthen the time it can stay on the shelf without spoiling. Trans fat is found in many foods, including most vegetable shortening, crackers, cookies, and snack foods.

Knowing about the three different types of fat in food is important. For good health, the U.S. Food and Drug Administration (FDA) recommends you eat a diet that is low in saturated and trans fats.

The **Daily Values (DV)** are ways of measuring the ingredients in food. The Daily Values are printed on nutrition labels. The DV percentage for fat tells how much fat is in the food compared with the total amount you need each day. A Daily Value of 5 percent or less of saturated fat is low. A DV of 20 percent or more is high. Table 10.2.1 below lists the saturated fats contained in several foods.

Table 10.2.1 Saturated Fats per Serving			
Product	**Common Serving Size**	**Saturated Fat (grams)**	**% DV for Saturated Fat**
Butter	1 tablespoon	7	35%
Candy bar	1 (40 grams)	4	20%
Doughnut	1	4.5	23%
Fast-food French fries	Medium (147 grams)	7	35%
Potato chips	Small bag (42.5 grams)	2	10%
Skim milk	1 cup	0	0%
Whole milk	1 cup	4.5	23%

Source: U.S. Food and Drug Administration

How Do Fads Affect Your Diet?

A fad is something that becomes popular for a short time. When you believe a food fad works, you may change your diet. For example, you might have heard that you should eat grapefruit six times a day for 2 weeks to lose weight. Grapefruit can be a healthy food, but eating too much of it is not healthy. Food fads usually focus on one food or on an unhealthy eating pattern. Your body needs nutrients from a variety of foods. Food fads can cause serious health problems.

Another example is the low-carb diet in which people reduce the number of carbohydrates they eat. Your body needs carbohydrates, so low-carb diets can be unhealthy.

There are many things to think about when choosing foods for your diet. Choosing good food and setting a healthy eating pattern will help your body get the nutrients it needs.

Decide for Yourself

Suppose you are planning a snack. Read the nutrition labels. Compare the information so you can choose the healthier snack.

On a sheet of paper, answer the following questions. Use complete sentences.

1. Which snack would you choose?

2. Why would you choose this snack? Explain your choice, using the nutritional information in both labels.

Wheat Crackers

Nutrition Facts

Serving Size 14 Crackers (22g)
Servings Per Container about 6

Amount Per Serving

Calories 110   Calories from Fat 10

Total Fat 1g
  Saturated Fat 0g
  Polyunsaturated Fat 0.5g
  Monounsaturated Fat 1.5g
Cholesterol 0mg
Sodium 110mg
Total Carbohydrate 21g
  Dietary Fiber 2g
  Sugars 2g
Protein 3g

Vitamin A 0%	Vitamin C 0%
Calcium 2%	Iron 6%

Nut Mix

Nutrition Facts

Serving Size 1 ounce
Servings Per Container about 20

Amount Per Serving

Calories 400   Calories from Fat 126

Total Fat 14g
  Saturated Fat 5g
  Polyunsaturated Fat 0.5g
  Monounsaturated Fat 2.5g
Cholesterol 0mg
Sodium 200mg
Total Carbohydrate 15g
  Dietary Fiber 5g
  Sugars 8g
Protein 6g

Vitamin A 0%	Vitamin C 3%
Calcium 5%	Iron 3%

Lesson 2 Review On a sheet of paper, write the word or phrase in parentheses that best completes each sentence.

1. Advertisers use words such as (low fat, high sugar, high calorie) to try to get you to buy their products.

2. Three types of fat are saturated fat, (unsaturated fat, vegetable oil, reduced fat), and trans fat.

3. One way to measure the amount of fat in food is to know its (calorie percent, Daily Value, weight).

On a sheet of paper, write the answers to the following questions. Use complete sentences.

4. **Critical Thinking** How would you advertise the value of a healthy diet to students at your school?

5. **Critical Thinking** How can you find out more about the health risks of a food fad?

▼◄▲▼◄▲▼◄▲▼◄▲▼◄▲▼◄▲▼◄▲▼◄▲▼◄▲▼◄▲▼◄▲▼◄▲▼◄▲▼◄▲▼◄▲▼

Health at Work

Dietary Aide

Dietary aides work in places such as hospitals and nursing homes. They work with dieticians to set good nutritional standards for patients. They may help prepare food for residents. They may also help plan menus, talk to patients about what they choose to eat, and keep diet records. Many dietary aides work on a tray line. They follow directions about what should go on each patient's meal tray. Then they deliver the trays. After a meal, they pick up the trays and return them to the kitchen. They record the amount of food that patients eat. Some dietary aides may help sort recyclables and trash, wash dishes, and do other clean-up tasks. Dietary aides are sometimes called food service workers or nutrition assistants.

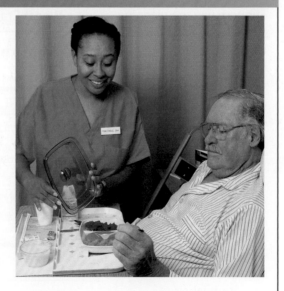

Dietary aides usually receive on-the-job training. Some may be asked to take special certification classes.

You know which nutrients your body needs, but you also need to know which foods contain these nutrients. To adjust your diet to your needs, you should know how many calories are in one serving of the foods you eat. This information is found on food labels. Food labels also list other things that are added to the foods you eat.

How Does the Government Make Sure Food Is Safe?

The government has agencies to make sure the foods you buy are labeled correctly and are safe to eat. These agencies set rules that companies must follow when they make food. The agencies have rules for how safe food must be, how clean the companies must be, how the companies advertise, how foods are labeled, and how the food is packaged.

The United States Department of Agriculture (USDA) is in charge of all programs that deal with making food. It conducts national food surveys to find out eating patterns in the United States. It is responsible for checking and grading meat and poultry.

The U.S. Food and Drug Administration (FDA) controls food and drug safety. It figures out which ingredients in the food are safe. The FDA also controls how food is labeled.

The Food and Nutrition Board of the National Research Council performs studies on the nutrients people need. It also suggests ways to help people meet those needs.

What Does a Food Label Tell You?

The government has set guidelines for what information must appear on a food label. The information includes what is in the package and how to store the food. Labels give the weight and lot number of the product. A lot number identifies a group of packages. Some labels say the product should be used by a certain date to be sure the product is fresh.

Figure 10.3.1 shows a sample food label. Food labels also must include information about the nutrients and contents of the product. These appear under the heading **Nutrition Facts.** Nutrition Facts tell the size of one serving and how many servings are in the package. Nutrition Facts also list the number of calories per serving, as well as the number of calories from fat.

The Nutrition Facts label also lists the Daily Value (DV) for each nutrient found in the food. The DV is based on a diet of 2,000 calories per day. For example, the DV for sodium is 2,400 milligrams (mg). The label in Figure 10.3.1 shows that the product has 250 mg of sodium per serving. Then it shows that the food has 10 percent of the DV for sodium. The Daily Value information helps you figure out how many nutrients you are getting in one serving of that food.

Under Daily Values, a food label must give the amounts of total fat, cholesterol, sodium, total carbohydrate, and protein. Amounts are given in grams (g) or milligrams. Next to the amount in grams or milligrams, the label shows the actual percent of Daily Value.

CHUNK LIGHT TUNA IN WATER

Nutrition Facts

Serv. Size 2 oz. drained (56g / about ¼ cup)
Servings about 2.5
Calories 60
  Fat Cal. 5

* Percent Daily Values (DV) are based on a 2,000 calorie diet.

Amount/Serving	%DV*	Amount/Serving	%DV*
Total Fat 0.5g	1%	**Total Carb.** 0g	0%
Sat. Fat 0g	0%	Fiber 0g	0%
Cholest. 30mg	10%	Sugars 0g	
Sodium 250mg	10%	**Protein** 13g	23%

Vitamin A 0% • Vitamin C 0% • Calcium 0% • Iron 2%
Niacin 20% • Vitamin B-6 8% • Vitamin B-12 20% • Phosphorus 8%

INGREDIENTS: LIGHT TUNA, WATER, VEGETABLE BROTH, HYDROLYZED CASEIN, HYDROLYZED SOY PROTEIN, SALT.

Figure 10.3.1 *Food label*

Link to ➤➤➤

Math

Figure 10.3.1 shows that a serving of tuna has 60 calories. This is about 3 percent of the Daily Value (DV) for calories. Which nutrients in the tuna provide more than 3 percent of the DV?

The Nutrition Facts label also must include the amount of vitamin A, vitamin C, calcium, and iron in the product. The label may list other vitamins and minerals. This information also is listed as a percent.

Finally, the label must list everything that is in the product, or the ingredients. The ingredients are listed in order by weight, from the most to the least. For example, on a can of soup, the first thing listed is water. That means there is more water in the soup than anything else. Some people must check the ingredients listed on labels carefully. If they have an allergy to a food, they can tell from the ingredients whether that food is included.

Additive

A substance added in small amounts to foods that changes them in some way

Preservative

A substance added to foods to prevent them from spoiling

Why is it important to be able to read and understand a food label?

All the information on the food label can be helpful in choosing food. If you are trying to limit something in your diet, such as sodium, look at the label. It will tell you what percent of sodium is in one serving. By using the information on the label, you can tell if the product is priced fairly. You can look at the price and the number of servings and decide how much each serving costs. You can then look at other brands to see which product is the best value.

What Are Food Additives?

A food **additive** is something added to food that changes it in some way. Additives change color, flavor, or texture. Additives such as sugars or salt are sometimes added to help prevent the food from spoiling. Sometimes, nutrients are added to foods. For example, vitamin C is added to some fruit drinks. Calcium is added to some fruit juices.

Some people question whether food additives are safe. The U.S. government has passed laws about food additives. The laws state that additives must be tested and must not be found to cause cancer in animals or humans. Food producers must test the additives and give their results to the FDA. The FDA decides whether the additive is safe.

Preservatives are also added to food. They keep bacteria from growing and spoiling the food. Preservatives such as sugar and salt are necessary, because many foods spoil quickly. Preservatives help by keeping canned, packaged, or frozen foods safe to eat.

In general, food additives are used in very small amounts. A person would have to eat a large amount of a food with additives to reach a dangerous level. Because foods are being processed more, it is a good idea to find out which additives are in the foods you eat often. You may decide to try to add more fresh foods to your diet.

Lesson 3 Review On a sheet of paper, write the letter of the answer that best completes each sentence.

1. The government agency that controls food labeling is the _____.

A Department of Agriculture
B Food and Nutrition Board
C Department of Education
D Food and Drug Administration

2. Ingredients on a food label are listed according to _____.

A calories   **C** weight
B Daily Value   **D** saturated fat

3. Daily Value percents are based on a diet of _____ per day.

A 2,000 calories
B three meals and a snack
C 2,000 carbohydrates and fats
D 500 grams

On a sheet of paper, write the answers to the following questions. Use complete sentences.

4. Critical Thinking How can you use labels to develop and track a personal health plan?

5. Critical Thinking How would you explain your point of view about food additives to someone who disagrees with you?

❖ ❖

Technology and Society

People lead busy lives. Planning meals and grocery shopping can be difficult. Healthy recipes for snacks, quick meals, or special diets can be found on the Internet. You can also find recipes from other cultures. Some people shop for groceries, special ingredients, or special cooking utensils on the Internet. Using the Internet can make meal planning faster and fun.

Chapter 10 SUMMARY

- A healthy eating pattern includes regular, balanced meals and nutritious snacks. A healthy eating pattern is important.

- Many things affect how you choose food. These include where you live, the time of year, the cost of food, and your cultural background. Association and stress also affect how you choose food.

- Companies use advertising to get people to buy their products.

- Fast food has become part of many people's regular eating patterns.

- Fad diets are diets that usually focus on a certain food. These diets can cause serious health problems.

- The U.S. government has set up agencies to make sure foods are labeled correctly and are safe to eat. They are the USDA, the FDA, and the Food and Nutrition Board of the National Research Council. The FDA is responsible for food labeling.

- Food labels provide information about the product. Labels include Nutrition Facts, Daily Value information, and a list of the product's ingredients. Food labels are helpful in choosing foods for your diet.

- Nutrition Facts tell serving sizes, number of servings in the package, and number of calories per serving.

- Additives are things that are added to foods to change them in some way. Some additives are preservatives that help prevent the food from spoiling. Additives are included in very small amounts.

Vocabulary

additive, 241	media, 233	preservative, 241
advertise, 233	Nutrition Facts, 240	product, 233
association, 231	organic food, 234	trans fat, 236
Daily Values (DV), 236		

Chapter 10 REVIEW

Word Bank

additive

advertises

association

Daily Value

media

Nutrition Facts

organic food

preservative

product

trans fat

Vocabulary Review

On a sheet of paper, write the word or phrase from the Word Bank that best completes each sentence.

1. Food grown without pesticides or unnatural fertilizers can be labeled as _____.

2. Something that changes the color of a food is a(n) _____.

3. A company _____ an item to draw attention to it.

4. A(n) _____ happens when a food reminds you of something you once did.

5. Something added to food to keep bacteria from growing is a(n) _____.

6. The _____ of a food is the percent of a nutrient that is found in a food.

7. You can find how much protein there is in a can of soup by looking at the _____.

8. The _____ includes TV, radio, the Internet, and magazines.

9. The purpose of advertising is to sell a(n) _____.

10. Processed vegetable oil is mostly made of _____.

Concept Review

On a sheet of paper, write the letter of the answer that best completes each sentence.

11. An ad that shows a child eating popcorn while watching a movie is using _____ to sell popcorn.

   A fast food   C claims of superior food

   B association   D peer pressure

12. The USDA is responsible for _____.

    A inspecting meat

    B inspecting health food stores

    C regulating the fast-food industry

    D suggesting new products

13. Nutrition facts on a food label show the ingredients and the _____ of the Daily Value of each nutrient.

    A kilogram   **B** percent   **C** milliliter   **D** calorie

14. Eating only cabbage soup for 2 weeks is an example of a(n) _____ diet.

    A trans fat   **B** nutritious   **C** fad   **D** organic

15. Two things that may affect which foods you choose are your cultural background and _____.

    A how old you are   **C** your interests

    B the weather   **D** the time of year

16. The most important meal of the day is _____.

    A dinner   **B** breakfast   **C** lunch   **D** a snack

Critical Thinking

On a sheet of paper, write answers to the following questions. Use complete sentences.

17. What is your definition of a healthy eating plan?

18. For a healthy diet, why should people know the nutritional value of fast foods?

19. How can food labels help someone with food allergies?

20. Your friend wants you to go on a fad diet with him or her. What would you tell your friend? Why?

Test-Taking Tip When you read test directions, say them in your own words to yourself to make sure you understand them.

International Red Cross

The International Red Cross is part of the world's largest network for helping people. This network is made up of 181 countries and includes many organizations.

The goal of the International Red Cross is to bring relief to people following a natural disaster. Its mission is to protect life and health for all people of the world. Each member country has equal status and carries equal responsibilities. Help is given without regard for political opinion, race, or religious beliefs.

Natural disasters come in many forms: crop failures, earthquakes, hurricanes, tsunamis, mudslides, and others. Natural disasters can affect thousands of people at the same time. Often they strike with little or no warning. Communities are destroyed. Often many lives are lost. Families are separated in the confusion brought on by the disaster. With little or no food, clean water, or medical supplies, malnutrition and disease are a constant threat to victims of natural disasters.

International Red Cross volunteers work within their own countries to bring relief to victims of natural disasters. Volunteer youth groups are an important part of this effort. The International Red Cross provides financial and technical support for relief efforts in individual countries.

This includes supplying natural disaster victims with additional volunteers, shelter, water, and food supplies. These organizations also help to reconnect families separated by a natural disaster. Often relief efforts last several months.

On a sheet of paper, write the answers to the following questions. Use complete sentences.

1. Why do you think the International Red Cross works with other organizations to help people after a natural disaster?

2. How are volunteers an important part of the International Red Cross?

3. Can you think of a recent natural disaster in which the Red Cross helped? Describe what the Red Cross did to help.

■ The U.S. government's Food Guide Pyramid shows how much and what kinds of foods to eat.

■ Your body needs six essential nutrients. Carbohydrates, fats, and protein are three nutrients that give your body energy. Vitamins, minerals, and water are three nutrients that help your body change food into energy.

■ Carbohydrates are starches and sugars that come mainly from plants. They provide much of the body's energy.

■ Fats are stored energy. Fats protect your organs and nerves. Too many saturated fats can lead to high levels of cholesterol in your blood. Some kinds of cholesterol can clog blood vessels.

■ Protein builds muscle and repairs tissue. Animal products and some plants give you protein. Protein is made of amino acids.

■ Your body needs vitamins in small amounts for normal growth and activity. Some vitamins can be stored in the body. Others cannot be stored.

■ Minerals are important in small amounts for fluid balance and digestion. Calcium, phosphorus, and iron are especially important minerals.

■ A healthy diet includes foods with all six essential nutrients. Not enough or too much of these nutrients can lead to health problems.

■ A healthy eating pattern includes balanced meals and nutritious snacks.

■ Many things affect how you choose food. These include where you live, the time of year, the cost of food, and your cultural background.

■ Advertisers use several ways to get people to buy their products.

■ Fad diets are diets that usually focus on a certain food. These diets can cause serious health problems.

■ The U.S. government has set up agencies to make sure foods are labeled correctly and are safe to eat. They are the USDA, the FDA, and the Food and Nutrition Board of the National Research Council.

■ Food labels include Nutrition Facts, Daily Value information, and a list of the product's ingredients. Nutrition Facts tell serving sizes, number of servings in the package, and number of calories per serving.

■ Additives are things that are added to foods to change them in some way. Some additives are preservatives that help prevent the food from spoiling.

Unit 3 R E V I E W

Word Bank

additive

association

calcium

carbohydrates

cholesterol

Daily Values (DV)

deficiency

protein

preservative

sodium

trans fat

unsaturated fat

Vocabulary Review

On a sheet of paper, write the word or phrase from the Word Bank that best completes each sentence.

1. Your body gets energy from _____, the starches and sugars that come mainly from plant food.

2. A nutrient that helps build muscle is _____.

3. People who do not eat a balanced diet are at risk of having a(n) _____.

4. A connection between a food and a memory is a(n) _____.

5. A mineral found in dairy products that helps keep your bones strong is _____.

6. Vegetable shortening and many cookies contain _____, which is made from processed vegetable oil.

7. Food producers must test a(n) _____ before it can be added to a food.

8. A(n) _____ is used to keep canned foods from spoiling.

9. Eating fish instead of red meat will replace saturated fat with _____.

10. The _____ are printed on food labels.

11. A mineral that helps control the amount of fluids in your body is _____.

12. A waxy, fatlike material that is important in making hormones is _____.

Concept Review

On a sheet of paper, write the letter of the answer that best completes each sentence.

13. Table sugar is _____.

   A fructose   **B** glucose   **C** lactose   **D** sucrose

14. The proteins that you must get from your diet are

_____.

A vitamins   **C** essential amino acids

B minerals   **D** complex carbohydrates

15. Many children want to eat fast food because they have seen _____ for the food.

A Nutrition Facts   **C** lot numbers

B TV advertisements   **D** serving sizes

16. The agency that checks and grades meat and poultry is the

_____.

A United States Department of Agriculture (USDA)

B U.S. Environmental Protection Agency (EPA)

C U.S. Food and Drug Administration (FDA)

D Food and Nutrition Board of the National Research Council

Critical Thinking

On a sheet of paper, write the answers to the following questions. Use complete sentences.

17. Many companies that sell vitamins use the word "daily" on the labels of vitamin pills. Why?

18. Suppose someone is recovering from a heart attack. Why might a doctor tell that person to eat less red meat?

19. Advertisements can affect a person's food choices. Describe a situation in which you or someone you know chose to eat something after seeing an advertisement. Was this a healthy choice? Explain your answer.

20. The Daily Values (DV) are based on a diet of 2,000 calories per day. Why is it important to include this amount (2,000 calories) on a Nutrition Facts label?

Unit 4

Preventing and Controlling Diseases and Disorders

When was the last time you were sick? Has it been so long ago that you cannot remember? This could be due to wise decisions you have been making about your health. Young adulthood is usually a time of excellent health. It is generally a time when your body is in peak physical form. However, young adulthood does not automatically mean good health. It is important for people of all ages to make healthy decisions. All people should do what they can to prevent disease.

Diseases affect how you feel in a number of ways. You can prevent many diseases by taking steps to protect yourself. In this unit, you will learn about causes and signs of disease. You will also discover how you can try to keep yourself from getting sick.

Chapters in Unit 4

Self-Assessment

Can you answer these questions?

☑ 1. What is an infectious disease?

☑ 2. What causes infectious diseases?

☑ 3. Why should you wash your hands frequently?

☑ 4. What are five ways that germs are spread?

☑ 5. How does AIDS affect the body?

☑ 6. What causes inherited diseases?

☑ 7. How do your skin, tears, and saliva help keep you from getting sick?

☑ 8. Why do people get some diseases only once?

☑ 9. Why does vaccination prevent some diseases?

☑ 10. Why is it important to be up to date on your vaccinations?

Disease—Causes and Protection

Have you ever wondered how you came down with the flu or got a cold? Have you wondered what your body does when you get sick? Your body has an amazing way of preventing many diseases. If you do get sick, your body fights the cause of the disease. When you know how diseases spread, you can take action to prevent getting or giving them.

In this chapter, you will learn the causes of diseases. You will also learn how the body fights diseases.

Goals for Learning

◆ To explain the causes of acquired diseases and inherited diseases

◆ To identify some of the body's barriers to infection

◆ To explain how the immune system works

◆ To recognize the importance of vaccinations

Inherit

To receive something passed down from parents

Acquire

To get after being born

Infectious

Passed from a germ carrier to another living thing

Communicable

Infectious

Influenza

A common illness known as the flu

Disease is a condition that harms or stops the normal workings of the body. A person can **inherit** or **acquire** a disease. An inherited disease is passed physically from parents to children. Acquired diseases are those that people get after they are born.

What Are Some Causes of Acquired Diseases?

Many diseases are acquired. Infections, human behaviors, or the environment cause an acquired disease.

When infection causes an acquired disease, the disease is **infectious.** Infectious means passed from a germ carrier to another living thing. Infectious diseases are often caused by germs that pass from person to person. They also can spread from food, water, or animals that carry germs. Another word for infectious is **communicable.** Infectious diseases such as **influenza,** or the common flu, often spread very easily. Here are the ways germs can be spread:

- through direct physical contact with an infected person

- by drops that an infected person coughs into the air

- by contact with an object that an infected person has used

- by contact with food or water with germs in it

- through the bites of infected animals, including insects

An acquired disease can also result from a person's behaviors. For example, eating healthy foods and getting regular exercise may help prevent heart disease. People who do not choose healthy behaviors are more likely to have heart disease. People may also tend toward heart disease because of heredity. For these people, choosing a healthy lifestyle is especially important.

An acquired disease can also come from the environment. For example, children living in older homes who eat lead-based paint chips can get lead poisoning. Nonsmokers who breathe others' cigarette or cigar smoke may get lung diseases, including cancer.

Why do you think people often get a cold or the flu within a couple of days after flying on an airplane?

What Are the Stages of Infectious Disease?

When a person acquires an infectious disease, it usually passes through certain stages. Figure 11.1.1 shows these stages. Germs that cause infectious diseases are **pathogens.** Pathogens include bacteria, fungi, and **viruses.** Viruses are small germs that reproduce only inside the cells of living things. Viruses cause the common cold, chickenpox, and influenza.

After a pathogen infects a person, the disease's first stage is the **incubation period.** This is the time it takes after infection for symptoms of the disease to appear. This period may be days, weeks, months, or even years.

The second stage is illness or getting well. If the body is able to defend, or fight off, the pathogens during incubation, a person may never become ill. The combination of body defenses that fights pathogens is the body's **immune system.**

Sometimes the body's defenses cannot fight off pathogens during the incubation period. Then the person becomes ill. The immune system continues to fight the illness. The third stage is recovery or death. The immune system successfully fights most infectious diseases and the person gets well. For example, if you get a cold, you are usually well again in about 10 days.

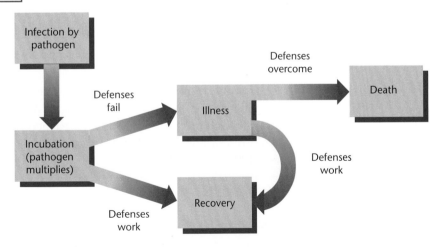

Figure 11.1.1 *Stages of infectious disease*

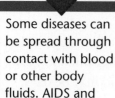

Antibiotic

Substance that can destroy the growth of certain germs

Some diseases can be spread through contact with blood or other body fluids. AIDS and hepatitis B and C are serious diseases that can be spread through the exchange of body fluids during sexual activity or other contact.

For some diseases, such as the common cold, there is no cure. Rest and plenty of liquids help a person get over a cold more quickly. **Antibiotics,** substances that can destroy the growth of certain germs, may be given for some diseases that bacteria cause. Antibiotics do not work against viruses. Sometimes bacteria change, and antibiotics do not work against them. This is one reason you may want to keep track of antibiotics you are treated with. You can determine whether they work.

A disease can affect the immune system itself. As a result, a person's defenses are weak or are not able to protect against other diseases. Even germs that normally are not pathogens can cause disease. People may then die from severe infections. In some people, disease of the immune system is inherited. In others, the disease is acquired. For example, AIDS is an acquired disease of the immune system.

What Are Some Causes of Inherited Diseases?

An inherited disease passes through the genes from parents to children. You cannot get an inherited disease any other way. There are three main causes for inherited diseases.

1. A single abnormal gene can cause diseases such as hemophilia. In this disease, blood does not clot normally. The person bleeds more than normal.

Link to ➤➤➤

Environmental Science

The environment can affect the rates of some infectious diseases. For example, mosquitoes carry several different types of infectious germs, such as West Nile virus. Mosquitoes breed in standing water. When rainfall in an area increases, the number of mosquitoes goes up. Diseases caused by germs carried by mosquitoes may increase.

---

2. A combination of many abnormal genes and environment can cause diseases such as diabetes and some cancers. **Deformities** also are caused this way. Deformities are abnormally formed body structures, such as cleft palate. In this disorder, the plates in the roof of an unborn baby's mouth do not close.

3. Abnormal chromosomes cause genetic disorders such as Down syndrome, a mental impairment. A chromosome may break or fail to divide properly. Genes can also be placed incorrectly on the chromosomes.

> *Deformity*
>
> *Abnormally formed body structure*

Decide for Yourself

Home or School?

Define the problem. You wake up one morning with a bad cold. Should you stay home or go to school? You have a big test today.

Come up with possible solutions. You can go to school. You can stay home and get plenty of liquids and rest.

Consider the consequences of each solution. If you go to school, you might feel worse, and you will spread pathogens. You might perform badly on your test. If you stay home, you will get well quicker and not spread pathogens. However, you will have to take a makeup test.

Put your plan into action. You decide to stay home and rest.

Evaluate the outcome. You feel much better in a couple of days. You do well on the makeup test. You feel good about yourself because you did not make other people sick.

On a sheet of paper, write answers to the following questions. Use complete sentences.

1. Have you ever been faced with a similar problem? If so, what did you decide to do?

2. What was your outcome?

3. Would you make the same decision in the future? Why?

Lesson 1 Review On a sheet of paper, write the word or phrase in parentheses that best completes each sentence.

1. Disease harms (abnormal, immune, normal) body function.

2. A disease that one person passes to another is (immune, inherited, acquired).

3. A combination of abnormal genes and environment can cause a (deformity, pathogen, virus).

On a sheet of paper, write the answers to the following questions. Use complete sentences.

4. Critical Thinking You have a friend who has a cold. He does not cover his mouth and nose when he sneezes. What advice would you give your friend?

5. Critical Thinking Is it possible for people with inherited diseases to have prevented them? Explain why or why not.

Health Myth

Myth: Antibacterial soap is better than regular soap at preventing diseases.

Fact: Washing the hands physically removes pathogens from the skin. Regular soap does this just as well as antibacterial soap. In addition, viruses cause the most common diseases. Antibacterial soap does not work against viruses.

Objectives

After reading this lesson, you should be able to

◆ explain how the body fights infection

◆ describe how the immune system works

◆ recognize the importance of vaccinations

Barrier

Something that blocks passage

Mucous membrane

The moist lining of the mouth and other body passages

Mucus

The fluid that mucous membranes produce

The human body has many ways to protect itself from disease and infection. Germs that are washed off the skin never enter the body. The body's physical and chemical **barriers** protect the body from infection. A barrier is something that blocks passage. The immune system also defends the body against disease.

How Does the Body Fight Infection?

Physical and chemical barriers are the first way your body protects itself from infection. These are the body's first line of defense. The skin and **mucous membranes** are physical barriers to infection. Mucous membranes are the moist linings of your mouth and other body passages. These barriers prevent pathogens from getting through your body's surface. The tiny hairs in your breathing passages are other physical barriers. These hairs whip rapidly back and forth to sweep pathogens and dust out of your body. Your body also has chemical barriers to infection. Saliva, tears, and sweat clear pathogens from your body's surface. Your stomach produces strong acids that kill pathogens that enter the digestive system. Urine carries pathogens out of your body. Tears, saliva, and **mucus** contain substances that fight pathogens. Mucus is the fluid that mucous membranes produce.

Link to ➤➤➤

Social Studies

In 1900, the number one cause of death in the United States was pneumonia. Pneumonia is a disease of the lungs. Today, the number one disease is heart disease. In 1900, 30 percent of all deaths in the United States occurred in childhood. Today, about 1 percent of all deaths occur in childhood. Throughout the 1900s, infectious diseases decreased because of antibiotics, childhood vaccinations, and public health improvements such as clean drinking water. Life expectancy has increased from 47 years in 1900 to 77 years today.

Sometimes, pathogens get past physical and chemical barriers. This can happen because of a break in the skin. If pathogens enter the bloodstream, they meet up with the second line of defense, which includes white blood cells. The white blood cells are part of the body's immune system. These cells travel to tissues and attack pathogens. **Inflammation** may also occur. Inflammation is the body's response to tissue damage. An area of the body that is inflamed may be red, warm, swollen, and painful.

How Does the Immune System Work?

You can practice many behaviors to keep your immune system healthy. Get the recommended amount of vitamins and minerals. Exercise regularly. Keep stress to a level you can manage. Get enough sleep.

The immune system is the body's final line of defense against infection. If pathogens enter the bloodstream, the blood makes **antibodies.** Antibodies are proteins that kill particular pathogens. If the correct antibodies are in the blood when an infection occurs, they can begin to fight it. They may knock out the infection during the incubation period. A person may never become sick.

Antibodies form in the blood in a number of ways. If you do become sick, antibodies that work against a pathogen develop during the course of the illness. These antibodies help fight the illness so that recovery is speeded up.

Some antibodies remain in the body after a person has recovered. These antibodies give you immunity so you will not get the disease again. For example, once you have mumps, you will not get the disease again. You are immune.

Health Myth

Myth: Vaccines are not necessary because the diseases they prevent are rare.

Fact: The reason some diseases are rare is because of vaccines. If vaccines were not given, more people would get the diseases. Countries that have low vaccination rates have high rates of diseases such as polio, measles, and diphtheria.

Immunization

The process of making the body immune to a disease

Vaccination

A means of getting dead or weakened pathogens into the body

Antibodies may also be in the blood as a result of **immunization,** or the process of making the body immune to a disease. A **vaccination** is a means of getting dead or weakened pathogens into your body. Vaccinations also can contain parts of organisms. A vaccination is usually an injection, or shot. A vaccination will not make you sick from the disease. However, your immune system will make antibodies against the bacteria or virus in the vaccine. For example, a vaccination against measles contains the weakened virus that causes measles. When you get a measles vaccination, your body makes antibodies against the measles virus. Then you are immune to measles.

Health in Your Life

Vaccinations—Not Just for Little Kids

Are you too old for vaccinations? No. Some vaccines are recommended for young people and adults. Adolescents need to make sure they receive the vaccinations shown in the list at right. The diseases these vaccines prevent can be very serious in teens and adults.

About 20 percent of children are not up to date on their vaccinations. They are at risk of getting diseases. Ask your family to help you make a list of all the vaccinations you have had and when you had them. If they are not up to date, see your doctor or local health department. Your school nurse can also help you locate places that offer vaccines.

On a sheet of paper, write the answers to the following questions. Use complete sentences.

1. Have you received all the vaccinations listed? Do you plan to get them? Why?

2. Use Internet or print sources to find more information about the diseases listed. What is tetanus? What is a common symptom of rubella?

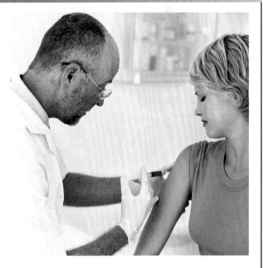

3. How can you communicate the importance of getting vaccinations to students in your school?

Vaccines Teens Need

- Varicella (chickenpox)
- Measles-Mumps-Rubella (MMR)
- Hepatitis B
- Tetanus-Diphtheria

?

Why do you think washing your hands is the best way to keep from getting pathogens?

Another way people get immunity is from their mothers during pregnancy. Babies are protected from the same infectious diseases as their mothers are. This is because antibodies pass from the mother to the baby through the placenta. Antibodies also pass to babies through breast milk. Babies have these antibodies until they are 6 to 12 months old. Then babies' own immune systems begin to take over.

Without the immune system, people would have many more diseases and infections. Your immune system is an important defense against disease.

Figure 11.2.2 *Babies get immunity from their mothers during pregnancy.*

Research and Write

Find out where free or low-cost vaccines are available in your community. Use the Internet or contact your local health department. Then make a brochure that explains what vaccines are, why they are important, and where people can get them. Place the brochure in your school library.

Lesson 2 Review On a sheet of paper, write the letter of the answer that best completes each sentence.

1. An example of a chemical barrier is _____.
   A the flow of urine
   B the outer layer of skin
   C strong acids in the stomach
   D tiny hairs in breathing passages

2. If you are immune to a disease, you _____.
   A have antibodies against the disease
   B must have been ill from the disease
   C will probably get the disease again
   D must have received a vaccination against the disease

3. One of the first ways that the body deals with pathogens is to _____.
   A make antibodies
   B become red, warm, and swollen
   C clear pathogens with saliva and tears
   D kill the pathogens during the incubation period

On a sheet of paper, write the answers to the following questions. Use complete sentences.

4. **Critical Thinking** Why is it important for school children to have certain vaccinations?

5. **Critical Thinking** Suppose you have the flu. Your brother gets it, too, but your sister does not. Why might your sister stay well?

❋ ❋

Technology and Society

Some people dislike getting vaccines because of the needle. Scientists are working on other ways to give vaccines. The day is not far off when people might get their vaccines from vegetables or skin patches. An influenza vaccine is now available that squirts up the nose. A liquid vaccine that was swallowed was used at one time against polio.

▼◄▲▼◄▲▼◄▲▼◄▲▼◄▲▼◄▲▼◄▲▼◄▲▼◄▲▼◄▲▼◄▲▼◄▲▼◄▲▼◄▲▼◄▲▼◄▲▼

Health at Work

Health Unit Coordinator

Health unit coordinators work in hospitals, clinics, and nursing homes. They perform nonnursing duties. They handle forms when patients enter or leave health care facilities. They enter doctors' orders on a computer. They communicate with other departments to order special diets, drugs, equipment, supplies, laboratory tests, and X rays. They may serve as receptionists on patient floors. Health unit coordinators may be called ward or unit secretaries, ward or unit clerks, or hospital service coordinators.

To become a health unit coordinator, a person needs a high school diploma and a 6-month to 1-year training program. Some employers require certification.

Health unit coordinators need excellent communication skills. They must be pleasant and businesslike when dealing with the public and coworkers.

- Diseases can be acquired or inherited.

- An acquired disease is caused by infection, human behaviors, or the environment.

- An acquired disease is infectious when infection causes it.

- Pathogens are the germs that cause infectious diseases.

- The first stage of infectious disease is the incubation period, which can last days, weeks, months, or years.

- If the body's immune system can fight off a pathogen, a person may never become ill.

- If the body's immune system cannot fight off a pathogen, a person becomes ill. The immune system continues to fight the illness, and a person usually recovers.

- The immune system fights pathogens by producing antibodies.

- Diseases of the immune system may cause people to become ill with organisms that are not normally pathogens.

- The body has physical and chemical barriers to infection. Some physical barriers are the skin and mucous membranes. Some chemical barriers are saliva, tears, mucus, and stomach acids.

- Antibodies get in the blood in a number of ways. Diseases or vaccinations build antibodies in the blood to fight infections. A baby gets antibodies through its mother's placenta and breast milk.

- A person may get an inherited disease through a single abnormal gene, a combination of many abnormal genes and environment, or an abnormal chromosome.

Vocabulary

acquire, 254	immune system, 255	inherit, 254
antibiotic, 256	immunization, 261	mucous membrane, 259
antibody, 260	incubation period, 255	mucus, 259
barrier, 259	infectious, 254	pathogen, 255
communicable, 254	inflammation, 260	vaccination, 261
deformity, 257	influenza, 254	virus, 255

Chapter 11 REVIEW

Vocabulary Review

Word Bank

acquired

antibodies

communicable

deformity

immune system

immunization

incubation period

infectious

inflammation

mucous
  membranes

mucus

pathogens

vaccination

virus

On a sheet of paper, write the word or phrase from the Word Bank that best completes each sentence.

1. An acquired disease is _____ when infection causes it.

2. Germs that cause infectious diseases are _____.

3. The first stage of infectious disease is the _____ .

4. The body's _____ produces antibodies.

5. The skin and _____ are physical barriers to infection.

6. Particular pathogens are killed by _____.

7. A shot of weakened or dead pathogens is a(n) _____.

8. Tears, saliva, and _____ are chemical barriers to pathogens.

9. A disease caused by infection, human behaviors, or the environment is _____.

10. Another word for infectious is _____.

11. A combination of many abnormal genes and environment can cause a person to be born with a(n) _____.

12. An area of the body that is red, warm, swollen, and painful is showing signs of _____.

13. After weakened pathogens are injected into the body, the process of _____ begins.

14. A germ that reproduces only within cells of living things is a(n) _____.

Concept Review

On a sheet of paper, write the letter of the answer that best completes each sentence.

15. An inherited disease is caused by _____.

   A pathogens   **C** personal behaviors

   B the environment   **D** genes from parents

16. A person can get an acquired disease from _____.

   A an infection

   B a single abnormal gene

   C abnormal chromosomes

   D many abnormal genes and the environment

17. The body's first line of defense includes _____.

   A antibodies   **C** stomach acids

   B vaccinations   **D** white blood cells

Critical Thinking

On a sheet of paper, write the answers to the following questions. Use complete sentences.

18. What do you think you could do to protect yourself from getting a cold from another person?

19. Why do you think making sure you get vaccinations is important?

20. Why are diseases of the immune system especially dangerous?

Test-Taking Tip Be sure you understand what the test question is asking. Reread it if necessary.

Self-Assessment

Can you answer these questions?

☑ 1. What is AIDS?

☑ 2. What causes AIDS?

☑ 3. Why are sexually transmitted diseases serious?

☑ 4. What is gonorrhea?

☑ 5. What is chlamydia?

☑ 6. What is syphilis?

☑ 7. What is genital herpes?

☑ 8. What are genital warts?

☑ 9. How can sexually transmitted diseases be prevented?

☑ 10. Which sexually transmitted diseases cannot be cured?

12 Preventing AIDS and Sexually Transmitted Diseases

Communicable diseases that are passed through sexual contact can be serious. A pregnant mother who is infected with a sexually transmitted disease can pass the disease to her baby. Some of these diseases can cause cancer or sterility. Some of them can be cured or treated with medicine. While some of these diseases cannot be cured, all of them can be prevented.

In this chapter, you will learn what causes AIDS, how it is acquired, and its symptoms. You will learn about infections that result when the immune system is weakened. You will learn about symptoms, treatments, and prevention of some common sexually transmitted diseases.

Goals for Learning

◆ To describe the causes of AIDS and how it is acquired

◆ To identify symptoms of AIDS and infections it causes

◆ To describe the symptoms and treatment of common sexually transmitted diseases

◆ To identify help or resources for people with sexually transmitted diseases

◆ To explain how sexually transmitted diseases can be prevented

A serious communicable disease is **acquired immunodeficiency syndrome (AIDS).** AIDS is a disorder of the immune system. The first cases of AIDS in the United States were identified in 1981. Since then, the disease has spread rapidly in the United States and throughout the world. Many people have died from it. Figure 12.1.1 shows the number of reported AIDS cases in the United States in 2003.

What Causes AIDS?

Human immunodeficiency virus (HIV) causes AIDS. HIV infects body cells and severely damages the human immune system. As a result, the body becomes open to **opportunistic pathogens.** These pathogens are germs that the body normally fights off. When the immune system is weakened, they cause infection.

Acquired immuno-deficiency syndrome (AIDS)

A disorder of the immune system

Human immuno-deficiency virus (HIV)

A virus that infects body cells and severely damages the human immune system, causing AIDS

Opportunistic pathogen

Germ that the body would normally fight off but that takes advantage of a weakened immune system

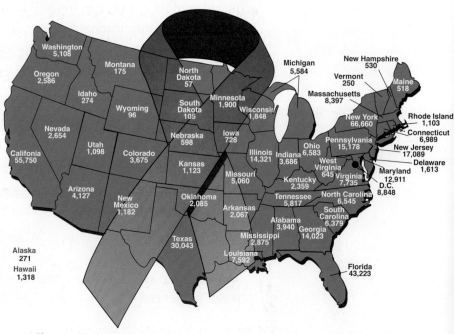

Figure 12.1.1 *Estimated numbers of people living with AIDS in the United States at the end of 2003*

Arts

When AIDS first came to public awareness, many people were afraid of those who had it. People thought they could get AIDS just from being near someone who had it. The movie *Philadelphia* tells the story of a lawyer whose firm fires him because he has AIDS. He sues the firm. The film shows how people were misinformed about AIDS and how it is acquired.

Health Myth

Myth: HIV affects only homosexual men and drug users.

Fact: HIV can affect anyone. Babies, heterosexual couples, and seniors have all been infected with HIV.

How Has AIDS Affected the World?

In the United States, more than half a million people with AIDS have died. Each year since 1989, there have been about 40,000 new cases of AIDS. An estimated 929,985 cases in total have been in the United States. Worldwide, more than 20 million people have died of AIDS since 1981. Young people from 15 to 24 years old account for half of all new HIV infections. Around the world, more than 6,000 young people become infected with HIV every day. In 2004, about five million adults and children became infected with HIV.

How Is AIDS Acquired?

Like all illnesses caused by a virus, AIDS is a communicable disease. HIV is spread in these ways:

1. Body fluids—HIV can be transmitted through blood, semen, vaginal secretions, and breast milk of infected people. It is spread through exchange of these fluids from one person to another. It has not been transmitted through fluids such as saliva, sweat, or urine.

2. Sexual activity—AIDS can be spread through sexual activity with an infected partner, including oral sex. Oral sex is any mouth-to-genital contact. Each new partner in turn can infect others.

3. Sharing needles among drug users—Any needle that is used for injection of a drug or medicine into the body has blood on it. Drug users who share needles risk getting HIV.

4. Mother to child—HIV can be passed from a mother to a baby before, during, or after birth. It can also be passed to a baby when the baby drinks the mother's breast milk.

A blood test often shows whether a person is infected with HIV or has AIDS. If people are not aware that they are infected with HIV, they do not realize that they may get or already have AIDS.

How Is AIDS Not Acquired?

AIDS is a serious disease that cannot be cured. Because of this, some people have fears about how it is acquired. These people are afraid to be around people with AIDS.

It is important to know that AIDS is not acquired by casual social contact. This is because HIV cannot survive outside of the body for very long. For that reason, touching, holding, or hugging a person with HIV or AIDS will not spread the disease. Contact such as shaking hands, hugging, kissing, crying, coughing, and sneezing does not spread AIDS.

AIDS is also not spread by sharing cups, dishes, and other eating utensils. Bathing in the same pool or hot tub has not been shown to spread AIDS. No evidence shows that bites from insects such as mosquitoes spread AIDS.

What Are the Symptoms of AIDS?

AIDS is an illness that can have a long incubation period. This means that a person infected with HIV may not show outward signs of AIDS for 6 to 10 years or longer. During that time, however, HIV is weakening the person's immune system.

When symptoms of AIDS appear, they are like symptoms of infection with HIV. Some of these symptoms are a feeling of weakness, chills and fever, night sweats, dry cough, and shortness of breath. Other symptoms are fatigue, stiff neck, headache, weight loss, skin rashes, diarrhea, and swollen glands. A person may also have sores in the mouth. The entire body may be swelled with fluid.

Because HIV weakens the immune system, people who are infected with it also can have other serious diseases. These are caused by the opportunistic pathogens that the body cannot fight against. For example, a person can have a certain kind of **pneumonia.** Pneumonia is a lung infection. Another serious disease can be **Kaposi's sarcoma,** a rare type of cancer. Still other serious problems can result from the attack of AIDS on the nervous system. The disease can also cause brain damage.

Figure 12.1.2 *AIDS is not acquired by casual social contact.*

How Safe Is the Blood Supply?

People sometimes need **transfusions.** A transfusion is the transfer of blood from one person to another.

AIDS can be acquired through infected blood. In 1985, a test was developed to detect HIV in blood. Since that time, all blood given for transfusions is tested. Blood can be used for transfusions only when the test for HIV is negative. Today, the U.S. blood supply is almost always safe. Some people who had blood transfusions before 1985 have been infected with HIV. These infections are now prevented by the HIV blood test.

Sometimes, people know in advance they need a transfusion. For example, they may have a surgery scheduled. They can give their own blood. Then the blood is set aside until it is needed.

Are Health Care Workers Safe from Acquiring AIDS?

Doctors, dentists, and other health care workers can be at risk for acquiring AIDS because they work with body fluids. These people may care for patients infected with HIV. Small cuts on the skin can provide a pathway for HIV to enter a health care worker's bloodstream.

Health care workers protect themselves through preventive measures such as wearing gloves and masks when working with body fluids. They treat every patient as though he or she may carry HIV or other pathogens.

Link to ≻≻≻

Social Studies

An area in Africa south of the Sahara Desert is the part of the world affected most by HIV and AIDS. More than 25 million people in the area are living with HIV. In 2004, AIDS killed about 2.3 million people there. Around 2 million children under the age of 15 have HIV. More than 12 million children have been orphaned by AIDS. Levels of economic well-being, education, and life expectancy in the area have always been lower than those in more developed nations. Since the AIDS outbreak, school enrollment has declined. AIDS is erasing much of the progress that had been made on life expectancy. Many workers have died. This has slowed economic growth. This makes it even harder for Africa to deal with the AIDS epidemic.

What Is the Future for People with AIDS?

At this time, AIDS is a disease with no vaccine and no cure. Some treatments increase the quality and length of life for people with AIDS. Eventually, however, all people with AIDS will die of the disease unless a cure is found. Scientists are researching many possible cures, but it may be years before they find one that works. For now, prevention is the only choice. Education has helped people slow down the spread of AIDS. AIDS infection can be prevented by avoiding contact with HIV-infected blood or other body fluids. Abstinence from sexual activity is one way to avoid this contact.

Lesson 1 Review On a sheet of paper, write the answers to the following questions. Use complete sentences.

1. What causes AIDS?

2. What are four ways that AIDS is acquired?

3. What are two diseases caused by opportunistic pathogens that a person with AIDS can get?

4. **Critical Thinking** Why is AIDS not acquired by casual social contact?

5. **Critical Thinking** Why do health care workers take precautions with all patients?

▼◄▲▼◄▲▼◄▲▼◄▲▼◄▲▼◄▲▼◄▲▼◄▲▼◄▲▼◄▲▼◄▲▼◄▲▼◄▲▼◄▲▼◄▲▼◄▲▼

Health at Work

Laboratory Assistant

Laboratory assistants work with medical technicians. Assistants look at samples of human urine, blood, and saliva. They look for organisms that cause disease. They report all organisms that are not normal. Laboratory assistants usually work in hospitals, clinics, and doctors' offices. They help to maintain equipment. If anything is not working properly, they report the problem.

Some 1-year programs are available, but a 2-year degree is usually needed.

Objectives

After reading this lesson, you should be able to

◆ name and describe five sexually transmitted diseases

◆ explain which sexually transmitted diseases can be cured

◆ explain how to avoid sexually transmitted diseases

Sexually transmitted disease

Any disease that is spread through sexual activity

Gonorrhea

A sexually transmitted disease

Any disease that is spread through sexual activity is a **sexually transmitted disease.** For example, AIDS is a sexually transmitted disease because it can be spread through sexual activity. In the United States, one in four people under age 21 has had a sexually transmitted disease. These diseases can be serious because they can cause other diseases if they are not treated. Millions of people around the world will have a sexually transmitted disease at some point in their lifetime. Even one sexual experience can pass a sexually transmitted disease from one person to another.

What Is Gonorrhea?

Gonorrhea is a sexually transmitted disease. One quarter of the people who have this infectious disease are between 10 and 19 years of age. It can also be transmitted to babies as they pass through the birth canal of an infected mother. Gonorrhea can cause an eye infection in babies that can lead to blindness.

In males, symptoms are a white discharge from the urethra and burning while urinating. From 20 to 40 percent of males, however, have no symptoms and do not know they are infected. Females may have a discharge from the vagina and some swelling and redness in the genital area. Most females, however, also have no symptoms and do not know they are infected. The gonorrhea bacteria can also infect the rectum and throat.

Gonorrhea used to be easy to treat with antibiotics. An antibiotic is a substance that can destroy the growth of certain germs.

Recently, some strains of gonorrhea have become resistant to some antibiotics. However, if a person thinks he or she may have been infected, clinics can still quickly diagnose and begin treating gonorrhea. All newborn babies are treated with a special eye medicine immediately after birth to prevent the eye infection.

Sterility

Inability to produce a child

Chlamydia

A sexually transmitted disease

Syphilis

A sexually transmitted disease

Chancre

A hard sore that is the first sign of syphilis

● ● ● ● ● ● ● ● ● ●

Technology and Society

Doctors are working to develop new drugs that will help people with sexually transmitted diseases. A new drug is tested in a clinical trial. The main purpose of a clinical trial is to make sure that the drug is safe and effective. A clinical trial helps doctors decide what information to put on the label for a drug.

If gonorrhea is not treated in males, it can lead to **sterility,** which is the inability to produce a child. If it is not treated in females, it can spread throughout the reproductive system. Untreated gonorrhea and other sexually transmitted diseases can cause an advanced infection that can lead to sterility in females.

Gonorrhea can spread to the bloodstream. Once there, the bacteria can infect other body parts. This can lead to heart valve problems and other diseases such as arthritis, a painful inflammation in the joints.

Gonorrhea is an important public health concern. Because many people do not have symptoms, they do not know they are infected and can spread the disease.

What Is Chlamydia?

The symptoms of **chlamydia,** another sexually transmitted disease, are similar to those for gonorrhea. For some females, symptoms may be pelvic pain and a discharge from the vagina. Usually, however, females have no symptoms. Males may have a discharge from the urethra and pain when they urinate. Chlamydia can be treated with an antibiotic.

Chlamydia can lead to sterility. Like gonorrhea, chlamydia can infect a baby as it passes through the birth canal. It can cause an eye infection that results in blindness.

What Is Syphilis?

Syphilis is a sexually transmitted disease that progresses in three stages if left untreated. The first stage of syphilis is a **chancre,** a hard sore with a small amount of yellow discharge. A chancre may be painful. The chancre is usually on the penis, anus, or rectum in men. It appears on the cervix and genital areas in women. It can also appear on the lips, tongue, tonsils, fingers, and mucous membranes. In this stage, the lymph glands may be swollen but not painful.

The second stage of syphilis appears 17 days to $6\frac{1}{2}$ months after infection, often as a rash that does not itch. A person has a feeling of discomfort, headache, aching bones, loss of appetite, and other symptoms.

During the third stage of syphilis, the symptoms disappear for many years. In about one-third of people with the disease, it progresses and affects the heart and brain.

Most people with syphilis become infected by sexual contact. Syphilis can also be passed from mother to baby through the placenta.

Figure 12.2.1 *Many states require that couples get tested for syphilis before they can get a marriage license.*

Many states require people to have a blood test for syphilis before they receive a marriage license. The test identifies people with the disease so that they can be treated with an antibiotic. Treatment also prevents the spread of infection to babies at birth.

What Is Genital Herpes?

Another sexually transmitted disease is **genital herpes.** It is a **chronic,** or lasting, disease. The main symptom of genital herpes is clusters of small, painful blisters in the genital area. The blisters break, heal, and then come back.

Genital herpes is spread by contact with someone who has it. Genital herpes can be spread even when blisters are not present. Avoiding contact with the pathogen that causes genital herpes can prevent this communicable disease. Contact can be avoided by abstaining from sex, including oral sex.

Genital herpes can cause other problems. Sometimes, repeated infections in females involve the cervix, which may lead to cancer of the cervix. Genital herpes can infect a baby passing through the birth canal, and can cause brain damage in the baby.

The disease has no cure. Medicines can control the symptoms of genital herpes. They speed up healing but do not get rid of the infection. Over time, the infections tend to be less severe, but genital herpes never goes away.

Why might periodic testing be necessary to be sure a person is free of sexually transmitted diseases?

What Are Genital Warts?

Genital warts are the result of an infection with human papilloma virus (HPV). These soft bumps appear in the genital area weeks or months after infection. They sometimes appear in clusters that resemble cauliflower. They can be raised or flat, small or large. About 5.5 million new cases of sexually transmitted HPV are reported every year. At least 20 million people in the United States are currently infected.

Genital warts are spread by skin-to-skin contact during sexual activity with an infected partner. There may be no symptoms of infection. People who are infected but have no symptoms can still spread the disease to a partner. Some types of HPV can cause cancer.

HPV has no cure. Further, there is no way to predict whether the warts will grow or disappear. They can be treated with medication, freezing, burning, or surgery. The only way to prevent an HPV infection is by avoiding direct contact with the virus.

What Help Is Available?

Except for genital herpes, genital warts, and AIDS, most sexually transmitted diseases can be cured when they are detected early. For diseases without a cure, medical treatment may make people more comfortable.

Many clinics concentrate on diagnosing and treating people who suspect they have a sexually transmitted disease. Health care workers know that the possibility of having a sexually transmitted disease can be difficult and embarrassing. They appreciate a person's strength and good judgment in seeking medical advice. They protect the identity of their patients.

You can get information about sexually transmitted diseases from doctors, local health departments, and family planning clinics. Also, the American Social Health Association (ASHA) gives free information. It also keeps lists of clinics and doctors who provide treatment for people with sexually transmitted diseases.

Genital warts

Bumps caused by a virus spread through sexual contact

Many people with sexually transmitted diseases have no symptoms. The only way a person can know for sure that he or she does not have a sexually transmitted disease is by being tested regularly.

?

Are you at risk for a sexually transmitted disease if you have only one sexual experience?

How Are Sexually Transmitted Diseases Prevented?

There are no vaccines that prevent sexually transmitted diseases. The body does not build up immunity to sexually transmitted diseases. Like all communicable diseases, they can be prevented by avoiding contact with the pathogens that cause them. The best prevention for sexually transmitted diseases is choosing abstinence from sexual activity. If two people are uninfected and have sexual activity only with their partners, they are not at risk for sexually transmitted diseases.

Decide for Yourself

There are ways to avoid a sexually transmitted disease. One is to be in a mutually faithful relationship with a partner who has been tested and found free of sexually transmitted diseases. The only sure way is to choose abstinence from sex.

There are many pressures on teens to have sex. Peer pressure can be strong. Teens may think that having sex will help them fit in and be popular. This pressure can make saying no hard. However, there is nothing cool about getting a sexually transmitted disease.

In addition to peer pressure, many messages in the media make casual sexual activity seem appealing. These messages are found in movies, TV shows, magazines, and advertisements. All of these show people having sex outside committed relationships. The problem is that these messages do not include the real danger of sexually transmitted diseases.

Here are some ways to say no to sexual activity:

1. Say no and repeat it as many times as needed to make your point.

2. Practice how to say no if someone pressures you. For example, if someone says "Everybody does it," respond with "I don't have to do what everyone else does."

3. If you get into a troublesome situation, walk away and stay away.

4. Stand tall, speak clearly, and look the other person in the eye. Your body language will express your choice.

On a sheet of paper, write the answers to the following questions. Use complete sentences.

1. What sometimes makes choosing abstinence hard?

2. Why should you practice saying no?

3. Why is using body language important to help express your choices?

Lesson 2 Review On a sheet of paper, write the word or phrase from the Word Bank that best completes each sentence.

1. Gonorrhea can lead to _____.

2. The symptoms for chlamydia are similar to the symptoms for _____.

3. The first stage of _____ is a chancre.

On a sheet of paper, write the answers to the following questions. Use complete sentences.

4. Critical Thinking What are some short-term problems that genital herpes causes?

5. Critical Thinking What are some long-term problems that genital herpes causes?

Health in Your Life

A Patient's Basic Rights

Everyone who wants medical treatment has certain basic rights. These include:

- You have the right to all information known about your illness or injury.

- You have the right to know about all the different treatment choices.

- Caregivers must have your informed consent to any treatment. This means that you understand what will happen before, during, and after the treatment.

- You have the right to privacy. This means that only caregivers who need to know about you will see your information.

- You have the right to be treated with dignity and respect.

- You have the right to use emergency services when needed.

- You have the right to refuse treatment.

On a sheet of paper, write the answers to the following questions. Use complete sentences.

1. Why is the right to privacy important?

2. Why is the right to use emergency services important to a person with no medical insurance?

3. How important would informed consent be to you if you were being treated in a hospital? Explain your answer.

- Acquired immunodeficiency syndrome (AIDS) is a disorder caused by the human immunodeficiency virus (HIV). HIV weakens the immune system.

- AIDS is spread through contact with certain body fluids, through sexual activity, by drug users sharing needles, and from mother to child.

- AIDS is not spread through casual social contact.

- The blood supply in the United States is safe because of a test for HIV. The test is used on all blood that is given for transfusions.

- Health care workers who are around body fluids and needles use preventive measures to protect themselves and patients.

- No cure is now available for AIDS. It can be prevented by avoiding contact with body fluids that may be infected with HIV.

- Any disease spread through sexual contact is a sexually transmitted disease.

- Gonorrhea has few symptoms. Antibiotics cure it, but untreated gonorrhea can lead to sterility.

- Chlamydia has symptoms and treatment similar to gonorrhea.

- Syphilis can progress in three stages if it is not treated. Antibiotics are used to treat syphilis.

- Genital herpes is chronic and has no cure.

- Genital warts are the result of an infection with human papilloma virus (HPV). HPV has no cure.

- People with sexually transmitted diseases can get treatment at clinics that protect their identity.

- All sexually transmitted diseases can be prevented by avoiding contact with the pathogen. The most reliable way to do this is by abstaining from sex, including oral sex.

Vocabulary

acquired immunodeficiency syndrome (AIDS), 270	genital warts, 278	pneumonia, 272
chancre, 276	gonorrhea, 275	sexually transmitted disease, 275
chlamydia, 276	human immunodeficiency virus (HIV), 270	sterility, 276
chronic, 277	Kaposi's sarcoma, 272	syphilis, 276
genital herpes, 277	opportunistic pathogen, 270	transfusion, 272

Chapter 12 REVIEW

Word Bank

AIDS

chancre

chlamydia

chronic

genital herpes

genital warts

human immunodeficiency virus (HIV)

Kaposi's sarcoma

opportunistic pathogens

pneumonia

sexually transmitted disease

sterility

syphilis

transfusion

Vocabulary Review

On a sheet of paper, write the word or phrase from the Word Bank that best completes each sentence.

1. The U.S. blood supply is tested for HIV, so a(n) _____ is safe.

2. AIDS is caused by _____.

3. When a person's immune system is weakened, it is open to _____, such as HIV.

4. Small bumps caused by a virus spread through sexual contact are _____.

5. A disorder of the immune system is _____.

6. Blisters that appear, break, heal and come back are symptoms of _____.

7. Two opportunistic infections that can appear as AIDS progresses are pneumonia and _____.

8. One in four people under age 21 in the United States has had a(n) _____.

9. Untreated gonorrhea can lead to _____, or the inability to have children.

10. A lung infection that often develops in AIDS patients is _____.

11. The sexually transmitted disease that progresses in three stages is _____.

12. Females with _____ have almost no symptoms.

13. Genital herpes is a(n) _____ infection because it never goes away.

14. The first symptom of syphilis is a(n) _____.

Concept Review

On a sheet of paper, write the letter of the answer that best completes each sentence.

15. A sexually transmitted disease that has no cure is

_____.

   A gonorrhea   **C** syphilis

   B chlamydia   **D** genital herpes

16. Before 1985, a person could get _____ from a blood transfusion.

   A gonorrhea   **C** genital herpes

   B AIDS   **D** syphilis

17. Babies can get a serious eye infection that is caused by

_____.

   A gonorrhea   **C** HIV

   B Kaposi's sarcoma   **D** pneumonia

Critical Thinking

On a sheet of paper, write the answers to the following questions. Use complete sentences.

18. Why are sexually transmitted diseases serious?

19. How do you think you could show caring and concern for a person infected with AIDS?

20. What would be the best way for you to avoid a sexually transmitted disease? Explain your answer.

Test-Taking Tip If you do not know the answer to a question, put a check mark beside it and go on. Then when you are finished, go back to any checked questions and try to answer them.

Self-Assessment

Can you answer these questions?

☑ 1. Why is it a good idea to be tested for high blood pressure?

☑ 2. How can you keep from getting diseases of the arteries?

☑ 3. What causes a heart attack?

☑ 4. What causes a stroke?

☑ 5. Which diseases are you more likely to get as you get older?

☑ 6. What are some risk factors and treatments for cancer?

☑ 7. How can you do a self-exam to check for cancer?

☑ 8. What are the symptoms of diabetes?

☑ 9. What causes epilepsy?

☑ 10. What are symptoms and treatments for asthma?

13 Recognizing Common Diseases

You can compare a healthy body to a musical band. Each system of your body is like an instrument that plays its own part. Each system is like part of the mix of music made by the band as a whole. Sometimes, though, a body system hits a "bad note." When a disease affects a body system, your body's "music" is interrupted. The disease can affect your body's overall health.

In this chapter, you will learn about heart and blood vessel diseases and why people get them. You will learn what causes cancer. You will discover the warning signs of this disease. You will also find out how cancer is treated. Finally, you will learn about diabetes, arthritis, epilepsy, and asthma, and how they are treated.

Goals for Learning

◆ To describe some cardiovascular diseases and what causes them

◆ To explain the causes, symptoms, warning signs, and treatments for cancer

◆ To explain the types of diabetes and treatment for the disease

◆ To describe arthritis, epilepsy, and asthma, as well as treatments for these diseases

Objectives

After reading this lesson, you should be able to

◆ explain what causes high blood pressure

◆ describe cardiovascular diseases and what might cause them

◆ discuss how a heart attack happens

◆ identify causes of a stroke

Cardiovascular

Relating to the heart and blood vessels

Arterial

Relating to the arteries

Hypertension

High blood pressure

Abnormality

A condition that is not usual

The group of diseases that affect your heart and blood vessels is called **cardiovascular** disease. More people die in the United States from these diseases than from anything else. Appendix C lists the numbers of deaths from cardiovascular disease. Some common cardiovascular diseases are high blood pressure and **arterial** diseases. Arterial diseases are diseases of the arteries. Arteries are blood vessels that carry blood from the heart.

You can decide to do things that will help prevent some of these diseases. These things include eating low-fat, low-sodium diets, exercising, and not smoking.

What Is High Blood Pressure?

Blood pressure is the force of your blood against your artery walls when your heart pumps. Blood pressure normally goes up when you exercise and down when you sleep or relax. If your blood pressure always remains too high, you have **hypertension,** or high blood pressure.

Artery walls become thicker if you have high blood pressure. If more pressure is in your arteries, your heart pumps harder than it normally does. If hypertension is not treated, it leads to other kinds of cardiovascular disease.

The exact cause of most hypertension is unknown. It can affect adults and children. For adults, stress, tobacco use, and a high-salt or high-fat diet raise the chances of having hypertension. Heredity also can affect high blood pressure. If one of your parents has high blood pressure, you might be likely to get it, too. For children, causes include kidney disease or an **abnormality** of blood vessels that the child is born with. An abnormality is an unusual condition.

Most people with hypertension do not know it. Its symptoms are not easy to see. The only way to find out if you have hypertension is to have your blood pressure checked by a health care professional.

High blood pressure cannot be cured. It can usually be controlled with medicine and diet. The medicine helps lower blood pressure. Eating a diet low in salt, sugar, cholesterol, and saturated fats can also help control blood pressure. Regular exercise is another measure that is good for lowering blood pressure.

What Are Some Diseases of the Arteries?

When you are born, the lining of your arteries is smooth. Over many years, fat can build up on artery walls. Usually, this happens because of foods you eat or heredity. Eventually, this fat buildup can harden like cement. This process is called **arteriosclerosis,** or hardening of the arteries. It is a chronic disease. This means it lasts for a long time. A chronic disease often causes major changes in your body. When your arteries harden, the arterial walls thicken and cannot move easily. When that happens, your blood cannot move around your body as it should.

Arteriosclerosis can cause many other diseases, including one called **atherosclerosis.** In atherosclerosis, your large and medium arteries get narrow because fat has built up along their walls. These narrowed arteries slow the flow of your blood to your heart. Your blood then gets too thick. You may get a blood clot. The fat deposits or a clot can block a blood vessel. If this happens, your heart does not get enough oxygen, or air. This is called a **heart attack.** Eating healthy foods can often prevent this buildup.

What Is a Heart Attack?

Like every muscle in your body, your heart muscle needs nutrients and oxygen. A heart attack occurs when the blood supply and nutrients to your heart are reduced or stopped. Suppose your blood supply is cut off for a life-threatening amount of time. Then muscle **tissues** get hurt and die. Tissue is body material made up of many cells. These cells are somewhat alike in what they are and what they do. How bad a heart attack is depends on how much tissue dies.

There are two kinds of cholesterol, LDL and HDL. LDL cholesterol is often called "bad" cholesterol. It can build up in your arteries and make a substance that leads to atherosclerosis. HDL cholesterol is often called "good" cholesterol. High levels of HDL cholesterol keep you from getting a heart attack by carrying cholesterol away from your arteries.

If a heart attack is mild, the heart can still function. Other arteries will do the work that the blocked arteries did. Scar tissue may form where the other tissue was hurt. Scar tissue does not move easily and does not contract when the heart contracts. That means the heart may never work again as well as it once did.

Machines can help people who have had a heart attack. For example, one machine can keep track of the sounds and electrical activity of the heart. Another machine can figure out how much the heart has been hurt.

Doctors can do **surgery** to open a blocked artery or make the blood go around it. During surgery, a doctor opens up a patient's body.

To replace a diseased heart, doctors can use the healthy heart of a person who has died and donated the heart. Sometimes artificial, or human-made, heart valves can take the place of diseased valves. A valve is the part of the heart that stops the return flow of blood. It does this by closing or folding.

Another option is to place a pacemaker next to the heart. A pacemaker is a small machine that makes the heart beat regularly.

There are other treatments besides these to help people who have had a heart attack. Medicine is one treatment. Changes in diet, exercise, and smoking are also part of the treatment.

Technology and Society

What if someone has a heart attack far away from a hospital? The heart attack victim may be saved by a portable defibrillator. This is a machine that can be carried or stored on airplanes, in places around the community, or in homes. Paddles or electrodes from the defibrillator are placed on the victim's chest. Small electronic shocks are sent to the heart. This helps get back a heartbeat rhythm. Then the blood can flow again.

Angina pectoris

Severe pain that happens when the heart does not receive enough blood

Stroke

A cardiovascular disease that happens when the blood supply to the brain is suddenly stopped

Health Myth

Myth: All people die soon after having a heart attack.

Fact: Many people live for many years after having a heart attack. Having a heart attack may make them change their diet and exercise plans and try to keep stress low.

What Is Angina Pectoris?

People with atherosclerosis may get **angina pectoris,** also called angina. It happens when not enough oxygen-rich blood reaches the heart. Often, painful angina happens before a heart attack.

You can have angina pain without actually having a heart attack. The pains, however, can seem like those of a heart attack. If you have angina, you can take medicine to get rid of the pain when it starts. You can also get rid of the pain by rest and relaxation. If you have angina, you may need to be less active at times. You also might need surgery to make your blood flow more easily.

What Is a Stroke?

A **stroke** happens when the blood supply to the brain is suddenly stopped. Arterial disease or a clot that is blocking an artery can stop the blood supply. High blood pressure may be one of the reasons a person has a stroke.

When the blood supply to your brain is stopped, some of your brain cells cannot work right. If these cells cannot get the blood and nutrients they need, they die. After a stroke, the part of your body that the dead brain cells controlled does not work any more. A stroke affects people differently. The effect depends on the part of your brain that is hurt. Some people notice almost no difference, while others may never be able to do certain things well again. It can take years to learn ways to make up for the damage that a stroke has caused.

Some new medicines can help lessen or do away with the effects of a stroke. A person must be treated within 6 hours of the stroke.

Link to ➤➤➤

Social Studies

A sphygmomanometer is a device used to check blood pressure. Early sphygmomanometers of the 1800s did not have a cuff. Later sphygmomanometers had cuffs, but the cuffs were too thin to be used to get a correct reading. Today's sphygmomanometers have a wide cuff that is placed around the middle of the upper arm. Health care professionals use the devices with a stethoscope to listen to how the blood is flowing.

Risk factor

A habit or trait known to increase the chances of getting a disease

Research and Write

Find and research the American Heart Association's Web site to learn more about heart disease. Make a poster that lists myths about heart disease. Explain why each one is a myth and what the truth is. Tell how people can guard against heart disease. Include drawings of a blocked artery and an artery that works properly.

What Are Some Cardiovascular Risk Factors?

A **risk factor** is a habit or trait known to increase your chances of getting a disease. Serious diseases, such as cardiovascular disease, have many risk factors. Some risk factors cannot be changed. Risk factors for cardiovascular problems that usually cannot be changed are:

- Family medical history—You may inherit the chance to have cardiovascular disease from your parents. You cannot change your genes. Knowing your family's medical history, however, can help you and your doctor figure out how high your risk is.

- Being male—Men have a greater risk of getting a heart attack before middle age than women do. After middle age, a woman's risk goes up.

- Aging—As you get older, the chance of having a heart attack is greater. More than half of all heart attacks happen to people who are age 65 or older.

- Race—Some races have a high risk of cardiovascular disease. For example, African Americans have an unusually high rate of hypertension.

How Can Cardiovascular Problems Be Prevented?

You can change the following risk factors to lessen your chances of having cardiovascular problems:

- Smoking—A person can lower the risk for cardiovascular problems by choosing not to smoke. Smoking can lead to hypertension and other cardiovascular diseases. A smoker is twice as likely to have a heart attack as a nonsmoker is. Death from a heart attack is also twice as likely for a smoker as for a nonsmoker. When a person quits smoking, his or her risk of cardiovascular disease quickly lessens.

Link to ➤➤➤

Math

Do you want to check your pulse? Use the tips of your first two fingers on one hand. Do not use your thumb because it has a pulse of its own. Place your fingertips on the inside of the wrist on your other hand. Press lightly. Count the number of beats for 10 seconds. Multiply by 6. The answer is your heart rate. Ask your health care professional to help you figure out your target exercising heart rate.

Word Bank

angina pectoris
arteriosclerosis
stroke

- High cholesterol—High blood cholesterol is another major risk factor for cardiovascular problems. Eating less saturated fats helps lower blood cholesterol levels. That means you should eat small amounts of animal fat, such as eggs, butter, and meat. You should exercise regularly, especially if cardiovascular disease runs in your family.

- Being overweight—Too much weight strains the heart and adds to cardiovascular problems. Also, it can raise blood cholesterol levels and blood pressure. Planning a balanced diet helps you keep to a healthy weight.

- Physical inactivity—Being inactive can make handling a sudden change in your blood pressure hard. Physical activity helps you handle these changes. Aerobic activities such as walking, running, swimming, or bicycling for 20 minutes every day can help. These activities help raise blood flow to your heart and strengthen it. Physical activity can also reduce mental stress, which may add to cardiovascular problems.

Lesson 1 Review On a sheet of paper, write the word or phrase from the Word Bank that best completes each sentence.

1. The terrible pain that comes with a short supply of blood to the heart is _____.

2. A cardiovascular disease that happens when the blood supply to the brain is stopped is a(n) _____.

3. Hardening of the arteries because of fat buildup is _____.

On a sheet of paper, write the answers to the following questions. Use complete sentences.

4. **Critical Thinking** Imagine you are a doctor. A young adult has come to you for medical advice. Both of the young adult's parents have hypertension. What would you tell the young adult?

5. **Critical Thinking** Write descriptions of the backgrounds and lifestyles of two people, one person who is at high risk for heart disease and one person who is at low risk for heart disease. Tell whose lifestyle is more like yours.

Tumor

A mass of tissue made from the abnormal growth of cells

Malignant

Harmful to health

Benign

Not harmful to health

Cancer is the second leading cause of death in the United States. For this reason, it can seem frightening to many people. Knowing about the causes and risk factors for cancer can help reduce people's fears.

What Causes Cancer?

An abnormal and harmful growth of cells in your body causes cancer. There are more than 100 different types of cancers. Some cancers are more harmful than others.

Cancer cells grow in your body in a wilder and more uncontrolled way than normal cells do. Cancer may invade normal tissues. This means the cancer gets in and spreads to other parts of your body. When cancer takes over normal tissues, those organs cannot work properly. Sometimes, the abnormal growth of cells forms a mass, or pile, of tissue called a **tumor.**

If the cells keep growing, the tumor is **malignant.** This means it is harmful to your health. When cancer gets in normal tissues and spreads to other organs, it becomes more harmful. Some tumors are not malignant. They are **benign.** They do not spread and are not harmful to your health. More than 90 percent of tumors are benign. For example, some tumors in the breast are benign. They are actually collections of cells filled with liquid. They are not cancerous and are usually harmless.

Where Does Cancer Develop?

Cancer can develop in any tissue of your body. It usually develops in some areas more than others. Table C.4 in Appendix C shows the most common places where people get cancer.

Once you get cancer, it can spread to other parts of your body. It can even spread to places in your body that are far from the original tumor. Cells from a malignant tumor can break away. They can get into your bloodstream.

These loose cancer cells reach other places in your body. There, they can grow into more tumors. Some cancers do not travel through your bloodstream. Instead, they spread by attaching themselves to nearby organs and getting inside them.

What Are the Symptoms of Cancer?

The symptoms of cancer depend on where it is in the body. For example, a person with lung cancer may have a cough that does not get better with treatment. A person with breast cancer may feel a lump in the breast. If the cancer has spread to the bones, a person may have back pain.

If cancer has moved into your blood, it may cause unusual bleeding. Cancer may attack blood. It may attack tissues that produce **lymph.** Lymph is a colorless liquid that feeds tissues. When your blood and lymph tissues are attacked, your immune system does not work properly. Then you can get other infections.

Not all symptoms for a particular cancer are easy to recognize. You may feel somewhat sick but may not have specific symptoms. Too much of a weight loss too quickly and a poor appetite may be possible symptoms of cancer.

Sometimes, changes in skin and in the way your body works can be warning signs of cancer. For example, blood in your feces may be a sign of cancer in the intestines. If the cancer grows, it may cause a change in your bowel habits.

The Seven Warning Signs of Cancer

C hange in bowel or bladder habits

A sore that will not heal

U nusual bleeding or discharge

T hickening or lump in the breast or elsewhere

I ndigestion or a hard time swallowing

O bvious change in a wart or mole

N agging cough or hoarseness

What Are the Warning Signs of Cancer?

Usually, cancer gives warning signs that can help in detecting the disease early. Read about the seven early warning signs in the box on the left. One sign, or a combination of signs, means there might be cancer.

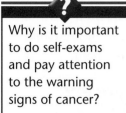

?

Why is it important to do self-exams and pay attention to the warning signs of cancer?

Finding cancer early is the most important thing for long-term survival. Talking about warning signs with a health care professional means you are more likely to be cured.

How Can You Do Self-Exams for Warning Signs of Cancer?

You can examine yourself for changes that may be early warning signs of cancer.

Females: Doing a Breast Self-Exam

Females should do a self-examination after each menstrual period, or once a month for older women. Breasts should be examined in front of a mirror, in the shower, or lying down. Females can stand in front of a mirror and look for any unusual shapes, dips, or lumps in the breasts.

For a breast exam in the shower or lying down, females can use the left hand to examine the right breast. They can then use the right hand to examine the left breast. The pads of the first three fingers should be used. Each breast is checked in a widening circle around the nipple until the entire breast is covered. Areas to check are the nipple, beneath the nipple, and the area between the armpit and breast. Look for unusual changes.

Males: Doing a Testes Self-Exam

Cancer of the testes is one of the most common cancers in males 20 to 35 years of age. Most testicular cancers are first found during self-examination. Males should do a self-examination of their testicles once a month. The best time for self-examination of the testes is immediately after a bath or shower. Gently roll each testicle between thumb and fingers, looking for any abnormal lumps.

Health Myth
Myth: Only women get breast cancer.
Fact: Men can also get breast cancer—though fewer men than women get the disease. Men have breast tissue and small amounts of the hormones women have. Men are more likely to die from breast cancer than women are. This is because men often do not consider or treat symptoms.

How Is Cancer Treated?

Now more than ever before, scientists are finding cures for cancer. For example, **Hodgkin's disease** is a lymph gland cancer that often affects young adults. With treatment, up to 90 percent of people with Hodgkin's disease can be cured.

There are as many treatments for cancer as there are types of cancers. Usually, one or more of three treatments is used to treat cancer. One common treatment for many kinds of cancers involves taking drugs that kill the cancer cells. This kind of treatment is called **chemotherapy.** Each kind of cancer may need a different type of drug.

A second kind of treatment is surgery to remove the abnormal growth of cells. The third kind of treatment for cancer is **radiation.** This involves sending energy in the form of waves. Radiation destroys cancerous tissue.

Often, cancer treatments give people side effects that make them very sick. For example, a person receiving chemotherapy may get an upset stomach. Even so, these treatments allow many people to survive cancer.

What Are the Risk Factors for Cancer?

Risk factors may cause cancer. If you know what the risk factors are, you can work to stay away from them.

- Cigarette and cigar smoke—Materials that cause cancer are called **carcinogens.** Carcinogens that cause the greatest number of deaths in America are found in cigarette and cigar smoke. As a result, smokers have a much higher risk for cancer than nonsmokers do. However, even nonsmokers can develop cancer from secondhand smoke.

- **Toxic** chemicals—Toxic chemicals are materials that are harmful to people or to the environment. Many chemicals used in industry, on farms, and in homes have been identified as toxic and are carcinogens.

- Radiation—While radiation is used to treat cancer, too much radiation can cause it. It is important to get X-rays only when you need them.

- Sunlight—Sunlight is a source of natural radiation that can cause skin cancer. For example, people who sunbathe or use tanning booths are a target of harmful radiation. That gives them a high risk for malignant melanoma, the most common form of skin cancer. See Appendix C.

- Heredity—The same genes that control heredity also control the growth and work of cells. Many people have cancers that run in their families. For example, daughters of women who have breast cancer have a higher risk of getting breast cancer.

- Viruses—Viruses can cause cancer in almost every living creature. A virus can get its genes into human chromosomes. This causes a **mutation,** or change, that leads to cancer. No cancer caused by a virus, however, can spread from person to person. Also, not everyone is open to cancers caused by viruses. Some people have a weakened immune system from AIDS, which is caused by HIV. Their systems are more open to cancer.

How Can You Avoid the Risk Factors for Cancer?

You can prevent many forms of cancer. You can stay away from the things and behaviors that are known to cause it. For example, keep away from cigarette smoke. Apply sunscreen before you go outdoors to help protect your skin. Use protective clothing such as long-sleeved shirts, wide-brimmed hats, and sunglasses. Try to stay away from toxic chemicals and X rays. If you have an inherited tendency to get certain kinds of cancer, see your doctor regularly.

Research and Write

Research hospital Web sites for disease prevention strategies. Learn how to prevent high blood pressure. Learn about pap smears and colorectal exams. Make a brochure to tell people about the importance of these preventive steps. Explain the age at which people should begin taking each step. Tell how often each step should be done.

Lesson 2 Review On a sheet of paper, write the answers to the following questions. Use complete sentences.

1. What is the difference between a malignant tumor and a benign tumor?

2. What are the seven warning signs of cancer?

3. What are the three types of treatments for cancer?

4. **Critical Thinking** Which patient would be more likely to get Hodgkin's disease—a 20-year-old or a 40-year-old. Why?

5. **Critical Thinking** What would you tell people in a presentation about how to avoid risk factors for cancer? How would you present the information?

Health in Your Life

Environmental Carcinogens

Things in the environment that can cause cancer are called environmental carcinogens. Scientists figure out whether something in the environment causes cancer by working in labs and doing studies.

One environmental carcinogen is secondhand smoke. It contains thousands of dangerous chemicals.

Asbestos is another known carcinogen. It was once used as insulation, a way to keep buildings warm or cool. Asbestos should immediately be removed by a professional if it is found in your home or school.

Mercury is another environmental carcinogen. Mercury is found in some kinds of fish from certain locations.

You can learn about many environmental carcinogens by checking the American Cancer Society (ACS) Web site.

You can also do more research in books and articles.

On a sheet of paper, write the answers to the following questions. Use complete sentences.

1. Before scientists studied the effects of smoking, there were many more smokers. Why do you think this is true?

2. Why do you think modern society has so many environmental carcinogens?

3. How do you think pollution affects the amount of carcinogens in food sources such as fish?

Objectives

After reading this lesson, you should be able to

◆ explain type I and type II diabetes

◆ recognize symptoms of diabetes

◆ discuss treatment for diabetes

Diabetes

A disease caused by lack of insulin in the body or when the body cannot use insulin effectively

Type I diabetes

A condition in which insulin is needed to stay alive

Coma

A condition in which a person loses consciousness

Diabetes is a chronic disease. It comes from not having enough insulin in your body. As you learned in Chapter 5, insulin is a hormone made in your pancreas. You can also get diabetes if your body is not using insulin properly. Insulin is important for growth because it is needed for the storage and release of energy.

Your digestive system turns carbohydrates into glucose. With the help of insulin, your body's cells use glucose for the energy they need. Without insulin, the cells cannot use the glucose. Then the sugar you eat stays in your bloodstream.

As diabetes gets worse, it makes changes in the blood vessels. Because of these changes, people with diabetes may lose their eyesight. Diabetes may hurt their kidneys and cause cardiovascular disease. It can also cause strokes or lessen the movement of the blood into the hands and feet. The two most common types of diabetes are type I and type II.

What Is Type I Diabetes?

Type I diabetes is also known as insulin-dependent diabetes. You have to take insulin to stay alive. This kind of diabetes usually starts in childhood. Your body may not be able to use glucose. This problem gives you high levels of glucose in your blood. When your high blood glucose level is not controlled, it can lead to a diabetic **coma.** When this happens, you pass out, or lose consciousness. A person who goes into a diabetic coma must be treated at once.

People with type I diabetes seem to have a defect in their immune system. Their immune systems kill the cells of the pancreas, which makes insulin. Type I diabetes symptoms include frequent urination and extreme thirst. Other symptoms are rapid weight loss, fatigue, and extreme hunger.

What Is Type II Diabetes?

Type II diabetes is also called noninsulin-dependent diabetes. It usually happens in adulthood after the age of 40. This is the most common type of diabetes. In type II diabetes, your pancreas makes insulin, but your body cells cannot use it right. Type II diabetes is milder than type I diabetes is. Type II diabetes has been linked to heredity, lack of activity, and **obesity,** or being very overweight.

Often, if you have type II diabetes, you do not know that your blood glucose level is high. Your symptoms may be blurry vision, slow-healing sores, and sleepiness. You may also have a tingling feeling in your hands or feet.

How Do You Know If You Have Diabetes?

There are two ways to check for diabetes. During a regular medical checkup, your health care professional can test your blood for glucose. If your blood glucose level is high, you may have diabetes. Your health care professional can also check your urine for glucose to test for diabetes. Normally, urine does not contain glucose.

What Is the Treatment for Diabetes?

If you have diabetes, you may get treated with insulin. You learn to measure the proper amount and give yourself insulin.

Some people with diabetes do not need to take insulin. A change in diet may keep their blood glucose at a safe level. For people who are obese, weight loss and exercise may treat the diabetes.

An important part of treatment for diabetes is learning which foods are safe to eat. If you have diabetes, foods with a lot of sugar can make your glucose level too high. If you have diabetes, you also must eat regularly, especially after taking insulin. You may need to eat nutritious snacks throughout the day. Insulin makes your blood sugar level go down. If you have an empty stomach, a shot of insulin could be dangerous.

Figure 13.3.1 *This teenager is using a glucose meter to check blood glucose levels.*

It could give you very low levels of glucose. The sugar that is found in orange juice or hard candy can quickly return your blood glucose level to normal.

The American Diabetes Association lists these as risk factors:

- being overweight or obese

- getting little or no exercise during the day

- being age 45 or older

- being a woman who has had a baby weighing more than 9 pounds at birth

- having a sister, brother, or parent with diabetes

If you have two or more of these risk factors, you are more likely to develop diabetes than the average person.

Decide for Yourself

Your friend has just learned that he has diabetes. His doctor has told him to test his blood during the day at school. He takes blood from his fingertip. Then he uses a small machine to tell if his glucose level is safe. He also has to eat a controlled diet.

Your friend has told you he is too embarrassed to test his blood at school. He does not want anyone to know he has diabetes. He does not plan to stop eating sugary foods. He says he has always loved these foods. He tells you that everyone will know something is wrong with him if he no longer eats them. He has begged you not to say anything to anyone. He thinks he will outgrow the problem.

On a sheet of paper, write the answers to the following questions. Use complete sentences.

1. Do you think your friend is right about outgrowing diabetes? Explain your answer.

2. What could you tell your friend to help him feel more comfortable about having diabetes? How could you help him deal with the things he must do?

3. Should you tell someone about your friend's problem? Explain your answer.

Lesson 3 Review On a sheet of paper, write the letter of the answer that best completes each sentence.

1. Diabetes comes from too little _____ or from the body not being able to use it.
   A urine
   B insulin
   C oxygen
   D fat

2. If a person with diabetes does not control the blood glucose level, the person might experience a(n) _____.
   A heart attack
   B asthma attack
   C seizure
   D coma

3. All of these are symptoms of type I diabetes EXCEPT _____.
   A lack of thirst
   B extreme hunger
   C fatigue
   D rapid weight loss

On a sheet of paper, write the answers to the following questions. Use complete sentences.

4. **Critical Thinking** A patient goes to a health care professional with a number of symptoms. These include sleepiness, tingling in the feet, blurred vision, and a sore that will not heal. Do you think this patient has type I or type II diabetes? What treatment do you think the health care professional will recommend? Explain your answer.

5. **Critical Thinking** Could a person with diabetes be on a swim team or play another team sport? Explain your answer.

Objectives

After reading this lesson, you should be able to

◆ discuss arthritis and its treatment

◆ understand epilepsy and its treatment

◆ recognize what to do when someone has a seizure

◆ discuss symptoms of asthma and how it is treated

Arthritis

A group of diseases that causes swelling of the joints

Rheumatoid arthritis

A condition in which the joints swell badly and become stiff and weak

Osteoarthritis

A condition in which the cartilage in the joints wears away

Cartilage

A cushion, or padding, in the joints

You have read about diabetes, which is a chronic disease. Most chronic diseases have no cure. With medical care, however, a chronic disease can be controlled. This lesson tells about three common chronic diseases.

What Is Arthritis and How Is It Treated?

Arthritis is a group of very painful diseases. They can cause your joints to swell and rub on the bones around them. Sometimes, your joints will not work if you have arthritis. There are two main types of arthritis. Together, they affect about 40 million Americans.

The first and most serious type of arthritis is **rheumatoid arthritis.** It is a harmful inflammation, or swelling, of your joints. In rheumatoid arthritis, your joints become stiff, swollen, and tender. If you have this disease, you may not be able to move your joints. You may feel weak and tired. Rheumatoid arthritis can include other tissues in your body and may cause them to be deformed, or misshapen. Usually, the treatment for rheumatoid arthritis includes drugs that help with the inflammation and pain.

The second and most common type of arthritis is **osteoarthritis.** In this kind of arthritis, the **cartilage,** or cushioning in your joints, wears away. When this happens, your bones rub against one another. This wear can change the makeup and shape of your joints. It can make your joints ache and feel sore. It can also make moving them hard. The same drugs that are used to treat rheumatoid arthritis have been used to treat osteoarthritis. New studies have shown that these drugs may cause problems. They may affect your body's natural way of fighting osteoarthritis.

When arthritis badly harms your joints, you may be able to have a joint replacement. This surgery gives you an artificial joint in place of the old one. Artificial joints work just like your body's own joints.

What Is Epilepsy and How Is It Treated?

Epilepsy is a chronic disease that affects 2.5 million Americans. It is caused by disordered brain activity. This is brain activity that sometimes gets mixed up. **Seizures** are usually a part of epilepsy. A seizure is a physical reaction to the mixed-up brain activity. There are two main kinds of epileptic seizures.

The most common kind of seizure is a **grand mal seizure.** If you have a grand mal seizure, you usually pass out and fall down. Your muscles get stiff, and your body shakes uncontrollably. During a grand mal seizure, you may lose control of your bladder and urinate. A grand mal seizure usually lasts about 2 to 5 minutes. Afterward, you may act strangely or be sleepy for a while. Often you do not remember the seizure.

The other kind of seizure is a **petit mal seizure.** If you have a petit mal seizure, you do not pass out. You may simply stare at something for a moment. You might drop something or act confused. A petit mal seizure lasts less than 30 seconds. Others nearby may not notice anything different. Only your own thinking is affected during a petit mal seizure.

Not all seizures are from epilepsy. A person is said to have epilepsy only after having two seizures without knowing why. While seizures may have many other causes, the cause of most seizures is not known.

The right medical care and prescribed medicine can help control seizures from epilepsy. In all other ways, a person with epilepsy can live a normal, active life.

Why is knowing what to do important when someone is having a seizure?

If someone has a seizure, follow these guidelines:

- Move nearby objects to protect the person.

- Loosen clothing such as buttoned collars or scarves around the person's neck.

- Place a cushion under the person's head.

- Turn the person's head to the side.

  - Do not put an object in the person's mouth.

  - Call for help if the seizure lasts more than 5 minutes.

What Is Asthma and How Is It Treated?

Asthma is a disease that makes breathing difficult. It is a respiratory, or breathing, disease. Many things cause asthma to act up. One cause is allergies. These may be allergies to mold, pollen (powdery material from plants), animal fur, or dust. Asthma affects some people during some seasons of the year more than other seasons. Strong feelings about something may also start an asthma attack.

Figure 13.4.1 *Allergies can cause you to sneeze and can cause an asthma attack.*

During an asthma attack, you may cough, wheeze, and be short of breath. Wheezing is a whistling-type sound that happens when breathing is hard. The linings of your bronchioles may make a great deal of mucus. Then the bronchioles tighten, and you have a hard time breathing. You may get scared about not being able to breathe and become even more stressed. People with asthma may have an attack as often as once every few hours or as rarely as once every few years.

Health Myth

Myth: People who have asthma should not exercise.

Fact: Exercise can be good for people who have asthma. Exercise helps them stay in good shape. Health care professionals tell patients with asthma to take their medicine before they exercise. Then it is safe for them to exercise.

You can get asthma at any age, but this disease often affects children. More than 20.3 million Americans have asthma, and about 6.1 million of those are under age 18. The overall number of people who have asthma is getting higher.

Many different medicines are used to treat asthma. Usually, you would breathe asthma medicine directly into your air passages. The medicine can quickly relieve your breathing problem. Sometimes stronger medicines are needed. Without treatment, asthma can be life threatening.

Health at Work

Ultrasound Technician

Using an ultrasound exam is a common way to find disease. An ultrasound technician performs an ultrasound exam. Sound waves are sent into the body. They bounce off body tissues and organs. This creates echoes. The echoes create a picture that shows if the tissues and organs are normal or abnormal. An ultrasound can help find many kinds of problems. These include problems related to heart disease, stroke, and cancer.

An ultrasound technician is trained to use ultrasound equipment and perform ultrasound exams. The technician makes and records the information from ultrasound exams. Then the information is given to a doctor. The technician does not tell patients what has been discovered in exams.

Usually, an ultrasound technician must complete a training program that lasts from 2 to 4 years.

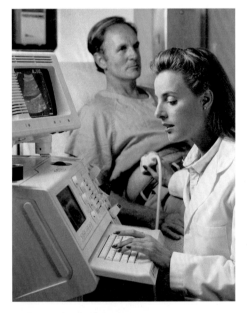

This training may be given through a college or a specialty school. Some hospitals or other health care clinics require that students get a special certification or license.

Use these search terms to find Internet sites with information about chronic diseases: "National Institutes of Health," "American Diabetes Association," "National Heart, Lung, and Blood Institute," "Arthritis Foundation," "Epilepsy Foundation," and "Asthma and Allergy Foundation of America."

Lesson 4 Review On a sheet of paper, write the word in parentheses that best completes each sentence.

1. Arthritis is a disease that swells the (blood vessels, joints, bronchioles) and may change how well they work.

2. An allergy to mold, pollen, animal fur, or dust can trigger an (asthma, epilepsy, osteoarthritis) attack.

3. The body has (bone, cartilage, muscle), which serves as a cushion in joints.

On a sheet of paper, write the answers to the following questions. Use complete sentences.

4. **Critical Thinking** One of your friends had an asthma attack for the first time last week. Now she is afraid she will have one every week. What can you tell her about the likelihood of having an asthma attack every week?

5. **Critical Thinking** A student just had a seizure and has passed out. Can you be sure this student has epilepsy? Explain your answer. Describe the two types of seizures in your explanation.

- Cardiovascular disease affects the heart and blood vessels. It is the leading cause of death in the United States.

- Hypertension, or high blood pressure, happens when your blood pressure regularly stays too high.

- Heart attacks happen when narrowed blood vessels do not send enough oxygen and nutrients to the heart.

- A stroke happens when the blood supply to the brain is cut off. Some brain cells may die. This affects the work of the part of the body these brain cells control.

- An abnormal, harmful growth of cells causes cancer and usually forms a tumor. Some tumors are malignant, or harmful. Others are benign, or not harmful.

- Cancer's symptoms depend on the body part that is involved. Most treatment involves chemotherapy, surgery, or radiation. Some risk factors for cancer can be avoided.

- In type I diabetes, a person depends on insulin to stay alive. In type II diabetes, the pancreas makes insulin, but the body cells cannot use it the proper way.

- Rheumatoid arthritis is a painful swelling of the joints. In osteoarthritis, cartilage wears away, causing the bones to rub against one another.

- Epilepsy comes from disordered, or mixed-up, brain activity. It often gives people seizures.

- Asthma makes breathing difficult. An allergy usually triggers an asthma attack, which can be controlled with medicine.

Vocabulary

abnormality, 286	coma, 298	petit mal seizure, 303
angina pectoris, 289	diabetes, 298	radiation, 295
arterial, 286	epilepsy, 303	rheumatoid arthritis, 302
arteriosclerosis, 287	grand mal seizure, 303	risk factor, 290
arthritis, 302	heart attack, 287	seizure, 303
asthma, 304	Hodgkin's disease, 295	stroke, 289
atherosclerosis, 287	hypertension, 286	surgery, 288
benign, 292	lymph, 293	tissue, 287
carcinogen, 295	malignant, 292	toxic, 295
cardiovascular, 286	mutation, 296	tumor, 292
cartilage, 302	obesity, 299	type I diabetes, 298
chemotherapy, 295	osteoarthritis, 302	type II diabetes, 299

Chapter 13 R E V I E W

Word Bank

arteriosclerosis

asthma

cartilage

chemotherapy

grand mal seizure

heart attack

hypertension

lymph

malignant

mutation

rheumatoid
  arthritis

stroke

tumors

type I diabetes

Vocabulary Review

On a sheet of paper, write the word or phrase from the Word Bank that best completes each sentence.

1. High blood pressure, or _____, happens when the heart pumps blood too hard.

2. The condition of hardening of the arteries is _____.

3. A _____ comes from a short supply of oxygen and nutrients to the heart.

4. When the supply of blood to the brain is cut off, a person could have a(n) _____.

5. An abnormal growth of cells that is harmful is a(n) _____ tumor.

6. A colorless liquid that feeds cells is _____.

7. A treatment that kills cancer cells is _____.

8. Abnormal cell growth can produce _____.

9. The kind of diabetes for which insulin is needed to stay alive is _____.

10. A virus can invade chromosomes and cause a(n) _____ that leads to cancer.

11. A painful swelling of the joints is _____.

12. A(n) _____ makes a person with epilepsy pass out.

13. An allergy to mold, pollen, animal fur, or dust may trigger a(n) _____ attack.

14. A cushion in the joints is _____.

Concept Review

On a sheet of paper, write the letter of the answer that best completes each sentence.

15. A risk factor for cardiovascular disease that CANNOT be controlled is _____.

    A weight   **C** smoking

    B heredity   **D** physical inactivity

16. Materials that cause cancer are called _____.

    A carcinogens   **C** mutations

    B viruses   **D** seizures

17. All of these words describe a mass of body tissue EXCEPT _____.

    A tumor   **C** artificial

    B benign   **D** malignant

Critical Thinking

On a sheet of paper, write the answers to the following questions. Use complete sentences.

18. Why is getting help as quickly as possible important for someone who has had a stroke?

19. What did you learn about how diet affects your health as you read this chapter? What surprised you the most about this?

20. How important do you think it is to know your family's medical history? Explain your answer.

Test-Taking Tip   Look for words in each question that tell you the correct form for the answer you should give. For example, some questions may ask for a *paragraph.* Others may ask for a *sentence,* and still others may ask for a *list.*

The Need for Vaccinations

In 2003, only 56 cases of measles were reported in the United States. Most of these people with measles had lived or traveled outside the United States. In 2003, about 30 million people got the measles in countries around the world. About 530,000 of these people died. Every year, tetanus kills 300,000 newborn babies. Pertussis, or whooping cough, kills nearly 300,000 people. All it takes to prevent these deadly infectious diseases are vaccinations. Why, then, do so many people get these diseases?

Many people in countries in Asia, Africa, Latin America, and islands near Australia do not get vaccinations because they lack the money. Another reason is that many areas do not have health services. There is no one to deliver and give the vaccinations. In some countries, the government does not think vaccinations are important.

However, this is slowly changing. Many groups around the world have joined together to deliver vaccinations to countries that cannot afford them. Their efforts are starting to work. In 1988, for example, 350,000 children were paralyzed with polio worldwide. In 2004, only about 1,200 people got the disease. From 1999 to 2003, the number of deaths from measles in Africa decreased by half.

The fight against polio and other infectious diseases shows what can happen when people work together. Smallpox, a deadly viral disease, was declared "wiped out" in 1980 because of vaccinations. One day, perhaps we can say the same for other diseases that vaccinations can prevent.

On a sheet of paper, write the answers to the following questions. Use complete sentences.

1. What must a country have in order to provide vaccinations for a large number of people?

2. Use the Internet or print resources to find more information about vaccinations around the world. What are three organizations that help people get vaccinations?

3. What are some ways to show that vaccinations have been effective in a country?

Unit 4 SUMMARY

- Diseases can be acquired or inherited.

- Pathogens are the germs that cause infectious diseases.

- If the body's immune system can fight off a pathogen, a person may never become ill. If the body's immune system cannot fight off a pathogen, a person becomes ill. The immune system continues to fight the illness, and a person usually recovers.

- The immune system fights pathogens by producing antibodies.

- A person may get an inherited disease through a single abnormal gene, a combination of many abnormal genes and environment, or an abnormal chromosome.

- Acquired immunodeficiency syndrome (AIDS) is a disorder caused by the human immunodeficiency virus (HIV). HIV weakens the immune system, leaving it open to other opportunistic pathogens.

- AIDS is spread through contact with certain body fluids, through sexual activity, by drug users sharing needles, and from mother to child.

- AIDS is not spread through casual social contact.

- Health care workers who are around body fluids and needles use measures to protect themselves and patients.

- No cure is now available for AIDS. It can be prevented by avoiding contact with body fluids that may be infected with HIV.

- All sexually transmitted diseases can be prevented by avoiding contact with the pathogen. The most reliable way to do this is by abstaining from sex.

- Cardiovascular disease affects the heart and blood vessels. It is a leading cause of death in the United States.

- Heart attacks happen when narrowed arteries do not send enough oxygen and nutrients to the heart.

- A stroke happens when the blood supply to the brain is cut off. Some brain cells may die. This affects the work of the part of the body these brain cells control.

- An abnormal, harmful growth of cells forms a tumor. Some tumors are malignant and others are benign.

- Cancer can affect any body part. Its symptoms depend on which part is involved. Most treatment involves chemotherapy, surgery, or radiation.

- In type I diabetes, a person depends on insulin to stay alive. In type II diabetes, the pancreas makes insulin, but the body cells cannot use it the proper way.

- Asthma makes breathing difficult. An allergy usually causes asthma, which can be controlled with medicine.

Vocabulary Review

On a sheet of paper, write the word or phrase from the Word Bank that best completes each sentence.

Word Bank

antibiotic

asthma

cardiovascular

chronic

diabetes

gonorrhea

heart attack

human immunodeficiency virus (HIV)

immune system

incubation period

pathogens

pneumonia

1. Bacteria, fungi, and viruses are all _____.

2. People who have AIDS often get _____, a lung infection.

3. A blocked blood vessel can lead to a(n) _____.

4. A symptom for males infected with _____ is a white discharge from the urethra.

5. A(n) _____ attack may be triggered by allergies.

6. The defenses that fight pathogens make up the body's _____.

7. Diseases that affect the heart and blood vessels are _____ diseases.

8. The chronic disease that comes from not having enough insulin in your body is _____.

9. During the _____, a person is infected but symptoms of the disease have not appeared yet.

10. Another term for "lasts a long time" is _____.

11. Drug users who share needles risk getting _____.

12. A substance that can destroy the growth of certain germs is a(n) _____.

Concept Review

On a sheet of paper, write the letter of the answer that best completes each sentence.

13. The human body's response to tissue damage is _____.

    A placenta   C type I diabetes
    B inflammation   D influenza

14. HIV often is transmitted from one person to another through _____.

A saliva   **C** blood

B urine   **D** sweat

15. The best prevention for sexually transmitted diseases is _____.

A having proper hygiene

B getting tested often

C eating a nutritious diet

D choosing abstinence from sexual activity

16. The cancer treatment that uses waves of energy to destroy cancerous tissue is _____.

A radiation   **C** angina pectoris

B obesity   **D** hypertension

Critical Thinking

On a sheet of paper, write the answers to the following questions. Use complete sentences.

17. In hospitals, there are places where patients with infectious diseases are not allowed to go. Why do hospitals have rules such as this?

18. In the early 1900s, thousands of people in the United States had the disease polio. Thanks to a vaccine, polio is extremely rare in the United States today. Why do you think the polio vaccine worked? Explain your answer.

19. About 25 million people in Africa were living with HIV at the end of 2004. How does fighting a disease on one continent help improve the lives of people who live on other continents?

20. Why is it important for people to understand epilepsy and be alert if one of their family members has epilepsy? Explain your answer.

Use and Misuse of Substances

Over-the-counter medicines and medicines given by doctors can help us fight and prevent illnesses. People should learn how to use their medicines wisely and safely. In this unit, you will discover details about drugs that help people. You will also learn about drugs that cause harm. It is important to learn the facts about different types of drugs. Then you can make wise decisions about how you will use them.

What do you think of when you hear the term *drug use*? Most people think only of illegal drugs. However, alcohol and nicotine in tobacco are also drugs—drugs that are legal for adults. You may be surprised to learn that legal drugs cause more deaths than illegal drugs cause.

Self-Assessment

Can you answer these questions?

☑ 1. What is a drug?

☑ 2. When is a drug thought of as medicine?

☑ 3. What are three purposes of medicine?

☑ 4. What are three ways medicine affects your body?

☑ 5. How does tobacco affect your body?

☑ 6. How does alcohol affect your body?

☑ 7. What are psychoactive drugs?

☑ 8. What effect do psychoactive drugs have on your body?

☑ 9. How does marijuana affect your body?

☑ 10. Why are anabolic steroids dangerous?

Chapter

14

Recognizing Medicines and Drugs

Have you ever played a word-association game? Someone says a word, and then you say the first word that comes to your mind. Each person might respond differently to the same word. For example, when you hear the word *drugs,* you might say "medicines." Someone else might say "illegal." Whether a drug is a medicine or an illegal substance, using it involves taking chances with your health. To keep from taking these chances, it is important to know whether a drug is safe. You must know how it can affect your mind and body.

In this chapter, you will learn about drugs that can help keep you from getting sick and drugs that may keep you healthy. You will learn about the harmful drug effects of tobacco and alcohol. You also will learn about the harmful effects of drugs that are illegal.

Goals for Learning

◆ To explain the types and purposes of medicines

◆ To describe how medicines are taken and possible problems with them

◆ To identify some cautions to follow when taking medicines

◆ To describe the effects of using tobacco and alcohol

◆ To explain the effects of psychoactive and other dangerous drugs

Medicine

A drug that is used to relieve, cure, or keep a person from getting a disease or problem

Prescription

A written order from a doctor for a medicine

Pharmacist

Druggist

Over-the-counter (OTC) medicine

Medicine that can be bought without a prescription

Side effect

Reaction to a medicine other than what it is intended for

From time to time, everyone gets sick. You may get simple aches and pains or something more serious. Sometimes, a drug or **medicine** is needed to help you get rid of pain and get you healthy again. Medicines are drugs that can relieve, cure, or keep you from getting a disease. Remember, a drug is something other than food that changes the way your mind and body work. All medicines are drugs, but not all drugs are used for medical reasons.

What Are the Types of Medicines?

The U.S. Food and Drug Administration (FDA) divides medicines into two types. The first type is **prescription** medicines. These can be gotten only with a written order from a doctor. Only a doctor can write a prescription. Only a **pharmacist** can fill a prescription. A pharmacist reads the prescription and makes sure it is given correctly to the patient. Pharmacists are highly trained druggists who work in drugstores.

The second type of medicines is **over-the-counter (OTC) medicines.** Anyone can buy these medicines without a prescription in drugstores and other stores.

Prescription medicines are generally stronger than OTC medicines. Because prescription medicines are strong, they may have unwanted **side effects.** Side effects are reactions to a medicine other than what it is intended for. Side effects can hurt you or help you. OTC medicines can have unwanted side effects. Because of possible side effects, reading the labels on OTC medicines is important. Reading the information that comes with both OTC and prescription medicines is especially important.

Young children should never take any kind of medicine without adult supervision. Even some of the most common OTC medicines can have side effects that could be serious. Some medicines should not be taken with other medicines. A doctor should always be told the names of all the medicines that a patient takes, including OTC medicines.

What Are Some Purposes of Medicines?

Both prescription and OTC medicines are used for many purposes. Usually, medicines are grouped according to why they are needed. Some of the reasons for the use of medicines are:

To get rid of pain—Medicines that a person takes to ease or get rid of pain are called **analgesics.** Some analgesics are mild. They work for minor pains such as a sore muscle. Most mild analgesics, such as aspirin or an aspirinlike drug, are OTC medicines. Other analgesics are powerful. They control serious pain, such as the pain you get after an operation. Powerful analgesics such as morphine are prescription medicines.

To control or destroy bacteria—Antibiotics are a kind of medicine that control infection by destroying bacteria. Sulfa drugs also reduce bacteria. Most antibiotics and sulfa drugs are prescription medicines. Some OTC medicines that can be rubbed on small wounds may contain a small amount of an antibiotic.

To make the heart and blood vessels healthy—Many different medicines treat problems of the heart and blood vessels. These medicines may slow your heartbeat, control blood pressure, widen veins and arteries, or control your heart's rhythm. These are all prescription medicines. New studies, however, show that aspirin, an OTC medicine, can help prevent heart attacks in some adults. Even so, adults should check with their doctor before taking aspirin for a heart condition.

All drugs have some side effects. With your doctor, talk about ways other than drugs that you may be able to treat an illness.

To prevent a disease—Vaccines are medicines that can keep you from getting different diseases by giving your body immunity, or a way of fighting the disease. For example, vaccinations keep you from getting diseases such as measles, mumps, and chicken pox. Vaccines are prescription medicines that you get at a doctor's office or at a health clinic.

To relieve symptoms of a disease—Medicines you take for the common cold are examples of medicines that can relieve symptoms. Cold medicines can relieve a sore throat or cough, dry up a runny nose and eyes, or reduce mucus. Most cold medicines are mild and can be bought over the counter.

To replace body chemicals—Some prescription medicines replace chemicals that the body cannot produce. For example, insulin is a prescription medicine. People with type I diabetes take insulin because their pancreas cannot produce it.

To lessen anxiety—Many medicines can reduce depression, anxiety, nervousness, and other mental health problems. Strong forms of these medicines are available only with a doctor's prescription. Milder forms, such as a mild sleep aid, can be bought over the counter.

How Are Medicines Taken?

Knowing the purpose of a medicine and how you should take it are important. Usually, a medicine is taken in the way that will start it working the fastest. For example, you may be told to swallow a medicine after a meal. Some medicines may upset your stomach. Taking some medicines with food may keep you from having an upset stomach. At times, you may take your medicine before a meal. This is because food may delay how quickly your body uses the medicine. Because of this, some medicines work faster on an empty stomach.

Sometimes, you receive medicines such as vaccinations as a shot. The medicine goes directly into a blood vessel or a muscle. Creams, lotions, and patches are put on the skin. The medicine in them is absorbed into the body through the skin. Other medicines are breathed in and go through the lungs first. For example, medicines for asthma are breathed in to help respiratory passages.

How Does a Medicine Affect Your Body?

Your size, weight, age, and how your body works make a difference in how a medicine affects you. For example, a short, thin adolescent may have unwanted side effects from a certain medicine. A tall, heavy adult may have few or no side effects from the same medicine. Your doctor figures out the amount of a medicine that is right for you. Sometimes, your doctor might have to give you more medicine or less so it works right and does not cause unwanted side effects.

Because each person's body chemistry is different, a medicine may affect each person differently. For example, most people can take penicillin for a bacterial infection. Some people, though, are allergic to penicillin and cannot take it. A doctor can prescribe another drug to take the place of penicillin.

What Are Some Problems with Taking Medicines?

The effects of medicine on your body can cause problems. For this reason, you always need to know the specific purpose of a medicine and how it should be taken. You also should know which medicines you cannot take to avoid problems. Four possible problems with taking medicines are having unwanted side effects, developing a strong need for a medicine, mixing medicines, and misusing medicines.

Many medicines cause unwanted side effects. For example, you may get a rash or a headache from taking a medicine. Some of these kinds of side effects are minor and hardly bother you. Other side effects, such as high blood pressure or irregular heartbeat, can be serious.

Sometimes, you can become **dependent** on a medicine. This is when you develop a need for the medicine. For example, a person may take a medicine to help him or her sleep. In time, the person may not be able to sleep without taking the medicine.

Mixing one or more medicines can cause problems. Sometimes, two different medicines cause you to get sick. Always check with your doctor before mixing OTC or prescription medicines with any other medicines.

Misusing medicines is a serious problem. A person can use a medicine incorrectly by taking more or less than the suggested amount. Taking two pills instead of one for a cold, for example, could cause a person to fall asleep while driving. Someone can misuse a medicine by taking it for a longer or shorter time than it should be taken. For example, if a person stops taking an antibiotic too soon, the infection may come back.

Another misuse of a medicine is taking it for a purpose other than its intended purpose. Although drugs are usually not used incorrectly on purpose, by misusing them, a person could get hurt or very sick.

How Does the Government Keep Medicines Safe?

The U.S. government has many laws and agencies to control the safety of medicines. Before a company can sell any medicine, the FDA makes sure the medicine is tested carefully to prove it does what it is supposed to do. The company must give the test results to the FDA. It must also write papers telling the purpose, ingredients, possible side effects, and other information about the medicine. The FDA then decides whether the medicine can be sold to the public. It also decides whether the medicine must be sold only with a doctor's prescription.

The FDA decides how medicines must be labeled. Labels must give the purpose of the medicine, the suggested amount, possible unwanted side effects, and cautions. Reading a label tells you whether taking the medicine is safe and how to keep from having any problems.

Health at Work

Pharmacy Technician

Pharmacy technicians work at hospital and community pharmacies. Pharmacy technicians order supplies. They help label drugs for homebound patients. They keep accurate records of all drugs and supplies. They might type and file reports and answer phones. Under a pharmacist's direction, they measure out or mix prescriptions. They enjoy helping people and working with the public. There is an increasing need for pharmacy technicians. Some pharmacy technicians receive on-the-job training. However, most states require licensing. A 2-year program at a community college can lead to getting a license.

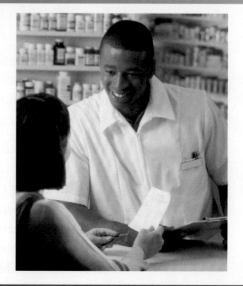

What Are Some Cautions When You Take Medicine?

The correct use of medicines can improve your health and life. Misusing medicines can cause serious problems. To be safe, follow these simple guidelines:

- Tell your doctor about any health problems you have. Tell your doctor about any other medicines you are taking before you get a new prescription.

- Follow the directions for taking a medicine exactly as they are given.

- Tell your doctor right away if you have any unwanted side effects from a medicine.

- Take medicines that are prescribed only for you. Be careful not to confuse one medicine with another.

- Store medicines correctly. Throw away old medicines.

- Do not mix medicines with other medicines, unless directed to do so by your doctor.

- Never mix medicines with alcohol.

Lesson 1 Review On a sheet of paper, write the word or phrase from the Word Bank that best completes each sentence.

Word Bank
medicine
over-the-counter medicines
side effects

1. Stomach upset or rashes are examples of unwanted _____ from some medicines.

2. All _____ can be bought without a prescription.

3. A(n) _____ is used to keep a person from getting a disease or to relieve a problem.

On a sheet of paper, write the answers to the following questions. Use complete sentences.

4. **Critical Thinking** Why is it important to read the label before taking any medicine?

5. **Critical Thinking** Why is knowing about the possible side effects of a medicine important?

Nicotine

A chemical in tobacco to which a person can become addicted

Stimulant

A drug that speeds up the central nervous system

Emphysema

A serious respiratory disease that makes breathing difficult

Some drugs change the way your body works in harmful, rather than helpful, ways. One drug that has harmful physical effects is tobacco.

Why Do People Use Tobacco?

People use tobacco for many reasons. Many teens and adults smoke to feel they fit in. Some people say smoking makes them feel relaxed. Teens may smoke because their friends smoke or because some TV programs make smoking look cool. They believe they can quit smoking before it harms their bodies. In reality, research shows that the younger people are when they start to smoke, the harder it is for them to stop.

The main reason people keep smoking is because of **nicotine,** a chemical in tobacco. People can get an addiction to nicotine. An addiction is a dependency, or a need for a habit-forming substance. Nicotine is in all forms of tobacco. That includes cigarettes, cigars, pipe tobacco, and smokeless tobacco. Smokeless tobacco is put between the cheek and gums and chewed.

What Are the Physical Effects of Tobacco?

The nicotine in tobacco is a **stimulant.** A stimulant speeds up your central nervous system. Even though people may believe that smoking relaxes them, nicotine makes the heart rate speed up. It raises blood pressure but narrows the blood vessels. Using tobacco for a long time also causes a buildup of material in your blood vessels. It can give someone a heart attack, stroke, and lung and other cancers. The buildup can cause lasting bronchitis and **emphysema.** Emphysema is a serious respiratory disease that makes breathing difficult.

When tobacco is burned, it creates thousands of other harmful chemicals besides nicotine. These chemicals include tars and other substances that form a thick, brown, sticky material in the lungs. Tars cripple and destroy the tiny parts in the bronchial tubes that help keep the lungs clean.

Studies show that most smokers begin smoking as teens. Studies also show that if people have not started smoking by the age of 18, they most likely never will smoke. Using the Internet and print resources, find information on the health risks of smoking during adolescence. What are the connections between smoking as a teenager and having health problems later in life? Create a class presentation that shows your research.

Tobacco smoke also makes gases, including carbon monoxide. This gas takes the place of the oxygen in the red blood cells, giving a person less oxygen. This lack of oxygen makes doing anything physical difficult. Other smoke-produced gases have poisonous chemicals in them that can give someone tumors and cancer.

Smokeless tobacco also can cause health problems. For example, it can rot teeth and cause gums to shrink so the teeth get loose and fall out. Smokeless tobacco can give a person white, leathery patches in the mouth that could turn into cancer.

How Does Smoke Affect Nonsmokers?

People who do not smoke but who breathe in other people's tobacco smoke also can be harmed. Many studies have shown that healthy people who do not smoke can get sick because of secondhand smoke. People can get respiratory diseases and cancers by breathing in smoke from burning cigarettes or cigars. People who do not smoke get these diseases because they breathe into their lungs many of the same harmful gases that smokers breathe in.

If you do not smoke, you still can get many of the same physical effects that smokers get. For example, you can get heart and lung problems. Your eyes may bother you, you can get headaches, and you might cough from the smoke. If you are sick, secondhand smoke can make you sicker. For example, if you already have a heart condition, breathing in smoke can make it worse.

Many studies have shown the dangers of breathing secondhand smoke. The health concern of secondhand smoke has caused changes in our society. Laws make smoking illegal in public places and on public transportation. Some cities do not let people smoke in restaurants. In other cities, you can ask to sit in nonsmoking areas of restaurants. Also, many workplaces have become smoke free. Each state decides how old someone must be to buy tobacco products. The federal government puts health warnings on the labels of tobacco products. It also has stopped tobacco advertising on television.

How Does Smoke Affect Unborn Babies?

Today, more than 17 percent of women ages 15 to 44 smoke while they are pregnant. Cigarette smoke is poison for unborn babies. Women who smoke are twice as likely as nonsmokers to have smaller babies. Recent research shows that tobacco smoke also affects brain growth. Babies born to mothers who smoked during pregnancy have a higher chance of developing attention deficit disorder (ADD) or of having lower intelligence levels. Babies born to mothers who smoke show a high chance of having upset stomachs. They also show signs of stress and drug **withdrawal.** This is a physical reaction to not having a drug in the body. For all of these reasons, women who are pregnant should not smoke. Pregnant women also should stay away from places with much secondhand smoke.

How Can People Stop Smoking?

As more people realize the problems that smoking causes, they are choosing to quit smoking. However, the addiction to nicotine is powerful. When people stop smoking, they will probably go through a period of withdrawal. During withdrawal from nicotine, a person may have a headache, be unable to sleep, and have a hard time focusing or concentrating. A person may be irritable and have some anxiety.

Help is available for people who choose to quit smoking. They can get skin patches or a special gum prescription from a doctor. These aids allow smokers to ease away slowly from their addiction to nicotine. Classes, support groups, and professionals also are available to help smokers quit smoking.

Link to ➤ ➤ ➤

Biology

Neurons, or nerve cells in the brain, pass on information. Chemicals called neurotransmitters carry the information from neuron to neuron. Nicotine attaches itself to one special neurotransmitter. When this happens in the brain, a person gets a feeling of pleasure and relaxation. Many people who smoke have a strong desire to experience these feelings again and again. The same kind of chemical release happens with cocaine. That is why both drugs are highly addictive.

Lesson 2 Review On a sheet of paper, write the word or phrase in parentheses that best completes each sentence.

1. The (tar, nicotine, oxygen) in tobacco is addictive.

2. People who do not smoke can still have smoke-related problems from (secondhand, primary, filtered) smoke.

3. Nicotine acts as a central nervous system (stimulant, pathogen, barrier).

On a sheet of paper, write the answers to the following questions. Use complete sentences.

4. **Critical Thinking** How does nicotine become addictive?

5. **Critical Thinking** Why should women who are pregnant stay away from places with a lot of smoke?

Health in Your Life

Breaking the Nicotine Habit

Nicotine addictions are hard to break. The effects of nicotine last from 40 minutes to 2 hours. Some people smoke many times during a day because they want to feel these effects. When people try to stop smoking, they may experience irritability, anxiety, depression, and a craving for nicotine. People who decide to quit smoking are taking the first step toward lifelong health. Think about this:

- Within 20 minutes of quitting smoking, blood pressure returns to normal.

- Within 2 to 12 weeks, circulation improves.

- Within 3 to 9 months, coughing and breathing problems get better.

- Within 10 years, chances of getting lung cancer are cut in half.

- Within 15 years, chances of a heart attack are the same as for someone who never smoked.

On a sheet of paper, write the answers to the following questions. Use complete sentences.

1. Why is an addiction to nicotine hard to break?

2. What might a smoker experience when he or she decides to quit smoking?

3. Why is quitting smoking a step toward lifelong health?

Depressant

A drug that slows down the central nervous system

Psychoactive

Affecting the mind or mental processes

Across America, alcohol is served in restaurants, bars, and bowling alleys and at sporting and community events. From the smallest town to the largest city, alcohol is easy to find and buy. It also is easily abused. About 14 million people in the United States abuse alcohol. Abuse of alcohol occurs when people drink too much alcohol or drink it too frequently.

Why Do People Use Alcohol?

Some people use alcohol to fit in with a particular group. Some people drink to make themselves feel better, to relax, or not to think about how they feel. In reality, alcohol does not help any of these things. Many teens try alcohol because their friends do it or because they have seen their parents drink. Some try it because of the ads they see on TV or in the movies.

You can become both physically and psychologically addicted to ethyl alcohol. This is the kind of alcohol that is found in wine, beer, and liquor. Alcohol is a **depressant,** a type of drug that slows down your central nervous system. It is also a **psychoactive** drug. Psychoactive drugs affect your mind, or mental processes.

It is a mistake to think that some forms of alcohol, such as beer or wine coolers, are safer than liquor. You can become just as addicted to beer or wine as you can to liquor.

How Does Alcohol Affect Your Body?

Alcohol has a negative effect on every major system in your body. Your body does not digest alcohol. It is absorbed directly from your stomach into your bloodstream. It is then carried throughout the body. How alcohol affects your body depends on several factors:

• the amount of alcohol you drink

• body size—the less you weigh, the more alcohol will affect you

• your sex—females are affected sooner than males

Link to >>>

Math

Blood alcohol concentration (BAC) is a measure of the percent of alcohol in the blood. A 0.10 BAC means a person has 1 part of alcohol for every 1,000 parts of blood. A 0.20 BAC means there is 1 part of alcohol for every 500 parts of blood. On average, one drink will cause a 0.04 increase in a person's BAC.

- whether your stomach is empty or full—food slows the effects of alcohol

- your previous experiences with alcohol

After entering your body, alcohol combines with oxygen in a process called oxidation. This happens mainly in your liver. Your liver can oxidize only about $\frac{1}{2}$ ounce of alcohol per hour. Drinking any amount of alcohol affects your judgment, vision, reaction time, and muscle control. Your blood alcohol concentration (BAC) begins to rise. Some short-term effects of alcohol are impaired driving ability, dizziness, flushed skin, dulled senses and memory, and a relaxed feeling.

With just one drink, you can rapidly lose muscle coordination and may not be able to perform simple activities such as walking a straight line. You cannot speak or think as clearly and your hearing and vision become less sharp. When you are affected physically in these ways, serious accidents such as car crashes can happen.

Long-term use of alcohol can cause serious diseases such as cancer of the liver, stomach, colon, and mouth. It can also damage the brain, pancreas, and kidneys. Long-term alcohol use can result in high blood pressure, heart attacks, strokes, and diseases of the liver. These health problems have costs to society.

What Is Fetal Alcohol Syndrome?

Drinking alcohol during pregnancy can cause fetal alcohol syndrome (FAS). Babies who have FAS are born with birth defects. These include unusual facial features and central nervous system disorders. In extreme cases, FAS can cause prenatal death—the baby dies before it is born. Babies who have FAS have difficulty learning and can have vision, hearing, and speech problems. Problems affecting the heart, kidneys, and bones also can occur. Older children with FAS have a greater chance of having problems in school. They are also more likely to be involved in crime.

FAS is a leading cause of birth defects. It is a permanent condition. However, it is entirely preventable. Only babies born to women who drink alcohol have FAS.

Intoxication

Excitement or stimulation caused by use of a chemical material

Alcoholism

A dependence on alcohol and lack of control in drinking

Binge drink

To drink alcohol heavily, then stop for a time, then drink heavily again

Health Myth

Myth: Beer contains less alcohol than does liquor such as whiskey.

Fact: The alcohol in beer is the same as in wine and liquor. The same amount of alcohol is found in 12 ounces of beer, 5 ounces of wine, or one shot ($1\frac{1}{2}$ ounces) of whiskey. Although there is a different amount of liquid in each of these three drinks, the total amount of alcohol is the same.

How Does Alcohol Affect Driving?

When a person's BAC rises to the point of **intoxication,** it can affect many things, including how you drive. Intoxication is excitement or stimulation caused by use of a chemical material. It means being drunk. In the United States, any person with a BAC of 0.08 is considered legally intoxicated. At this level, it is against the law to drive a car.

Alcohol affects your judgment, lessens your attention level, and causes you to get sleepy. Alcohol also cuts down your reaction time and makes it hard to judge your speed and distances. Drinking and driving can lead to death. In the United States, an average of one alcohol-related vehicle death occurs every 30 seconds. Among teenagers, alcohol-related accidents are the number one cause of death. A person with a BAC of 0.04 is twice as likely as a nondrinking driver to be in a fatal car crash. The chances rise to three times as likely for a person with a BAC of 0.08.

Driving drunk has many negative consequences, including paying heavy fines and losing a driver's license for 6 months to 1 year. People who are stopped for driving drunk may have to spend time in jail and be evaluated for **alcoholism.** Alcoholism is a dependence on alcohol and lack of control in drinking.

When Is a Person an Alcoholic?

The main sign of alcoholism is that a person cannot control his or her drinking. Alcoholics are physically and mentally dependent on alcohol. They cannot manage stress without alcohol, and they cannot stop drinking each time they start. Some alcoholics drink on a daily basis. Others **binge drink,** or drink heavily and then stop for a while before drinking heavily again.

People who start drinking at an early age have a greater chance of becoming alcoholics. Among teens who use alcohol, about 38 percent said they had tried their first drink by eighth grade. Studies show that more than 43 percent of teenagers who start drinking before the age of 14 become alcoholics. If a member of a family is an alcoholic, other family members have an increased chance of getting the disease.

In your state, what are two of the penalties for people convicted of drunk driving?

People can recover from alcoholism if they stop drinking. Often medical and psychological help is needed for an alcoholic to recover from the disease.

Lesson 3 Review On a sheet of paper, write the answers to the following questions. Use complete sentences.

1. What are five physical effects of alcohol on the body?

2. Why should women who are pregnant not drink alcohol?

3. What is binge drinking?

4. **Critical Thinking** Do you know anyone who has either driven drunk or been a victim of a drunk driver? Describe what happened.

5. **Critical Thinking** Why is alcoholism thought to be a disease, not just a behavior problem?

Decide for Yourself

Drinking alcohol can affect your grades, your friendships, and how well you do at sports. Drinking can cause vomiting, severe headaches, and death from accidents or alcohol poisoning. Teens who drink are more likely to have unprotected sex and engage in other high-risk behaviors.

Studies show that one out of every 30 high school students drinks daily. Four out of every 10 sixth-grade students feel pressure to drink alcohol. You must be age 21 to drink legally. If you are caught drinking before you are age 21, you can be fined, lose your driver's license, or be put in jail.

Here are some ways to avoid drinking:

- Become friends with people who choose not to drink.

- Get involved with school activities.

- Leave a party or event if you see people your age drinking.

- Say no when someone offers you an alcoholic beverage. Keep saying no even if you are being pressured to have a drink.

- Do not allow friends to drink and drive. Find a ride home for your friend with someone who has not been drinking.

On a sheet of paper, write the answers to the following questions. Use complete sentences.

1. How much pressure to use alcohol do you think teens experience? Explain your answer.

2. Why is it important to know how to say no to drinking alcohol before you go to a party?

3. What law do you think should be passed that might help stop underage drinking?

Stimulants, depressants, narcotics, and hallucinogens are psychoactive drugs. Each one makes a person behave or think differently. Some psychoactive drugs can be used as prescription medicines under a doctor's direction. Buying these drugs without a prescription is against the law. Some psychoactive drugs have no medical use and are made and bought illegally. Buying or selling these drugs is a felony, a serious crime. If a person is found guilty of a felony, he or she can spend a long time in prison. In some states, people found guilty of a felony lose the right to vote.

What Are the Effects of Stimulants?

Stimulants are one kind of psychoactive drug. Stimulants speed up the body's central nervous system. They speed up breathing and heart rate, and they raise blood pressure. People can become dizzy and not want to eat. People also may have headaches, blurred vision, sweating, and sleeplessness. In large amounts, stimulants can make the heart beat irregularly and cause other problems. Breathing in or injecting stimulants can raise blood pressure so high that a person has a stroke or high fever. People could have heart failure and die. People can also become physically dependent on stimulants.

Figure 14.4.1 *People who are dependent on stimulants can feel tired and depressed when the drugs wear off.*

Stimulants change the way the mind works. They provide a feeling of energy and fool people into thinking they are not tired. These feelings can cause someone to become psychologically and physically dependent on stimulants. The dependence begins when the effect of the drug wears off and the person feels tired and depressed. Then the person wants the drug to get back the same feeling of energy again.

The nicotine in tobacco is a stimulant. Descriptions of two other stimulants follow.

Amphetamines

Amphetamines are synthetic, or human-made, stimulants. This means they are made from chemicals in a laboratory. These drugs speed up heart rate and breathing. They will make a person anxious and not want to eat or sleep.

Doctors do not prescribe amphetamines as much as they once did. Doctors may still prescribe them for certain diseases.

Illegal amphetamines are used to lose weight, stay awake and alert, or do better in sports. They are also used to cancel out the effects of depressants. *Speed, ice, crank,* and *crystal* are a few of the names used for an amphetamine called **methamphetamine** or *meth.* Methamphetamine is an addictive amphetamine. A person can become hooked on meth the first time he or she uses it. Meth can cause liver, kidney, lung, and brain damage. It can also cause a stroke or heart failure, which can cause death.

Cocaine

Cocaine is a stimulant that comes from the leaves of the coca plant. It is made into a white powder. This highly addictive drug is now illegal, but at one time it was used for medical purposes. Like other stimulants, cocaine gives a person a lot of energy. The feeling of energy is actually increased heart rate, blood pressure, and breathing. In large amounts, it may cause shaking, seizures, and heart and respiratory failure. These problems can be life threatening. Dependence on cocaine happens quickly— sometimes the first time it is used.

Cocaine dependence can greatly harm physical and mental health. Usually, cocaine is inhaled, or snorted, through the nose. It is absorbed through the mucous membranes and enters the bloodstream. The drug tightens the blood vessels in the nose, making it feel dry. Constant use can wreck the wall that separates the nasal passages. People who use cocaine all the time stop eating properly. They often get malnutrition. If a user has a heart problem, cocaine will make it worse. It also can raise the chances of getting a heart attack. People who inject cocaine risk getting AIDS if they share needles with other cocaine users.

Amphetamine

A central nervous system stimulant

Methamphetamine

A highly addictive, illegal amphetamine

Cocaine

A highly addictive illegal stimulant

Cocaine also affects mental health. Using cocaine gives a false feeling of confidence for the first few minutes. That feeling is often followed by depression. To keep from getting depressed, people will use more and more of the drug to get the same feeling of confidence. When that happens, people quickly build up **tolerance** to cocaine. Tolerance occurs when larger amounts of a drug are needed to get the same effect a person used to get with less drugs. Cocaine affects people mentally, too. Some people say they have felt as if insects were crawling under their skin. Others get confused and have hallucinations, or imagine things or events that are not really there.

Crack is a form of cocaine that is smoked. It is made when cocaine is mixed with baking soda to form lumps that look like rocks. Sometimes, people mix the rocks with ether and then set fire to them so the drug can be smoked. This is called freebasing. A big danger of freebasing is setting off an explosion and uncontrolled fire.

Like other forms of cocaine, the effects of crack last only a few minutes. Like other forms, too, people can become extremely addicted to it. The same health problems from using cocaine are even worse with crack.

What Are the Effects of Depressants?

Depressants are a second kind of psychoactive drug. They slow down the central nervous system. Depressants sedate, or calm, a person. They lower blood pressure, heart rate, and metabolic rate. Using large amounts of depressants can make a person sleepy, not think clearly, lose muscle control, and nauseous. An **overdose,** or too much, of a depressant may give a person heart, lung, or kidney failure. It can even put people in a coma and kill them. Depressants can create both physical and psychological dependence.

If people use alcohol and other depressants together, they are taking great chances with their health. This combination can severely depress the central nervous system, causing death.

Sedative-hypnotic drug

A prescribed depressant that lessens anxiety or helps a person sleep

Barbiturate

A category of sedative-hypnotic drugs

Tranquilizer

A category of sedative-hypnotic drugs

Narcotic

A pain-killing drug made from the opium poppy and in laboratories

When a woman uses depressants while she is pregnant, her baby may be born dependent on the drugs. At birth, the baby also may have signs of withdrawal from the depressants. Also, babies can be born with birth defects and have long-term behavioral problems.

Some people use depressants to handle stress, but that is very dangerous. Tolerance to depressants builds up quickly. Within a few weeks of regular use, depressants lose their effectiveness and no longer work. By that time, people may be dependent on the drugs and need more of them. People may feel worse than when they started using the depressants. People who continue to use more depressants may die, depending on the amount of these drugs and the way they are used.

Sedative-hypnotic drugs are depressants prescribed by a doctor to lessen anxiety (sedatives) or help a person sleep (hypnotics). There are three categories of sedative-hypnotic drugs— **barbiturates,** minor **tranquilizers,** and major tranquilizers.

What Are the Effects of Narcotics?

Narcotics are a third kind of psychoactive drug. Used as pain relievers, narcotics are made from the opium poppy and in laboratories. Some common medicines that are narcotics are morphine and codeine.

Morphine is given to help people with the pain that they get after an operation. It is also given to patients in the painful later stages of cancer. Codeine is used to help with pain and to control coughing.

Narcotics act as strong depressants on the central nervous system. At first, narcotics produce a feeling of well-being. After that, they cause sleepiness, nausea, and sometimes vomiting. An overdose of narcotics makes the breathing shallow, causes cold, damp skin and seizures. It can result in a coma and even death. Usually, a strong physical dependence and tolerance happen with narcotics. The symptoms of withdrawal are so painful that people continue to use narcotics so they do not have to go through withdrawal.

Heroin

An illegal narcotic made from morphine

Hallucinogen

A psychoactive drug that confuses the central nervous system and makes a person see, hear, feel, and experience things that are not real

Flashback

Experiencing the effects of a drug without using it again

Ecstasy

An illegal, psychoactive drug

Heroin, which is illegal to make or use in the United States, is a narcotic made from morphine. Babies of mothers who use heroin may be born early or dead. Babies who are born addicted to heroin may go through severe withdrawal pain. People who inject heroin with a used or dirty needle can get blood poisoning or HIV. A heroin overdose can cause death.

What Are the Effects of Hallucinogens?

Hallucinogens are a fourth kind of psychoactive drug. These drugs confuse the central nervous system. They change the way the brain handles information from the sense organs, including information about sight, hearing, smell, and touch. Because they change thoughts and moods, hallucinogens make things appear to be what they are not. Physically, they can cause the pupils to dilate and can raise body temperature, blood pressure, and heart rate. A person who uses hallucinogens may feel weak and sick.

The mental dangers of hallucinogens are worse than their physical effects. People may feel anxious, confused, or terrified, and may get panic attacks. Because hallucinogens twist people's thinking, people may do something that hurts either themselves or someone else.

Hallucinogens can cause permanent brain damage. For example, users may have **flashbacks.** That means experiencing the effects of the drug without using it again. Because the drug stays in a person's body, flashbacks can happen at any time for the rest of a person's life.

Hallucinogens are illegal and have no medical use. Some hallucinogens are human-made drugs known as street drugs. These dangerous drugs can leave poisonous materials in the brain and may damage the way it works.

Ecstasy is a psychoactive drug much like methamphetamine. It is also much like a hallucinogen. Ecstasy changes a person's mood and metabolism. It is addictive. People using ecstasy get the same harmful effects on their body as they would with cocaine or an amphetamine.

How can you use peer pressure in a good way to keep your friends from using drugs?

LSD

A human-made hallucinogen

PCP

A human-made hallucinogen

LSD, perhaps the best-known human-made hallucinogen, was originally used in research to treat mental illnesses. LSD did not cure any mental problems, however, but often caused additional ones. LSD is both illegal and dangerous.

PCP may be the most dangerous human-made hallucinogen. This is because its effects are different for everyone. It may give one person memory problems, another person depression, and a third person violent behavior. A person who takes a large dose of PCP may have seizures, a coma, and heart and lung failure.

Lesson 4 Review On a sheet of paper, write the letter of the answer that best completes each sentence.

1. A drug that speeds up the central nervous system is called a(n) _____.
   A depressant
   B overdose
   C stimulant
   D narcotic

2. A person who uses cocaine quickly builds up a(n) _____ to it.
   A tolerance
   B intoxication
   C withdrawal
   D immunity

3. Narcotics act as a strong _____ on the central nervous system.
   A tolerance
   B withdrawal
   C stimulant
   D depressant

On a sheet of paper, write the answers to the following questions. Use complete sentences.

4. **Critical Thinking** Why are stimulants, such as amphetamines, very harmful to use?

5. **Critical Thinking** Why are the mental effects of hallucinogens especially dangerous?

Objectives

After reading this lesson, you should be able to

◆ list five effects of marijuana use

◆ explain how inhalants affect the body

◆ explain how anabolic steroids are used both medically and illegally

Marijuana

A drug from the hemp plant, Cannabis sativa

THC

The psychoactive chemical in marijuana

Some drugs are dangerous to use because of their effects on your body and your mind. Many of these drugs are also illegal.

What Is Marijuana?

Marijuana is a drug that comes from the hemp plant, called *Cannabis sativa.* It is illegal to grow or use marijuana. Because hemp leaves and buds have an intoxicating effect, some people smoke, drink, or eat them. Marijuana contains more than 400 chemicals, one of which is called **THC.** THC has a strong psychoactive effect that can make a person dependent on it.

THC is harmful because it may remain in the body's tissues for up to 30 days. It stays mainly in the brain, kidneys, liver, lungs, and reproductive organs. Using marijuana for a long time may harm all of these organs. Also, THC harms proper growth and division of cells.

Marijuana affects each person differently. It can act like a central nervous system depressant, a pain reliever, or a hallucinogen. Marijuana can lower body temperature and raise blood pressure and heart and pulse rates. It makes the eyes red and makes a person hungry. Driving and movement skills lessen after a person uses marijuana.

Marijuana affects how a person functions mentally by weakening memory, concentration, and judgment. As a result, a person's schoolwork may suffer. People can experience mood changes with the first use of marijuana. People who use marijuana may not care about things they once did.

Studies show that using marijuana has serious health problems, including lung disease. For example, marijuana smokers breathe in the smoke deeply and try to hold it in their lungs for a long time. This can damage the lungs. In addition, marijuana smoke can give a person cancer and may make the immune system less effective when fighting disease and infection.

What Are Inhalants?

Inhalant

A chemical that is breathed in

Designer drug

A drug with a slightly different chemical makeup from a legal drug

Look-alike drug

A drug made from legal chemicals to look like a common illegal drug

Inhalants are chemicals that people breathe into their bodies. Some inhalants may be used to help with pain. Other inhalants are used for a hallucinogenic effect. Chemicals with a hallucinogenic effect are generally found in products that are not used as drugs. Some examples of these products are glues, gasoline, spray paints, markers, hair spray, nail polish, air freshener, and other products. Using an inhalant for a different purpose than it is meant for is considered illegal drug use.

Using inhalants can harm a person's mind and body by depressing the central nervous system. People who use inhalants may have slurred speech, poor judgment, confusion, dizziness, headaches, and hallucinations. They may even pass out. Some physical effects of using inhalants are sneezing, coughing, sniffing, and nosebleeds. Inhalants can cause more serious damage, including permanent brain damage. People who use a lot of inhalants can die immediately because they suffocate, or stop breathing.

What Are Designer and Look-Alike Drugs?

A **designer drug's** chemical makeup is like the chemical makeup of a legal drug. Drug dealers, however, make designer drugs slightly different from the original drug. They are usually many times stronger. Many designer drugs act like narcotics. An example of a designer drug is china white, which imitates heroin.

Look-alike drugs are made from legal chemicals to look like other illegal drugs. They may contain anything. For example, people who think they are buying an amphetamine may be getting a depressant.

Making and using all designer and look-alike drugs is illegal. Because people really do not know what is in these drugs, someone using these drugs could easily overdose. Even small doses can raise blood pressure and heart rate. These drugs can act like poison in the body. People who mix look-alike drugs with other drugs have a good chance of dying.

What Are Anabolic Steroids?

Anabolic steroids are human-made drugs that are like the natural male sex hormone, testosterone. When used medically, anabolic steroids help people who do not make enough testosterone naturally. Major League Baseball is one of many organizations that has strict rules banning anabolic steroids. Athletes sometimes abuse anabolic steroids to do better at their sport. By abusing these drugs, athletes may get bigger and stronger.

Anabolic steroids can have both physical and mental effects on the body. They can cause high blood pressure, heart and kidney disease, or life-threatening liver cancer. If a person uses these drugs as an adolescent, the bones may stop growing and the person might not reach normal adult height. Males may get bald, have their testes shrink, and make less sperm. In females, breasts may shrink, facial hair may grow, the voice may deepen, and head hair may thin. Both males and females may never be able to have children after using steroids.

Although steroids generally are not used to change mood, they can have bad mental effects. In both sexes, steroids can cause violence. Other mental effects are anxiety, depression, sudden mood swings, and hallucinations.

Lesson 5 Review On a sheet of paper, write the answers to the following questions. Use complete sentences.

1. For how long does THC remain in the body after use and where is it stored?

2. Why is inhaling and holding marijuana in your lungs harmful?

3. What effect do inhalants have on the body?

4. **Critical Thinking** Why are look-alike drugs more dangerous than the drugs they copy?

5. **Critical Thinking** How can anabolic steroids be both helpful and harmful?

- A drug is something other than food that changes the way the mind and body work. All medicines are drugs, but not all drugs are used for medical reasons.

- Medicines are bought with a doctor's prescription or over the counter without a prescription.

- Medicines are grouped according to their purpose.

- Body size, weight, age, and how your body works influence how a medicine affects you.

- Taking medicines as directed will help you avoid unwanted side effects and dependence.

- The U.S. government controls the safety of medicines.

- The nicotine in tobacco is an addictive stimulant.

- Nonsmokers who breathe in secondhand smoke can have the same health problems that smokers have.

- Alcohol is an addictive central nervous system depressant and psychoactive drug.

- Alcoholism is a disease that comes from dependence on alcohol.

- Using tobacco or alcohol can result in serious diseases involving the heart, lungs, and other body organs.

- Stimulants, depressants, narcotics, and hallucinogens are all addictive psychoactive drugs. Stimulants speed up the central nervous system, and depressants and narcotics slow it down. Hallucinogens confuse the central nervous system.

- Marijuana, inhalants, designer drugs, look-alike drugs, and anabolic steroids are dangerous and addictive drugs.

Vocabulary

alcoholism, 330
amphetamine, 333
anabolic steroid, 340
analgesic, 319
barbiturate, 335
binge drink, 330
cocaine, 333
crack, 334
dependent, 321
depressant, 328
designer drug, 339
ecstasy, 336
emphysema, 324

flashback, 336
hallucinogen, 336
heroin, 336
inhalant, 339
intoxication, 330
look-alike drug, 339
LSD, 337
marijuana, 338
medicine, 318
methamphetamine, 333
narcotic, 335
nicotine, 324
overdose, 334

over-the-counter (OTC)
  medicine, 318
PCP, 337
pharmacist, 318
prescription, 318
psychoactive, 328
sedative-hypnotic drug, 335
side effect, 318
stimulant, 324
THC, 338
tolerance, 334
tranquilizer, 335
withdrawal, 326

Chapter 14 R E V I E W

Word Bank

alcoholism
anabolic steroids
analgesic
depressants
emphysema
flashbacks
inhalants
intoxicated
nicotine
overdose
pharmacist
THC
withdrawal

Vocabulary Review

On a sheet of paper, write the word or phrase from the Word Bank that best completes each sentence.

1. Only a(n) _____ can fill a prescription written by a doctor.

2. A medicine that helps get rid of pain is a(n) _____.

3. Drugs that slow down the central nervous system are _____.

4. All forms of tobacco have _____ in them.

5. A serious disease that affects the lungs and can come from smoking is _____.

6. A person who has a blood alcohol concentration of 0.08 is legally _____.

7. People who cannot control their drinking have _____.

8. People can _____ on a drug, which means they have taken too much.

9. Glue, markers, gasoline, and hair spray are examples of _____.

10. Babies born addicted to heroin go through _____ when they are born.

11. People who use hallucinogens may have _____ for the rest of their lives.

12. The _____ in marijuana remains in the brain and other body organs for up to 30 days after use.

13. Adolescents who use _____ may stop growing early.

Concept Review

On a sheet of paper, write the letter of the answer that best completes each sentence.

14. Three purposes of medicine include getting rid of pain, keeping disease away, and _____.

A replacing body chemicals   **C** causing withdrawal

B causing side effects   **D** creating mood swings

15. Smokeless tobacco is dangerous because it can lead to _____.

A kidney problems   **C** a slower heart rate

B carbon monoxide poisoning   **D** cancer

16. Alcohol and tobacco are both psychologically and physically _____.

A stimulants   **C** depressants

B addictive   **D** psychoactive

17. Anabolic steroids are human-made drugs that are like _____.

A depressants   **C** hallucinogens

B narcotics   **D** testosterone

Critical Thinking

18. How do alcohol, tobacco, and other drugs affect the central nervous system?

19. Why do you think some people never misuse drugs and others become dependent on them?

20. Why do you think alcoholism or any drug dependence could be thought of as a family disease?

Test-Taking Tip Read test questions carefully to pick out those questions that are asking for more than one answer.

Self-Assessment

Can you answer these questions?

☑ 1. How can friends and family members express concern about a person's drug use?

☑ 2. What is the cost to society of drug dependence?

☑ 3. How can you refuse when pressured to use drugs?

☑ 4. What are the signs of drug dependence?

☑ 5. How could you identify drug treatment programs in your community?

☑ 6. What activities can young people do instead of using drugs?

☑ 7. How does drug dependence by a family member affect other family members?

☑ 8. How does stress contribute to drug use?

☑ 9. How can you help friends avoid drug use?

☑ 10. What is the drug dependence recovery process?

Chapter

15 Dealing with Drug Dependence

Everyone is faced with choices and problems in life. People who choose drugs usually are struggling with problems. They may see drug use as a quick solution. However, drug use never provides the solutions to life's problems. In fact, drug use adds to them.

Understanding the problems that drug dependence brings is important. Knowing about solutions for drug dependence is equally important. Perhaps most important is knowing about healthy choices, or alternatives, to drug use.

Goals for Learning

- ◆ To explain physical and psychological drug dependence
- ◆ To identify the main pattern and signs of drug dependence
- ◆ To describe how drug dependence costs the family and society
- ◆ To explain the steps in recovery from drug dependence
- ◆ To identify resources for help overcoming drug dependence
- ◆ To use refusal skills when pressured to use drugs
- ◆ To describe healthy alternatives to drug use

Objectives

After reading this lesson, you should be able to

◆ explain physical and psychological drug dependence

◆ identify the main pattern and signs of drug dependence

◆ recognize how drug dependence affects the family

◆ describe how drug dependence costs society

Dependence on alcohol and other drugs is a serious problem. It affects not only individuals but also families and society. Understanding more about this dependence and its costs is important.

What Is Drug Dependence?

Drug dependence is a need for a drug that results from using the drug once in a while or for a long time. Other names for drug dependence are *addiction* and *substance abuse disorder*. Drug dependence can be physical, psychological, or both. Psychological drug dependence affects the mind and behavior.

Physical Drug Dependence

Physical drug dependence happens when the body develops tolerance to a drug and goes into withdrawal when drug use is stopped. The body begins to develop tolerance as a person uses more of a drug. If people develop tolerance for one drug, they may develop tolerance for other drugs as well. When people who have developed tolerance suddenly stop taking a drug, they go into withdrawal. Withdrawal is the physical reaction to the sudden absence of a drug in the body. Generally, symptoms of withdrawal are the opposite of the effects of the drug. Suppose a person is dependent on alcohol or another depressant. If the person suddenly stops using the drug, the central nervous system speeds up. Suppose a person who is dependent on a stimulant, such as an amphetamine, suddenly stops taking it. The central nervous system slows down.

Heredity may influence whether people become physically dependent on drugs. For example, the risk for alcoholism runs in families. Research studies have proved that the tendency to become addicted to alcohol is genetic. However, this does not mean that people with these genes will always become addicted. For example, people who know that alcoholism runs in their families can avoid drinking alcohol.

The drugs that produce the strongest physical dependence are narcotics, barbiturates, and alcohol. Withdrawal from narcotics is extremely painful. A person in withdrawal from alcohol or barbiturates can die without medical care.

Psychological Drug Dependence

Psychological dependence on a drug happens when people believe they need the drug to feel good or avoid the pain of personal problems. The dependence usually begins when people have personal problems. People may have low self-esteem, for example, or get along poorly with their family members. When they use a drug, they notice that its effects lessen their emotional pain.

When the effect of the drug wears off, the emotional pain comes back. To avoid this pain, people use the drug again to escape their feelings. These people may then begin to have a mental desire to use the drug. Even if they stop using the drug, they may still feel a psychological need for it.

Generally, drugs that produce a psychological dependence are psychoactive drugs. Examples are alcohol, marijuana, cocaine, heroin, and amphetamines. These drugs change the way people think. They can also produce physical dependence.

A drug can result in just physical or just psychological dependence. Usually, however, both types result. The symptoms of dependence are different for each drug. All drugs that produce dependence have one thing in common. They create a need to use more of the drug to feel good or avoid pain.

Link to ➤ ➤ ➤

Language Arts

Writer Langston Hughes wrote the poem "Junior Addict," published in 1961. He describes an African American boy who uses drugs perhaps because of how he feels African Americans have been treated in America. The boy may find strength and hope if he can feel pride in his heritage.

What Are the Main Pattern and Signs of Drug Dependence?

The main pattern and signs of drug dependence seem to be the same for all drugs that cause dependence. The main pattern is that people's lives center on the drug. When people start using drugs, their behavior and personalities change. They spend their time thinking about the drug and how to get it. They spend more time using the drug and recovering from its effects. After they recover, the pattern starts again. Over time, the pattern is set. People become dependent on the drug.

Some signs of drug dependence appear in Table 15.1.1. People who have only one or two of the signs may not have a drug problem. If they show many of these signs, however, they may have a drug problem. Lesson 2 describes ways to get help.

Table 15.1.1 Signs of Drug Dependence	
changes in how a person looks	reduced energy and ambition
major changes in behavior	loss of interest in favorite activities or hobbies
changes in choice of friends	borrowing money
sudden mood changes	trouble with the police
angry or aggressive behavior	drop in performance at school or work
loss of memory and concentration	many school or work absences and tardiness
lying, cheating, and stealing	becoming angry or resistant when discussing drug use

How Does Drug Dependence Affect the Family?

Being able to recognize signs of drug dependence may be especially important for family members. As people become more dependent on drugs, their behavior and personalities change. These changes greatly affect families.

Enabling

Actions of a friend or family member that help a person continue to use drugs

Family members cannot predict the behavior of the people who are drug-dependent. They sometimes try to protect the dependent family members. For example, family members may tell other people that someone in the family is sick when the person actually is drunk. They may make excuses for a drug user's actions. They may lie for the person or provide money to buy drugs. These actions actually help the person to continue using drugs. This is called **enabling.** The family keeps the drug user from having to face the effects of his or her behavior.

Enabling usually happens in an attempt to protect the family image. In some cases, a family member is afraid of the drug user. However, enabling winds up hurting everyone. The person using drugs continues getting deeper into drug dependence.

Figure 15.1.1 *Sudden mood changes or changes in behavior can be a sign of drug dependence.*

Enabling also delays getting help for the drug user. As the problem goes on, the emotional well-being of family members is affected. Children growing up in families with drug dependence often feel stress and are abused.

How Does Drug Dependence Cost Society?

Drug dependence affects not only the family but also society. Alcohol and other drug dependence costs the United States billions of dollars each year. Expenses include lost work time, lost jobs, car crashes, crime, and health problems. As a result, everyone must pay higher taxes. They also must pay for higher insurance and health care costs.

Drug dependence costs more than money—it costs lives. Car crashes in which alcohol is involved are the leading cause of death among teens.

Drug dependence costs not only present lives but also future lives. Pregnant women who use drugs run the risk of giving birth to drug-dependent babies. Women who drink alcohol when they are pregnant may have babies who are smaller than normal. These babies also may have defects that cannot be reversed. They may be mentally slow or have deformities. Mothers who use cocaine during pregnancy may give birth to babies who are dependent on cocaine. These babies do not like to be held. They fail to respond to other humans. They are likely to have physical and behavior problems throughout their lives.

Drug dependence can increase the risk of acquiring AIDS and other sexually transmitted diseases. Young people who use drugs are more likely to have sex than people who do not use drugs. Many drug users report using alcohol or other drugs when they have sex. In addition, people who inject drugs and share needles have a higher risk for acquiring AIDS.

Drug dependence can have criminal consequences. Being convicted for selling or using drugs can have serious and long-term effects. A person who has been convicted of selling or using drugs may be sent to prison and pay large fines. A convicted drug user cannot get loans or grants for college. In some states, a person who has been convicted of drug use may lose the right to vote or hold office. The person may not be able to train as a nurse, pharmacist, teacher, or other professional. Getting employment may be difficult.

Research and Write

Work in small groups to locate sources of information on the Internet and in your community on alcohol and other drugs. Determine whether these sources are reliable. Then make a brochure that tells other teens where they can find reliable information on alcohol and other drugs. Place the brochure in the school library.

Lesson 1 Review On a sheet of paper, write the answers to the following questions. Use complete sentences.

1. When does physical drug dependence happen?

2. When does psychological drug dependence happen?

3. What are three signs of drug dependence?

4. **Critical Thinking** A friend tells you that she suspects her brother is drinking alcohol. She is doing his homework for him. Are the friend's actions helpful? Explain.

5. **Critical Thinking** A classmate says drugs should be legal because they do not hurt anyone but the person using the drugs. What would you say to this classmate?

Health in Your Life

Media, Culture, and Drug Use

You are watching sports on TV. A commercial shows people drinking beer. The beer company wants you to think that you will have fun and fit in if you drink its beer. Every day, you are surrounded by media messages that try to influence you to use drugs. Movies and TV programs show people using alcohol and other drugs.

Culture also influences drug use. If a person's community or peers accept drug use, a person is more likely to use drugs.

When you resist media and cultural influences, you do not let them control you. You can avoid movies or events that promote drug use. You can use positive peer pressure to help others avoid drug use. You can be a role model, remind your friends of future goals, and choose fun activities that do not involve drugs.

On a sheet of paper, write the answers to the following questions. Use complete sentences.

1. How might talking about future goals help friends avoid drug use?

2. How can you resist negative cultural influences on drug use?

3. A friend wants you to go with her to a party where beer will be served. You are not old enough to drink alcohol. You do not want to drink. How can you use positive peer pressure in this situation?

Detoxification

Removing addictive drugs from the body

People who are dependent on drugs can take positive steps to recover. Many programs are available to help people stop using drugs.

How Do People Recover from Drug Dependence?

The process of recovery from drug dependence includes three main steps. The first step requires a person to recognize that he or she has a problem with drugs.

The second step in recovery is **detoxification,** or removing addictive drugs from the body. Detoxification should take place in a hospital under medical care to avoid serious problems.

The third step in recovery is learning to live day to day without drugs. This is a long-term process. Treatment counselors help a drug user understand his or her behavior and attitude. The person becomes healthier emotionally. The person learns healthy ways to handle problems through decision-making and problem-solving skills.

The process of recovery never stops, because drug dependence cannot be cured in the way that some diseases can be cured. However, drug dependence can be treated successfully so that people can lead healthy lives. Abstinence is the goal of recovery. This means that a person never uses drugs again. Sometimes, the recovering drug user goes back to using drugs. Even so, the person can still achieve recovery and the goal of abstinence.

❊❊❊❊❊❊❊❊❊❊❊❊❊❊❊❊❊❊❊❊❊❊❊❊❊❊❊❊❊❊❊❊❊❊❊

Technology and Society

In research studies, scientists studied the effects of alcohol on animals' brains. The animals' brain cells did not respond normally to a brain chemical that produces feelings of pleasure. The animals drank alcohol to produce those feelings. Gene therapy caused the cells to respond normally to the chemical. As a result, the animals drank less alcohol. In time, this therapy may be used to help treat people with alcoholism.

What are some of the support groups that meet in your community?

Where Can Individuals and Families Get Help?

Successful treatment programs set up a plan to help each individual. Each person may respond differently to treatment. For this reason, trained professionals use several different methods to help a person. All treatment programs help a person overcome drug dependence. The places where a person gets help may depend on the drug he or she used. It also depends on how long the person used it and on his or her desire for help. Some types of treatment resources or centers are described here.

Counseling

Most schools have counselors or a student assistance program. Students can talk over concerns about drug use—their own, a friend's, or a family member's. Counselors at community mental health centers can help by directing people to treatment centers. They also can provide help and encouragement after treatment or for family members.

Support Groups

A common place for treatment is support groups. These are groups in which members help one another. Alcoholics Anonymous (AA) was the first organization to offer support groups. The goal of treatment for AA members is never to drink again. AA believes that people with alcoholism are responsible for managing their disease day by day. The group is based on the buddy system. That means that each person in AA has a sponsor. The sponsor is available around the clock to help the person deal with the desire to drink.

AA has three other groups for family members of people with alcoholism. Al-Anon is a support group for adult family members. Alateen is for 12- to 18-year-olds. Alatot is for 6- to 12-year-olds. Members help one another deal with the problems of living with someone who has alcoholism.

Two other support groups are Cocaine Anonymous and Narcotics Anonymous. You can locate all of these support groups by searching online or the phone directory.

Many organizations and businesses have programs to reduce drug use. They may have policies that drug users can lose their jobs. Employers may conduct drug testing. Many programs provide information about drug use. They also refer employees who use drugs to treatment and support services.

Residential Treatment Centers

An individual can go to a regular hospital, a mental health hospital, or a center. The individual lives in such a center, called a **residential treatment center,** during treatment. The person receives help from health professionals who are trained in treating drug dependence. Different centers may focus on certain age groups or steps in treatment. For example, some centers may treat only adolescents.

The doctors, social workers, and counselors in these centers use the medical approach to treatment. That means they slowly take the drug-dependent person off a drug. Sometimes, these professionals use medicines to help individuals get through withdrawal.

Some treatment centers are run by state or local governments. Others are privately owned. Centers that the government runs may be less expensive than privately owned centers. In either case, a person's health insurance plan may cover treatment in these centers.

Halfway Houses

Sometimes, when people leave a treatment center, they go to a **halfway house.** These houses provide shelter and food for recovering individuals as they ease back into society. People may stay in a halfway house to adjust to drug-free living. They must stay off drugs while staying there.

Outpatient Treatment Centers

Some individuals receive treatment in an **outpatient treatment center.** These centers are for people who can function without drugs while recovering from their drug dependence. Usually, people live at home while they get treatment for a few hours each day at the center. This kind of treatment generally lasts longer than residential treatment.

Lesson 2 Review On a sheet of paper, write the word or phrase in parentheses that best completes each sentence.

1. The first step in recovery from drug dependence is (detoxification, recognizing a problem, learning to live without drugs).

2. A place where a recovering drug user can live while easing into society is a (halfway house, support group, medical hospital).

3. Removing addictive drugs from the body is (counseling, detoxification, abstinence).

On a sheet of paper, write the answers to the following questions. Use complete sentences.

4. **Critical Thinking** Why is learning healthy ways to deal with problems important for recovering drug users?

5. **Critical Thinking** Whom could you talk to if you thought a friend had a problem with drugs?

▼◀▲▼◀▲▼◀▲▼◀▲▼◀▲▼◀▲▼◀▲▼◀▲▼◀▲▼◀▲▼◀▲▼◀▲▼◀

Health at Work

Substance Abuse Counselor

Substance abuse counselors work with people who are dependent on alcohol or other drugs. The counselor's goal is to break the dependence. The counselor helps people identify behaviors and problems related to the dependence. Counselors may work with an individual, the individual and the family, or groups of people who need counseling. Substance abuse counselors may work in halfway houses, hospitals, residential treatment centers, and state and local government agencies. Some counselors are self-employed. A substance abuse counselor must have more than a 4-year degree to be licensed or certified. A person with a 4-year degree can work as a counseling aide.

Resistance skill

A way to resist negative peer pressure

Eating a balanced diet every day increases energy levels and maintains normal brain chemistry. A person who has normal brain chemistry can cope better with stress and other problems.

There are many ways to avoid ever starting to use drugs. You can refuse offers from people trying to get you to use drugs. You can choose healthy alternatives to drug use.

How Do You Refuse Drugs?

One main reason adolescents use drugs is peer pressure. **Resistance skills** are ways to resist negative peer pressure. One way for anyone feeling pressure to use drugs is to say no and walk away. Another way is to avoid places where you know or suspect drugs are being used. For example, if you know there will be drugs at a party, you simply do not go.

Here are some other refusal techniques.

• Change the subject. Refuse an offer of drugs and then talk about something else.

• Give honest reasons for not using drugs. For example, you could say you want to be in control of your life rather than having drugs control your life.

• Keep repeating that you do not want to use drugs.

• Give facts about why the drugs will harm you and why you will not use them.

• Choose to spend time only with people who do not use drugs.

How Can You Get Help?

Getting help for stress and other problems can help people avoid drug use. This is especially important for people with a family member who uses drugs. Those people need to know that they are not responsible for the drug user's behavior. They also need to realize that they are responsible for their own behavior.

People can get help to avoid drug use by talking with a trusted, trained person. Sometimes, supportive friends can help. Sources of help are parents, school counselors or nurses, teachers, and other adult family members.

Many hotlines are also available, such as the National Drug and Alcohol Treatment Hotline run by the Center for Substance Abuse. This service can link people with treatment in their own community.

What Are Some Alternatives to Drug Use?

Using drugs to deal with problems is a risky choice that never solves the problems. Here are some activities that can help you be part of a group and have fun. These activities can increase your self-esteem. You can make them part of your lifestyle.

- Do something physically active. Exercise can improve mental and physical fitness, reduce stress, and increase energy. It also gives you a sense of accomplishment. You might try a dance or martial arts class.

- Get involved in an important cause that helps others and adds purpose to your life. You might volunteer at a hospital or for an environmental cleanup.

- Join an interest or activity group with people who share common concerns. You might start a new hobby, work on the school newspaper, or help organize a walk for charity.

- Work at a part-time job. You will get a paycheck and the pleasure of doing a job well. A job can help increase your feelings of self-worth, self-esteem, and self-confidence.

- Choose entertainment that promotes mental and physical health. You might choose movies, books, and magazines that do not feature violence or drug use.

- Support efforts by your school and community to prevent drug use. Join a committee to develop your school's drug policy. Find out how you can participate in community prevention programs and activities.

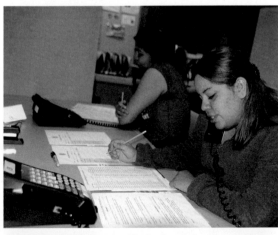

Figure 15.3.1 *Getting help for drug dependence can start with a call to a substance abuse hotline.*

Who is someone you admire who does not use illegal drugs?

Lesson 3 Review On a sheet of paper, write the answers to the following questions. Use complete sentences.

1. What are two techniques for refusing drugs?

2. Name three alternatives to drug use.

3. What is one main reason adolescents use drugs?

4. **Critical Thinking** What is a reason you would give someone for not using drugs?

5. **Critical Thinking** Who are two people you could turn to if you needed help to avoid drug use?

Decide for Yourself

The best way to avoid the negative effects of drugs is to avoid situations where drugs are being used. However, you may not always be able to do so.

Suppose you are at a party at a friend's house. Your friend says, "Hey, I found these pain killers in my parents' medicine cabinet. You can get a high with no bad effects because they're not illegal."

You say, "No, I don't want to take them."

He replies, "Well, everyone else here is taking them. What's the matter with you?"

You respond, "It doesn't matter to me what other people are doing. I don't want to take them. I want to be in control of my mind and body. These pills are prescription medicine. They could make me vomit or go into a coma. I don't want to get sick."

Your friend keeps pressuring you, and you keep saying no. You decide to leave the party.

On a sheet of paper, write the answers to the following questions. Use complete sentences.

1. How many resistance skills can you identify in the situation? Name them.

2. What other resistance skills could you use in this situation?

3. Who is making the most reasonable argument here—you or your friend? Explain your answer.

Chapter 15 S U M M A R Y

- Drug dependence can be physical, psychological, or both.

- In physical drug dependence, the body develops tolerance to a drug and then withdrawal when the drug use is stopped. Heredity may influence whether people become physically dependent on drugs.

- In psychological drug dependence, people believe they need a drug to feel good or avoid the pain of personal problems. Psychoactive drugs produce psychological drug dependence.

- Drug use usually results in physical and psychological drug dependence.

- The main pattern of drug dependence is that a person's life centers on a drug. The more signs of drug dependence a person shows, the greater are the chances the person is drug dependent.

- Enabling is the effort of friends or family members to protect a drug user from the results of drug use. Enabling delays admitting the problem and getting help. It hurts everyone.

- Drug dependence costs society in dollars, present lives, and future lives.

- Drug dependence can increase the risk of acquiring AIDS and other sexually transmitted diseases. Using drugs can have criminal consequences.

- People can recover from drug dependence, although they can never be cured. The three main steps in recovery are admitting the problem, detoxification, and learning to live every day without drugs.

- Treatment in support groups involves members helping one another stay drug free. Support groups help people who live with or are close to a drug-dependent person.

- Some people live in residential treatment centers during treatment. Others live in halfway houses for a short time after treatment. Some live at home when going to outpatient treatment.

- People can avoid drugs by using resistance skills. They can talk with trusted adults when they are having problems or feel stress. There are many healthy alternatives to drug use.

- Hotlines provide information about sources of help for drug dependence.

Vocabulary

detoxification, 352	halfway house, 354	residential treatment center, 354
enabling, 349	outpatient treatment center, 354	resistance skill, 356

Chapter 15 R E V I E W

Vocabulary Review

Word Bank

detoxification

enabling

halfway house

outpatient
  treatment center

residential
  treatment center

resistance skills

On a sheet of paper, write the word or phrase from the Word Bank that best completes each sentence.

1. Individuals who live in the place where they are treated are in a(n) _____.

2. Helping someone to keep using drugs is _____.

3. Getting addictive drugs out of the body is _____.

4. Saying no to drug use is one of several _____.

5. A(n) _____ provides help for recovering individuals as they ease back into society.

6. Individuals who live at home while they are treated go to a(n) _____.

Concept Review

On a sheet of paper, write the letter of the answer that best completes each sentence.

7. Support groups help _____.
   A children only   **C** family members
   B drug users only   **D** counselors

8. All of these actions enable drug users EXCEPT _____ them.
   A lying for   **C** making excuses for
   B getting treatment for **D** giving money to

9. Another name for drug dependence is _____.
   A withdrawal   **C** substance abuse disorder
   B detoxification   **D** tolerance

10. A good alternative to drug use is to _____.
    A avoid exercise   **C** keep to yourself
    B try a new hobby   **D** stop watching TV

11. A drug user's parent _____ his behavior.

    A may feel stress from   **C** is able to control

    B can predict   **D** is responsible for

12. If you use resistance skills, you _____.

    A are physically active   **C** refuse offered drugs

    B resist getting help   **D** give in to peer pressure

13. Treatment for a drug user can happen at a _____.

    A halfway house   **C** drug user's home

    B support group   **D** residential treatment center

14. All drug-dependent people _____.

    A can be cured   **C** have enabling families

    B have stable personalities **D** have a drug tolerance

15. The effects of drugs on unborn babies _____.

    A are rarely serious   **C** may include deformities

    B can usually be reversed **D** last only a few years

Critical Thinking

On a sheet of paper, write the answers to the following questions. Use complete sentences.

16. A friend confides in you that her mother has a drinking problem. What would you say to this friend?

17. How might a drug-free person end up paying for drug use?

18. Suppose a friend told you he would not be your friend any longer unless you drank alcohol. What would you say?

19. What are some benefits of a drug-free lifestyle?

20. How does being involved in a loved one's treatment for drug dependence benefit family members?

Test-Taking Tip Try to answer all questions as completely as possible. When asked to explain your answer, do so in complete sentences.

Drug Trafficking

Drug trafficking is the buying and selling of illegal drugs. It is a big business. Out of about 185 million drug users in the world, about 25 million are in the United States. Cocaine, heroin, marijuana, and methamphetamine are some of the illegal drugs that come into the country by air, land, and sea. Some illegal drugs also are produced in the United States.

Many U.S. government agencies are responsible for detecting the movement of illegal drugs across American borders. The U.S. Coast Guard watches over drug trafficking by air and sea. The U.S. Customs Service searches the country's borders. It also monitors people and luggage coming into the country on commercial flights. One of the most successful customs programs is the Canine Enforcement Program. Dogs such as Labrador retrievers, golden retrievers, and German shepherds are trained to detect narcotics. These dogs found almost 2 million pounds of narcotics in 2004.

Though drug trafficking is still a huge problem, it has been decreasing in the United States. The United States works with many other countries to try to stop drug production.

However, focusing on drug trafficking alone cannot solve the problem. People must be educated about the dangers and consequences of drug use. Efforts must continue to help drug users never use drugs again. When the demand for drugs decreases, the supply decreases.

On a sheet of paper, write the answers to the following questions. Use complete sentences.

1. How would the amount of drugs coming into the United States change if fewer people used drugs? Explain your answer.

2. Suppose you are going to write a letter to your state representatives. You want to urge them to support funding to reduce drug trafficking from other countries. What would you write in your letter?

- A drug is something other than food that changes the way the mind and body work. All medicines are drugs. However, not all drugs are used for medical reasons.

- Taking medicines as directed will help you avoid unwanted side effects and dependence.

- Using tobacco or alcohol can result in serious diseases involving the heart, the lungs, and other body organs.

- The nicotine in tobacco is a stimulant. People can become addicted to nicotine.

- Nonsmokers who breathe in secondhand smoke can have the same health problems that smokers have.

- Alcohol is an addictive depressant, and it is a psychoactive drug. Psychoactive drugs affect the mind.

- Alcoholism is a disease. Alcoholism is a dependence on alcohol.

- Stimulants, depressants, narcotics, and hallucinogens are all addictive psychoactive drugs. Stimulants speed up the central nervous system. Depressants and narcotics slow down the central nervous system. Hallucinogens confuse the central nervous system.

- Marijuana, inhalants, designer drugs, look-alike drugs, and anabolic steroids are dangerous and addictive drugs.

- In physical drug dependence, the body develops tolerance to a drug and then withdrawal when the drug use is stopped. Heredity may influence physical dependence.

- In psychological drug dependence, people believe they need the drug to feel good or avoid the pain of personal problems. Psychoactive drugs produce psychological drug dependence.

- The main pattern of drug dependence is that a person's life centers on a drug. The more signs of drug dependence a person shows, the greater are the chances the person is drug dependent.

- Enabling is the effort of friends or family members to protect a drug user from the results of drug use. Enabling delays admitting the problem and getting help. Enabling hurts everyone.

- Drug dependence can increase the risk of acquiring AIDS and other sexually transmitted diseases. Using drugs can have criminal consequences.

- People can recover from drug dependence, although they can never be cured. The three main steps in recovery are admitting the problem, detoxification, and learning to live every day without drugs.

- People can avoid drugs by using resistance skills.

Word Bank

detoxification

enabling

hallucinogen

inhalant

nicotine

outpatient
 treatment center

over-the-counter
 medicine

psychoactive

resistance skill

side effect

stimulant

tolerance

Vocabulary Review

On a sheet of paper, write the word or phrase from the Word Bank that best completes each sentence.

1. Anyone can buy a(n) _____ without a prescription.

2. A reaction to a medicine other than what it is intended for is a(n) _____.

3. An addictive chemical in tobacco is _____.

4. A drug that speeds up the central nervous system is a(n) _____.

5. A(n) _____ drug is one that affects your mental processes.

6. A type of chemical that is breathed in is a(n) _____.

7. If a person needs more cocaine to get the same effect that once occurred with less cocaine, the person has developed a(n) _____ to the drug.

8. A drug that confuses the central nervous system and can make the user hear things that are not real is a(n) _____.

9. In the process of recovery from drug dependence, _____ should take place in a hospital.

10. Someone who lies to protect a drug user is _____ the drug addiction.

11. A(n) _____ is a place for people who can function without drugs while recovering from their drug dependence.

12. An effective way to resist negative peer pressure is a(n) _____.

Concept Review

On a sheet of paper, write the letter of the answer that best completes each sentence.

13. A type of psychoactive drug that slows down the central nervous system is a(n) _____.

   A depressant   **C** amphetamine

   B hallucinogen   **D** anabolic steroid

14. Aspirin and other over-the-counter medicines that get rid of pain are _____.

   A hallucinogens   **C** inhalants

   B anabolic steroids   **D** analgesics

15. The physical reaction to the sudden absence of a drug in the body is _____.

   A tolerance   **C** withdrawal

   B emphysema   **D** intoxication

16. A(n) _____ dependence exists when an alcohol addict believes that she must drink to feel good.

   A psychological   **C** physical

   B look-alike   **D** enabling

Critical Thinking

On a sheet of paper, write the answers to the following questions. Use complete sentences.

17. Why is a person who is addicted to alcohol at risk for having liver problems? Explain your answer.

18. Why do some employers require job seekers to take a drug test? Do you think this is fair?

19. The word *anonymous* describes something that is not named or identified. Why do you think the support group Alcoholics Anonymous uses that name?

20. In your school or community, what are some healthy activities that are alternatives to drug use?

Unit 6

Injury Prevention and Safety Promotion

The last time you rode a bicycle, did you wear a helmet? In some places, people are ticketed for not wearing a helmet when riding a bike. How about seatbelts? Do you always wear a seatbelt while riding or driving in a vehicle? Wearing a helmet and fastening your seatbelt are two ways to reduce risk of injury. There are many more.

Many Americans might find life today riskier than ever before. Yet the number of years we are expected to live continues to rise. This is because we have discovered new ways to stay safe and live longer. Through laws, education, and technology, communities are working to provide a safe environment. What will you learn in this unit? You will discover things you can do to help yourself, your family, and your community be safe. You will learn ways to reduce risks of injuries at home and away.

Chapters in Unit 6

Self-Assessment

Can you answer these questions?

☑ 1. Who is at the greatest risk for injuries from falls?

☑ 2. How can electrical outlets cause fires?

☑ 3. What are two fire safety devices?

☑ 4. How can the risk of poisoning be reduced?

☑ 5. What is OSHA?

☑ 6. What is survival floating?

☑ 7. How can the number of vehicle crashes be reduced?

☑ 8. Why are bicyclists and motorcyclists at greater risk for injury than riders in cars?

☑ 9. How can people prepare for a hurricane?

☑ 10. How can people prepare for a tornado?

Reducing Risks of Injury

Everyone faces risks of injury every day, both at home and away from home. These injuries range from falls to motor vehicle crashes. People today are more aware of risks in their lives than ever before. They are also more aware of the steps they can take to reduce the risks. Laws, education, and technology have all helped to increase the safety of the individual, the family, and the community. Identifying some common risks and learning what can be done to reduce those risks also increases safety. With that knowledge, you can lower both the chances and the results of injuries to yourself and others.

In this chapter, you will learn how to reduce common risks at home, away from home, and on the road. You will also learn what you can do to prepare for and stay safe during natural disasters.

Goals for Learning

◆ To describe ways to reduce the risks of falls, fire, poisoning, and electrical shock at home

◆ To identify ways to reduce risks at work and during recreational activities

◆ To explain how to reduce the risks of vehicle crashes and increase bicycle and motorcycle safety

◆ To describe ways to stay safe during common natural disasters

Objectives

After reading this lesson, you should be able to

◆ identify safety hazards in the home

◆ identify ways to reduce the risk of falls

◆ discuss ways to reduce the risk of fire, poisoning, and electrical shock

Put together a first aid kit for your home. Put it in a place that you can reach quickly.

Everyone would like to think that home is a safe place, but accidents do happen there. People make nearly 21 million medical visits each year because of accidental injuries at home. Nearly 18,000 people die from their injuries. Fortunately, a large number of accidents at home can be avoided.

Most injuries that occur at home are the result of falls. Other causes of injuries at home are fires, poisoning, and electrical shock. Many of these injuries can be prevented. In each case, you can take steps to reduce the risks involved.

How Can the Risk of Falls Be Reduced?

Everyone can trip and fall, but young children and older people are especially at risk. Stairs are a dangerous place for falls. To make stairways safer, they should be well lit, in good repair, and free of litter. Tightly secured handrails, carpeting, and nonskid strips all can help prevent falls on stairs.

Bathtubs and showers are common places where people fall. To make tubs and showers safe, grip bars can be installed to provide a handle. Nonskid mats or stickers on the bottom of bathtubs also can help prevent falls.

Spills or objects scattered on floors cause people to slide or trip and fall. Spills should be cleaned up when they happen. In addition, fastening throw rugs in place can prevent people from tripping and falling. Keeping toys and other objects off floors and all pathways is another preventive measure.

People often fall from unstable chairs, boxes, or piles that they stand on to reach high places. A safe stepladder or step stool is a better choice than a wobbly chair or box.

How Can the Risk of Fire Be Reduced?

Making sure electrical outlets are not overloaded is one way to prevent electrical fires. Another way is to check for bad wiring or damaged electrical cords. A licensed electrician can fix these problems.

Smoke detector

A device that sounds loudly when it senses smoke or high amounts of heat

Fire extinguisher

A portable device containing chemicals that put out small fires

Keep fuel or fire starters away from sources of heat and out of the reach of children. Store all flammable liquids in tightly closed containers away from heat, including a fireplace. Also, keep matches or lighters out of the reach of small children.

Fires in fireplaces and chimneys are often the cause of house fires. To prevent this, place a screen in front of a fireplace when a fire is burning. Also, a fire in a fireplace should be attended at all times. Fires in chimneys can be prevented by having them cleaned each year.

Space heaters and furnaces can cause fires in homes. Clean all heating units regularly and check to be sure they are operating safely. Only use extension cords that match the requirements of a space heater.

Loose-fitting clothing and many materials can easily catch fire near an open flame. Be careful around burning candles, fireplaces, and grills when people wear such clothing. Someone should always watch something cooking on the stove.

Link to ➤➤➤

Social Studies

In 2004, employers spent $38 billion for injuries that their workers had at home. The costs included health insurance, life insurance, sick leave pay, and disability. Costs for hiring and training new employees also play a part. An injury that causes a hospital stay can cost an employer nearly $20,000.

What Are Some Fire Safety Devices?

If a fire does start, a smoke detector and a fire extinguisher can help. A **smoke detector** is a device that sounds loudly when it senses smoke or high amounts of heat. It warns people so they can take action immediately. A house should have at least one smoke detector on every level and in each bedroom. To make sure the batteries work, test smoke detectors every month. Change the batteries twice a year.

A **fire extinguisher** is a portable device containing chemicals that put out small fires. Keep an extinguisher in the kitchen, since many fires can start from spills on the stove or in the oven. Almost everyone in a family can learn when and how to use a fire extinguisher.

What Can Be Done If a Fire Starts?

Use a fire extinguisher only to put out small fires. A small fire is one that stays in the area where it started. For example, a fire extinguisher can put out a fire in a wastebasket, furniture cushion, or small appliance.

Does your school have regular fire drills? What else could your school do to make sure your school is safe from fire?

A person should know how to use a fire extinguisher correctly. The person's back should always be to an escape route in order to leave quickly if necessary.

Sometimes, small fires can be put out in other ways. For example, baking soda can put out a small grease fire on a stove or in an oven. Putting a tight lid on a pan that has a grease fire in it cuts off oxygen to the fire. Do not use water on a grease fire, because it makes the fire spread.

People should not attempt to fight fires that they cannot easily extinguish. In case of a large fire that cannot be extinguished, it is best to be prepared ahead of time by taking these actions:

- Have regular fire drills, including a drill as if everyone were asleep in bed.

- Have a signal that alerts everyone to a fire drill. For example, someone could press the "test" button on the smoke detector.

- Drop to the floor on hands and knees and crawl to a door. Stay close to the floor where there would be less smoke and more oxygen.

- Feel the door and doorknob to check for warmth. If a door is hot, everyone should take a second escape route, such as a window.

- Stop, drop, and roll on the ground if clothing has caught fire.

- Get out of the house at once without stopping to take belongings. Then go to a designated meeting place.

- Call the fire department from a neighbor's home.

How Can the Risk of Poisoning Be Reduced?

A poison causes injury, illness, or even death when it enters the body. Most poisonings happen with babies and young children, because they put so many things in their mouth. Sometimes, two different medicines or drugs interact and cause poisoning. Taking too much of a drug is the main cause of poisoning in 15- to 24-year-olds.

Most risks of poisoning can be reduced in these ways:

- Store medicines and household products in their original containers out of children's reach.

- Never run a car or other engine powered by gasoline or oil in a closed garage. These engines release poisonous gas.

- Inspect the yard for such plants as poison ivy, poison oak, and poison sumac. Find out how to remove them safely.

- Keep the poison control center number by the phone.

Another type of poisoning is food poisoning. This occurs when a person eats food containing certain types of living things, including some kinds of bacteria. Most cases of food poisoning are mild and last only a few days. Other cases require medical care. Some forms of food poisoning can be prevented by cooking and handling food properly.

How Can the Risk of Electrical Shock Be Reduced?

Electrical shock is a flow of electric current through the body. Electrical shock may cause serious burns, injuries to organs, and even death.

Here are some ways to avoid electrical shocks:

- Never use an electric appliance if the floor, your body, or your clothing is wet.

- Pull on the plug, not the cord, when disconnecting appliances.

- Stay away from power lines that are down.

- Never touch a power line, and make sure that no object, such as a ladder, touches a power line.

- Cover electrical outlets with safety plugs.

- Have only a licensed electrician repair appliances and wiring.

- Unplug electrical appliances that are not working properly.

Electrical shock

A flow of electric current through the body

What Are Some Other Household Dangers?

Some parts of homes are dangerous and are common sources of injuries. These parts are safety **hazards.** You can act to prevent injuries. Doorknob covers and locks can keep children away from hazardous areas such as swimming pools and bathrooms. Window guards and safety netting can prevent falls from windows. Injuries from sharp edges of furniture and fireplaces can be reduced by the use of corner and edge bumpers. Window blind cords should be cut short enough that children cannot reach them. Children can be choked or strangled by the cords.

Special devices placed on faucets and showerheads can prevent burns. Doorstops and door holders can help prevent hand injuries. Burning candles can be fire hazards. They should be watched carefully and never left unattended.

If firearms are in the home, they should be kept in a locked place. Guns should be unloaded and locked in a separate place from the ammunition.

Safety When Caring for Children

Watching young children carries many responsibilities for safety. These guidelines can help avoid risks when you are watching young children.

- Know how to contact parents and know when they will return.

- Have emergency and neighbors' phone numbers nearby.

- Learn family rules for playing inside.

- Keep your full attention on the children.

- Keep children away from appliances, matches, cleansers, soap, medicine, and bodies of water.

Lesson 1 Review On a sheet of paper, write the answers to the following questions. Use complete sentences.

1. Where are two places that people commonly fall in the home?

2. What are two fire safety devices that can help keep you safe if a fire starts in your home?

3. For what kind of fires should a fire extinguisher be used?

4. **Critical Thinking** How can you help your family reduce injuries from a fall? How can your family help you?

5. **Critical Thinking** How can you help your family reduce the danger of a fire? How can your family help you?

Health in Your Life

Planning Escape Routes

Do you know how you would get out of your home in case of a fire? Follow these guidelines to make a plan of escape from every room of your home.

Draw a floor plan of your home. Show escape routes from each room to use in case of fire. Include an emergency meeting place that your family has chosen outside your home.

Decide who will assist anyone in your family with special needs during the escape.

Post the floor plan where every family member can review it once in a while. Make sure each family member is familiar with the routes and the emergency meeting place.

Beneath the floor plan, write the names of two people whose homes you can go to in case of emergency.

On a sheet of paper, write the answers to the following questions. Use complete sentences.

1. How can your family members help you make these escape plans?

2. Where will you post these escape plans?

3. What can your family do to make sure all family members can use the plan?

Objectives

After reading this lesson, you should be able to

◆ identify ways to avoid injuries in the workplace and at school

◆ identify ways to avoid drowning

◆ discuss water and sports safety

Injuries occur not only at home but also in the workplace and during recreational activities. You can reduce your risk for these injuries.

How Can Injuries at Work Be Reduced?

If you have a job, you may already know about job safety. Every year, nearly four million U.S. workers have disabling injuries on the job. More than 5,000 workers die. In addition, millions of work hours are lost every year because of work-related injuries and illnesses. Expenses for injuries and lost productivity cost employers hundreds of billions of dollars each year.

Many occupational injuries and illnesses can be prevented. A U.S. government agency that seeks to protect the safety and health of American workers is the Occupational Safety and Health Administration (OSHA).

Health at Work

Industrial Safety Specialist

Industrial safety specialists work for OSHA. OSHA's mission is to save lives, prevent injuries, and protect the health of American workers. Industrial safety specialists make sure companies correct unsafe conditions. Safety specialists might discover dangerous asbestos materials in a building. They may convince workers to practice industrial safety activities. All workers need to understand how to be safe. Industrial safety is challenging because of the many rules. Industrial safety specialists must be concerned with waste disposal, environmental safety, pollution, and health hazards.

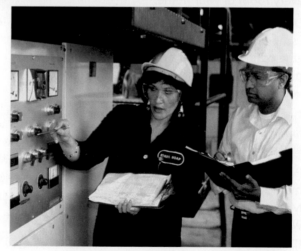

A 4-year college degree is usually required to become an industrial safety specialist. Continuing education also is necessary to keep up with changes on the job.

OSHA sets standards for industrial safety and provides education about safety procedures. For example, OSHA sets standards for noise and fire safety, protective clothing and safety gear, and safe levels of certain substances. It then works with employers and employees to make sure that these standards are met.

Employers are responsible for reducing risks of injury to employees by informing them of possible dangers on the job. They also must remove dangers in the workplace, train workers properly, and make employees aware of safety regulations.

Employees also can reduce the risks of injuries on the job. Getting necessary rest helps employees be alert at work and avoid injuries. Employees need to follow all safety procedures, learn how to use equipment properly, and wear any required protective clothing or devices.

How Can Risks of Injuries at School Be Reduced?

Injuries can happen at school, though many of them are preventable. For example, falls can happen at school. To prevent them, report spills and slippery places, such as worn stair edges, to a teacher or janitor. Do not run in the halls, especially when it is raining outside and the floors are wet.

Fires can break out at school. Pay attention during fire drills. Know where stairways and exits are located. Do not use elevators during a fire. Try to help people with disabilities get out of the building.

Your backpack can cause an injury. Do not use it as a portable locker. Backpacks should weigh no more than 15 to 20 pounds. Use both straps when carrying your backpack. Readjust the straps every time you put on your backpack.

How Can Recreational Injuries Be Reduced?

Everyone enjoys some kind of recreation. Every day, however, people are injured or die while engaging in recreational activity. Water and sports safety are special concerns.

Water Safety

Drowning is the third most common cause of accidental death in the United States. Drowning most often occurs among people between the ages of 15 and 24. It usually results from swimming and boating accidents, often when people have been drinking alcohol.

Knowing how to swim can prevent drowning. Swimming classes usually are offered through schools, at community pools, or through community recreation programs.

A technique that can help prevent drowning is called **survival floating.** This technique helps victims in warm water conserve their energy while they wait to be rescued. Figure 16.2.1 shows how survival floating works.

Drowning can be prevented in other ways. Before going out in a boat, people should check the weather conditions and make sure the boat is in good repair. No one in a boat should ever drink alcohol. Everyone in a boat should wear an approved life jacket or life preserver at all times. If a boat overturns, passengers should stay with the boat until help arrives.

Figure 16.2.1 *Survival floating*
Left: In the float position, rest face down for several seconds. Let arms and legs dangle.
Right: Slowly tilt head back so it clears the water. Exhale and take a new breath while pressing arms down and bringing legs together. Return to the float position.

Here are some other water safety guidelines that can help prevent drowning:

- Swim only in places where a lifeguard is on duty and follow any posted water safety rules.

- Dive only where you know water is a safe depth.

- If a strong current pulls you away from shore, swim at a diagonal angle toward the shore and try not to panic.

- If you see a swimmer in trouble, yell for help immediately. Do not attempt to rescue someone who is in danger of drowning unless you have had special training.

- Heed any warning signs to stay off thin ice. Signs should be posted if walking or skating on the ice is safe.

- If ice begins to crack while you are on it, lie down and crawl away from the crack to safety.

Sports and Recreational Safety

Injuries to people engaging in sports activities are very common. In fact, many doctors treat only sports injuries. You can prevent many sports accidents by following these simple guidelines:

- Know how to use recreational or sports equipment properly and safely as it was intended to be used. Make sure all equipment is working properly.

- Wear the protective gear that is required or recommended for a sport.

- Learn the skills needed to do the activity.

- Learn and follow any recommended safety guidelines, including proper warm-up and cooldown exercises.

- Do not try to do more than you are able or know how to do.

- If you fall while skating or biking, try to curl up into a ball and roll as you fall. This will decrease the chance of injuries.

- When camping, always make sure someone knows where you will be. Take plenty of food and water. Never camp alone.

Lesson 2 Review On a sheet of paper, write the letter of the answer that best completes each sentence.

1. Backpacks should not weigh more than _____.
   A 5 to 10 pounds
   B 10 to 15 pounds
   C 15 to 20 pounds
   D 20 to 25 pounds

2. A U.S. government agency that seeks to protect the health of workers is the _____.
   A Occupational Health and Safety Administration
   B Department of Justice
   C Department of Health and Human Services
   D Council on Environmental Quality

3. The third most common cause of accidental death in the United States is _____.
   A strangulation
   B drowning
   C falling
   D fire

On a sheet of paper, write the answers to the following questions. Use complete sentences.

4. **Critical Thinking** Why is it important for employees to learn how to use equipment properly?

5. **Critical Thinking** Suppose a person fell out of a boat and did not know how to swim. How could that person keep from drowning?

Motor vehicle crashes cause the highest number of deaths among 16- to 24-year-olds in the United States. Fortunately, safe driving practices can prevent many of these crashes.

How Can Vehicle Crashes Be Reduced?

The best prevention for vehicle crashes is to take a driver's training course to learn safe driving skills and habits. Students in these courses learn road rules and defensive driving skills. They learn to watch out for drivers who make mistakes. They learn to adjust for unsafe road conditions.

A critical safe driving habit is observing and maintaining the speed limit. When road conditions are wet or icy, traveling below the posted speed allows safe handling of a vehicle. Reducing speed on dirt roads and on damaged pavement is also important.

Wearing a seat belt at all times can reduce injuries if an accident does occur. Both drivers and riders should buckle their seat belts securely. Small children should always be buckled into car seats that meet specific state requirements.

Never use alcohol or other drugs and then drive. Never ride with a driver who is under the influence of alcohol or other drugs.

To avoid crashes:

• Maintain the vehicle properly.

• Maintain good vision by clearing moisture and ice from windows. Make sure windshield wipers and defroster fans work properly.

• To see and be seen, use headlights from dusk until just after sunrise and in rain, snow, and fog.

• Leave enough distance between you and the vehicle in front of you so you can stop quickly and safely.

• Avoid driving when your judgment might be clouded because of frustration, stress, anger, or other strong emotions.

Should school buses be equipped with seat belts?

How Can You Stay Safe on a School Bus?

Here are some tips for staying safe while riding a bus to or from school.

- When waiting for the bus, stay away from traffic and do not play in the street.

- Wait until the bus has stopped and the door has opened before stepping into the street.

- When on the bus, stay quietly in your seat. Loud talking or other noise can distract the bus driver.

- Never put your head, arms, or hands out of the window.

- Keep the aisles clear.

- Wait for the bus to stop completely before leaving your seat to get off.

- If you have to cross the street in front of the bus, walk ahead of the bus until you can see the driver before crossing. Make sure the driver can see you. Do not cross the center line of the road until it is safe for you to do so.

- Stay away from the bus's wheels at all times.

Figure 16.3.1 *Wearing seat belts reduces injuries in car crashes.*

Link to ➤➤➤

Arts

The movie *Passion Fish* is about a soap opera star who is injured in a car accident. She goes home to Louisiana to deal with her life in a wheelchair. One of her nurses has problems of her own. The movie shows how these two women become friends and help each other heal.

How Can Bicycle and Motorcycle Safety Be Increased?

Bicyclists and motorcyclists are hard to see and are less protected than people riding in closed vehicles. These reasons and human error increase their risk for accidents. Hundreds of thousands of people are injured or die each year in bicycle and motorcycle accidents.

Both bicyclists and motorcyclists should wear the proper safety helmets. They should obey all traffic rules. They should never grab a moving vehicle and should always keep a safe following distance. In addition, bicyclists should follow these guidelines:

- Make safe turns and cross intersections with care. Signal all turns with the left arm straight out for a left turn and the forearm up for a right turn.

- Some roads have bicycle lanes. Use these lanes when possible.

- Ride single file as far to the right as possible with the flow of traffic, not against it.

- Wear bright clothing to be seen in daylight and reflective clothing to be seen at night.

- Use the right safety equipment and make sure the bike is in good repair.

Motorcyclists should follow these safety tips:

- Follow the rules for getting a motorcycle permit or license in your state.

- Learn to drive a motorcycle properly and safely before taking it on the road.

- Be sure that the motorcycle has working lights, reflectors, and rearview mirrors.

- Make sure the motorcycle is in good repair and have it inspected regularly.

- Wear proper clothing for protection and to avoid getting it caught in moving parts.

- Be especially careful driving on wet surfaces.

Lesson 3 Review On a sheet of paper, write the word or phrase in parentheses that best completes each sentence.

1. The best prevention for vehicle crashes is a (driving course, reflector, safe distance).

2. It is important to (increase, maintain, reduce) speed with dangerous road conditions.

3. Bicyclists and motorcyclists are less (noisy, alert, protected) than people in closed vehicles.

On a sheet of paper, write the answers to the following questions. Use complete sentences.

4. **Critical Thinking** How do the tips for preventing vehicle crashes apply to school buses? What can you do to make your school bus ride safe?

5. **Critical Thinking** Why is it important for bicyclists to ride single file?

Decide for Yourself

In the United States, more than 500,000 people are injured riding bicycles each year. In 1999, 750 of these people died. More than 25 percent of the deaths were of children ages 5 to 15. More than 95 percent of those killed were not wearing helmets. About 140,000 children visit emergency rooms each year for head injuries they receive while bicycling.

Helmets are the most important safety equipment you can wear while bicycling. A helmet protects your skull and brain if you fall. Helmets vary in quality, however. The most important thing in choosing one is to find one that fits you properly. The strap should keep the helmet from sliding to one side or to the back.

Other safety equipment includes gloves to protect your hands if you fall. Pads can protect your knees and elbows.

Putting a flag and electric lights on your bike will help drivers of cars and other vehicles see you. Reflective materials on the bike or on clothing help, but lights are the best.

On a sheet of paper, write the answers to the following questions. Use complete sentences.

1. Why is wearing a helmet important?

2. Why is finding a helmet that fits important?

3. Suppose a friend plans to ride a bike home from your house after dark without lights or reflectors. What would you say to your friend?

Hurricane

A severe tropical storm with heavy rains and winds above 74 miles per hour

Tornado

A funnel-shaped column of wind with wind speeds up to 300 miles per hour

Natural disasters are sudden emergencies that result from causes in nature. Some natural disasters can be predicted. Others cannot be predicted. People who have no warning can be injured or killed in natural disasters, which cause millions of dollars in damage. With warning and preparation, however, people can survive these disasters with few or no injuries.

How Can People Prepare for a Hurricane?

A **hurricane** is a severe tropical storm with heavy rains and winds above 74 miles per hour. Most hurricanes can be predicted. They affect the southern and eastern coasts of the United States. When a storm begins to develop, the National Weather Service sends out a hurricane watch or warning. A watch means that a hurricane may occur. A warning means that one is expected within the next 24 hours. People can use radios, TVs, or the Internet to get updates and instructions. In dangerous situations, people are told to quickly leave certain areas.

To prepare for a hurricane, tape or board windows and bring in items from outside. If advised to leave your home, go to a designated place until conditions are safe again. Before leaving home, shut off water, gas, and electric power. Avoid any downed power lines to prevent being killed by electric shock. If the hurricane is close, do not drive. Stay indoors on the downwind side of the house or building.

How Can People Prepare for a Tornado?

Another natural disaster involving high winds and heavy rain is a **tornado.** A tornado is a funnel-shaped column of wind with wind speeds up to 300 miles per hour. Usually, tornadoes happen in the central and southern parts of the United States. These dangerous storms can be predicted. The National Weather Service sends out a tornado watch when weather conditions make it possible for tornadoes to form. A tornado warning is issued when a tornado is formed and is threatening a certain area.

Figure 16.4.1 *Tornadoes can cause serious damage and injury.*

If you are in the area of an approaching tornado, take shelter at once. Go to the basement and stay there. If you do not have a basement, go to the center of the house on the lowest floor. Crouch or lie flat in a closet or bathtub and cover your head. People who live in mobile homes should go to a tornado shelter. If there is no shelter, they should leave their homes and head for low, protected ground.

If you are outside and you have time, move away from a tornado at right angles to its path. If the tornado is too close, lie facedown in a ditch or the nearest low spot.

Technology and Society

People in many areas of the country can dial 911 to speak with emergency fire and police services. New technology is being developed to alert people to natural disasters. The technology enables the National Weather Service to make more than 1,000 calls per minute to people in targeted areas.

Flood

A natural disaster that occurs when a body of water overflows and covers normally dry land

Flash flood

A dangerous flood that occurs suddenly without warning because of heavy rains

Earthquake

The shaking caused when the major slabs of rock in the earth's crust shift and move

How Can People Prepare for a Flood?

A **flood** is a natural disaster that occurs when a body of water overflows and covers normally dry land. Floods may result from severe rainstorms or from unusually heavy winter snowmelts in the spring. Most floods can be predicted hours to days in advance. Occasionally, however, very heavy rains cause dangerous **flash floods** suddenly and without warning.

If people live in flood areas, they need to know where to go if they are ordered to move to high ground. If they have time before leaving, they should turn off gas, electricity, and water in their homes. They should also move their belongings to an upper floor if they have one.

During a flood, do not try to walk across a stream where water is at or above knee level. Do not drive over flooded roads or land. If your car stalls because of floodwater, leave it and go to higher ground at once.

After a flood, do not touch electrical equipment in wet areas. Throw away any foods or liquids that the floodwater touched. Drink only bottled or boiled water until you are told the water supply is safe again.

How Can People Prepare for an Earthquake?

Another type of natural disaster is an **earthquake.** An earthquake happens when plates—major slabs of rock in the earth's crust—shift and move, causing the earth to shake. Most earthquakes in the United States occur along the West Coast. Scientists cannot yet predict when an earthquake will occur. Even though earthquakes cannot be predicted, people in earthquake areas can prepare emergency plans.

To prepare for an earthquake, store emergency supplies such as food, water, flashlights, extra batteries, and a first aid kit. Learn where the main gas valve is in a house or building and know how to shut it off. Either move or secure pictures and mirrors so they will not fall off the walls.

During an earthquake, duck under a strong table or desk and cover your face and head if you are indoors. Hold this position until the shaking stops. Stay away from glass and do not use elevators or stairs. If you are driving, move to the shoulder of the road, stop, and stay in the car. Do not stop under bridges, overpasses, or power lines. If outside, stay in a clear space away from buildings, walls, trees, and power lines.

After an earthquake, turn off the gas valve if you smell gas to avoid a fire from a broken gas line. Stay away from downed power lines and keep out of damaged buildings.

How Can People Prepare for a Blizzard?

A natural disaster that occurs in winter is a **blizzard.** A blizzard is a violent snowstorm with winds above 35 miles per hour that lasts for at least 3 hours. The temperature during a blizzard is at or below 20°F, and there is almost no visibility. The National Weather Service can predict blizzards, which occur mainly in the northern plains of the United States.

During a blizzard, stay in your home or a warm shelter. Do not travel even short distances. If there is a medical emergency, call 911 or alert local authorities for help. If the heat goes out in your home, dress in layers of warm clothing and sleep under several blankets. Turn off water main and open taps to avoid frozen water pipes.

If you live in an area where blizzards occur, carry emergency gear in your vehicle during the winter. Emergency gear includes blankets, flashlights, snacks, warm mittens and hats, extra socks, and warm boots. If your vehicle becomes stuck during a blizzard, stay in it. Run the vehicle only a few times each hour for heat. Clear away snow from the tailpipe to keep car exhaust out of the vehicle. Keep moving and stay awake to keep from freezing.

Keep a supply of new batteries for radios and flashlights on hand at all times.

How Can People Prepare for Lightning Strikes?

Another natural disaster is a **lightning** strike. Lightning is an electrical discharge that commonly occurs during thunderstorms. Lightning is dangerous because it can strike and kill people. The National Weather Service can predict thunderstorms, which occur in certain seasons in most areas of the United States.

During a thunderstorm, stay indoors or in a closed vehicle. Unplug electrical equipment and use telephones with cords only in an emergency. (Cell phones are safe during thunderstorms.) If you are outdoors, find shelter away from trees, tall objects, and water. That is because lightning usually strikes tall objects or water. Lie down in the lowest possible place if you cannot get to shelter. Whether indoors or outdoors, stay away from metal objects during a thunderstorm.

How Can Communities Prepare for Disasters?

Usually, communities have plans to follow in case of natural disasters. For example, if a tornado or severe storms are approaching, sirens sound to alert people to take shelter. People who make these plans usually include police, hospital, fire, and public health representatives. The planners may also include local Red Cross, United Way, and the Federal Emergency Management Agency (FEMA) representatives. FEMA is part of the U.S. Department of Homeland Security. FEMA's purpose is to help people before, during, and after a disaster.

The agencies these people represent can teach people how to prevent accidents, as well as how to respond in disasters. Many of these agencies offer courses to train people for emergencies. For example, the Red Cross offers courses in first aid and lifesaving.

Word Bank

blizzard
flash flood
lightning

Lesson 4 Review On a sheet of paper, write the word or phrase from the Word Bank that best completes each sentence.

1. A _____ occurs suddenly and is caused by heavy rains.

2. To avoid injury by _____, you should use telephones with cords only in an emergency during a thunderstorm.

3. A _____ lasts longer than 3 hours.

On a sheet of paper, write the answers to the following questions. Use complete sentences.

4. Critical Thinking How are hurricanes and tornadoes alike and different?

5. Critical Thinking How is hurricane preparation different from earthquake preparation?

Chapter 16 SUMMARY

- Serious falls can happen at home. Installing simple equipment and using some preventive measures can help you avoid falls.

- Fires caused by electrical problems, fuel and fire starters, space heaters and furnaces, and open flames can all be prevented.

- Every home should have one or more smoke detectors and fire extinguishers.

- A few simple measures can prevent poisoning or electrical shocks.

- The Occupational Safety and Health Administration (OSHA) sets standards for safety in the workplace. Employers are responsible to reduce and remove dangers in the workplace. Employees can reduce risks by following procedures and requirements.

- Learning to swim can prevent drowning. Survival floating and following other water safety guidelines also can prevent drowning.

- Sports injuries can be prevented by using equipment properly, wearing protective gear, and learning necessary skills.

- Learning safe driving skills and habits, maintaining the speed limit, and driving according to conditions all help prevent vehicle crashes. Wearing a seat belt can reduce injuries if a crash occurs. Following other tips can help avoid crashes.

- Bicyclists and motorcyclists can be seriously injured in an accident because they are less protected than people in larger vehicles. Wearing helmets, following the rules of the road, and taking other preventive actions can reduce risks of accidents.

- Natural disasters cannot be prevented and may or may not be predictable. People can be prepared and take protective steps in case of hurricanes, tornadoes, floods, earthquakes, blizzards, or lightning strikes.

Vocabulary

blizzard, 388	flash flood, 387	lightning, 389
earthquake, 387	flood, 387	smoke detector, 371
electrical shock, 373	hazard, 374	survival floating, 378
fire extinguisher, 371	hurricane, 385	tornado, 385

Chapter 16 R E V I E W

Word Bank

blizzard

earthquake

electrical shock

fire extinguisher

flash flood

flood

hazard

hurricane

lightning

smoke detector

survival floating

tornado

Vocabulary Review

On a sheet of paper, write the correct word or phrase from the Word Bank that best completes each sentence.

1. A(n) _____ is a portable device containing chemicals that put out small fires.

2. A flow of electric current through the body is _____.

3. An unprotected electrical outlet is a safety _____.

4. A technique to conserve energy in warm water while waiting to be rescued is _____.

5. When there is smoke or excess heat, a(n) _____ sounds.

6. A(n) _____ occurs when water covers land that is normally dry.

7. A(n) _____ is a flood that occurs suddenly.

8. A violent snowstorm is a(n) _____.

9. A(n) _____ is a funnel-shaped column of wind.

10. A(n) _____ has winds above 75 miles per hour.

11. Preparation for a(n) _____ includes anchoring heavy items that might fall.

12. An electrical discharge that occurs during a thunderstorm is _____.

Concept Review

On a sheet of paper, write the letter of the answer that best completes each sentence.

13. The federal government agency in charge of disaster aid is _____.

    A OSHA   **C** FEMA

    B the FBI   **D** the National Weather Service

14. Most injuries that occur at home are the result of _____.

    A drowning   **C** poisoning

    B falls   **D** fire

15. A natural disaster in which people must seek higher ground is a _____.

    A flood   **C** hurricane

    B blizzard   **D** tornado

16. A natural disaster in which people must go to basements or lower floors is a _____.

    A flood   **C** hurricane

    B blizzard   **D** tornado

17. Electrical fires can be caused by _____.

    A burning candles   **C** overloaded outlets

    B gas stoves   **D** dirty chimneys

Critical Thinking

On a sheet of paper, write the answers to the following questions. Use complete sentences.

18. Which home safety tips are your responsibility? Which are the responsibility of adults in your home?

19. You may have heard the caution that you "should not fool with nature." Why do you think this is especially true during natural disasters?

20. Which parts of school and school bus safety can you control? Which are under someone else's control?

Test-Taking Tip   After you have completed a test, reread each question and answer. Ask yourself: Have I answered the question completely?

Self-Assessment

Can you answer these questions?

☑ 1. What are the basic guidelines for first aid?

☑ 2. When should you call 911 and what information should you provide?

☑ 3. What laws protect people who help others in emergencies?

☑ 4. What should be placed in a first aid kit?

☑ 5. How can you help someone who is choking?

☑ 6. How can you help someone who has stopped breathing?

☑ 7. How can you help someone who is in shock?

☑ 8. How can you help someone who is bleeding heavily?

☑ 9. How can you help someone who has been poisoned?

☑ 10. For what types of injuries do you know how to give first aid?

17 Applying First Aid to Injuries

I n an emergency, it is important to closely follow certain rules for giving first aid. In some emergencies, first aid skills can mean the difference between life and death. If you know first aid, you can spot the signs of a serious illness or injury. Then you will be able to do the proper things to help someone. Giving the right first aid can help make sure that these illnesses or injuries do not become more serious.

In this chapter, you will learn the basic guidelines for first aid. You will also find out about laws that protect you if you help someone who needs first aid. You will learn the signs of choking, respiratory failure, cardiovascular failure, shock, and serious bleeding. You will learn how to give first aid for life-threatening emergencies, poisoning, and common injuries.

Goals for Learning

◆ To identify basic guidelines for first aid

◆ To describe first aid steps in five life-threatening emergencies

◆ To explain first aid for poisoning and common injuries

First aid is immediate emergency care. It is given to a sick or injured person before professional medical care arrives. Performing the proper emergency steps can lessen the pain and seriousness of someone's injuries. It can even save a life.

What Are the Basic Guidelines for First Aid?

The most important thing to do for someone in an emergency is to remain calm. Then you will be better able to follow these guidelines:

1. Look around at your immediate surroundings to see if there are any dangers to either one of you. Move the person only in case of danger, such as drowning or fire. Make sure you will be safe while helping the person.

2. Find out if the person is conscious, or awake. Tap on the person's shoulder. You can also loudly ask if the person is all right. If he or she is not conscious, do not leave. Ask someone else to call for help. If you are alone, quickly make the call. Then immediately return to take care of the person.

3. Check whether the person is breathing. Make sure he or she has a pulse and open airway. If not, try to clear the airway and perform rescue breathing. Rescue breathing is described in Lesson 2 of this chapter.

Objectives

After reading this lesson, you should be able to

◆ explain the basic guidelines for first aid

◆ understand how to help someone who needs first aid

◆ discuss Good Samaritan laws

◆ describe universal precautions

First aid

Immediate emergency care given to a sick or injured person before professional medical care arrives

What can you do at home to prepare for a medical emergency? List what every family member should know, such as the location of a first aid kit.

Research and Write

Research the American Red Cross. Find out who started this organization and for what reason. Write a report that includes how many people the Red Cross helps each year. Include the kinds of emergencies in which the Red Cross helps. Also, include information about how the Red Cross is run and the people who work for the Red Cross.

Latex

A kind of rubber used to make thin gloves for health care professionals

Practice knowing when to use 911 with younger brothers or sisters. Ask: "What happens if the adult at home is hurt and cannot tell you what is wrong?" Explain: "Dial 911. Tell your name. Tell our address. Tell what is wrong. Don't hang up."

4. If the person is conscious, ask permission to give help. Check the person's whole body for any other injuries. Check for emergency medical identification, such as a tag, bracelet, or card. This identification will tell any medical problems the person may have. These problems may include a heart condition, diabetes, or allergies to medicines.

5. Check for bleeding. If you have **latex** gloves, put them on. Latex gloves are very thin gloves made of a special type of rubber. You have probably seen them in a doctor's office or hospital. The latex gloves will help protect you. After you put them on, press down on the wound. This will help stop the bleeding. If you do not have latex or plastic gloves, you can use several layers of cloth or a sheet of plastic to protect yourself from the blood.

6. If no one has called for help, call 911 or 0 for the operator. Explain that you need emergency medical help. Be prepared to say where you are and tell important details about the person you are helping. Answer any questions you are asked. Listen carefully to everything you are told to do. Stay on the line until the operator ends the call.

After you have done these things, stay with the person. Explain that more help is on the way. Do your best to keep the person from getting too cold or too warm. Shade him or her from sunlight. Loosen any tight clothing around the neck area if you can, but be careful not to move the person's spine or neck. Use common sense and do only what you have been trained to do. Make sure your help will not hurt the person.

Link to ➤➤➤

Social Studies

In 1797, French doctor Dominique-Jean Larrey went to Italy to treat injured French soldiers. He used "flying ambulances." These were wagons pulled by horses. The wagons could quickly take the wounded from the battlefield to get medical care. Larrey's ideas led to the kind of ambulances in use today.

What Are Good Samaritan Laws?

To protect people who help others in emergencies, many states have **Good Samaritan laws.** These laws state that rescuers use common sense and skills within their training. You can get this training in first aid classes. These classes are offered through groups such as the American Red Cross and the American Heart Association. You are not expected to risk your own life when you help someone else.

What Are Universal Precautions?

Medical workers protect themselves by using **universal precautions.** Universal precautions keep workers from having contact with another person's blood or other body fluids. These actions help lessen the risk of passing on diseases such as AIDS.

Here are some universal precautions:

- Workers wear latex gloves and other protective gear, such as masks.

- Workers are careful to properly throw away any materials that have come in contact with body fluids. These materials may include bandages and **dressings.** Dressings are layers of cloth and other materials that protect a wound.

- Workers carefully wash their hands after they finish.

If you ever give first aid, you should follow these rules. They protect both you and the person you are helping.

Health in Your Life

Protecting Your Family

Here is a list of ways to protect family members during emergencies:

- Keep cleaning items and medicines in the boxes and bottles they came in. Keep them in separate places. Never store gasoline or other poisonous items in soft-drink bottles.

- Keep all medicines and cleaning items out of the reach of children.

- Mark all poisonous items with a sticker that shows children should stay away. This includes cleaning items. Poison control centers may have these stickers available at no charge.

- Place nonskid mats in bathtubs.

- Do not give or take medicine if you just woke up and the room is still dark. Wait until you turn on the lights and are fully awake.

- Put together a first aid kit. The American Red Cross recommends that you put the following items in your kit: activated charcoal (use only if told to by a poison control center); adhesive tape; antiseptic ointment; bandages (several sizes); blanket; cold pack; disposable latex gloves; gauze pads and roller gauze (several sizes); hand cleaner; plastic bags; scissors and tweezers; small flashlight and extra batteries; syrup of ipecac (use only if told to by a poison control center).

On a sheet of paper, write the answers to the following questions. Use complete sentences.

1. Why do you think it is important to keep cleaning items and medicines in the boxes and bottles they came in?

2. Why do you think it is important to place nonskid mats in bathtubs?

3. Why do you think it is a good idea to have disposable latex gloves in a first aid kit?

Lesson 1 Review On a sheet of paper, write the answers to the following questions. Use complete sentences.

1. What is the most important thing to do in an emergency?

2. How can you find out if a person is conscious?

3. What are Good Samaritan laws?

4. **Critical Thinking** Suppose you are helping someone who is not conscious. What is one reason you might leave the person alone?

5. **Critical Thinking** What is the purpose of using universal precautions?

Health at Work

911 Operator

A 911 operator answers calls for people who need emergency services. The operator asks questions to find out information.

In an emergency, the operator types the information into a computer. Then emergency help is sent.

It is important for a 911 operator to think fast and make decisions quickly. The operator can offer support until help arrives.

Usually, a 911 operator must have a high school diploma. Knowing how to work with computers and do office work sometimes is needed. Often, training is done on the job. A special certification might also be needed.

In first aid, it is important to treat life-threatening conditions before treating anything else. Choking, inability to breathe, heart attack, shock, and serious bleeding can all be life threatening. Minutes can mean the difference between life and death for people with these conditions. Knowing what to do before help arrives can make that difference.

What Is First Aid for Choking?

Thousands of children and adults choke to death each year. Often, food or some other object blocks the airway or throat. It is important to recognize the **universal distress signal** for choking. This signal is known in many different places by people who speak many different languages. Someone who grabs the throat with the hand or hands is choking. Look at Figure 17.2.1. Other signs of choking include gasping, a weak cough, and inability to speak. A person may get pale or blue skin and pass out.

Choking is sometimes mistaken for a sign of a heart attack. Before giving first aid, always ask if a person is choking. If the person choking can still speak or cough, allow him or her to try to cough up the object. Never pound on the person's back to try to force out the object. This can make the problem worse.

If the person choking cannot speak, cough, or breathe, perform the **Heimlich maneuver.** Firm, upward thrusts, or squeezes, just below the rib cage force air from the lungs. This pushes the object out of the throat.

Universal distress signal

A sign made by grabbing the throat with the hand or hands to show a person is choking

Heimlich maneuver

A way of giving firm upward thrusts below a person's rib cage to force out an object from the throat

Figure 17.2.1 *Someone using the universal distress signal for choking needs help immediately.*

The Heimlich maneuver is shown in Figure 17.2.2A:

1. Stand behind the person choking and wrap your arms around the person's waist.

2. Make a fist with one hand.

3. Place the thumb side of your fist against the middle of the person's abdomen above the navel but below the ribs.

4. Use your other hand to grab your fist. Give quick, upward thrusts into the abdomen.

5. Repeat this until the object is forced out.

If the blockage is not removed and the person passes out, lower the person face up on the floor. Open the person's mouth and check the throat for the object. Use the finger sweep shown in Figure 17.2.2B. To do the finger sweep:

1. Grasp the person's tongue and lower jaw between your thumb and fingers and lift the jaw.

2. Use your other index finger in a hooking action at the back of the tongue. Sweep the object out of the airway.

3. If this does not work, begin rescue breathing, which is described on the next page.

If you are alone and begin to choke, you can give yourself the Heimlich maneuver. Put your hands in the position shown in Figure 17.2.2A. You also can lean over with your stomach pushing into a firm object, such as a chair.

A. The Heimlich maneuver

B. The finger sweep

Figure 17.2.2 *First aid for choking*

What Is First Aid for Respiratory Failure?

Choking is one reason people stop breathing. Other reasons include electrical shock and drowning. **Respiratory failure,** or not breathing, is a life-threatening emergency. Signs that a person is not breathing are no noticeable breathing movement and blue fingernails, lips, and tongue.

Rescue breathing is needed when a person stops breathing, but the person's circulation and pulse continue. Rescue breathing puts oxygen from a rescuer's lungs into an unconscious person's lungs. Figure 17.2.3 shows the steps in rescue breathing, which is also called **mouth-to-mouth resuscitation.** The best way to learn how to do this is in your health class or another training class.

What Is First Aid for Cardiovascular Failure?

When a person's heart or circulatory system stops working, it is a life-threatening emergency. The cardiovascular system may fail because of electrical shock, poisoning, drug overdose, or heart disease. It may also fail because a blood vessel is blocked, as in a stroke.

A. Tap on the person's shoulder or loudly ask, "Are you all right?" This will help you find out if the person is conscious. If the person is unconscious, send someone to call 911 for help.

B. Tilt the person's head back and lift the chin to open the airway.

C. Look, listen, and feel for breathing for 5 to 10 seconds.

D. Keep the person's head tilted back and pinch the nose shut.

E. Take a normal breath. Then seal your lips around the person's mouth and give him or her two full breaths. For babies, seal your lips around both the mouth and nose. Then give gentle breaths once every 3 seconds.

F. Check for a pulse on the side of the neck for 5 to 10 seconds. If you find a pulse, recheck breathing. Continue rescue breathing as necessary.

Figure 17.2.3 *The steps in rescue breathing*

Cardiac arrest

A condition in which the heart has stopped beating and there is no pulse

Cardio-pulmonary resuscitation (CPR)

A procedure for cardiovascular failure

Chest compression

When doing CPR, the act of pressing against the chest over and over

?

Suppose you need to give CPR. You are nervous. How can you calm down?

Signs of cardiovascular failure include a hard time breathing, an irregular pulse, a damp face, and pale or blue skin. The person may stop breathing altogether. If a person's heart has stopped beating and there is no pulse, he or she is in **cardiac arrest.** If a person shows these signs, call 911 immediately.

As you wait for help to arrive, you can perform **cardiopulmonary resuscitation (CPR).** This involves both rescue breathing and **chest compressions,** or presses. The goals of CPR are to open the person's airway and restore breathing and circulation. To perform CPR, follow these basic steps, which are shown in Figure 17.2.4:

1. Find the proper hand position.

- Locate the notch at the lower end of the person's breastbone.

- Place the heel of your other hand on the breastbone, next to your fingers.

- Remove your hand from the notch and place it on top of your other hand.

- Use only the heels of your hands, keeping your fingers off the person's chest.

2. Give compressions to the person in the following way:

- Position your shoulders over your hands.

- Compress, or press down on, the person's breastbone $1\frac{1}{2}$ to 2 inches. Do 30 compressions in about 10 seconds.

- Compress down and up smoothly, keeping your hand in contact with the person's chest at all times.

- After every 30 compressions, give the person two full breaths.

The best way to learn and practice CPR is in your health class or another training class.

Figure 17.2.4 *Cardiopulmonary resuscitation (CPR)*

What Is First Aid for Shock?

Shock can be a life-threatening emergency. It is a physical reaction to a serious injury, such as bleeding or a heart attack. When a person is in shock, the circulatory system fails to send enough blood to the body. Because shock can lead to death, steps should be taken at once to treat shock.

To tell if a person is in shock, look for specific signs. Signs of shock include a very fast or slow pulse, fast or slow breathing, and large pupils. Other signs are weakness, thirst, and an upset stomach. They may include cold and damp skin, as well as pale or blue skin.

If a person is in shock, call 911 for help at once. Then use these first aid steps for shock until help arrives:

1. Keep the person lying down. Raise the person's legs about 12 inches to help return blood to the heart. Do not raise the legs, however, if you think the person's neck or spine is injured.

2. Maintain the person's normal body temperature. Use blankets or other warm covers.

3. Do not give the person any food or water.

What Is First Aid for Serious Bleeding?

Because serious bleeding can cause shock or death, it must be controlled quickly. If you are going to help someone who is seriously bleeding, you must do four things:

1. Stop the bleeding.

2. Protect the wound from infection.

3. Treat the person for shock.

4. Get emergency help immediately.

If you are helping someone with serious bleeding, you should first take steps to protect yourself. Latex gloves, plastic gloves, or a sheet of plastic can give you this protection. Several layers of cloth also offer protection.

Sterile

Free from bacteria

Pressure point

A place on the body where an artery can be pressed against a bone to stop bleeding in an arm or a leg

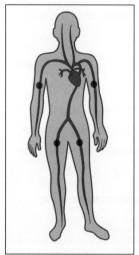

Figure 17.2.5 *Pressure points for the arms and legs*

Word Bank

choking

respiratory failure

shock

After protecting yourself, follow the steps below to control serious bleeding.

1. Cover the wound with a **sterile** bandage or clean cloth. A sterile bandage is free from bacteria.

2. Use the palm of your hand to put direct pressure on the wound. If blood soaks through the first dressing, leave it there and add more dressings. Continue doing this until the bleeding stops.

3. Elevate, or raise, the wound above the level of the person's heart.

Usually, bleeding can be stopped with direct pressure and elevation. If bleeding continues, you may need to apply pressure at a **pressure point.** This is a place where an artery can be pressed against a bone. The purpose of using pressure is to control the flow of blood and stop bleeding in an arm or a leg. To apply pressure on one of these points, use your fingers or the heel of your hand. Press the artery toward the nearest bone and hold it there until help arrives. This will prevent the person from losing more blood. Figure 17.2.5 shows where the pressure points are for the arms and legs.

Lesson 2 Review On a sheet of paper, write the word or phrase from the Word Bank that best completes each sentence.

1. Rescue breathing is the kind of help you give when someone has _____.

2. The Heimlich maneuver is used to help someone who is _____.

3. Signs of _____ include large pupils, very fast or slow pulse, damp skin, and thirst.

On a sheet of paper, write the answers to the following questions. Use complete sentences.

4. **Critical Thinking** Why should people who are not doctors know the Heimlich maneuver?

5. **Critical Thinking** What might you do to help you remember how to give CPR?

After reading this lesson, you should be able to

◆ recognize the correct first aid steps to take when someone has been poisoned

◆ understand first aid treatment for a variety of problems

◆ discuss emergency treatment needed when a person has been in extreme temperatures

Oral poisoning

Poisoning that happens after a harmful material is swallowed

Inhalation poisoning

Poisoning caused by breathing in harmful fumes

Fume

Gas

Someone trained in first aid can recognize signs of poisoning, fainting, burns, and other problems. Then the right help can be offered.

What Is First Aid for Poisoning?

Poisons may be swallowed, breathed in, or absorbed through the skin. In any case, medical help should be found quickly after first aid is given. Some poisoning can be life threatening.

Oral Poisoning

Oral poisoning happens when a harmful material, such as a household cleaner, is swallowed. Signs of oral poisoning include sudden severe abdominal pain, upset stomach, and vomiting. The person may become sleepy and lose consciousness. The person may have chemical burns on the lips and a chemical odor on the breath. A container of a poisonous material may be nearby.

If a person has swallowed a poison, call your local poison control center immediately. Give as much information as you can, including the person's age. Also tell how much you think the person weighs. Give the name of the poison you think was swallowed. The poison control expert will tell you what to do and send emergency workers if they are needed.

Inhalation Poisoning

Inhalation poisoning happens when someone breathes in harmful **fumes.** Fumes are gases. Signs of inhalation poisoning include headache and dizziness followed by unconsciousness.

Link to ➤➤➤

Biology

When a person swallows poison, how does it get into the bloodstream? The poison enters the throat. It is pushed into the stomach by the muscles and moves to the small intestine. Villi absorb chemicals from the small intestine. The villi contain small blood vessels that are connected to the rest of the bloodstream. Poisonous chemicals move from the villi into the bloodstream.

Contact Poisoning

Poisoning that happens when harmful materials are absorbed through the skin

Fainting

Short-term loss of consciousness caused by too little blood to the brain

Rabies

A serious disease that affects the nervous system

Someone who has breathed in poison should get fresh air or be moved out of the area immediately. If the person is unconscious, check for a pulse and breathing. If the person is not breathing, perform rescue breathing or cardiopulmonary resuscitation (CPR). Be careful not to breathe in any harmful fumes yourself. If your own safety is in danger, do not try to help the person. Instead, call for help at once.

Contact Poisoning

Contact poisoning happens when harmful materials are absorbed through the skin. Poisons may be absorbed from plants such as poison ivy and from household cleaning products. Poisons may also be absorbed from lawn and farm chemicals, such as fertilizers. Signs of contact poisoning include a bad rash, swelling, blisters, itching, and burning. Immediately take off any clothes that have come in contact with a poison. Wash the skin with soap and large amounts of water. Applying calamine lotion may get rid of the itching for a while.

What Other Problems Need First Aid?

Fortunately, most problems that need first aid are less serious than those described in Lesson 2. First aid can ease the pain of these problems. It can prevent them from becoming more serious. You can read about a number of these problems below.

Fainting

Fainting is a short-term loss of consciousness caused by too little blood to the brain. Signs that a person is about to faint include pale skin, perspiration, and dizziness. Usually, the person regains consciousness in a minute or two. To give first aid to a person who has fainted, have the person lie flat. Then elevate the person's feet. Another way to help is to bend the person over so the head is lower than the heart. Loosen any tight clothing and sponge the face with cool water. If the person does not regain consciousness, call 911.

Bites and Stings

Animal bites—Bites from dogs and other animals can give diseases such as **rabies** to humans. Rabies is a serious disease that affects a person's nervous system.

Fracture

A broken bone

Splint

An unbendable object that keeps a broken arm, leg, or finger in place

Some people think that minor dog and cat bites should not be treated. This is not true. Even small bites can easily get infected. It is important to treat them in the same way a more serious bite would be treated.

To help, first control any bleeding from the animal bite. Then wash the wound with soap and water. Finally, apply a dressing. If possible, have animal control workers catch the animal. Then it can be tested for rabies. Do not try to catch the animal yourself. Follow up later by calling your local health department to find out if the animal had rabies. This will tell you whether the person needs treatment for rabies or other diseases.

Snakebites—Only four kinds of snakes in the United States are poisonous. These are rattlesnakes, copperheads, water moccasins, and coral snakes. Snakebites can cause serious problems and even death. Snakebites should be treated at once. Get the person with a snakebite to a hospital right away or call 911. In the meantime, keep the person calm, still, and lying down. This keeps the venom, or the animal's poison, from traveling throughout the body. Keep the affected part of the body still. Make sure it is lower than the person's heart.

Insect stings—Some people are allergic to stings from bees, wasps, and hornets. These people may have a life-threatening reaction to a sting. Use the edge of something firm or your fingernail to scrape away the stinger. Do not pull out the stinger. Pulling out the stinger could force the poison under the skin. Wash the area with cold water. Apply vinegar or a paste of baking soda and water. These applications help lessen the swelling and pain. Watch for signs such as vomiting, upset stomach, a hard time breathing, or an irregular heartbeat. If you see any of these signs, call 911 immediately. If the person stops breathing, begin rescue breathing.

Bone and Joint Injuries

If you think someone has a broken bone, or **fracture,** check for crookedness, swelling, bruising, loss of movement, and serious pain. Keep the body part in the same position in which you found it. Make a **splint.** A splint is an unbendable object that keeps a broken arm, leg, or finger in place. If the bone has broken through the skin, cover the wound with a sterile dressing. Be careful not to press on the bone. If you think the person has a broken neck or back, do not move him or her. Call 911 at once.

Sprain

The tearing or stretching of tendons or ligaments that connect joints

A **sprain** occurs when the tendons or ligaments that connect joints together get torn or stretched. The joints are parts of the body where bones are connected. Usually, sprains occur at wrists, knees, or ankles. A person with a sprain should avoid moving that part of the body. To lessen swelling, the injured part of the body should be raised. An ice pack or a cold pack should be placed on the injury. Then it is important to get medical attention.

Figure 17.3.1 *A person with a sprain should place an ice pack or a cold pack on the injured part.*

Burns

There are three types, or degrees, of burns. First-degree burns are the least serious. They hurt only the outer layer of the skin. Some sunburns are first-degree burns. Second-degree burns affect the top layers of skin. Bad sunburns may cause second-degree burns. Third-degree burns go through all the layers of skin to the tissues underneath.

First aid for first-degree and second-degree burns is the same. First, stop the burn by getting the person away from its source. Next, cool the burn with large amounts of cool water. Then without cleaning the burn, cover it. As a cover, use a dry, loose, sterile dressing or a sheet. This will help keep the burn from getting infected. For third-degree burns, call 911 immediately. Stay with the person and watch for signs of shock.

Objects in the Eye

If there is an object in the eye, do not rub. Flush the eye by pouring large amounts of water over it. Start the flushing at the corner of the eye near the nose. This may remove the object. If the object will not come out, get medical help.

Health Myth

Myth: In a burn emergency, you should put butter or ice on the burn.

Fact: Butter does not help to treat a burn. Ice can actually be harmful. It can create a cold burn in addition to the burn the person already has.

Health Myth

Myth: If someone has a nosebleed, pinch the nose and lean the head back.

Fact: Leaning the head back does not help. It can cause blood to run down the throat. Then the blood can enter the stomach. This could make the person vomit.

Nosebleeds

For a small nosebleed, have the person sit and lean forward. The person should breathe through the mouth. Direct pressure should be placed on the bleeding nostril for 10 minutes. A cold cloth across the bridge of the nose may help. If these steps do not stop the bleeding, get medical help.

Exposure to Extreme Heat and Cold

Heat exhaustion usually comes from hard physical work in a very hot place. Signs of heat exhaustion include weakness, heavy sweating, muscle cramps, headache, and dizziness. To give first aid, remove the person from the heat. Loosen the person's clothing, cool him or her with wet cloths, and offer cool water to sip. Call 911 if the person becomes unconscious.

Heatstroke may happen when a person stays in high heat too long. The main sign of heatstroke is a lack of sweating. Other signs include high body temperature, red skin, vomiting, confusion, a very fast pulse, and sudden unconsciousness. Call 911 immediately and follow the same steps for treating heat exhaustion.

Hypothermia is a serious loss of body heat that comes from being in the cold too long. It happens most often in cold, damp weather. It often happens when a person is tired and is not dressed warmly. Signs of hypothermia include shivering, slurred speech, and below-normal body temperature.

Hypothermia can cause death. If the person is not breathing, perform rescue breathing. Have someone call 911 immediately. Then remove wet clothing and dry the person. Slowly warm the person with blankets or other heat sources. Give the person warm liquids to drink. Watch the person until help arrives.

Frostbite is a tissue injury that comes from being out in extreme cold without proper clothing. It usually affects the hands, feet, ears, or nose. Skin that has frostbite looks gray or yellowish and feels numb, cold, and doughy. To treat frostbite, slowly rewarm the affected area by placing it in warm water. Do not rub the area. Cover it with clean, dry bandages and get medical help.

Some people are afraid to go to an emergency room. They do not know what to expect when they get there. Research to find out what people can expect when they go to an emergency room. Create a brochure that explains what to expect.

Lesson 3 Review On a sheet of paper, write the letter of the answer that best completes each sentence.

1. Inhalation poisoning happens when someone _____ a harmful material.

A breathes in   **C** spits out

B touches or holds   **D** chews and swallows

2. A _____ burn extends through all layers of skin.

A first-degree   **C** third-degree

B second-degree   **D** fourth-degree

3. For a bee sting, you should NOT _____.

A wash the sting with cold water

B pull out the stinger quickly

C apply a paste of baking soda

D watch for an upset stomach

On a sheet of paper, write the answers to the following questions. Use complete sentences.

4. Critical Thinking If something is in the eye, why should the eye not be rubbed?

5. Critical Thinking Give an example of a time that someone might get heat exhaustion. What are two ways the heat exhaustion might have been prevented?

Decide for Yourself

You and a friend are walking through the neighborhood on your way to a party. Your friend steps on a wet rock, his foot slides off the rock, and he falls down. When he falls, his ankle twists and makes a popping sound. You help your friend stand up and ask him if he is hurt. He says, "No, I'm fine. It's no big deal." Your friend begins to limp, but he still wants to attend the party. He says that he will put an ice pack on his ankle when he returns home after the party.

On a sheet of paper, write the answers to the following questions. Use complete sentences.

1. Does your friend have a good plan of treatment for his injury? Explain your answer.

2. Should you convince your friend to get medical treatment? If so, what would the treatment be? Explain your answer.

3. Should you call 911? Should you call anyone else? Explain your answer.

- In an emergency, stay calm, find out whether the person is conscious and breathing, look for injuries, and call 911 for help.

- Good Samaritan laws protect people who help others in emergencies.

- Following universal precautions helps rescuers from coming in contact with blood and other body fluids and protects wounds from dirt and infections.

- Choking, failure to breathe, cardiovascular failure, shock, and serious bleeding all can be life-threatening emergencies.

- The Heimlich maneuver is used when someone is choking to force an object out of the throat.

- Rescue breathing puts oxygen from the rescuer's lungs into an unconscious person's lungs.

- A person in cardiovascular failure has a hard time breathing and an irregular pulse. A person whose heart has stopped beating and has no pulse is in cardiac arrest. Cardiopulmonary resuscitation (CPR) is needed for both.

- Shock happens when the circulatory system fails to get enough blood to the body. First aid goals are to return blood to the heart and maintain a normal body temperature.

- Immediate direct pressure over a wound is the first step in first aid for serious bleeding.

- The local poison control center can give instructions to treat poisoning.

- First aid can treat fainting, bites and stings, bone and joint injuries, burns, nosebleeds, heat exhaustion, and frostbite.

Vocabulary

cardiac arrest, 404	Good Samaritan laws, 398	pressure point, 406
cardiopulmonary resuscitation (CPR), 404	heat exhaustion, 411	rabies, 408
	heatstroke, 411	rescue breathing, 403
chest compression, 404	Heimlich maneuver, 401	respiratory failure, 402
contact poisoning, 408	hypothermia, 411	shock, 405
dressing, 398	inhalation poisoning, 407	splint, 409
fainting, 408	latex, 397	sprain, 410
first aid, 396	mouth-to-mouth resuscitation, 403	sterile, 406
fracture, 409		universal distress signal, 401
frostbite, 411	oral poisoning, 407	
fume, 407		universal precautions, 398

Chapter 17 REVIEW

Word Bank

cardiac arrest

fainting

fracture

frostbite

heatstroke

hypothermia

inhalation
  poisoning

oral poisoning

pressure point

rabies

rescue breathing

shock

universal distress
  signal

universal
  precautions

Vocabulary Review

On a sheet of paper, write the word or phrase from the Word Bank that best completes each sentence.

1. A disease a person can get when bitten by an infected animal is _____.

2. To lessen their risk of catching diseases, medical workers use _____.

3. The transfer of someone's breath to a person who cannot breathe is _____.

4. Grabbing the throat with the hand or hands is the _____ for choking.

5. The main sign of _____ is a lack of sweating.

6. When the circulatory system does not get enough blood to the body, a person may experience _____.

7. People can press on a(n) _____ to stop someone's bleeding.

8. Chemical burns on lips and chemical odor on the breath are often signs of _____.

9. A person who has breathed in harmful fumes has _____.

10. A person who is in _____ has no heartbeat and no pulse.

11. A serious loss of body heat from being outside too long in cold, damp weather is _____.

12. To treat _____, slowly warm the affected area.

13. A temporary loss of consciousness, or _____, can happen when the brain gets too little blood.

14. Crookedness, swelling, bruising, loss of movement, and pain are signs of a(n) _____.

Concept Review

On a sheet of paper, write the letter of the answer that best completes each sentence.

15. Always ask before helping if you think someone is choking because choking is sometimes mistaken for _____.

A frostbite   **C** a heart attack

B fainting   **D** hypothermia

16. The condition LEAST likely to be life threatening is _____.

A contact poisoning   **C** cardiovascular failure

B shock   **D** a nosebleed

17. To treat heat exhaustion, do NOT _____.

A loosen the person's clothing

B apply warm cloths to the person's neck

C give the person a glass of water to sip

D take the person inside or into the shade

Critical Thinking

On a sheet of paper, write the answers to the following questions. Use complete sentences.

18. How can you prepare to give emergency first aid?

19. What did you learn about emergency treatment in this chapter that surprised you the most? What might you do as a result? Explain your answer.

20. Why might you be less likely to be afraid to help in an emergency now? Explain your answer.

Test-Taking Tip After you have taken a test, review it and ask yourself "Do my answers show that I understood the question?"

Self-Assessment

Can you answer these questions?

☑ 1. What is violence?

☑ 2. How can conflict lead to violence?

☑ 3. How does violence affect people?

☑ 4. What are three causes of violence?

☑ 5. What types of violence are teens most concerned with?

☑ 6. What are five ways to manage anger?

☑ 7. What does a mediator do?

☑ 8. How can people avoid conflict?

☑ 9. What does a peacemaker do?

☑ 10. What are three ways communities can fight crime?

Preventing Violence and Resolving Conflicts

You see violence on TV. You read about it in newspapers or on the Internet. Even the words to some songs are violent. You may ask why violence is in your health book, too. The answer is simple. Violence has become a health topic. It is a growing danger for young people. We all need to understand violence. Then we can prevent it, keep ourselves healthy, and help protect our friends and loved ones.

In this chapter, you will learn about the causes of violence. You will think about how violence affects its victims. You will read about the high cost of violent acts. You will learn how people can avoid violence. You will learn how victims of violence can get help. Finally, you will gain an understanding of how communities can fight crime.

Goals for Learning

◆ To define *violence* and describe its costs

◆ To identify warning signs of conflict

◆ To identify the causes of violence

◆ To explain ways to prevent violence and find answers to conflicts

What Is Violence?

Violence is actions or words that hurt people or damage things. Violence can take away a person's sense of safety and feelings of self-worth.

Violent behavior may be as simple as pushing, hitting, or name-calling. Violence can involve damaging someone's property. It can involve the deadly use of a weapon. Violence is shown on TV and on the Internet. Many movies include violent scenes and violent special effects. Violence also is a part of many popular video games.

Violence can begin in many different ways. A small difference of opinion can quickly become violent. Violent fights can be about money or drug abuse. People can become the **victims** of family violence. A victim is a person who has had a crime committed against him or her. This can cause great harm to one or more family members. Parents may become violent toward each other. Parents also can become violent toward their children. Often, violent people experienced violence when they were children.

Some violence has no real target. People damage property by spraying paint, throwing rocks, or perhaps setting fires. Sometimes, people are hurt. Other violent acts, such as drive-by shootings, cause the deaths of innocent people.

Gang violence is a growing problem in the United States. Gang members commit many acts of violence. More than 21,000 known gangs are in the United States. Most large cities have gang-related crime. Gangs also are a problem in many small cities, in suburbs, and in the country.

Many people who commit crimes know their victims. Most murders occur between people of the same race. Teen crime is a big concern. In 2002, about 5.7 percent of male teens ages 16 to 19 were victims of violent crimes. The rate for females in that age group was 3.8 percent. Violent crimes are committed more often against teens than against any other age group.

Objectives

After reading this lesson, you should be able to

◆ explain the short-term and long-term effects of violence

◆ look at how conflict and violence are alike and different

◆ identify the most likely victims of violence

◆ describe the cost of violence to victims and society

Victim

A person who has had a crime committed against him or her

How Is Conflict Different from Violence?

Conflict is a disagreement, or difference of opinion, between two or more people who have different ideas. Conflict can turn into violence. Disagreements among people are normal. Letting conflict turn into violence is not normal.

Conflict may be minor, ongoing, internal, or major. You may have a minor conflict with a friend because you hurt the friend's feelings. Your parents may have a minor conflict with each other. These kinds of conflicts can be about doing chores, handling money, or managing family problems.

Many conflicts are ongoing. For example, you may have some constant disagreement with a brother or sister. Sports teams compete against each other. They have an ongoing conflict about which team will win.

You may have a conflict within yourself about making a difficult decision. This is an internal conflict. Maybe someone wants you to go somewhere. You really want to go, but if you go, you will have to give up something else.

Major conflicts can take a long time to resolve. Often, patience and compromise are needed to fix a major conflict. You may face major conflicts with your friends or at home. If you accept others and have respect for everybody's differences, you will have fewer conflicts. If you handle major conflicts well, your conflicts likely will not become violent.

Conflict

A difference of opinion between two or more people who have different ideas

Compromising, or each person giving up some things they want, is often needed to settle conflicts peacefully.

Link to ➤➤➤

Language Arts

The musical *West Side Story* is loosely based on the play *Romeo and Juliet* by William Shakespeare. *West Side Story* is about two enemy gangs. The Sharks are Puerto Rican and the Jets are white. Tony, who once was a Jet, falls in love with Maria, the sister of a Shark. Maria and Tony try to get away from the violence between the two gangs, but fail.

What Is the Trend in Violent Crime?

Violent crime affects everyone. In 1990, almost 2 million people were the victims of violent crimes. In 2003, that number had dropped by 700,000 people. Except for drug-related crimes, the crime rate in the United States has been going down. Table 18.1.1 below shows the percentage of each age group that have been victims of violent crime. This includes violent crimes committed by teens ages 12 to 17. Drug-related crimes among people older than 17, however, keep going up.

Table 18.1.1 Victims of Violent Crime (approximate percentage of each age group)							
Year	Age Group						
	12–15	16–19	20–24	25–34	35–49	50–64	65+
1990	10%	10%	9%	6%	3%	1%	0.4%
1991	9	12	10	5	4	1	0.4
1992	11	10	10	6	4	1	0.5
1993	12	11	9	6	4	2	0.6
1994	12	12	10	6	4	2	0.5
1995	11	11	9	6	4	1	0.6
1996	10	10	7	5	3	2	0.5
1997	9	10	7	5	3	1	0.4
1998	8	9	7	4	3	2	0.3
1999	7	8	7	4	3	1	0.4
2000	6	6	5	3	2	1	0.4
2001	6	6	4	3	2	1	0.3
2002	4	6	5	3	2	1	0.3
2003	5	5	4	3	2	1	0.2
2004	5	5	4	2	2	1	0.2

Source: U.S. Department of Justice, Bureau of Justice Statistics, Criminal Victimization in the United States, various years.

What Are the Costs of Violence?

Violence has many costs. One cost is money. Other costs are physical and emotional harm to people.

The victims of violent acts may be hurt permanently. For example, they may have brain damage or become paralyzed. When people are paralyzed, they are unable to move their arms or legs. Victims of violence can also suffer mental health problems. They may always be afraid, angry, or sad. The costs of treating physical and mental health problems can add up to thousands of dollars for each victim.

The friends and relatives of victims often feel sad and angry, too. They may have to take care of the victim. In some cases, they may have to help pay medical costs.

People who commit violent acts may feel guilty about what they have done. They often feel worse about themselves than they did before the crime. Someone who is arrested for a violent act has to go to court and may go to prison. A criminal record or a violent past may limit future job and housing opportunities.

People who see violence may pay a different kind of price. They may lose their peace of mind and may never feel safe again.

Link to ➤➤➤

Math

The same information used to create a table also can be shown in pie graphs, bar graphs, or line graphs. Line graphs show trends.

The information from Table 18.1.1 was used to create this line graph. The graph shows that most victims of violent crime were younger than 24 during these years. The highest number of victims were teenagers.

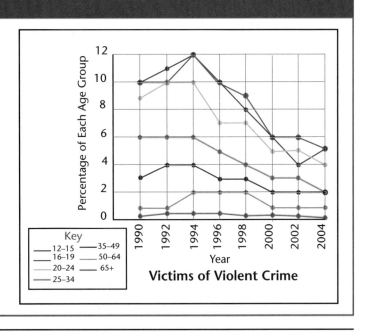

Victims of Violent Crime

All people end up paying for crime. The costs of police protection, courts, and prisons go up each year. The government often raises taxes to cover these costs. No matter where, how, or why violence happens, everyone in some way becomes a victim.

Health in Your Life

Cycle of Family Violence

Family violence rarely happens only once. Instead, it often happens in a cycle. Victims of family violence often feel ashamed. Some may feel that they are somehow to blame or deserve the abuse. The cycle of family violence has four phases.

Phase 1: This is a time when tension rises. Minor conflicts between family members explode. The victim feels that he or she has to be very careful about saying or doing anything in the home.

Phase 2: Abuse occurs. The victim is abused physically or verbally. The victim might be slapped, kicked, threatened with weapons, or sexually abused. Usually, no one else sees the violence.

Phase 3: The abuser apologizes and shows sadness for what he or she has done. The abuser promises that it will never happen again. The abuser may give gifts to the victim. The abuser may argue about how violent he or she was or say the victim is making a big deal out of nothing.

Phase 4: The victim again is afraid to say or do something that might set off the abuser. The cycle starts over. The next time is often worse than the last. The time between phases can also shorten, so the abuse happens more often.

Abuse victims must realize that no one has the right to hurt another person. People who experience family violence can take steps to protect themselves and others:

- Talk to a trusted person about the abuse.

- Have a plan in place to leave if someone in the home becomes violent. Have a bag of clothes ready to take when leaving.

- Know where to find community shelters. Know their phone numbers in order to call for help.

- Keep a written record of when and how the abuse happens.

- Remember the cycle of violence when an abuser promises that he or she will never become violent again.

- Call the police or 911 for help when in danger. Acts of violence are crimes.

On a sheet of paper, write your answers to the following questions. Use complete sentences.

1. What is the cycle of family violence?

2. Why is understanding this cycle of violence important?

3. What is an important thing to know about how often family violence occurs?

Lesson 1 Review On a sheet of paper, write the answers to the following questions. Use complete sentences.

1. What is violence?

2. Where are some places violence can occur?

3. Which age group has the highest number of violent crime victims?

4. **Critical Thinking** What is the difference between conflict and violence?

5. **Critical Thinking** How does violence affect a community?

▼◀▲▼◀▲▼◀▲▼◀▲▼◀▲▼◀▲▼◀▲▼◀▲▼◀▲▼◀▲▼◀▲▼◀▲▼◀▲▼◀▲▼◀▲▼◀▲▼

Health at Work

Victim or Witness Advocate

People who are victims of crime often feel alone, scared, and sad. They may wonder if anyone can ever be trusted again. Victim or witness advocates work with the county or state justice system. They help victims of crime know their rights under the law. They help victims get restraining orders. A restraining order is a court order that keeps the person who causes harm from coming near the victim.

Victim or witness advocates also help victims with court matters. For example, advocates tell victims when court hearings will take place. Advocates also help victims make victim statements. Victim statements are taken into consideration when a person is sentenced for a crime.

Victim or witness advocates can help survivors of a family member who was murdered get needed services. They can also help victims find resources that will help them return to living a normal life.

Objectives

After reading this lesson, you should be able to

◆ explain five causes of violence

◆ identify teen-related crimes

◆ describe three ways to keep from becoming a victim

How Can Conflict Be Recognized?

You may think that you can simply steer clear of all conflict, but that is not easy. Everyone faces times in which conflict can occur. Once you learn to identify the signs of conflict, you will be better able to avoid it. You will be better able to end the conflict and keep it from getting violent. Here are some warning signs of conflict:

- shouting
- name-calling
- spreading rumors
- giving the "silent treatment"
- using insults
- giving mean looks
- making fun of someone
- getting others to take sides
- making threats or threatening gestures
- pushing or hitting

Health Myth

Myth: All abused and neglected children will become violent adults.

Fact: Abused and neglected children do not necessarily become violent adults. As children move into their teen years, the abuse and neglect they experienced may not cause them to become violent.

What Causes Violence?

In 2003, there were 5.4 million victims of violent crimes in the United States. Some people blame the media for some of these violent crimes. Movies and TV programs often include both verbal and physical violence. For some people, all of the violence in the media makes violence seem like a normal part of life.

Violence within a family is especially harmful for young children. Children who live with violence may grow up thinking violence is the way to solve problems. Many criminals were the victims of family violence. Violent behavior became part of their lives.

A physical workout, such as running, jogging, walking, or another exercise program can help you deal with anger. The exercise can calm you and help you relax.

Does the media make violence attractive?

Many people buy guns as protection for themselves and their families. They usually do not plan to use them. However, just owning a gun increases the likelihood of being involved in a violent incident. Unfortunately, the more violence occurs, the more people buy guns and the more violence increases.

All schools are gun-free zones. Schools have very strict policies against bringing guns, knives, and other weapons onto school property. Some schools have metal detectors to help enforce these policies.

Alcohol and other drugs make people act in dangerous ways. They also can prevent a person from using good judgment. About one-third of all victims of violent crime believe the person committing the crime used alcohol or other drugs. About one-fourth of all crimes were committed to get money for drugs.

Members of gangs often have troubled lives. A gang may give them a feeling of belonging. Gang members often wear certain colors or clothes, or have tattoos that show they are members of a specific gang. About 6 percent of all violent crime is gang related. Victims of gang crime are often young.

When people have problems, it can cause them great stress and make them feel depressed and angry. People who usually show good judgment may turn to violence during these stressful times.

Sometimes, people take part in violence to show how loyal they are to a group. Some people will go against their own better judgment because of a group. Giving in to such negative peer pressure can get in the way of a person's ability to make good decisions.

Prejudice is a negative opinion that is formed without having enough information or experience. Prejudice means judging people you do not know based on their race, sex, sexual preference, cultural background, or religion. This sometimes leads to hate crimes. Hate crimes are violent acts against people who belong to a particular group. In 2003, more than 9,000 people were the victims of hate crimes. About half of all these hate crimes involved race.

Health Myth

Myth: Most people are raped by strangers.

Fact: Almost 80 percent of all rapes are committed by people the victims know. The majority of rapes happen in the victims' homes. The same number of rapes happen during the day as at night. Statistics show that one in every six women and one in every 33 men have been victims of rape.

A person who has been insulted or hurt may want revenge, or a way to get even. Revenge may become more violent than the act that caused it. This can be especially true in school. Prejudice, rumors, name-calling, and comments about someone's personal life can lead to violent results. For example, revenge for name-calling may be shoving or tripping. Revenge for the shoving or tripping may be a fistfight. Revenge for the fistfight may be a fight with weapons.

Sexual Harassment

Sexual harassment happens when a person makes unwanted sexual comments or physical advances to another person. Sexual harassment can happen anywhere, including school and the workplace. What is important is the effect the harassment has on the victim, not what the harasser meant to do. It is sexual harassment if someone's comments, suggestions, or physical advances make a person uncomfortable.

About 40 to 70 percent of women and 10 to 20 percent of men believe they have been sexually harassed at work. Students also report high rates of sexual harassment. Yet many victims of sexual harassment choose not to report the harassment.

If you are the victim of sexual harassment, make it clear to the harasser that you find the sexual harassment offensive and uncomfortable. Keep a record of when the sexual harassment happens. If the harassment continues, make a formal complaint to a trusted teacher, counselor, or job supervisor about it.

What Kinds of Crimes Happen to Teens?

Most teenagers are not violent. However, many teenagers become the victims of different kinds of violence. About one-third of all victims of violent crimes are teens. Murder rates are the highest among people ages 18 to 24. Murder is the second leading cause of death among people ages 15 to 24. Other violent crimes that happen to teens and young adults include robbery, beating, and **rape.** Rape is the unlawful act of forcing a person to have sex.

Several drugs are considered date rape drugs. Date rape drugs are put into victims' drinks by their dates. The drugs cause a victim to become mentally confused and not know what is happening. This makes it hard for the victim to fight against the rapist. In addition to rape, these drugs can cause serious physical problems for the victim.

Rape

Teens ages 16 to 19 are more than three times as likely as other people to be victims of rape, attempted rape, or some other type of **sexual assault.** Sexual assault is any forced sexual contact. Many rape victims are under the age of 12. Reporting a rape is often very hard for the victim. Experts think that only about half of all rapes are reported. Often, victims of rape are embarrassed or afraid of being blamed for the rape. Sometimes, they know the rapist and are afraid of getting the person in trouble. They may be scared their rapist will come after them again. Many communities have police officers who are trained to help and talk to rape victims.

Dating Violence and Sexual Exploitation

Sometimes, young people become the victims of dating violence. For example, a person may use threats or aggressive behavior to try to gain control. The person might touch his or her date even if the touching is not wanted. Any touching that is not wanted is abuse.

Some teens are the victims of **date rape,** which is committed by someone with whom the victim socializes. If a person says no or tells his or her date to stop making sexual advances, the person should stop. Warning signs that date rape might happen include threats, insults, controlling behavior, and unwanted touching.

Unwanted sexual contact is always wrong. This type of act does not show the basic respect that every person deserves. Date rape carries serious consequences. People who commit date rape are often expelled from school, charged with a crime, or both.

Another crime that happens to some teens and younger children is **sexual exploitation,** a form of sexual abuse. Sexual exploitation of children happens when an adult forces a young person to do something related to sexual activity. These forced acts include prostitution and taking part in child pornography. The adult involved makes money from this exploitation. Like all sexual abuse, the sexual exploitation of children is illegal. People found guilty of sexual exploitation go to prison.

Figure 18.2.1 *At night, walk quickly and confidently in well-lighted areas with someone you know.*

Here are some ways to keep from becoming a victim of a crime:

- Do not walk alone at night. Walk only in areas or places you know and move quickly and confidently. Stay in well-lighted areas.

- If you are being followed, walk quickly to a place where there are other people.

- Carry a cell phone, if possible.

- Keep out of gangs by becoming involved with school or community activities.

- If dating someone you do not know well, stay out of places where you and your date are alone.

- When driving, park only in well-lighted areas, never pick up strangers, and keep your car doors locked.

Lesson 2 Review On a sheet of paper, write the letter of the answer that best completes each sentence.

1. About 6 percent of all violent crime is _____.
   A a hate crime   **C** drug related
   B gang related   **D** caused by family members

2. Hate crimes always involve _____.
   A date rape   **C** only race
   B nonviolent acts   **D** prejudice

3. The second leading cause of death among people ages 15 to 24 is _____.
   A murder   **C** accidents
   B drug abuse   **D** natural causes

On a sheet of paper, write the answers to the following questions. Use complete sentences.

4. **Critical Thinking** What would make you feel sexually harassed?

5. **Critical Thinking** What can you do in your daily life to keep from becoming the victim of a crime?

Objectives

After reading this lesson, you should be able to

◆ list three ways to manage anger

◆ describe how to resolve conflict

◆ identify seven things a mediator does to help resolve a conflict

You get angry sometimes. Everyone does. A relative, a friend, or someone you hardly know may offend you. You may be angry about something you said or did. When you are angry, your heart beats faster and your blood pressure rises. Your muscles tense. Your face may look strained and red. Anger is a natural feeling. It causes people to feel aggressive and defensive. Anger is important for survival, but it can cause problems if you do not know how to handle it.

How Can Anger Be Managed?

Managing your anger the right way will help you feel in control. Here are three ways to manage your anger:

• Take a deep breath to calm yourself before you say anything. Say what you need to say in a clear and calm way. Do not curse or use threatening words. Be respectful of the person you are angry with. Also, think about how you hold your body. Shaking your fist or taking a step toward a person shows aggression.

• Control your anger. Breathe deeply. Tell yourself to relax. Picture yourself in control. Think about how you are holding your body. Looking angry might make the other person become defensive and perhaps aggressive. Try to stay calm. Calmly ask the person to explain the problem. Listen quietly. Use humor if you can. Do not be sarcastic.

• Hold back your anger. Think of something positive instead of what is making you angry. Doing this will help calm you. It is important that you later talk with the person about what made you angry. You might also exercise or work on a project, such as mowing the lawn or cleaning your room.

It is important to understand what causes you to get angry. It also is important to control how you react. Acting angrily at the other person often makes things worse.

How Can Conflict Be Avoided?

Sometimes, the best way to deal with a conflict is to walk away. Ask yourself: Is it really such a big deal? Is the conflict based on a rumor that may not be true? How will I feel if I just forget about it? Think about what is happening. Maybe the other person is having some serious problems at home or at school. Perhaps the person never meant to cause a conflict. Let it go, and realize that the other person will be easier to get along with at another time.

Remember that movements you make and words you use in one culture may mean something very different in another culture. Understanding this will lessen conflict between people from different cultures.

During conflict, people may feel insulted or misjudged. Good listening skills are important. Asking the right questions to clear up any misunderstandings is also important. Do not let your anger get in the way of figuring out what the other person is trying to say. Good communication and listening can keep conflict from getting violent.

How Can Conflicts Be Resolved?

Some conflicts cannot be ignored. When you have to get to the bottom of a conflict, talking with the person alone is best. Having other people around raises the chance that things will get out of control. Do not talk when the other person has been drinking alcohol or using other drugs.

As you explain your feelings, try to remain calm and keep your feelings under control. Using put-downs will not help you resolve the conflict peacefully. Focus on your feelings rather than what the other person is doing. Give the other person a chance to do the same thing. If you have had a part in hurting the other person, do not be afraid to say, "I'm sorry."

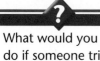

What would you do if someone tried to start a fight with you and would not let you walk away?

Research and Write

Do you feel your school is safe? What would you do if you saw violence at your school? What kind of school safety plan does your school have? Write a report on safety at your school. Interview teachers and students for your report, and include a visual presentation, such as a poster, brochure, or video.

Mediator

Someone who helps people find a solution to a conflict

Negotiation

Ability to help people reach a compromise

How Can You Help Others Stay Out of Fights?

If other people get into a fight, do not cheer them on. Often, people in conflict feel they have to follow through when others are watching.

Let people know that you respect them for being able to walk away from a fight. Give respect to someone who is strong enough to apologize.

There may be times when you can put pressure on friends not to fight. Let them know you think they should solve their problems peacefully.

You may be able to help as a **mediator.** A mediator is someone who helps others find a solution to a conflict. To successfully mediate a conflict:

• Let both people know that you are not taking sides.

• Set some rules, such as using calm, reasonable talk.

• Let each person say his or her feelings without being interrupted.

• Allow each person to ask reasonable questions of each other.

• Encourage both people to figure out different ways to solve the problem.

• Ask both people to discuss each way and to agree on one idea.

• Work at finding a compromise. Do not let them give up without really trying.

Many schools have peer mediation programs. In these programs, counselors train students to help one another resolve conflicts. **Negotiation,** or the ability to help people reach a compromise, is an important part of peer mediation programs. Find out if your school has such a program.

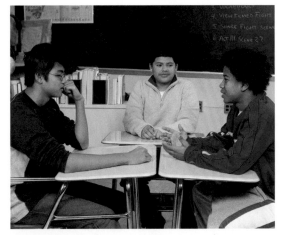

Figure 18.3.1 *Peer mediators help others find solutions to conflicts.*

How Can a Person Get Help with a Conflict?

When you have a serious conflict, you need to get help. Talk with your parents or a peer mediator, teacher, or counselor. If they cannot help you, they can probably send you to someone who can.

You may hear that a friend has plans for a violent act. You may not want to tell anyone about your friend's plans. Remember, it is always important to stop someone who plans to do harm. Talk with a parent or other trusted adult who may be able to help your friend.

Lots of people have conflicts. Asking for help does not mean that you are weak. It just means that you care enough about yourself and other people to take control of your life.

Decide for Yourself

Some people think that the only way to resolve a conflict is to fight. Being able to resolve a conflict instead of fighting is a sign of strength and control. Conflict resolution skills give you control in a situation. They lessen the chance of violence among teens and adults.

Steps to Conflict Resolution

1. Set the ground rules. Agree to discuss the problem without cursing or name-calling. Avoid accusing the person with whom you are arguing.

2. Allow the person to describe the argument. Listen to how the person feels. Often the conflict is not about what happened but about how a person feels about what happened.

3. Decide what both of you agree on.

4. List the ways you can resolve the conflict. You may find no agreement on what caused it.

5. Think of a solution in which both of you win. Compromise is important at this point. For example, if you disagree on whether you have taken something that belongs to the other person, find a mediator who will make a plan that will be fair to both of you.

6. Come to a specific agreement. Write it down if necessary. Work with a mediator or trusted person to make sure the agreement works.

On a sheet of paper, write your answers to the following questions. Use complete sentences.

1. Why are good listening skills needed during conflict resolution?

2. Why is avoiding name-calling important during conflict resolution?

3. Which of the conflict resolution steps will be the most difficult for you? Which step will be the easiest?

How Can Communities Help Fight Crime?

Communities are taking steps to fight crime. One way is the Neighborhood Crime Watch. In this program, volunteers are trained to look for unusual activity and crimes that are being committed. Then they report what they see to police. Often, neighbors post signs and stickers that warn would-be criminals that neighbors are watching.

Because many crimes happen at night, community leaders in many places are making important changes. For example, they are planning more nighttime activities for young people. They are putting in bright lights at nighttime hangouts such as playgrounds and parking lots. Some cities have teen curfews that do not allow teenagers on the streets after a certain hour. More people are being added to the police force in some places.

Some other community actions to reduce crime are:

- setting up neighborhood centers where agencies can provide counseling help, recreation, and vocational training

- improving or adding streetlights to help police and neighborhood watch programs

- putting security systems in stores to let police know if a robbery is taking place

- finding and training neighbors to take care of children in danger

- providing crime awareness education to teach people how not to become victims of crime

Technology and Society

Each year, more than 700 million people fly from one part of the country to another. Each person who wants to get on a plane must go through a series of safety and security checks. This includes checking for sharp metal objects or chemicals that might mean the person has a bomb. Airport security works to prevent violence and terrorist attacks. The Department of Homeland Security controls airport security systems.

Many lawmakers are working for tougher punishments for those found guilty of violent crimes. You may wish to write your local lawmakers with your ideas about how your community can better fight crime.

Schools in many cities now have full-time security guards. The students in these schools must pass through metal detectors. Some schools have video cameras to watch hall activity. Many school districts are hiring more counselors to help students in trouble. Students can work together with teachers and counselors to make sure that their school is safe. Some schools have student-run safety committees. Perhaps the most positive move that many schools have made is to teach courses in accepting and respecting one another. Teens can choose to be peacemakers rather than troublemakers.

Lesson 3 Review On a sheet of paper, write the word or phrase in parentheses that best completes each sentence.

1. Using a (mediator, offender, troublemaker) to resolve conflicts is often helpful.

2. One way to stay out of a fight is to (disagree, push, mediate).

3. An important part of conflict resolution is (time pressure, compromise, fault).

On a sheet of paper, answer the following questions. Use complete sentences.

4. **Critical Thinking** What is one way you could help others stay out of a fight?

5. **Critical Thinking** What is the best way for you to control your anger?

Chapter 18 SUMMARY

- Violence never solves problems but makes new ones that are usually worse.

- Conflicts are disagreements between two or more people with different ideas. Conflicts may be minor, ongoing, internal, or major. A disagreement is normal conflict, but conflict that becomes violent is not normal.

- Costs of violence are permanent injuries, mental health problems, hurt to loved ones, lost peace of mind, and money that everyone must pay.

- Knowing the signs of conflict helps people avoid or resolve conflicts and reduces the likelihood of violence.

- Some causes of violence are the media, growing up with violence, alcohol and other drugs, and gangs. Other causes are personal problems, group loyalty, prejudice, and revenge.

- Robbery, beating, murder, and rape are crimes that often happen to teens.

- Everyone feels anger at times. People can deal with anger to keep minor conflicts from becoming violent.

- At times, the best way to deal with conflict is to walk away from it. Avoiding conflict shows strength, not weakness.

- Talking with a mediator is one of the best ways to resolve conflict. Both sides in a conflict must remain calm, not insult each other, and focus on feelings rather than actions.

- Two ways to help others not get into fights are not to watch the fight and to respect the person who can walk away from it. You also can pressure others not to fight, and you can act as a mediator.

- Talking with a parent, mediator, teacher, or school counselor can help resolve a conflict. It is always important to stop someone who plans to do harm.

- Neighborhood Crime Watch and other programs help communities fight crime. Local, state, and national lawmakers are making tougher punishments for crime. Schools are taking many actions to fight crime.

Vocabulary

conflict, 419	negotiation, 431	sexual exploitation, 427
date rape, 427	rape, 426	sexual harassment, 426
mediator, 431	sexual assault, 427	victim, 418

Chapter 18 REVIEW

<table>
<tr><td>

Word Bank

conflict

date rape

mediator

negotiation

rape

sexual assault

sexual exploitation

sexual harassment

victim

</td></tr>
</table>

Vocabulary Review

On a sheet of paper, write the word or phrase from the Word Bank that best completes each sentence.

1. Forced sex with someone the victim socializes with is _____.

2. A disagreement between people is a _____.

3. Injury is one cost for a _____ of violence.

4. A person who forces another person to have sexual intercourse is committing _____.

5. Unwanted sexual comments are a type of _____.

6. Someone who helps people compromise is practicing _____.

7. As a _____, you can help work out conflicts.

8. Using a person sexually to make money is _____.

9. Any forced sexual contact, including rape, is _____.

Concept Review

On a sheet of paper, write the letter of the answer that best completes each sentence.

10. A negative opinion formed without enough information is _____.

   A a solution   **C** an educated guess

   B prejudice   **D** a theory

11. Violence includes actions or words that hurt people or damage things and _____.

   A cause conflict   **C** result in conflict resolution

   B are not a big deal   **D** help negotiation

12. Some warning signs of conflict are pushing, name-calling, shouting, and _____.

   A staying calm   **C** asking for a mediator

   B walking away   **D** spreading rumors

13. The first step in conflict resolution is _____.

    A asking for a mediator   **C** setting the ground rules

    B compromising   **D** listing ideas

14. One way to lessen your chances of being a victim of rape is to _____.

    A walk alone at night

    B avoid being alone with a date

    C date only people you know

    D get in a car with someone you do not know

15. A conflict at home over not doing chores is _____.

    A minor   **B** internal   **C** ongoing   **D** major

16. A conflict that takes a long time to resolve is _____.

    A minor   **B** internal   **C** ongoing   **D** major

17. Many people who commit crimes _____ their victims.

    A know   **C** have never met

    B date   **D** are related to

Critical Thinking

On a sheet of paper, answer the following questions. Use complete sentences.

18. What do you think is the most serious cause of violence? Explain your answer.

19. What effects does violence have on a person?

20. What can you do as a mediator to resolve a conflict?

Test-Taking Tip Review your corrected tests. You can learn from mistakes you made earlier.

Doctors Without Borders

Doctors Without Borders is an international volunteer group. It is made up of doctors, nurses, experts on clean water, and other professionals. Together, they bring medical aid to people affected by emergencies around the world. This includes both natural and human-made emergencies such as floods, earthquakes, and civil war. Doctors Without Borders volunteers can quickly set up mobile operating rooms complete with medical supplies. They also provide tents, cooking kits, and blankets for people affected by emergencies.

Doctors Without Borders began in 1971. Today, the organization responds to more than 3,800 medical missions each year. Along with its emergency programs, Doctors Without Borders sets up worldwide vaccination programs. Volunteers construct wells for clean drinking water. Volunteer doctors perform life-saving operations. They also treat people with infectious diseases such as AIDS and tuberculosis.

Doctors Without Borders has public education programs that help others understand what it is like to live in a refugee camp, be malnourished, or live without medicine. The organization is funded by private donations.

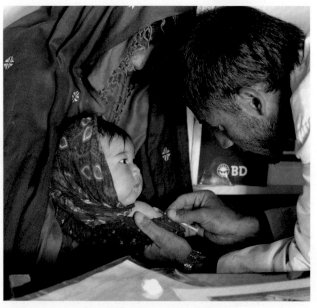

Today, more than 3 million people donate funds to help Doctors Without Borders provide medical aid to people in need.

On a sheet of paper, write the answers to the following questions. Use complete sentences.

1. How are the volunteers of Doctors Without Borders important to world health?

2. Why is clean water important for the work of Doctors Without Borders?

3. Why is getting quick medical help to people affected by emergencies important?

■ Fires caused by electrical problems, fuel, space heaters, furnaces, and open flames all can be prevented.

■ Every home should have one or more smoke detectors and fire extinguishers.

■ The Occupational Safety and Health Administration (OSHA) sets standards for safety in the workplace. Employers are responsible for removing dangers in the workplace.

■ Learning to swim, survival floating, and following water safety guidelines can prevent drowning.

■ Learning safe driving skills and habits, maintaining the speed limit, and adjusting to conditions all help prevent vehicle crashes. Wearing a seat belt can reduce injuries if a crash occurs.

■ Wearing helmets, following the rules of the road, and taking other preventive actions can reduce risks of accidents for bicyclists and motorcyclists.

■ People can take protective steps in cases of natural disasters such as hurricanes, tornadoes, floods, earthquakes, and lightning strikes.

■ In an emergency, stay calm, find out whether the person is conscious and breathing, look for injuries, and call 911 for help.

■ Good Samaritan laws protect people who help others in emergencies.

■ Following universal precautions prevents rescuers from coming into contact with blood and other body fluids. These precautions also protect wounds from dirt and infections.

■ The Heimlich maneuver is used to force an object out of the throat when someone is choking.

■ Rescue breathing puts oxygen from the rescuer's lungs into an unconscious person's lungs.

■ A person in cardiovascular failure has a hard time breathing and an irregular pulse. A person whose heart has stopped beating and has no pulse is in cardiac arrest. Cardiopulmonary resuscitation (CPR) is needed for both.

■ Immediate direct pressure over a wound is the first step in first aid for serious bleeding.

■ Knowing the signs of conflict helps people avoid or resolve conflicts and reduces the likelihood of violence.

■ At times, the best way to deal with conflict is to walk away from it. Avoiding conflict shows strength, not weakness.

■ Talking with a parent, mediator, teacher, or school counselor can help resolve a conflict.

■ Neighborhood Crime Watch and other programs help fight crime.

Unit 6 REVIEW

Vocabulary Review

On a sheet of paper, write the word or phrase from the Word Bank that best completes each sentence.

Word Bank

cardiopulmonary resuscitation (CPR)

date rape

electrical shock

first aid

hazard

Heimlich maneuver

hurricane

mediator

oral poisoning

sexual harassment

sterile

survival floating

1. Using an electric appliance when your clothing is wet can result in _____.

2. Rescue breathing and pressing on a person's chest are both parts of _____.

3. When performing the _____, upward thrusts are made below a person's rib cage to force an object out of the throat.

4. A severe tropical storm with heavy rains that strikes the eastern coast of the United States is a(n) _____.

5. When a person makes unwanted physical advances or says sexual things that make another person uncomfortable, it is an act of _____.

6. A clean bandage that is free from bacteria is _____.

7. One technique that can prevent a person from drowning is _____.

8. When a person swallows a harmful material, he or she could suffer from _____.

9. A(n) _____ is someone who helps others find a solution to a conflict.

10. Immediate emergency care given to an injured person before professional medical care arrives is _____.

11. A person who forces a friend to have sex is committing _____.

12. Leaving books or toys on stairs creates a(n) _____ in the home.

Concept Review

On a sheet of paper, write the letter of the answer that best completes each sentence.

13. A small grease fire can be put out with _____.

   A water   **C** oxygen

   B baking soda   **D** milk

14. A person riding a bicycle at night should wear _____ clothing.

   A dark   **C** reflective

   B loose   **D** lightweight

15. When medical professionals wear protective masks and latex gloves, they are using the _____.

   A universal precautions   **C** pressure points

   B Good Samaritan laws   **D** universal distress signal

16. People use _____ when they compromise.

   A conflict   **C** anger

   B prejudice   **D** negotiation

Critical Thinking

On a sheet of paper, write the answers to the following questions. Use complete sentences.

17. Why should a person never camp alone?

18. Suppose you and a friend are giving first aid to a boy who is seriously bleeding from a cut on his forearm. Your friend suggests that you raise the boy's injured arm above his heart. Do you think this is a good idea? Explain your answer.

19. Why do you think frostbite usually affects the hands, feet, ears, or nose but not other body parts?

20. What is something that could cause violence in your community? How could this issue or situation be handled so that violence does not occur?

Unit 7

Health and Society

Do you buy products with environmentally safe packaging? Do you volunteer for causes that promote public health? Do you recycle on a regular basis? We all have a responsibility to promote public health and protect our environment. As people who buy and use goods and services, we can choose products that protect the environment. As members of a community, we can help to promote public health.

When buying goods and services, we are faced daily with decisions that affect us physically, socially, and emotionally. These decisions cover a wide range of choices. We might be choosing health care. We might be shopping for food. We might be looking for a way to prevent water pollution. This unit will show how you can make wise health choices. You will learn to promote public health and protect the environment.

Chapters in Unit 7

Self-Assessment

Can you answer these questions?

☑ 1. Where is the nearest clinic at which people in your neighborhood can get treatment?

☑ 2. What kind of health insurance do your parents or guardians have?

☑ 3. What are your health care professional's qualifications?

☑ 4. What steps should you take if you buy a product that does not work?

☑ 5. How do you decide what health products to buy?

☑ 6. What are some kinds of health professionals?

☑ 7. What is the difference among health care facilities?

☑ 8. What types of health insurance are available?

☑ 9. What are some situations in which you should see a doctor?

☑ 10. How can people lower health care costs?

19 Consumer Health

People buy health products and services every day. Health products and services affect your physical and emotional well-being. From the soap you wash with to the sunscreen you use, you buy health products. You buy services when you see a health care professional such as a doctor, dentist, or nurse.

Making wise choices when buying health products and services takes effort. You need to learn how to judge the products and services you use. You need to find out when and where to seek health care. You need to know how to pay for health care.

In this chapter, you will learn what influences people's health choices and how to choose products and services. You will find out when you need to seek health care from a professional and where to find it. You will learn how health care expenses are paid.

Goals for Learning

◆ To explain the advantages of making wise health choices

◆ To describe what influences people's health choices

◆ To describe ways to judge products and services and correct problems with them

◆ To decide when self-care or professional treatment is best

◆ To identify sources of health care

◆ To explain ways to pay for health care

Objectives

After reading this lesson, you should be able to

◆ explain the advantages of being a wise consumer

◆ discuss consumers' rights

◆ recognize influences on consumers' choices

◆ judge health products and services

◆ describe how to correct problems with products and services

Consumer

Someone who buys goods or services

Part of promoting your own health is being a wise **consumer.** A consumer is someone who buys goods or services. For example, you buy goods such as grooming products or over-the-counter medicines. You buy services such as dental or medical care.

What Advantages Does a Wise Consumer Have?

Being a wise consumer has several advantages. First, you protect and improve your health. You avoid buying products that are useless or that may be harmful. You recognize symptoms that signal the need for health care and get the help quickly.

Second, you save money. This means getting the best product or service for the least money. Saving money takes some research, but it pays off in the long run. Consumer publications or reviews online help you compare features and prices of different products.

Third, you gain self-confidence. Speaking up for your rights means taking care of yourself. For example, you can make a complaint to the proper source about a product that does not work. You can usually get your money back or have the product replaced.

Figure 19.1.1 *To make a wise choice, compare prices and ingredients before you buy.*

What Influences Consumers' Choices?

Many factors influence consumers' choices. These include advertising, family and friends, and price. Being a wise consumer means that you judge these factors before you buy. You spot misleading advertisements. You keep in mind that what is right for another person may not be the best product for you. You compare prices.

Businesses use different media sources to advertise their products. You may see or hear ads on television, radio, billboards, newspapers, magazines, and the Internet. Advertisers may use strategies that influence people without their realizing it. For example, you may keep singing a catchy tune that you have heard to advertise a product. Perhaps a famous actor or athlete you admire is promoting the product. Without thinking about the reason, you may buy that product.

The media may influence family and community health, as well as personal health. For example, suppose one parent buys personal care products for the family. If an ad influences that person to buy a certain product, the health of everyone in the family is affected by using the product.

Here are ways to analyze advertising techniques. Ask yourself the following questions before buying a health product. Use the answers to help you decide whether to buy the product.

1. Is the advertisement from a reliable source?

2. Is the health information given in the ad correct?

3. What are the ingredients in the product? Are they effective?

4. What are the health benefits of the product? What are the side effects?

5. Is the advertiser trying to influence my emotions to buy this product?

Another influence on consumers is the advice or opinions of family, friends, and the community. For example, if your friend tells you that a shampoo has solved his dandruff problem, you may decide to try it.

You also might buy a product because your family has always used it. Your community might put messages on the radio and in the newspaper to encourage people to visit a new neighborhood clinic.

Price also influences choices. Brand-name products are familiar but usually cost more than lesser-known brands. The size of a product and the store where a product is purchased also affect price. For example, the cost of a product in a convenience store may be higher than in a drugstore or discount store.

How Does Quackery Influence Consumers?

Quackery is the promotion of medical products or services that are unproved or worthless. Each year, Americans spend billions of dollars on products that claim to cure diseases. People with chronic diseases such as cancer and arthritis often become victims of quackery. People who are overweight or who want to look younger also are targets. At best, people waste their money on these products and services. At worst, people delay getting proper medical treatment.

How Can Products and Services Be Judged?

You can use a set of standards, or criteria, to help you judge products and services. Use these criteria every time you choose a product or service. They will help you be a wise consumer.

1. Look at the cost benefits. Suppose you want to purchase a pair of running shoes. You need to compare the features with the price on several different brands. Decide which features you really need. Do not pay for features you do not need.

2. Consider recommendations. You can find reviews of exercise equipment and personal grooming products on the Internet and in consumer magazines. A doctor usually can offer information about a product or service. Word-of-mouth recommendations from family and friends can be helpful. Keep in mind, however, that what is right for another person may not work for you.

3. Watch for false or misleading claims. Avoid any product or service that promises a cure or immediate results. Using library sources or the Internet, do research to make sure the health information given about the product or service is correct.

4. Look at the ingredients. Federal law says that manufacturers must include certain information on the label of every food, drug, and cosmetic or grooming product. Suppose you buy medicine for your allergy symptoms. Your doctor has told you to look for a certain ingredient, so you look for a product that has that ingredient.

5. Compare prices. Compare the price of products with their weight, volume, or count to find the best value. Generic, or nonbrand-name, products are usually less expensive than brand-name products. If two products have the same ingredients, then the generic product is the better buy.

How Can a Consumer's Problem Be Corrected?

In addition to federal laws, such as for labeling products, states have their own consumer protection laws. These laws protect consumers against false or misleading advertising. Consumers have the right to complain about products that do not work. They can often get their money back. If you buy a product that does not work or have a bad experience with a health care provider, you can take these actions:

1. Write a letter or send an e-mail to the company that sold the product or provided the service. Politely explain what you bought and the problem with it. Ask for your money back or for a fair exchange. If you call, write down the names of people you talked with, the dates, and what they said they would do. Calling does not always protect your rights. A letter or an e-mail is a record that you complained and so it better protects your rights.

Keep copies of all sales receipts, letters, and other papers when trying to correct a consumer problem.

2. If you do not get a satisfactory response, write a letter to an agency listed on the next page. To get the addresses of government agencies, look in the phone book or on the Internet. In the letter, give the details of your problem. Send a copy of this letter to the company or person the complaint is against. Keep a copy for your records. If you do not get a response within 6 weeks, send a follow-up letter with a copy of the first letter.

Decide for Yourself

Define the problem. You are sitting in class at the end of the day. You have a scratchy throat. You are sneezing and your nose begins to run. You realize you have a cold. You know that cold medicines cannot cure a cold. However, they can help relieve symptoms. You go to the drugstore after school. The over-the-counter medicines you look at contain one or all of the ingredients in the chart below.

Come up with possible solutions. (1) Choose the cheapest medicine. (2) Choose the medicine that has everything, because you are getting more for your money. (3) Choose the medicine that has only the ingredients to relieve your symptoms.

Consider the consequences of each solution. (1) The cheapest medicine may not contain the right ingredients for your cold. (2) The medicine that has everything has medicine you do not need. (3) The medicine that is right for your cold may be more expensive than some of the other medicines.

Put your plan into action. You make your choice, buy the medicine, and use it.

Evaluate the outcome. Decide whether you made the best decision for yourself.

On a sheet of paper, write the answers to the following questions. Use complete sentences.

1. Which solution would you choose?

2. How do you think you would evaluate the outcome of your decision?

Ingredients in Cold Medicines	
Analgesics	for headache and body aches
Decongestants	for stuffy nose
Antihistamines	for sneezing and runny nose
Expectorants	for causing coughing to clear bronchial passageways
Suppressants	for reducing coughing

Sources of Help for the Consumer

- Complaints about a product or service, false advertising, or irresponsible behavior:

    Better Business Bureau (Check the phone book for the local bureau.)

    Your state attorney general's office (Complaint forms usually are available on the Internet.)

- Complaints about false advertising:

    Federal Trade Commission

- Complaints about foods, drugs, or cosmetics:

    U.S. Food and Drug Administration or your state Department of Agriculture

    U.S. Food Safety and Inspection Service or your state Department of Agriculture

- Complaints about dangerous products:

    U.S. Consumer Product Safety Commission

Lesson 1 Review On a sheet of paper, write the answers to the following questions. Use complete sentences.

1. What are three advantages of being a wise consumer?

2. What are two standards to help you judge products and services?

3. What is the first thing you should do to complain about a product or service?

On a sheet of paper, write the answers to the following questions. Use complete sentences.

4. **Critical Thinking** You see an ad for expensive shampoo. Actors with beautiful hair say they use the shampoo. How are the advertisers trying to influence you?

5. **Critical Thinking** Why might people who have chronic diseases be targets of quackery?

Scoliosis

A condition in which the spine is abnormally curved

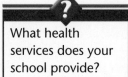

What health services does your school provide?

Wise health consumers know when to use self-care. They also know when it is best not to act as their own doctor.

When Is Self-Care the Best Action?

Self-care means that you take action to prevent health problems. Good nutrition, regular exercise, and safety practices help to prevent illness or injuries. Not smoking and not breathing in secondhand smoke also are preventive measures. You practice prevention when you avoid tobacco, alcohol, or illegal drug use. Maintaining a healthy body weight helps to prevent heart and joint problems.

You can use self-care for ordinary colds and other minor illnesses. The key word is *ordinary.* For example, good self-care for an ordinary cold is to drink plenty of liquids and get extra rest. Minor illnesses and injuries that do not get better within a few days require professional, or expert, help.

What Health Services Do Schools Offer?

You might receive certain health services through your school. School health services differ from school to school. Some schools do not have a school nurse. Other schools have health centers with a doctor and nurses. Only 14 states require that a school have a school nurse. Many school districts have school psychologists. Some may have social workers.

School health services differ depending on the medical experts available and the cost of services. School counselors and psychologists help students with emotional or social problems. School nurses may provide care for students with disabilities and emergency care for all students. Nurses may provide information on staying well and preventing disease.

School nurses may also conduct health screenings. These may include screenings of vision, hearing, and blood pressure. School nurses may also do **scoliosis** screening. Scoliosis is a condition in which the spine is abnormally curved.

Taking part in any health screenings your school gives is important. This helps health professionals identify conditions that may need treatment. It also helps you keep track of changes in your health.

When Should People Seek Professional Help?

Sometimes, not treating your health problem yourself is the best choice. Here are some examples of situations for which you should seek professional help:

- an injury that is more than a minor cut or bruise or a minor blow to the head

- any unusual bleeding, such as blood in the urine or feces

- any severe pain, such as in the abdomen, or a severe headache

- a patch of skin or a mole that has changed shape or color

- a minor problem, such as a cold, flu, cough, sore throat, or body aches, that lasts more than a week

- vomiting that lasts more than a day

- a fever of 103°F for any length of time or a fever of 100.5°F for longer than 3 days

- depression that lasts more than a few days or having thoughts of suicide or harming yourself

Who Are Some Health Care Professionals?

There are many different kinds of health care professionals. A **primary care physician** treats people for usual problems. For example, a primary care physician may perform checkups or prescribe medicine for a throat infection. A **specialist** is a doctor who works only in a certain branch of medicine. Some types of medical specialists and the types of health problems they treat are listed at left.

A **nurse practitioner** is a registered nurse with special training for providing primary health care. Nurse practitioners perform checkups, detect usual illnesses, and check on chronic conditions.

Doctors sometimes refer people to other kinds of health care providers. For example, a physical therapist helps people regain use of their muscles. A registered dietitian provides nutritional counseling for people with illnesses or special dietary needs.

Regular medical and dental checkups are important. So are vaccinations. Checkups include screening for health problems. Checkups help doctors and dentists prevent problems and find problems early so that treatment is not delayed.

Finding a doctor you are comfortable with may be as simple as asking someone to recommend one. You can get the names and qualifications of physicians in your area from several sources. These include your family's health insurance provider, local medical associations, or directories in the public library or on the Internet. Look for these qualifications:

- a certificate from the appropriate board in the person's field

- an association with a teaching hospital, dental school, or medical center

- experience in treating your particular health problems

- someone who answers your questions and with whom you feel comfortable.

Some health conditions are common in members of the same family. Before you visit a doctor the first time, ask your parents or guardian to help you prepare a family history of health problems. Share this information with your doctor.

What Are Some Health Care Facilities?

People see health care professionals in different kinds of places. A **health care facility** is a place where people go for medical, dental, and other care. A dental or medical office is one kind of health care facility. Primary health care is provided in these offices. Primary health care includes checkups and tests to identify diseases and problems. It also includes treatment of common illnesses and injuries.

How can you find out more about a health care professional's qualifications?

Outpatient clinics provide health care for people who do not need to stay overnight. Outpatient clinics offer primary health care. They also offer same-day surgery, meaning the patient has surgery and goes home the same day. Most clinics treat all kinds of medical problems. Others have a certain focus, such as adolescent health.

Other facilities provide **inpatient** care for overnight or longer. Patients can receive nursing care and **rehabilitation**—therapy needed to recover from surgery, illness, or injury.

A hospital is a facility that provides complete health care services. People can receive both outpatient and inpatient care at a hospital. General hospitals provide care for all kinds of illnesses and injuries. Students preparing to be health care professionals receive training in teaching hospitals.

Research hospitals conduct medical studies. Specialty hospitals, such as children's hospitals, deal only with certain illnesses or groups of patients.

Hospital emergency rooms and some urgent care centers offer walk-in emergency care 24 hours a day. These centers are required by law to treat people who do not have health insurance.

Long-term care facilities, such as nursing homes, offer 24-hour nursing care. These facilities are not just for elderly people. Younger people who cannot live independently because of a disability may live there. People recovering from surgery or a serious illness may stay there for a few days or weeks. A **hospice** is another kind of long-term care facility for people who are dying from diseases such as AIDS or cancer.

What Questions Should You Ask Yourself About a Doctor?

- Does the doctor ask about my health problem and history?

- Does the doctor listen carefully and answer all my questions?

- Do I feel comfortable with the doctor?

- Does the doctor give me enough time and attention?

- Does the doctor clearly explain the purpose of tests and procedures? Does the doctor clearly explain test results or diagnoses?

- Does the doctor encourage me to take preventive action?

- Is the doctor willing to refer me elsewhere when necessary?

Lesson 2 Review On a separate sheet of paper, write the word or phrase in parentheses that best completes each sentence.

1. Self-care is appropriate for (unusual bleeding, vomiting more than a day, a cold).

2. A professional who works only in a certain branch of medicine is a (primary care physician, specialist, nurse).

3. A person who needs short-term physical therapy after surgery might stay for a few days in a(n) (outpatient clinic, hospice, nursing home).

On a sheet of paper, write answers to the following questions. Use complete sentences.

4. **Critical Thinking** What are three actions you take every day to practice self-care?

5. **Critical Thinking** Besides starting treatment early, what is another benefit of finding health problems early?

Health in Your Life

Communicating with Your Doctor

How well you communicate with your doctor is an important part of your health care. Doctors depend on you to talk about your symptoms so they can determine what is wrong. Many teens have questions about sensitive subjects, but they are too embarrassed to ask. Write down your questions before your visit. Then you can read the questions or have the doctor read them.

Make sure you understand your doctor's instructions. Do not be afraid to ask your doctor to repeat an explanation or to tell you again how to take a prescribed medicine. Taking an active role also means that if you feel uncomfortable with a certain doctor, you choose another one.

On a sheet of paper, write answers to the following questions. Use complete sentences.

1. How might your health care be affected if you feel uncomfortable with your doctor?

2. Your doctor prescribes a medicine for you, but you are not sure why. What do you ask your doctor?

After reading this lesson, you should be able to

◆ explain how different kinds of health insurance work

◆ describe ways individuals can lower health care costs

◆ identify a patient's rights

Health insurance

A plan that pays a major part of medical costs

Deductible

The first part of each year's medical expenses before the insurance company makes payments

Health care is expensive. Therefore, understanding the ways in which people pay for health care is important. Some people pay directly for medical expenses. However, most people cannot afford to do this. **Health insurance** is a less expensive way to pay for health care. Health insurance is a plan that pays a major part of medical costs. These costs may include medicines, surgery, tests, hospital stays, and doctors' visits. Health insurance covers major medical expenses that people otherwise could not afford. The main kinds of health insurance are private and government supported.

How Does Private Health Insurance Work?

With a private health insurance plan, people pay for a policy themselves. Individuals regularly pay a premium, or fee, to an insurance company for a policy. In exchange, the insurance company pays part or all of their health care expenses.

Many employers offer a group plan as a job benefit to workers. Usually, the premiums are lower when people join the plan as a group. Employers usually pay the largest amount. Workers pay a smaller amount each month.

In both plans, each individual usually pays a **deductible.** A deductible is the first part of each year's medical expenses before the insurance company makes payments. If you have a $200 deductible, you must pay the first $200 on your medical expenses each year. For all other expenses that year, the insurance company pays a certain percentage. You pay the rest. For example, suppose you have an additional $1,200 in health care expenses one year. The insurance company pays 80 percent, or $960. You pay the remaining 20 percent, or $240.

Some insurance policies pay only a fixed amount for some procedures or services. They may not cover other procedures or services. For example, some insurance policies may pay 50 percent for eyeglasses. They may pay nothing for a hearing aid. The individual must pay for anything that is not covered.

Research and Write

Work in small groups to research what Congress is doing on a national level to improve access to health insurance for all Americans. Write a letter to your state's senators expressing your opinion on what can be done.

How Does Managed Care Work?

Managed care is another type of private health insurance. In managed care, an organization is the go-between for the patient and the physician. Managed care tends to cost less than other private insurance. There are two common kinds of managed care.

Health Maintenance Organizations

A **health maintenance organization (HMO)** is a form of managed care in which the organization controls how health care is delivered and what it costs. Members can be individuals or employers. They pay a fixed amount each month. There are two types of HMOs. Group HMOs require members to go to certain clinics or medical offices. Independent practice associations (IPAs) provide members with a list of doctors and hospitals from which to choose.

HMOs have advantages and drawbacks. HMOs provide preventive health care such as regular physical exams, well-baby care, and routine vaccinations at no extra charge. Private insurance usually charges for preventive care. However, HMO members are limited in their choice of health care providers. Waiting time for appointments can be long. People cannot see a specialist unless their primary care doctor refers them. Members must usually pay all expenses for seeing doctors who do not belong to the HMO.

Preferred Provider Organizations

A **preferred provider organization (PPO)** is a form of managed care that has fewer rules and more choices of doctors than an HMO has. The doctors are paid a separate fee for each service. Patients pay a fixed amount per visit, and the insurance company pays the rest. Like an HMO, members have a list of doctors who belong to the organization. However, members can go directly to a specialist without a referral. PPOs are generally more expensive than HMOs but less expensive than most private insurance plans.

What Is Government Health Insurance?

Government health insurance includes several kinds of insurance for special groups of people. This insurance is paid by federal, state, or local funds.

Medicare is health insurance for people age 65 or older. It also covers some people under age 65 with certain disabilities. Medicare pays for some medical expenses. People must pay the rest themselves or with additional private insurance.

Medicaid is health insurance for people whose incomes are below a certain level. Medicaid is different from Medicare in that it has no age requirement. It is paid for by state and federal taxes. Individual states operate Medicaid and determine the benefits they will offer. Some people qualify for both Medicare and Medicaid.

The State Children's Health Insurance Program (SCHIP) provides health care for children of low-income parents. The parents make too much money to qualify for Medicaid but generally less than a certain amount. Individual states run this program.

How Else Does Government Pay for Health Care?

The U.S. Public Health Service (USPHS) oversees the Medicare, Medicaid, and SCHIP programs. The following list describes several more branches of the USPHS:

- The National Institutes of Health (NIH) provides money for research on health and illness. Universities, hospitals, and private institutes conduct the research.

- The Centers for Disease Control and Prevention (CDC) is responsible for the control and treatment of communicable diseases. This includes diseases such as the flu and sexually transmitted diseases.

- The Food and Drug Administration (FDA) enforces laws for the safety, effectiveness, and labeling of food, drugs, and cosmetics.

- The Substance Abuse and Mental Health Services Administration (SAMHSA) oversees programs to prevent and treat alcoholism, drug addiction, and mental illness.

- The Health Resources and Services Administration (HRSA) supports mother and child health programs, community health education, and training programs for health care workers.

State and local health departments also provide health care services through tax money. These may include vaccinations, blood pressure screening, and vision tests. These services are provided at little or no cost. State and local health departments also operate centers for people with mental and physical disabilities.

How Can Individuals Lower Health Costs?

The cost of health care in the United States continues to increase every year. Fewer people are able to afford health insurance. Leaders at the state and national level are working to address the problem. However, individuals can do the following to lower health care costs:

- Choose outpatient health care whenever possible. The most costly medical treatment is inpatient care. One low-cost place is a *neighborhood clinic.* These clinics offer many health care services at a low fee. *Alternative birthing centers* (ABCs) usually employ certified nurse-midwives to deliver babies. They offer care for low-risk pregnant women before and after giving birth. The cost is much less than delivery in a hospital. *Hospices* provide dying patients with the medical care they need to live out the rest of their life comfortably. The costs for hospice care are lower than for hospital care.

- Educate yourself and become more active in your own health care. Eat right, exercise, and avoid alcohol, tobacco, and other drugs. Preventing diseases is a major way of keeping down health care costs.

- Ask your doctor to prescribe a generic drug when possible.

Link to ➤➤➤

Social Studies

The number of people age 65 and older is expected to almost double in the United States between 2000 and 2030. Because about 80 percent of older adults have at least one chronic condition, this increase may lead to higher health care costs.

❀ ❀ ❀ ❀ ❀ ❀ ❀ ❀ ❀ ❀

Technology and Society

Fluoride is a substance that helps prevent cavities. In 1945, communities began adding fluoride to public water supplies. For every $1 that is spent on fluoridation, $38 in dental treatment costs are saved. Fluoridation, dental sealants, and toothpaste with fluoride can prevent nearly all cavities.

- Advocate for family and community health. You might volunteer for a charitable health organization, such as the American Lung Association or the American Cancer Society. You also might keep informed about health issues that affect your community. Write a letter or e-mail to your local and state representatives to support available, affordable health care for everyone.

- Take part in health promotion programs that your employer offers. Many employers promote healthy nutrition, physical activity, and avoiding or quitting smoking. Companies can save almost $5 for every $1 spent on these programs. Some companies save millions of dollars in health costs by helping employees prevent chronic diseases.

What Are Your Rights as a Patient?

The Patients' Bill of Rights was developed by a committee appointed by President Bill Clinton in 1997. Many health plans have adopted these rights and responsibilities. The list below summarizes these rights.

Patients' Bill of Rights

1. the right to accurate information about your health plan, health care providers, and health care facilities

2. the right to choose your health care providers

3. the right to receive emergency services without regard to ability to pay

4. the right to know your treatment choices and to take part in decisions about your care

5. the right to considerate and respectful care, without discrimination

6. the right to talk in confidence with health care providers and to have your health care information kept private

7. the right to a fair, fast, and unbiased review of any complaint you have about your health care

Lesson 3 Review On a sheet of paper, write the word or phrase from the Word Bank that best completes each sentence.

1. Health care paid by the government for low-income people is _____.

2. The first part of each year's medical expenses an individual pays to a health insurance company is a _____.

3. HMOs and PPOs are two types of _____.

On a sheet of paper, write the answers to the following questions. Use complete sentences.

4. **Critical Thinking** How does preventing chronic diseases help keep down health care costs?

5. **Critical Thinking** Suppose a person has a stroke and needs rehabilitation. The person is expected to be able to live independently. To which health care facility might the person go right after leaving the hospital?

▼◀▲▼◀▲▼◀▲▼◀▲▼◀▲▼◀▲▼◀▲▼◀▲▼◀▲▼◀▲▼◀▲▼◀▲▼◀▲▼◀▲▼◀▲▼◀▲▼◀▲▼◀▲▼

Health at Work

Medical Records Technician

A career as a medical records technician may be for you if you want to work in a health facility and can pay close attention to details. Medical records technicians organize patient information. Technicians translate disease names and treatments into coding systems. The information is then entered into a computer. Technicians need to be orderly and detailed. They need excellent keyboarding skills. Technicians may work in hospitals, clinics, health agencies, insurance companies, nursing homes, and other health facilities. Medical records technicians usually have a 2-year degree. Most employers require technicians to take an exam that qualifies them as registered health information technicians (RHITs).

- Some influences on choices of health consumers are advertising, price, and recommendations of family or friends.

- Criteria to help judge products and services are to look at the cost benefits, consider recommendations, watch for false or misleading claims, look at the ingredients, and compare prices.

- Preventing and taking care of ordinary colds and minor illnesses are wise forms of self-care.

- School nurses may provide care for students with disabilities. They may provide information on staying well and preventing disease.

- Health care professionals include primary care physicians, specialists, nurse practitioners, physical therapists, and registered dieticians.

- Qualifications to look for in a health care professional are board certificates, associations, and experience. The person's comfort with the professional is also important.

- Some health care facilities are dental or medical offices, outpatient clinics, and inpatient facilities for nursing care and rehabilitation. Other health care facilities are hospitals, urgent care centers, nursing homes, and hospices.

- People can pay for health care costs through private individual or group insurance plans. Health maintenance or preferred provider organizations offer less expensive health care.

- Government-supported health insurance includes Medicare for people over age 65, Medicaid for low-income people, and SCHIP for children in low-income families.

- Individuals can help lower health costs. They can choose low-cost outpatient facilities when possible. They can practice prevention, buy generic medicine, and advocate for family and community health. They can also take part in workplace health promotion programs.

Vocabulary

consumer, 446	inpatient, 455	preferred provider organization (PPO), 458
deductible, 457	managed care, 458	primary care physician, 453
health care facility, 454	Medicaid, 459	quackery, 448
health insurance, 457	Medicare, 459	rehabilitation, 455
health maintenance organization (HMO), 458	nurse practitioner, 453	scoliosis, 452
hospice, 455	outpatient clinic, 454	specialist, 453

Chapter 19 R E V I E W

Word Bank

consumer

health insurance

HMOs

hospice

inpatient

Medicare

nurse practitioner

outpatient clinic

PPOs

primary care
  physician

quackery

rehabilitation

scoliosis

specialist

Vocabulary Review

On a sheet of paper, write the word or phrase from the Word Bank that best completes each sentence.

1. People are influenced by _____ when they buy a product that claims to cure a disease such as cancer or arthritis.

2. A(n) _____ is a type of physician who treats people for usual problems.

3. A nurse who provides primary health care is a(n) _____.

4. A facility that provides health care for people who do not stay overnight is a(n) _____.

5. A person who stays overnight or longer in a health care facility is receiving _____ care.

6. Someone recovering from surgery may need _____.

7. Many employers offer _____ as a job benefit.

8. Some people under age 65 with certain disabilities may be covered by _____.

9. When someone buys a product, the person is a(n) _____.

10. School nurses may conduct screenings for _____.

11. A person who is dying may stay in a(n)_____.

12. Members of _____ must visit a primary care physician first before seeing a specialist.

13. Members of _____ may visit a specialist without a referral from primary care physicians.

14. A(n) _____ is a doctor who works only in a certain branch of medicine.

Concept Review

On a sheet of paper, write the letter of the answer that best completes each sentence.

15. You are a wise consumer when you _____.

  A buy the least expensive medicine

  B buy generic drugs when available

  C use only the products your best friend uses

  D buy products advertised by your favorite actor

16. You should see a doctor if you _____.

  A have a mild headache

  B bruise your foot on a rock

  C are coughing when you have a cold

  D are depressed for several weeks

17. One form of government health insurance is _____.

  A Medicare   **B** an HMO   **C** a PPO   **D** a hospice

Critical Thinking

On a sheet of paper, write the answers to the following questions. Use complete sentences.

18. If a person had a disease that could not be cured, why do you think quackery might appeal to the person's emotions instead of reason?

19. What might be one reason that the cost of health care has become so high?

20. Why is it important to recognize how advertisers of health products and services are trying to influence you?

Test-Taking Tip When taking a matching test, match all the items that you know go together for sure. Cross out these items. Then try to match the items that are left.

Self-Assessment

Can you answer these questions?

☑ 1. What are some public health goals the U.S. government has set?

☑ 2. What are some public health problems in the United States?

☑ 3. Why is poverty linked to public health problems?

☑ 4. Why is homelessness a community health problem?

☑ 5. What are some groups of people who are at high risk for health problems?

☑ 6. What are some basic health services?

☑ 7. What are some worldwide health concerns?

☑ 8. What organizations help make vaccinations available?

☑ 9. What does a public health department do?

☑ 10. What does the World Health Organization do?

20 Public Health

The health of a community is important because it can affect each individual's personal health. To promote a community's health and well-being, each individual, family, and neighborhood can help. People do this when they become aware of public health problems and cooperate to solve them. Every effort, no matter how small, can affect the health and well-being of individuals and of the whole community.

In this chapter, you will learn about public health problems in the local, national, and international communities. You will learn how the public health system works to solve problems, promote health, and prevent disease. You will learn how you can help promote public health.

Goals for Learning

◆ To identify public health problems nationally and internationally

◆ To describe community, state, national, voluntary, and international public health services

◆ To explain the role of health promotion and disease prevention in public health

◆ To identify individual opportunities to promote public health

467

Objectives

After reading this lesson, you should be able to

◆ identify some national public health problems

◆ describe epidemics

◆ discuss poverty, homelessness, and environmental factors as public health concerns

◆ describe some worldwide health concerns

Public health

The practice of protecting and improving the health of a community or a nation

Epidemic

The rapid spread of a communicable disease that affects large populations at the same time

Health is more than a personal concern. Health is a concern of whole communities and countries. **Public health** is the practice of protecting and improving the health of a community or a nation. Public health uses such means as preventive medicine, education, and control of communicable diseases to respond to health concerns.

Every 10 years, the U.S. government sets public health goals on which it works over the coming 10-year period. These include the following general goals based on some national public health problems:

• to provide equal health care for all Americans, including children, adolescents, older people, and individuals with disabilities

• to increase health and quality of life for older Americans

• to increase the ability of all Americans to be able to use preventive health services

What Are Some National Public Health Problems?

You already know that violence and alcohol and other drug abuse are public health problems in the United States. The spread of disease is another problem. Poverty, homelessness, availability of health services, and environmental factors also are public health problems.

Epidemics

When a communicable disease spreads rapidly, affecting large populations at the same time, it is called an **epidemic.** In the United States, epidemics are not as common as they once were. For example, polio was an epidemic in the 1940s and 1950s. The polio vaccine has nearly eliminated the disease. Nevertheless, epidemics still happen. For example, AIDS has reached epidemic levels in many countries.

Link to >>>

Art

In the movie *Restoration,* a doctor helps to battle the Great Plague of 1665 in England. This bubonic plague epidemic killed 15 percent of London's population.

Throughout history, organizations such as the Centers for Disease Control and Prevention (CDC) have gathered statistics related to national health. Epidemics have killed thousands of people in the United States. Table 20.1.1 shows the number of people who died in some of the worst epidemics in the United States.

Table 20.1.1 Deaths from the Worst Epidemics in the United States			
Date	Disease	Number Who Died	Total U.S. Population at the Time
1832	cholera	7,340	13,000,000
1878	yellow fever	20,000	49,000,000
1900–1904	typhoid	20,520	76,000,000
1900–1904	tuberculosis	140,600	76,000,000
1916	polio	7,000	99,000,000
1918	influenza	550,000	102,000,000
1949–1952	polio	6,000	151,000,000
1985–2005	AIDS	more than 500,000	248,000,000– 296,000,000

Tooth decay is one of the most common infectious diseases among U.S. children. It may cause pain, poor appearance, and weight loss.

Poverty

Poverty is a public health concern because it puts people at high risk for serious health problems. Many experts believe that poverty can lead to health problems.

When people cannot afford a balanced diet with the right nutrients, malnutrition and other health problems may result. When people cannot afford health care or health insurance, many of their health problems are not treated effectively, if at all.

Poverty is the main reason that many children go without vaccinations and other health care. When pregnant women do not get proper care before a baby is born, both mother and baby can have health problems. Babies may have low birth weight or slowed mental function. To have a healthy pregnancy, mothers should follow these guidelines:

- See a doctor or other health care provider from the start of the pregnancy.

- Do not use tobacco, alcohol, or other drugs.

- Eat healthy foods, including fruits, vegetables, low-fat milk, eggs, cheese, and grains.

- Exercise sensibly.

- Have the baby checked by a doctor or health care provider right after birth and throughout childhood.

- Clean the baby's gums and teeth to prevent tooth decay.

Homelessness

Homelessness is a community health problem related to poverty. On any given night, about 600,000 Americans are without shelter. Of those, 40 percent are families with children. About 39 percent of homeless people are under age 21.

Health Myth

Myth: The United States has the best health care in the world.

Fact: Americans spend about $2\frac{1}{2}$ times as much for health care as other developed nations. However, the United States has fewer doctors per person, higher infant mortality rates, and lower than average childhood immunization rates than other developed nations.

Figure 20.1.1 *Volunteer food assistance programs help poor and homeless people.*

Tuberculosis

A communicable lung disease

Health disasters such as heat waves do not affect everyone equally. Poor people and elderly people are often the worst hit.

Research and Write

Using the Internet, research the topic of Americans who do not have health insurance. Prepare an oral report on how this lack of insurance affects dental care, doctor visits, and hospital visits. Explain possible solutions to these problems.

People may become homeless because of domestic violence. When homeless shelters are overcrowded, parents and their children sometimes return to an abusive household. Children cannot attend school regularly. They frequently go without any health care.

In some homeless shelters, communicable diseases such as **tuberculosis**—a lung disease—are a growing problem. Poor hygiene also is a problem for homeless people. The other health problems that affect poor people also affect homeless people.

Getting Health Services

High-risk groups of people often are not able to get basic health services. Poor people and homeless people are two high-risk populations. Teenage parents and their children, people with mental health problems, and elderly people also are high-risk groups. People with disabilities and recent immigrants to the United States are other high-risk groups.

Lack of transportation may limit basic health services. For example, in rural areas, nearby health services are often not available.

Basic health services include vaccinations and medical care for women during pregnancy. Basic health services also include screening for health problems such as breast cancer. Nutritional counseling and exercise and fitness programs for elderly people are other basic health services. In addition, elderly people often need assistance meeting their daily needs. When the population over age 65 increases, even more health resources will be needed for elderly people.

People who provide health services need to be sensitive to cultural differences. Sometimes, people with health problems cannot speak the same language as the nurse or doctor they contact. In such cases, a trained interpreter, not a family member, should translate. Also, some ethnic groups are more open to problems such as alcoholism or depression. Members of different ethnic groups sometimes metabolize medications differently. This can lead to problems with finding the correct dosage.

Environment

The release of harmful chemicals into the environment is a public health concern. These chemicals harm the food people eat, the water they drink, and the air they breathe. This damage increases the risk of health problems. Some geographical areas are more affected than others. In some areas, for example, cancer rates or the number of **birth defects** are high. Birth defects are deformities or impaired functions of the body that are present from birth.

Decide for Yourself

Adults can get many diseases. Several of these can be prevented by vaccinations. These diseases include influenza (flu), tetanus, and pneumococcal disease.

Flu is a contagious respiratory disease. In the United States, more than 200,000 people are hospitalized with flu complications every year. About 36,000 people die. To help prevent flu, you can get a vaccination every year.

Tetanus is a disease of the nervous system. It leads to muscle contractions in the face, which is why the disease is also called lockjaw. Another symptom of tetanus is severe muscle spasms throughout the body. It causes death in 30 to 40 percent of cases. After high school, you should get a tetanus shot every 10 years.

Pneumococcal disease can lead to serious infections of the lungs, the blood, and the covering of the brain. Each year pneumococcal disease kills more people than all other vaccine-preventable diseases combined. For many people, one vaccine is all that is needed to make them immune to pneumococcal disease.

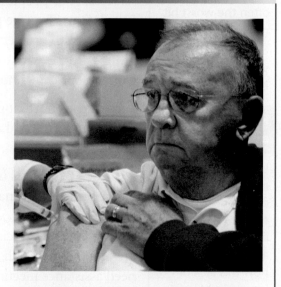

On a sheet of paper, write the answers to the following questions. Use complete sentences.

1. Which of the diseases mentioned do you think is the worst? Explain your answer.

2. Why do you think it is important for elderly people to get flu vaccinations?

3. Why do you think many adults do not get vaccinations?

Research and Write

Using the Internet, research obesity as an American public health problem. Write two pages on its causes and effects.

?

Which public health problem do you think should be given the highest priority?

What Are Some Worldwide Health Concerns?

Developing nations often have little money and low standards of living. Developing nations may not have laws or the resources to protect the environment. When these conditions exist, people cannot meet their basic needs for food, water, and shelter. Problems such as hunger and malnutrition can result. Poverty, AIDS, environmental damage, and diseases such as malaria are public health concerns in many developing nations. Natural disasters and war also are concerns of worldwide public health.

Lesson 1 Review On a sheet of paper, write the answers to the following questions. Use complete sentences.

1. What are three goals for public health in the United States?

2. Why is poverty a public health concern?

3. What are two high-risk groups of people who may have trouble getting health services?

4. **Critical Thinking** Why is health a public concern rather than just a personal concern?

5. **Critical Thinking** Why do you think epidemics in the United States are not as common as they used to be?

Technology and Society

A virus causes poliomyelitis (polio). Polio destroys nerve cells that control muscles. It makes the legs, arms, or body unable to move. It makes swallowing, talking, and breathing difficult. Polio usually occurs in children. In 1943, the best-known person with polio was President Franklin D. Roosevelt. The same year, polio killed 1,151 people in the United States.

In 1954, Jonas Salk developed a polio vaccine. After many laboratory tests, Pittsburgh schoolchildren were vaccinated. In 1955, the medicine was tested in 44 states. Salk said polio would be very rare before long. He was right. By 1969, few people died from polio. The epidemic was over.

Sanitation

Measures related to cleanliness that protect public health

Health Myth

Myth: All bottled water is better than tap water.

Fact: City tap water and bottled water are both highly regulated and monitored for quality. Some, but not all, bottled water is purer and safer than some tap water.

Have you ever gotten a vaccination at a school, neighborhood health center, or local drugstore? How was that vaccination made possible? Public health agencies, nonprofit groups, and individuals support organized preventive efforts to ensure the public's health. Most of these health services are provided to individuals at the community level.

What Are Some Community and State Health Services?

All states have public health departments. Most cities and counties also have health departments. These departments make sure that laws relating to disease and **sanitation** are observed. Sanitation refers to measures related to cleanliness that protect public health. Sanitation tasks include inspecting restaurants, making sure water is clean and safe, and tracking down sources of communicable diseases.

Community and state health departments also work to provide medical care for low-income individuals. The departments provide vaccination programs, routine tests, and physical examinations. They also may provide visiting nurse and nutrition programs, community clinics, and community education programs. For example, community education programs may target young mothers and their babies, focusing on nutrition and education. Senior centers and aging and nutrition programs assist elderly people. School-based and school-linked clinics and services provide students with health care.

Federal and state governments provide local communities with funds to operate prevention and treatment programs. Most local programs, however, are funded through local taxes and private charities.

What Are Some National Health Services?

The Department of Health and Human Services (HHS) is the U.S. government agency with the largest responsibility for public health. HHS gathers and analyzes health information, sets health and safety standards, and sponsors education and research. HHS includes these divisions:

- Centers for Medicare and Medicaid Services (CMS)—controls Medicaid and Medicare

- Centers for Disease Control and Prevention (CDC)—collects and distributes information about public health problems

- Administration for Children and Families (ACF)—oversees programs for low-income families and people with disabilities

- National Institutes of Health (NIH)—conducts research, promotes disease prevention, and carries out national health policies

- Food and Drug Administration (FDA)—regulates food, drugs, medical devices, and blood products

The Environmental Protection Agency (EPA) is another government agency concerned with public health. It sets policy for and monitors the quality of the water and air.

The Occupational Safety and Health Administration (OSHA) and the Consumer Product Safety Commission (CPSC) are government agencies concerned with public health. They set guidelines for safe exposure to toxic substances for workers and consumers.

Link to ⋗⋗⋗

Social Studies

Public concern about pollution led to the establishment of the Environmental Protection Agency (EPA) in 1970. The EPA creates and enforces regulations to protect the environment. When a regulation is being created, the EPA requests that members of the public comment on it. The EPA relies on these comments to develop the final wording of the regulation.

These government agencies fund research and conduct monitoring tasks. They also issue **government regulations.** These are rules that businesses must follow to protect public health. For example, the FDA regulates the ingredients in foods and their labeling. It makes sure that any advertising claims about the effects of a drug are true. Funding for these national health agencies and programs comes from federal income taxes.

Health in Your Life

Identifying Health Services in Your Community

Find out about the different programs for disease prevention, health promotion, and treatment available in your community. List local health agencies and organizations. Check with parents, counselors, librarians, or teachers for ideas. You could also search the phone book, newspaper, or Internet. Work with a partner to gather information about the agencies. Call each agency and ask about the items below. Prepare for the interview in advance. You might record the answers.

- name, address, and phone number of agency
- days and hours of operation
- types of services and health professionals on staff
- who qualifies for services and the fees charged
- whether the services are confidential
- languages in which the services are offered

Use the information to compare the services.

On a sheet of paper, write the answers to the following questions. Use complete sentences.

1. Are there parts of your community in which some services are not available?

2. Do several agencies provide the same services?

3. Do you know anyone who might benefit from knowing about these services? Who are they?

Centers for Disease
Control and
Prevention

Department of
Health and
Human Services

Food and Drug
Administration

Lesson 2 Review On a sheet of paper, write the phrase from the Word Bank that best completes each sentence.

1. The U.S. government agency with the largest responsibility for public health is the _____.

2. The _____ regulates food, drugs, medical devices, and blood products.

3. The _____ collects and distributes information about public health problems.

On a sheet of paper, write the answers to the following questions. Use complete sentences.

4. **Critical Thinking** Why do you think it is important to have local, as well as national, health services?

5. **Critical Thinking** Why do you think it is necessary for the FDA to monitor drug advertising claims?

▼◀▲▼◀▲▼◀▲▼◀▲▼◀▲▼◀▲▼◀▲▼◀▲▼◀▲▼◀▲▼◀▲▼◀▲▼◀▲▼◀▲▼◀▲▼

Health at Work

Home Health Aide

Living at home is important for most people, especially when they are ill. Home health aides help sick people stay at home by performing routine tasks for them. Aides might change bed linens, prepare meals, clean, do laundry, and run errands. Aides help bathe and clean people. Aides may read aloud or play games with sick people. They may give massages and other treatments.

Usually, health care agencies employ home health aides. Some hospitals run home care programs that employ home health aides. In some cases, individuals hire an aide.

Home health aides should know CPR. Federal law requires home health aides to pass a test covering a wide range of areas. A person can receive training before taking this test. Some states also require home health aides to be licensed.

Objectives

After reading this lesson, you should be able to

◆ discuss how voluntary organizations aid public health

◆ explain how health promotion aids public health

Many nonprofit voluntary health organizations respond to public health needs. Voluntary public health agencies are funded by contributions from individuals and businesses.

What Voluntary Agencies Provide Health Services?

Voluntary organizations that provide health services include the American Heart Association, the American Cancer Society, and the American Lung Association. These groups provide public health support through education programs. Usually, these organizations focus on a single disease. The efforts of these voluntary organizations have helped Americans learn preventive health measures. Anyone can volunteer to assist the efforts of these groups.

In many communities, people with common concerns meet for support and education. Self-help groups provide support. For example, they support people with organ transplants or those who are recovering from an emotional illness.

What Are Some International Health Services?

Recall that you learned about the WHO in the Health in the World feature on page 92. You read about the International Red Cross in the Health in the World feature on page 246.

Ridding the world of hunger, providing relief after major disasters, and fighting epidemics are shared efforts of the world. One organization that plays a major role in these efforts is the United Nations (UN). Programs of UN agencies such as the World Health Organization (WHO) work to provide public health services.

Other UN agencies provide worldwide health services. The United Nations International Children's Emergency Fund (UNICEF) provides vaccinations, school food programs, and health centers for children. It also helps train nurses. The Food and Agriculture Organization (FAO) works in developing countries to improve food production and to distribute food.

The United States also sponsors efforts for international public health. Organizations such as the Peace Corps and the U.S. Agency for International Development (USAID) are two examples. The International Red Cross is the world's largest private international public health organization. It provides aid such as food, clothing, medical care, and temporary shelter to victims of natural disasters.

How Do Health Promotion and Prevention Help?

A healthy population locally, nationally, and internationally has obvious benefits. Healthy people produce more on the job. Health promotion and disease prevention reduce the demands on the health care system. Preventive health care costs less than treatment of illness. Thus, health promotion and disease prevention are goals of many policy makers.

Education for health promotion focuses on sexually transmitted diseases, violence, physical fitness, nutrition, and substance abuse prevention. Those efforts may target specific groups at risk or whole communities. A community-wide nutrition education program, for example, can encourage individuals to lower their fat intake and exercise regularly.

Prevention organizations that work with specific groups are called **advocacy groups.** Advocacy groups may provide health services themselves, or they may help remove health care barriers. They do this by working to change government policies that prevent some people from receiving health care.

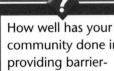

How well has your community done in providing barrier-free environments for people in wheelchairs?

Nationally, advocacy groups encourage passage of civil rights laws. For example, laws have been passed that guarantee special education programs in public schools for all children who have disabilities. Advocacy also has produced laws that protect the rights of elderly people.

Many businesses have health promotions for their employees. These businesses educate employees on how to live a healthier life. They encourage people to adopt better health practices concerning diet and exercise. Research has shown that these work-site programs can reduce sick days and health care costs.

How Can You Promote Public Health?

People get involved in health promotion in their community for many reasons. One reason is that disease prevention and health promotion save society money by preventing illness. Another reason is that communities organized to provide mutual support and promote health have fewer problems, including less crime and drug abuse. A third reason is that individuals increase their self-esteem as they work to improve the health of others.

To get involved, you could investigate existing community resources to identify your community's health needs. You could then choose a place to volunteer. For example, you could volunteer to help with a food drive or get people to sponsor you in a benefit walk for homeless people. You could write letters to lawmakers, asking for changes. You might join a health advocacy group.

Your school also has resources for promoting public health. The school nurse has access to a wide variety of educational materials. Your health teacher also does. You can find a wealth of information on the Internet.

Lesson 3 Review On a sheet of paper, write the word or phrase in parentheses that best completes each sentence.

1. Voluntary public health agencies are funded by (only businesses, the government, charitable contributions).

2. Programs of UN agencies mainly target (developing, large, tropical) countries.

3. Prevention organizations that work with specific groups are (international, advocacy, disaster aid) groups.

On a sheet of paper, write the answers to the following questions. Use complete sentences.

4. **Critical Thinking** Look up the word *advocate* in a dictionary. How does its meaning apply to the goals of an advocacy group?

5. **Critical Thinking** What are some examples of how you can promote public health?

- Public health means protecting and improving the health of a community or nation.

- Epidemics are public health problems because communicable diseases spread rapidly and affect large populations at the same time.

- Poverty puts people at high risk for health problems. It especially affects children's health.

- Communicable diseases and poor hygiene are major problems for homeless people.

- Poor people, homeless people, and teen parents and their children may have difficulty getting basic health services. Elderly people and people with disabilities or mental health problems also can have difficulty.

- Chemicals in the environment that harm food, water, and air increase the risk of public health problems.

- Poverty, low standards of living, hunger, malnutrition, AIDS, environmental damage, diseases, natural disasters, and war are international public health problems.

- Local and state public health departments make sure that laws relating to disease and sanitation are observed. Public health departments also provide medical care for low-income people.

- The U.S. Department of Health and Human Services gathers and analyzes health information, sets health and safety standards, and sponsors education and research.

- Nonprofit voluntary health organizations provide education programs in most communities.

- The United Nations, some U.S. organizations, and the International Red Cross provide public health services internationally.

- Health promotion and disease prevention through education and advocacy groups reduce costs and relieve demands on the health care system at every level.

- Individuals can promote public health by volunteering, writing letters to lawmakers, and joining public health advocacy groups.

Vocabulary

advocacy group, 479	government regulation, 476	sanitation, 474
birth defect, 472		tuberculosis, 471
epidemic, 468	public health, 468	

Chapter 20 REVIEW

Word Bank

advocacy group

birth defect

epidemic

government regulations

public health

sanitation

tuberculosis

Vocabulary Review

On a sheet of paper, write the word or phrase from the Word Bank that best completes each sentence.

1. The practice of protecting and improving the health of a community or nation is _____.

2. When an infectious disease spreads rapidly and affects many people, it is a(n) _____.

3. One communicable lung disease is _____.

4. Local and state health departments make sure that laws relating to disease and _____ are observed.

5. The Department of Health and Human Services helps develop _____.

6. A deformity present at birth is a(n) _____.

7. A goal of a(n) _____ is to change government health policies.

Concept Review

On a sheet of paper, write the letter of the answer that best completes each sentence.

8. A factor that puts people at higher risk for serious health problems is _____.

  A having health insurance   **C** advocacy

  B poverty   **D** clean air

9. High-risk groups include _____ because often they cannot get basic health services.

  A young adults   **C** people in large cities

  B factory employees   **D** homeless people

10. On any given night, the number of people who are homeless in the United States is about _____.

  A 6,000   **C** 600,000

  B 60,000   **D** 6,000,000

11. People may become homeless because of _____.

    A lack of transportation   **C** domestic violence

    B epidemics   **D** malnutrition

12. Basic health services include _____.

    A vaccinations   **B** shelter   **C** surgery   **D** transportation

13. A type of prevention organization is a(n) _____ group.

    A international **B** environmental **C** advocacy **D** charitable

14. Businesses' work-site programs can reduce _____.

    A sick days   **B** epidemics   **C** poverty   **D** disabilities

15. Poverty can result in _____.

    A malnutrition   **C** high birth rate

    B multiple sclerosis   **D** healthy pregnancies

16. A growing problem in homeless shelters is _____.

    A polio   **B** tuberculosis   **C** advocacy   **D** cholera

17. People at high risk for not getting basic health services include _____.

    A insured people   **C** single people

    B high-income people   **D** teenage parents

Critical Thinking

On a sheet of paper, write the answers to the following questions. Use complete sentences.

18. Discuss three international public health problems.

19. How do natural disasters cause public health problems?

20. What are two benefits of health promotion and disease prevention?

Test-Taking Tip   When you answer multiple-choice questions, read all of the options first. Then eliminate the ones that are not correct.

Self-Assessment

Can you answer these questions?

☑ 1. What is the balance of nature?

☑ 2. How does the balance of nature happen?

☑ 3. How can human activity change the balance of nature?

☑ 4. How does air pollution affect health?

☑ 5. How does air pollution affect Earth?

☑ 6. What effect does acid rain have on animal and plant life?

☑ 7. What are five causes of water pollution?

☑ 8. How does deforestation affect health?

☑ 9. What is noise pollution?

☑ 10. How can the environment be protected?

Environmental Health

The environment is made up of natural resources. Natural resources include Earth's air, water, land, and living things. Earth's natural resources work together. What happens to any one resource can directly affect other resources. For example, an oil spill in the ocean near Alaska can affect the fish and animals that live in and along the Alaskan coastline. Earth's environment is protected when its natural resources are protected.

In this chapter, you will learn about people's effect on the environment. You will learn how the environment affects your health. You will learn about ways people can protect the environment. You also will learn about ways the government protects the environment. Protecting the environment is one way to protect your health.

Goals for Learning

◆ To explain how the environment affects health
◆ To identify causes of air and water pollution
◆ To describe other environmental problems
◆ To identify actions that protect the environment

Health and the Environment

Objectives

After reading this lesson, you should be able to

◆ explain the term *balance of nature*

◆ describe three ways to disturb the balance of nature

◆ explain how damage to the environment affects health

◆ explain why understanding the effects of pollution on the environment is important

All living things depend on their environment for their needs. The environment is a system of natural resources, including air, land, water, plants, and animals. Living things depend on air, water, and land to live and grow.

What Is the Balance of Nature?

Humans contribute to the environment, just as the environment contributes to humans. For example, humans breathe out carbon dioxide. Plants need carbon dioxide to live and grow. Plants in turn give off oxygen, which humans need to live and grow. When all parts of the environment contribute to one another in this way, a healthy balance of nature is maintained. When any part of the environment is hurt or destroyed, this balance is changed.

Figure 21.1.1 *Natural and human-made changes, such as forest fires, affect the balance of nature.*

What Disturbs the Balance of Nature?

Natural events are always disturbing the balance of nature. Earthquakes, volcanoes, hurricanes, fires, and floods sometimes cause serious damage. However, nature usually recovers. In fact, the changes that natural events cause can be good for the environment over time.

Humans also can disturb the balance of nature. For years, humans have changed the environment by building houses, farming, and using Earth's resources. As the number of people on Earth grows, more demands are made on its resources. For example, metals and minerals are taken from the ground and used for many things. Coal and oil are used to heat homes and fuel cars and trucks. Trees are cut to make houses and paper.

Most fires destroy life. Prairie fires, however, are good for prairies. The roots of prairie plants grow deep into the ground. For this reason, fire does not harm them. Prairie fires prevent brush and trees from taking over the prairie. After a fire, prairies are alive with prairie plants.

Changes in the environment that humans cause can upset the balance of nature for many years. Mining can make the land unusable. Stripping the land of trees can cause **soil erosion.** Soil erosion happens when the soil is moved by wind, water, or ice. Using harmful chemicals also can make the land unsafe for people and animals.

How Does Environmental Damage Affect Health?

The wastes that people make have an immediate effect on health. Human waste usually does not cause problems because it is broken down in nature. Factories, however, can give off dangerous chemicals and other harmful wastes. When these harmful wastes get into the air or water or are buried under the ground, they cause **pollution.** Pollution happens when harmful materials get into the soil, water, or air. For example, an oil spill on the water can kill fish and birds that live there. If that water is used in people's homes, they are also affected.

Pesticide

A chemical used to kill bugs

Fragile

Easily broken, destroyed, or damaged

Pollution can be so harmful that it puts human life in danger. For example, chemicals are used in factories that make products for people to use every day. These same chemicals can make the factory workers sick. Wastes from factories, power plants, and cars can harm the air and water that people need to live. Pollution can be especially harmful to a growing fetus. For example, **pesticides** are chemicals that are used to kill bugs. Studies have shown that pesticides can pass from a mother's blood to the fetus. Some chemicals are known to cause cancer. Others cause brain and nerve damage or have an effect on how a fetus develops.

Why is the environment so fragile?

How Can Understanding the Effects of Pollution Help?

Damage to the environment can be turned around. The first step is understanding the problem. There is only so much of Earth's resources. Someday the resources will run out. Many people understand that the environment that gives us life— rivers, forests, soil, and air—is **fragile,** or easily damaged. The conditions that are needed to keep humans alive—air, water, animals, and soil—are all linked together. Keeping this fragile existence going is an important health issue.

Link to ➤➤➤

Math

On average, every person in the United States throws out about 4 pounds of trash each day. About how much trash does one person throw out in a year?

Most trash ends up in special places set aside for garbage. These places have low-lying ground where waste is buried between layers of dirt. Some trash decomposes much faster than other trash. Trash that takes many years to decompose can pollute the land over time.

Ecology

The study of how living things and the environment work together

People have begun to make changes to protect the environment. For example, lakes that were once believed to be dead have been brought back to life through careful management. The fish and plants that once lived there are coming back. The lives of bald eagles were once in danger. After the use of certain pesticides was stopped, the numbers of bald eagles grew.

Whole new branches of science that deal with protecting the environment have come about. **Ecology,** for example, is the study of how living things and the environment work together and depend on each other. Clinical ecology is a new science that deals with the harmful effects of human-made and natural materials on humans.

Word Bank

balance

environment

flood

Lesson 1 Review On a sheet of paper, write the word or phrase from the Word Bank that best completes each sentence.

1. All living things depend on their _____ to live.

2. All parts of the environment add to the _____ of nature.

3. One natural event that disturbs the balance of nature is a(n) _____.

On a sheet of paper, write the answers to the following questions. Use complete sentences.

4. Critical Thinking How can humans cause pollution?

5. Critical Thinking Why is it important to maintain the balance of nature?

Research and Write

Humans have had a critical effect on the environment. Visit the library and research a plant or animal that no longer exists because of what humans have done. How did humans affect the plant or animal? Make a poster about what you learn.

Photochemical smog

A form of air pollution

Bronchitis

A lung disease that makes breathing hard and causes coughing

Every day, you breathe in about 16,000 quarts of air. If the air you breathe is polluted, toxins get into your body. If you breathe in polluted air over months or years, your lungs may be damaged. Air pollution can affect your health, whether you are outdoors or indoors.

What Causes Outdoor Air Pollution?

The main cause of outdoor air pollution is burning. Whenever a material is burned, harmful gases get into the air. For example, factories that burn oil and coal make smoke. Cars and trucks that burn gas make a kind of smoke called exhaust. Other sources of air pollution are tobacco smoke, furnaces that burn waste, and leaf burning.

How Does Outdoor Air Pollution Affect Health?

Hydrocarbons are materials made of hydrogen and carbon. They are found in the exhaust that comes out of cars and trucks. They are also found in natural gas and other liquid fuels that get into the air. Hydrocarbons in the air can sting your nose and throat and make your eyes water. Some hydrocarbons can cause cancer.

Photochemical smog occurs when sunlight mixes hydrocarbons and nitrogen oxides together. Photochemical smog makes ozone. Ozone is a gas. Ozone found in the air you breathe keeps your body from getting oxygen from the lungs to your bloodstream. It can hurt your respiratory system and give you lung diseases such as asthma. It can also cause emphysema and **bronchitis,** a lung disease that makes breathing hard. Ozone can irritate your eyes.

Carbon monoxide is a poisonous gas that has no color or smell. It is found in the exhaust of cars and trucks. It is also found in tobacco smoke. Breathing in carbon monoxide affects the red cells in your blood. It keeps you from getting enough oxygen to your other body cells. This can result in headaches, dizziness, blurred vision, and tiredness. Over many years, carbon monoxide can make heart and lung disease worse.

Fossil fuel

A material that is made from plant or animal remains that can be burned

Particulate

Tiny piece of solid material

Sulfur dioxide is a poisonous gas that gets into the air from factories and power plants that burn **fossil fuels.** Fossil fuels are burnable materials such as coal, oil, and natural gas that form in the earth from plant or animal remains. Sulfur dioxide can irritate your eyes, throat, and lungs, making breathing hard. It makes asthma, emphysema, and bronchitis worse.

Particulates are tiny pieces of solid materials such as dust, ash, dirt, and soot that float in the air. Some particulates carry gases and pesticides that can harm your body when you breathe them in. Particulates may bother your eyes, nose, throat, and lungs.

Lead is an example of a particulate. Leaded gasoline raises the amount of lead in the air. Only unleaded gasoline can be used in the United States. Leaded gasoline is still used in other countries. Lead gets into your bloodstream through your lungs or gets absorbed into your skin. Too much lead can cause high blood pressure, loss of appetite, and damage to your brain and nervous system.

Outdoor air pollution affects everyone. In some areas, a smog alert is given when there is a lot of pollution in the air. People with serious health problems should stay indoors on days when the air is poor. Even healthy people should not do heavy exercise on those days.

Many large cities post ozone codes. Some cities show the ozone codes in the chart at the right on electric message boards. Some cities put daily ozone levels on the Internet.

Ozone Codes	
Air Quality Rating	**Air Quality Index (AQI)**
Green—good	0–50
Yellow—moderate	51–100
Orange—unhealthy for sensitive groups	101–150
Red—unhealthy	151–200
Purple—very unhealthy	201–300

How Does Indoor Air Pollution Affect Health?

Air inside homes and buildings also can affect health. This can happen when homes and buildings are closed up too tightly. Window and door seals are made to save energy and keep the outside air from getting in. Sometimes what happens, though, is that no new air gets in. All of the pollution is trapped inside the home or building.

Some building materials and household chemicals are toxic. For example, some glues used in wood furniture and paneling give off harmful gases. Household chemicals such as paints, drain cleaners, and pesticides give off gases that can cause respiratory problems. A building material that gives off particulates when crumbled is **asbestos.** Asbestos is a material that was used in older homes and buildings. Moving asbestos around puts tiny bits of it into the air. Asbestos can cause lung cancer. Asbestos is rarely used today. State laws say that workers must follow rules when removing asbestos from public places, such as schools.

There are other indoor air pollutants. Tobacco smoke causes respiratory and other problems for both smokers and nonsmokers. Broken heaters and appliances such as ovens and refrigerators can allow carbon monoxide and nitrogen dioxide to get into the air. **Radon** is another gas with no smell or color that comes from the radioactive decay of radium underground. Radon can be a serious indoor air pollutant when it gets into houses through walls and basement floors. Radon may cause lung cancer.

Indoor air pollution can make it hard for you to breathe, give you a cough that will not go away, and bother your nose and throat. Some indoor air pollutants can cause lung and respiratory diseases. Some indoor air pollutants can cause certain cancers. Indoor air pollution also can bother your eyes and give you an upset stomach and headaches. Some people cannot sleep. They might also get depressed, dizzy, cranky, and tired when they breathe in certain pollutants.

Greenhouse effect

The warming of Earth's atmosphere

Ozone layer

An area above Earth that guards and protects Earth from the sun's harmful rays

Link to ➤➤➤

Earth Science

Global warming refers to a worldwide climate change. Some scientists say that there is less Arctic ice than there once was. They conclude that less Arctic ice means that temperatures around the world are rising. Temperatures have been rising over the past 100 years. Some scientists believe global warming will upset the balance of nature and make serious changes in the weather.

How Does Air Pollution Affect Earth?

Air pollution affects not only people's health but also adds to long-term changes in Earth's atmosphere. Air pollution causes harm in several ways.

The Greenhouse Effect

Many scientists believe that all the carbon dioxide in the air is causing Earth to act like a greenhouse. A greenhouse is warm and damp inside. It has a glass ceiling that traps the sun's heat. A carbon dioxide cloud caused by air pollution surrounds Earth. This cloud acts like the glass ceiling in a greenhouse, trapping heat and dampness. The result is that Earth's atmosphere is warm, which allows life to exist on Earth. This is called the **greenhouse effect.**

Even small rises in the temperatures around the world affect rainfall everywhere. Less rainfall in some areas could cause crops to fail and make more deserts. More rainfall in other areas could cause serious floods and soil erosion. Sea levels could rise, flooding areas along the coast and mixing saltwater with freshwater.

The Ozone Layer

Scientists think that air pollution has made the **ozone layer** thinner. The ozone layer is an area 6 to 30 miles above Earth. It is made of naturally occurring gases. It guards and protects Earth from the sun's harmful rays. In 1985, scientists discovered a hole the size of the United States in the ozone layer over Antarctica. Later studies found an ozone loss over the Arctic polar region.

Scientists know that natural events such as volcanoes can affect the ozone layer. They also think that chlorofluorocarbons (CFCs) in the atmosphere have an effect. CFCs are chemicals that once were used in refrigerators and air conditioners. CFCs stay in the atmosphere for years. They turn ozone molecules into oxygen molecules. Oxygen molecules cannot protect Earth from the sun's harmful rays. Because of this, most products with CFCs are no longer used in the United States.

A thinner ozone layer allows more of the sun's harmful rays to reach Earth. These rays may damage crops, forest growth, animal life, and human health.

Acid Rain

Acid rain is precipitation—rain, snow, sleet, or hail—that contains large amounts of sulfuric or nitric acids. Sulfur and nitrogen from cars, trucks, factories, and home heating mix with the dampness in the air to form sulfuric and nitric acids. These acids spread through the atmosphere and come back to Earth in the form of acid rain. Acid rain may fall far from where the acids were made. For example, factories in the Midwest make large amounts of these acids. The acid rain falls as far away as the Southeast, New England, and eastern Canada.

Acid rain harms rivers, lakes, and water and plant life. As the water gets full of acid, fish do not lay eggs and may die. Water with a lot of acid pulls mercury and lead out of the lake beds and into the water. When the mercury and lead get into the fish, they become unsafe for humans to eat. In Germany, major forests have been destroyed by acid rain.

Lesson 2 Review On a sheet of paper, write the letter of the answer that best completes each sentence.

1. The main cause of air pollution is _____.
   A acid rain   **C** photochemical fog
   B burning   **D** ozone

2. A building material that gives off cancer-causing particulates is _____.
   A ozone   **C** coal
   B radon   **D** asbestos

3. A rise in the amount of carbon dioxide causes _____.
   A acid rain   **C** the greenhouse effect
   B the ozone layer   **D** photochemical smog

On a sheet of paper, write the answers to the following questions. Use complete sentences.

4. **Critical Thinking** What do you think causes the most air pollution?

5. **Critical Thinking** What can be done to lessen air pollution?

Sewage

Liquid and solid waste from drains and toilets

While three-quarters of Earth's surface is covered with water, only a small fraction of that water is freshwater. Most of Earth's water is in oceans, which contain saltwater. Saltwater cannot be used for drinking or growing crops. Freshwater is as important as air is in supporting human life.

Groundwater is water beneath Earth's surface. Groundwater is the largest source of freshwater. It supplies springs and wells. People depend on groundwater for drinking, cooking, and bathing. Groundwater is an important natural resource. It must be kept clean and free of pollution.

What Causes Water Pollution?

For many years, countries have dumped their wastes into oceans, lakes, and rivers. Many of these wastes cannot be broken down. They stay there for a long time and do permanent harm. Waste from factories, drains and toilets, oil leaks and spills, farm and household chemicals, and acid rain are the most common ways water gets polluted.

Factory Wastes

Toxic materials from factories cause water pollution when they get into the water supply. Most factory wastes such as mercury, lead, and acids cannot be broken down. Often the wastes were dumped into bodies of water or into groundwater. Mining has also caused a great deal of water pollution in the United States. The federal and state governments have passed laws to stop factories from polluting freshwater.

Sewage

Sewage is waste from drains and toilets. Most sewage comes from human body wastes. Sewage contains bacteria and life-forms that can cause disease. If sewage gets into groundwater and bodies of water such as ponds, lakes, and rivers, it can kill animals and plants. Humans can get diseases such as typhoid fever and cholera from water that has been polluted with sewage.

In 1977, the U.S. government passed a law that said sewage in the United States had to be treated before it was put into the environment. As a treatment, tiny helpful life-forms were added to the sewage to break down bacteria and harmful life-forms. Since then, the U.S. government has passed other clean water laws. In 1987, for example, it made stronger laws about sewage treatment and how clean the water had to be. More changes to the law were made in the 1990s and more recently. It is the job of the Environmental Protection Agency (EPA) to make sure factories do not break any clean water laws.

Oil Leaks and Spills

The worldwide need for oil and petroleum, which is a mixture of hydrocarbons, is great. To meet the need, large oil tankers move a large amount of oil and petroleum across oceans. Sometimes, these tankers leak, causing oil spills on the water. The spills kill animals and leave behind carcinogens. These carcinogens can affect humans.

Agricultural Runoff

Farmers use chemicals to make plants grow better. They use pesticides and herbicides to control bugs and weeds. When it rains, these chemicals run off into streams, rivers, lakes, and groundwater. The fertilizers speed up the growth of **algae,** a large group of plants that live in water. These plants quickly use up the oxygen supply in the water so other plants and fish cannot live. Rain runoff can also wash the chemicals in the fertilizers into the local water supply. When these chemicals get into water, they can kill fish in nearby rivers and lakes. They can also ruin the groundwater that people drink.

Figure 21.3.1 *Oil spills kill animals and leave behind carcinogens.*

Wastes from animals also make agricultural runoff that is harmful to the environment and humans. U.S. and state governments watch the effects of agricultural runoff. They give researchers money to find ways of preventing water pollution that agricultural runoff causes.

Household Chemicals

Some household cleaners contain chemicals that are harmful to plants and humans if they get into the water supply. Many cleaning products now must be sold without these harmful chemicals. For example, laundry soaps must now be sold without phosphates. They must be able to break down in the environment and not pollute water sources. Even so, reading labels on household products to learn how to throw them away safely is important.

Decide for Yourself

Some communities have strong laws about the environment. For example, some communities do not allow gasoline to be sold on a lakefront. Other communities may have rules for motorboats that are on a lake. Still other communities may give out fines for polluting the water. It may be against the law in some places to throw trash into a lake or allow farm runoff to reach a river or stream.

Polluting a community can mean that there is trash in a park or on a street. It could also mean there is air or water pollution from factories. Every community, small and large, has some type of pollution problem. What can you do as a person or as a class to make your community cleaner?

Steps to Environmental Health

1. First, find the problems. Think about how you can make your community cleaner. List the problems you find.

2. Decide on a problem you feel you can correct.

3. Create a plan to correct the problem. You may need the help of other students. You may need to work with community officials. Decide how long it will take and who must be involved for the project to be a success.

4. Carry out your plan.

5. Decide how successful you were.

On a sheet of paper, write your answers to the following questions. Use complete sentences.

1. How hard was it to decide on a community project? Explain your answer.

2. Whom did you need to involve for your project to be successful?

3. Do you think the problem would not have existed if there was already a law in place? Explain your answer.

How Can Freshwater Be Conserved?

Many places do not have a lot of freshwater. Therefore, protecting it is important. One way to protect freshwater is to conserve it, or use it carefully.

Here are some ways you can conserve water:

- Take showers no longer than 5 minutes.

- Fill the tub only halfway when you take a bath.

- Wet the toothbrush when you brush your teeth and turn off the water until you rinse.

- Wait to run the clothes washer or dishwasher until there is a full load.

- Fix leaking faucets.

Lesson 3 Review On a sheet of paper, write the word or phrase in parentheses that best completes each sentence.

1. The largest supply of freshwater is (clean water, groundwater, saltwater).

2. Factory wastes such as mercury and acid (can, cannot, might) be broken down.

3. Agricultural runoff comes from pesticides, (herbicides, germicides, petroleum), and animals.

On a sheet of paper, write the answers to the following questions. Use complete sentences.

4. **Critical Thinking** Why is agricultural runoff harmful to places where freshwater is found?

5. **Critical Thinking** What are three habits you can change to help conserve water? Which habit will be the hardest to change?

Objectives

After reading this lesson, you should be able to

◆ explain how world population affects health

◆ explain how pollution affects health

◆ describe what is meant by hazardous waste

◆ identify three symptoms of radiation sickness

Deforestation

Cutting down and clearing trees

Famine

A time when there is not enough food for people

The world's growing population is a problem for the environment. So is **deforestation,** which is the cutting down and clearing of trees. Solid waste, noise pollution, and radiation can also affect the environment. Because these problems affect the environment, they also can affect people's health.

How Does Population Size Affect Health?

The world's population is more than 6 billion people. Growing enough crops to feed so many people is a concern. See Table C.7 in Appendix C. Many countries have already gone through long periods of **famine,** a time when there is not enough food for people. Famines in Africa, for example, have come after long periods without enough rainfall to grow crops.

Many concerns seem to come from the growing world population. The more people there are on Earth, the more cars, trucks, and factories there will be. With more cars, trucks, and factories, there will be more air pollution. The more air pollution there is, the more global warming there will be, and the ozone layer may get thinner. If the ozone layer becomes thinner, more harmful rays from the sun will get into the atmosphere. With more harmful rays, more people will get skin cancers. You can see that everything in the environment is connected.

How Does Deforestation Affect Health?

Some people believe that long periods with no rain and the famine in Africa came from deforestation. Over history, two-thirds of the world's forests have been lost to deforestation. Some African countries have lost all of their forests to make room for people, crops, and cattle.

Solid waste

Garbage, trash

Earth needs trees to keep its fragile balance. When people cut down forests to help support a growing world population, rains wash away the topsoil. The soil underneath does not hold water well. Soon the land cannot support the growth of crops. This causes famine and human suffering.

Tropical rain forests cover only about 6 percent of Earth's surface. However, they include half of all Earth's plants. Because of deforestation, only half of Earth's original rain forests are left. Each year, people burn millions of acres of tropical rain forest. Rain forest trees are burned or cleared to plant crops, to raise cattle, or to sell the wood.

Destroying tropical rain forests affects human and environmental health. Plants in the rain forests give us more than one-quarter of the medicines we use. Also, rain forest plants may hold the key to new medicines. Rain forest plants act as Earth's lungs by taking in carbon dioxide. Too much carbon dioxide adds to global warming.

How Does Solid Waste Affect Health?

Developing nations get rid of few materials because there are not many resources. In more developed nations, people tend to throw things away after a short time. Then they buy more. In the United States, for example, people dump billions of tons of **solid waste**—garbage or trash—each year. Getting rid of solid waste has an effect on the environment and therefore, on human health.

Research and Write

Wetlands such as swamps and marshes make a good home for plants and animals. Wetlands are important in flood control. More than half of all U.S. wetlands have been lost. Today, scientists are making new wetlands. Using the Internet, research wetlands in the United States. Make a graph showing what you learned.

Many communities have dumped solid waste in **landfills.** Landfills are low-lying ground where waste is buried between layers of dirt. One problem, however, is that landfill space is running out in the United States. Another problem is that toxic materials called **hazardous waste** are sometimes dumped. Hazardous waste can be harmful to the environment, human health, and other living things. Factories are the largest makers of hazardous waste. Toxic materials that come from hazardous waste sometimes leak into nearby ground and pollute the groundwater.

Sometimes, people notice the effect of polluted groundwater right away. Other times, the effect is not noticed for years. For example, between the late 1930s and early 1940s, a factory in Love Canal, New York, dumped toxic chemicals into the ground. Later, people built homes there. In 1978, heavy rains flooded basements in those homes. People noticed oily liquids in the floodwater. Hazardous wastes had leaked into the soil and groundwater. The homes were polluted, and all the people had to move.

Every person can help to reduce hazardous waste. Paint, car batteries, and car oil can be thrown away separately from the rest of the garbage. Check with your community to learn how to dispose of hazardous waste.

How Does Noise Pollution Affect Health?

As the population and number of factories have risen, so has noise. Noise pollution happens when sounds in the environment become too great. Listening to too much loud noise over a long time can cause **sensorineural deafness.** This is a hearing loss in which the tiny cells in the inner ear are destroyed. Many Americans have sensorineural deafness that comes from noise pollution. Too much noise also may cause stress and problems such as high blood pressure, tension, anger, and tiredness.

How Does Light Pollution Affect Health?

Light pollution is the glow you see above a city at night. As communities have grown, so has their use of light in parks, streets, and factory areas. Although many people think lights are needed to make places safe, other people do not like this light. Environmental studies have shown that this light is harmful for some animals. When an area is light all the time, animals that are most active at night get confused. Migrating birds have been known to fly into lighted towers. Some communities are taking steps to lessen the glow in the night sky. Others are using special lights that shine downward but guard against light that goes up.

How Does Radiation Affect Health?

Radiation sends energy in the form of waves. It happens naturally in the environment. Usually, people are exposed only to low levels of radiation, such as X-rays. Some factories use high levels of radiation. Nuclear power plants, for example, use radiation to make electricity for homes and businesses. People who work in nuclear power plants are exposed to high levels of radiation.

Too much radiation may cause cancer in humans. People who are exposed to very high levels of radiation may get **radiation sickness.** Some symptoms of radiation sickness are upset stomach, vomiting, headache, diarrhea, hair loss, and tiredness. Radiation sickness can lead to death. The U.S. government sets exposure safety rules for people who work with or near radiation.

Nuclear power plants are carefully controlled. Still, accidents have happened at these plants. For example, an accident happened in 1986 in the nuclear plant at Chernobyl in the former Soviet Union. Many people died immediately. Others died of radiation sickness weeks later. Wind carried radiation across much of Europe. Some scientists believe that many Europeans will die of cancer because of what happened. Today, the villages and forests around Chernobyl are deserted and unsafe. It was the worst nuclear accident ever.

> **Radiation sickness**
>
> *Sickness caused by being around high levels of radiation*

Lesson 4 Review On a sheet of paper, write the answers to the following questions. Use complete sentences.

1. What are two effects of a growing world population?

2. What is deforestation?

3. How can groundwater become polluted?

4. **Critical Thinking** Why are nuclear power plants both a resource and a danger?

5. **Critical Thinking** Which type of pollution do you believe is the greatest danger to health? Explain your answer.

✿ ✿

Technology and Society

Agriculture biotechnology is science's way of making better plants and animals. Agriculture biotechnology has been used to make new medicines. It also has helped farmers use less pesticides and herbicides. The Environmental Protection Agency (EPA) and the Food and Drug Administration (FDA) are in charge of biotechnology. Food that is created through biotechnology must be tested before it can be sold.

Protecting the environment is everyone's job—the world community, governments, businesses and factories, local communities, and individuals.

What Laws Protect the Environment?

The U.S. government has passed several laws to protect the environment. All of these laws are also meant to protect human health.

The Clean Air Act was first passed in 1970 and has been changed several times since then. It says how much air pollution there can be. It also makes each state have a plan to meet its standards.

The National Environmental Policy Act requires federal agencies to think about how their plans and activities will affect the environment. Before an agency can begin a new project, it must file an environmental impact statement. This statement explains how the project will affect the environment. The agency also must hold public meetings about the effect of the project on the environment. Many states have passed similar laws.

Congress has passed other environmental laws. These laws set standards for water safety and ways to get rid of solid and hazardous wastes. They require polluters to manage the cleanup of chemical spills and toxic waste.

How Do Governments Protect the Environment?

In the United States, the Environmental Protection Agency (EPA) writes and carries out the environmental laws Congress passes. Its job is to protect the environment.

Because so many environmental problems affect the entire world, nations have joined together to try to solve the problems. For example, an international meeting in Senegal in 2005 looked at ways to keep from thinning the ozone layer. Many nations have agreed to stop using chlorofluorocarbons (CFCs) and other materials that may thin the ozone layer.

In 1992, the United Nations (UN) General Assembly started the Conference on Environment and Development. It brought together leaders from 178 countries. They talked about ways to live well and protect the environment at the same time. Today, the UN keeps looking for ways to protect the environment.

What Are Future Environmental Plans?

Scientists are working on ways to protect the environment from further harm. For example, they are searching for ways to use solar energy, or energy from the sun. Solar energy is a clean and environmentally safe energy source. Wind energy is another energy source. Most of our oil, gas, and electricity now comes from fossil fuels. If we used solar and wind energy, we would lessen our use of fossil fuels. Some scientists say we could lessen it as much as 70 percent.

Scientists have also found other fuels to lessen exhaust from cars and trucks. One of these fuels is ethanol, or alcohol made from corn—a renewable resource. Some states already use ethanol mixed with regular gasoline. Hydrogen and natural gas are two other kinds of fuels. Hybrid cars use a mix of gasoline and electricity. These cars save gasoline and lessen harmful emissions, or exhaust. Clean energy, such as solar energy, may one day be a common way to power cars.

California has passed a law that says new cars have to use less energy. Other states have high-occupancy vehicles (HOV) lanes. HOV lanes encourage people to ride to work together. Having fewer cars on the road is one way to lessen car exhaust. Some states have laws about how much exhaust cars can make. In these states, cars must pass an emissions test every year.

Health Myth

Myth: Biodegradable items do not harm the environment.

Fact: When they are thrown away, biodegradable items release methane into the atmosphere as they break down. Methane is one of several greenhouse gases. A good option is to use biodegradable products that can be turned into compost. A better option is to use recyclable products or products that come in refillable containers.

How Can You Help Protect the Environment?

Everything you do makes a difference. Every individual can work to protect the environment. Here are some actions you and others can take to protect the environment:

- Walk, ride a bike, take the bus, or carpool to school or work.

- If you drive, keep your car tuned up, have the exhaust equipment checked regularly, and keep tires properly inflated.

- Buy a car that gets good gas mileage.

- Turn off lights when you leave a room.

- Keep air conditioning at a steady temperature on the automatic setting, and keep windows and doors closed.

- Set the furnace at a steady low temperature—perhaps 68 degrees Fahrenheit—and wear layers of clothing.

- Take shorter showers.

- Do not run hot water if you do not need to.

- Use fewer things that need to be thrown away. For example, use a glass cup instead of a paper or plastic cup, or use cloth towels instead of paper towels.

- Recycle newspapers, cans, bottles, plastic, and paper. Find out what recycling services are in your community. Reuse items such as paper clips, too.

- Buy only what you need.

- In general, buy products that have the least amount of packaging. Buy products that have refillable containers, such as beverages in glass bottles.

- Look for products with the recycled symbol. This symbol shows that recycled materials were used in making them.

- Find other products for your home that do not contain toxins. For example, instead of using oven cleaners with lye, use baking soda and water. Wash windows with white vinegar and water.

- If you must buy household products with toxins in them, throw them away, using the instructions on the package.

- Write to lawmakers about your concerns for the environment.

- Plant some trees to take in more carbon dioxide and reduce the greenhouse effect.

Health in Your Life

Recycling

Recycling means reusing materials instead of buying new ones. Recycling saves natural resources and makes less solid waste. Newspapers, cardboard, aluminum cans, glass, and some paper can be recycled. Many communities pick up recyclable products at the curb. Other communities have recycling centers. In many communities, people can get cash for aluminum and other metals.

Scientists have found ways to make materials like plastic from biodegradable materials such as corn. Plastic made from hydrocarbons takes hundreds of years to biodegrade. Plastic made from corn, however, takes about 47 days to biodegrade. Plastic cups made from corn can be crushed into compost after use. The compost becomes dirt. Combining recycling with biodegradable plastics helps to lengthen the life of landfills. It also protects the environment.

Each community needs to have a plan to recycle and use packaging that can biodegrade into compost when possible.

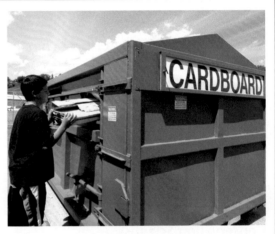

What recycling plan does your community have? Can the plan be improved? How can you help your community save natural resources?

On a sheet of paper, write your answers to the following questions. Use complete sentences.

1. What is recycling?

2. What products can be recycled?

3. How can mixing recyclable products and products that can biodegrade into compost help the environment?

Lesson 5 Review On a sheet of paper, write the word or phrase in parentheses that best completes each sentence.

1. The (UN, EPA, CDC) makes sure factories follow clean air and water laws.

2. An example of a renewable resource is (corn, aluminum, gasoline).

3. One way to help protect the environment is to (recycle, throw away, buy more) items.

On a sheet of paper, write the answers to the following questions. Use complete sentences.

4. **Critical Thinking** How do state laws about car exhaust help protect the environment and keep people from getting sick?

5. **Critical Thinking** Why do scientists keep trying to find new ways to protect the environment?

Health at Work

Conservation Scientist

Conservation scientists find ways to make the best use of the land without harming the environment. There are different types of conservation scientists. Some look for ways to keep water supplies clean. Others find the best use of farmland or manage cattle ranges. Still others work directly with animal management.

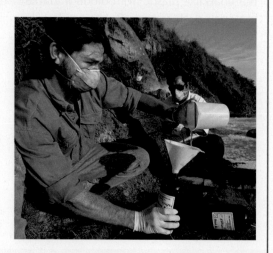

A conservation scientist needs to have a 4-year college degree in ecology, environmental science, forestry, or some related field. Along with working in the field, a conservation scientist must know how to write reports and be able to work with others to solve problems.

Chapter 21 SUMMARY

- When all parts of the environment work together, a healthy balance of nature is maintained.

- Human activity has upset the balance of nature by overusing Earth's resources and producing pollution.

- Because pollution can put human health and life in danger, people are finding some solutions.

- Burning is the main cause of outdoor air pollution. Cars, trucks, and factories make the most air pollution.

- Hydrocarbons, nitrogen oxides, ozone, carbon monoxide, and particulates are some outdoor air pollutants.

- Some indoor air pollutants are gases and particulates from building materials and household chemicals, tobacco smoke, broken appliances, and radon.

- Respiratory and lung problems are common health effects of air pollution.

- Results of air pollution on Earth are the greenhouse effect, thinning of the ozone layer, and acid rain.

- Since the supply of necessary freshwater is limited, saving and protecting it is important.

- Some causes of water pollution are factory wastes, sewage, oil leaks and spills, agricultural runoff, and toxic chemicals.

- The growing world population has caused many environmental problems, including deforestation, solid waste, noise pollution, and radiation.

- The federal and state governments have passed several laws that protect the environment.

- Nations and individuals can take many actions that help protect the environment, including using energy and water carefully.

Vocabulary

acid rain, 494	fragile, 488	pollution, 487
algae, 496	greenhouse effect, 493	radiation sickness, 502
asbestos, 492	hazardous waste, 501	radon, 492
bronchitis, 490	landfill, 501	sensorineural deafness, 501
deforestation, 499	ozone layer, 493	sewage, 495
ecology, 489	particulate, 491	soil erosion, 487
famine, 499	pesticide, 488	solid waste, 500
fossil fuel, 491	photochemical smog, 490	

Chapter 21 R E V I E W

Word Bank

acid rain

asbestos

deforestation

ecology

fossil fuels

hazardous waste

ozone layer

particulates

pesticides

pollution

radiation sickness

radon

sewage

Vocabulary Review

On a sheet of paper, write the word or phrase from the Word Bank that best completes each sentence.

1. A gas produced by radioactive radium is _____.

2. Wastes that cannot be broken down in nature make _____.

3. The study of how living things and the environment work together is _____.

4. Schools and other buildings no longer use _____ as a building material.

5. The _____ keeps the sun's rays from harming Earth.

6. Farmers use _____ to get rid of bugs.

7. Typhoid fever and cholera are diseases people get from water polluted with _____.

8. Cutting down and clearing away all the trees in an area is _____.

9. When you breathe in _____, they can harm your body.

10. Toxic materials dumped in landfills are _____.

11. Many people who lived near Chernobyl died from _____.

12. The remains of dead animals are used for _____.

13. Snow and sleet that contain harmful chemicals as they fall are examples of _____.

Concept Review

On a sheet of paper, write the letter of the answer that best completes each sentence.

14. Earthquakes, volcanoes, and floods can upset the _____.

    A ozone layer   **C** chlorofluorocarbons

    B creation of oxygen   **D** balance of nature

15. A slow warming of Earth's atmosphere is called _____.

    A acid rain   **C** radiation sickness

    B the greenhouse effect   **D** chlorofluorocarbons

16. One cause of water pollution is _____.

    A sewage   **C** wetlands

    B famine   **D** groundwater

17. The destruction of tropical rain forests affects both human health and _____.

    A landfills   **C** environmental health

    B deforestation   **D** solid waste

Critical Thinking

On a sheet of paper, write the answers to the following questions. Use complete sentences.

18. What can people do to lessen noise pollution?

19. What do you think is the most important action people can take to protect air quality?

20. What role do you think government should play in protecting the environment?

Test-Taking Tip When taking a short-answer test, first answer the questions you know. Then go back to spend time on the questions about which you are less sure.

HEALTH IN THE WORLD

Health Care and Aging

About 60 percent of people over age 65 live in developing countries such as Chile, China, and India. Worldwide, older people as a percentage of the total population is increasing. One reason for this increase is lower birthrates. Another reason is improvements in public health and medical technology, such as vaccinations. These improvements help people live longer. Between 2000 and 2025, the number of people age 60 and over will double to 1.2 billion.

Health care costs for older people are higher than for younger people. About 80 percent of Americans over age 65 have at least one chronic condition such as diabetes, heart disease, or cancer. People with chronic diseases make more doctor visits, take more prescription medicines, and get other medical treatments. In addition, people with chronic diseases sometimes have disabilities their disease causes.

Leaders of many countries are working to address the problem of increased health care costs as their populations age. The World Health Organization (WHO), for example, holds conferences on aging. Policies are being developed to help older people live a healthier lifestyle and improve access to health services.

In the United States, the Centers for Disease Control and Prevention (CDC) promotes healthy behaviors in people of all ages, including older people. These include getting regular exercise, keeping a healthy weight, staying involved with family and community, and not smoking. The WHO calls these behaviors lifestyle choices for active aging. People who practice healthy behaviors throughout their lives tend to have a lower risk of chronic diseases as they age.

On a sheet of paper, write the answers to the following questions. Use complete sentences.

1. What do you think is the main reason that the population of older people is increasing?

2. Why do you think disabilities in older people add to health care costs?

3. How do young people who reduce their risk of chronic disease help to reduce health care costs in the future?

Unit 7 SUMMARY

- Criteria to help judge products and services are to look at the cost benefits, consider recommendations, watch for false or misleading claims, look at the ingredients, and compare prices.

- Health care professionals include primary care physicians, specialists, nurse practitioners, physical therapists, and registered dieticians.

- Qualifications to look for in a health care professional are board certificates, professional associations, and experience. The patient's comfort with the professional is also important.

- People can pay for health care costs through private individual or group insurance plans. Health maintenance organizations (HMOs) and preferred provider organizations (PPOs) offer less expensive health care.

- Government-supported health insurance includes Medicare for people over age 65, and Medicaid for people whose incomes are below a certain level. Another government program is the State Children's Health Insurance Program (SCHIP) for children of low-income parents.

- Individuals can help lower health care costs. They can choose low-cost outpatient facilities when possible. They can practice prevention, buy generic medicine, and advocate for family and community health. They can also take part in workplace health promotion programs.

- Groups of people who may have difficulty getting basic health services include poor people, elderly people, and homeless people. Teen parents and their children, and people with mental health problems are also included.

- Local and state public health departments make sure that laws relating to disease and sanitation are observed.

- Health promotion and disease prevention through education and advocacy groups reduce costs and relieve demands on the health care system.

- Burning is the main cause of outdoor air pollution. Cars, trucks, and factories make the most air pollution.

- Some results of air pollution are the greenhouse effect, acid rain, and thinning of the ozone layer.

- Some causes of water pollution are factory wastes, sewage, oil leaks and spills, and agricultural runoff.

- The growing world population has caused many environmental problems, including deforestation, solid waste, noise pollution, and light pollution.

- Nations and individuals can take many actions that help protect the environment. Recycling materials, conserving energy, and using water carefully can help.

Unit 7 REVIEW

Vocabulary Review

On a sheet of paper, write the word or phrase from the Word Bank that best completes each sentence.

1. Health insurance for people whose incomes are below a certain level is _____.

2. A person who pays for a service or buys a product is a(n) _____.

3. A period of _____ is a time when there is not enough food for people.

4. Restaurant owners who make sure that their kitchen equipment is cleaned properly are following laws related to _____.

5. Precipitation that contains large amounts of sulfuric or nitric acids is _____.

6. Therapy needed to recover from surgery, an illness, or an injury is _____.

7. Education programs, the use of preventive medicine, and the control of diseases are all parts of _____.

8. Before a vaccine for polio was developed, there was a(n) _____ in the United States because thousands of people had this disease.

9. A(n) _____ is an area where waste is buried between layers of dirt.

10. The slow warming of Earth's atmosphere is the _____.

11. A prevention organization that helps specific groups of people get health services is a(n) _____.

12. A doctor that a patient visits for a regular checkup is a(n) _____.

Concept Review

On a sheet of paper, write the letter of the answer that best completes each sentence.

13. If your health insurance plan has a $300 _____, you must pay the first $300 of your medical costs.

    A PPO   **B** hospice   **C** deductible   **D** premium

14. To have a healthy pregnancy, a mother should avoid _____.

    A fruits   **B** exercise   **C** cheese   **D** tobacco

15. One voluntary public health organization that has education programs is the _____.

    A Food and Drug Administration

    B American Heart Association

    C National Institutes of Health

    D Consumer Product Safety Commission

16. One of the problems with deforestation is that it can lead to _____.

    A oil leaks   **C** light pollution

    B soil erosion   **D** radiation sickness

Critical Thinking

On a sheet of paper, write the answers to the following questions. Use complete sentences.

17. Why would a primary care physician tell a patient to visit a specialist? Describe a situation in which this might happen.

18. Why do you think the spread of tuberculosis might be a problem in a homeless shelter? Explain your answer.

19. How has the balance of nature been disturbed in your community? What were the results?

20. Do you think the problem of solid waste will be better or worse in the year 2050? Explain your answer.

Figure A.1 *The Skeletal System*

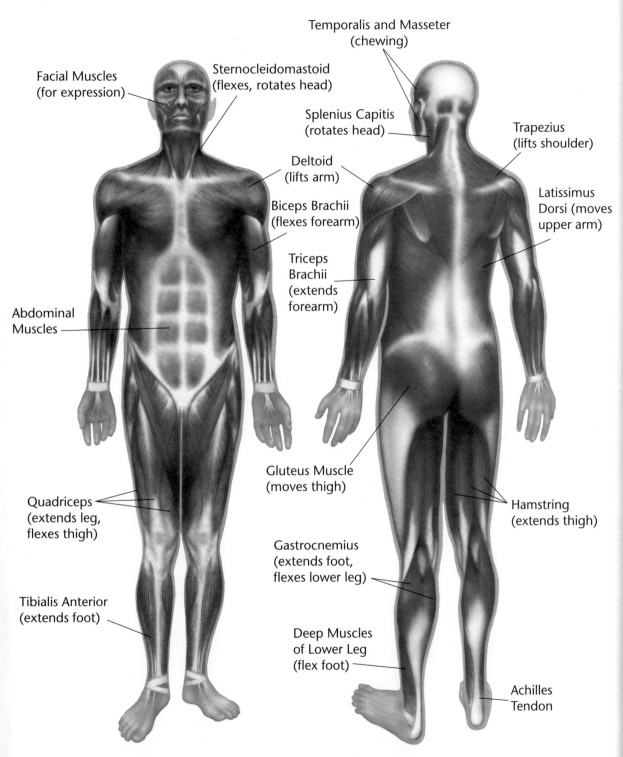

Figure A.2 *The Muscular System*

Figure A.3 *The Nervous System*

Figure A.4 *The Circulatory System*

Appendix B: Nutrition Tables

Table B.1 The Six Essential Nutrient Classes

Nutrient	Best Food Sources	Why They Are Needed
Proteins		
	Cheese, eggs, fish, meat, milk, poultry, soybeans, nuts, dry beans, and lentils	To promote body growth; to repair and maintain tissue
Carbohydrates		
	Bread, cereal, flour, potatoes, rice, sugar, dry beans, fruit	To supply energy; to furnish heat; to save proteins to build and regulate cells
Fats		
	Butter, margarine, cream, oils, meat, whole milk, nuts, avocado	To supply energy; to furnish heat; to save proteins to build and regulate cells; to supply necessary fat-soluble vitamins and other nutrients
Minerals		
Calcium	Milk, cheese, leafy green vegetables, oysters, almonds	To give rigidity and hardness to bones and teeth; for blood clotting, osmosis, action of heart and other muscles, and nerve response
Iron	Meats (especially liver), oysters, leafy green vegetables, legumes, dried apricots or peaches, prunes, raisins	To carry oxygen in the blood
Iodine	Seafood, iodized salt	To help the thyroid gland regulate cell activities for physical and mental health
Vitamins		
Vitamin A	Whole milk, cream, butter, liver, egg yolk, leafy green vegetables, dark yellow fruits and vegetables	To promote health of epithelial tissues and eyes; to promote development of teeth
Thiamin	Present in many foods, abundant in few: pork, some animal organs, some nuts, whole grains, yeast, dry beans, and peas	To promote healthy nerves, appetite, digestion, and growth; for metabolism of carbohydrates
Riboflavin	Milk, glandular organs, lean meats, cheese, eggs, leafy green vegetables, whole grains	To promote better development, greater vitality, freedom from disease; to aid metabolism of carbohydrates, fats, and proteins
Niacin	Lean meats, liver, poultry, peanuts, legumes, yeasts	To promote good digestion, healthy skin, and a well-functioning nervous system
Vitamin C	Citrus fruits, strawberries, tomatoes, broccoli, cabbage, green peppers	To enhance iron absorption; for deposit of intercellular cement in tissues and bone
Vitamin D	Milk, salmon, tuna	To help absorb and use calcium and phosphorus
Water		
	Drinking water, foods	To supply body fluids; to regulate body temperature

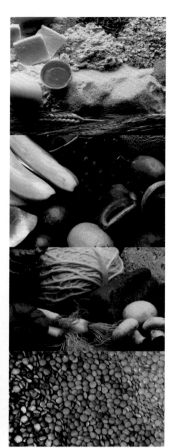

Table B.2 Fiber Content of Selected Foods

Food	Serving Size	Dietary Fiber (g)
Grains		
Bread, white	1 slice	0.6
Bread, whole wheat	1 slice	1.5
Oat bran, dry	⅓ cup	4.5
Oatmeal, dry	⅓ cup	2.7
Rice, brown, cooked	½ cup	2.4
Rice, white, cooked	½ cup	0.8
Fruits		
Apple, with skin	1 small	2.8
Apricots, with skin	4	3.5
Banana	1 small	2.2
Blueberries	¾ cup	2.9
Figs, dried	3	5.3
Grapefruit	½	1.6
Pear, with skin	1 large	5.8
Prunes, dried	3 medium	1.7
Vegetables		
Asparagus, cooked	½ cup	1.8
Broccoli, cooked	½ cup	2.4
Carrots, cooked, sliced	½ cup	2.1
Peas, green, frozen, cooked	½ cup	4.3
Potato, with skin, raw	½ cup	1.5
Tomato, raw	1 medium	1.0
Legumes		
Beans, white, cooked	½ cup	5.8
Kidney beans, cooked	½ cup	6.9
Lentils, cooked	½ cup	7.8
Lima beans, canned	½ cup	6.6
Peas, blackeye, canned	½ cup	5.6
Pinto beans, cooked	½ cup	7.4

Table B.3 Calcium and Fat Content of Dairy Products*

Product	Calories	Fat (grams)	Calcium (milligrams)
Skim milk (also called nonfat or fat free)			
Plain	86	0	301
Chocolate	144	1	292
1% milk (also called lowfat or light)			
Plain	102	$2\frac{1}{2}$	300
Chocolate	158	$2\frac{1}{2}$	288
2% milk (now called reduced fat, not lowfat)			
Plain	121	5	298
Chocolate	179	5	285
Whole milk			
Plain	150	8	290
Chocolate	209	8	280
Buttermilk (lowfat)	100	2	300
Buttermilk (whole)	150	8	300
Sweetened condensed milk	246	7	217

*All nutrition information is based on a 1-cup serving, except sweetened condensed milk, which is based on a quarter-cup serving.

Appendix C: Fact Bank

Frame Size

To determine your frame size:

1. Extend your arm in front of your body bending your elbow at a 90° angle to your body. (Your arm will be parallel to your body.)

2. Keep your fingers straight and turn the inside of your wrist to your body.

3. Place your thumb and index finger on the two prominent bones on either side of your elbow. Measure the distance between the bones with a tape measure or calipers.

4. Compare to the medium frame chart below. Select your height based on what you are in 1-inch heels. If you are below the listed inches, your frame is small. If you are above, your frame is large.

Elbow Measurements for Medium Frame		
Sex	**Height in 1-Inch Heels**	**Elbow Breadth**
Male	5'2"–5'3"	$2\frac{1}{2}$"–$2\frac{7}{8}$"
	5'4"–5'7"	$2\frac{5}{8}$"–$2\frac{7}{8}$"
	5'8"–5'11"	$2\frac{3}{4}$"–3"
	6'0"–6'3"	$2\frac{3}{4}$"–$3\frac{1}{8}$"
	6'4"	$2\frac{7}{8}$"–$3\frac{1}{4}$"
Female	4'10"–4'11"	$2\frac{1}{4}$"–$2\frac{1}{2}$"
	5'0"–5'3"	$2\frac{1}{4}$"–$2\frac{1}{2}$"
	5'4"–5'7"	$2\frac{3}{8}$"–$2\frac{5}{8}$"
	5'8"–5'11"	$2\frac{3}{8}$"–$2\frac{5}{8}$"
	6'0"	$2\frac{1}{2}$"–$2\frac{3}{4}$"

Table C.1 Top 10 Fat-Blasting Exercises			
Activity	Calories Burned (per 30 minutes)	Activity	Calories Burned (per 30 minutes)
Bicycling, vigorous (15 MPH)	340	Spinning class (indoor cycling)	312
Jogging (10- to 12-minute miles)	340 to 272	Jumping rope, slowly	340
Swimming, vigorous	340	Tennis, singles	240
Cross-country ski machine	323	Hiking, uphill	238
Inline skating	238	Walking, uphill (3.5 MPH)	204

Table C.2 Recommended Height and Weight for Women			
Height (feet/ inches)	Small Frame	Medium Frame	Large Frame
4'10"	102–111	109–121	118–131
4'11"	103–113	111–123	120–134
5'0"	104–115	113–126	122–137
5'1"	106–118	115–129	125–140
5'2"	108–121	118–132	128–143
5'3"	111–124	121–135	131–147
5'4"	114–127	124–138	134–151
5'5"	117–130	127–141	137–155
5'6"	120–133	130–144	140–159
5'7"	123–136	133–147	143–163
5'8"	126–139	136–150	146–167
5'9"	129–142	139–153	149–170
5'10"	132–145	142–156	152–173
5'11"	135–148	145–159	155–176
6'0"	138–151	148–162	158–179

Weights at ages 25–59 based on lowest mortality. Weight in pounds according to frame (in indoor clothing weighing 3 lb; shoes with 1-inch heels)

Table C.3 Recommended Height and Weight for Men			
Height (feet/ inches)	Small Frame	Medium Frame	Large Frame
5'2"	128–134	131–141	138–150
5'3"	130–136	133–143	140–153
5'4"	132–138	135–145	142–156
5'5"	134–140	137–148	144–160
5'6"	136–142	139–151	146–164
5'7"	138–145	142–154	149–168
5'8"	140–148	145–157	152–172
5'9"	142–151	148–160	155–176
5'10"	144–154	151–163	158–180
5'11"	146–157	154–166	161–184
6'0"	149–160	157–170	164–188
6'1"	152–164	160–174	168–192
6'2"	155–168	162–178	172–197
6'3"	158–172	167–182	176–202
6'4"	162–176	171–187	181–207

Weights at ages 25–59 based on lowest mortality. Weight in pounds according to frame (in indoor clothing weighing 5 lb; shoes with 1-inch heels)

The Five Leading Causes of Death in the United States by Age Group

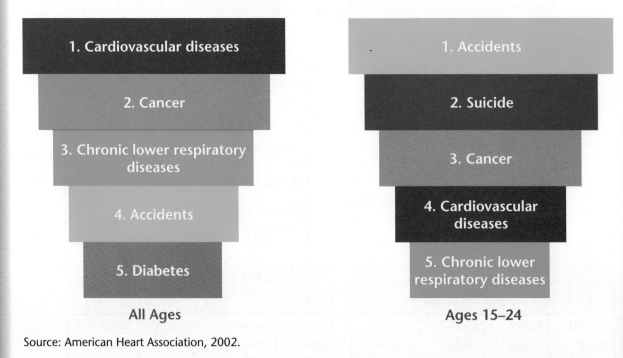

All Ages

1. Cardiovascular diseases
2. Cancer
3. Chronic lower respiratory diseases
4. Accidents
5. Diabetes

Ages 15–24

1. Accidents
2. Suicide
3. Cancer
4. Cardiovascular diseases
5. Chronic lower respiratory diseases

Source: American Heart Association, 2002.

Table C.4 Estimated U.S. Cancer Cases for 2004			
Men	Percentage of 699,560 Total Cases	Women	Percentage of 668,470 Total Cases
Prostate	33%	Breast	32%
Lung and bronchus	13%	Lung and bronchus	12%
Colon and rectum	11%	Colon and rectum	11%
Urinary bladder	6%	Uterus	6%
Melanoma of skin	4%	Ovary	4%
Non-Hodgkin's lymphoma	4%	Non-Hodgkin's lymphoma	4%
Kidney	3%	Melanoma of skin	4%
Oral cavity	3%	Thyroid	3%
Leukemia	3%	Pancreas	2%
Pancreas	2%	Urinary bladder	2%
All other sites	18%	All other sites	20%

Source: American Cancer Society, 2004.

The ABCDs of Melanoma

Melanoma is usually curable if you find it early. Follow this ABCD self-examination guide adapted from the American Academy of Dermatology.

■ *A is for asymmetry*—Symmetrical round or oval growths are usually benign. Look for irregular shapes where one half is a different shape than the other half.

■ *B is for border*—Irregular, notched, scalloped, or vaguely defined borders need to be checked out.

■ *C is for color*—Look for growths that have many colors or an uneven distribution of color. Generally, growths that are the same color all over are usually benign.

■ *D is for diameter*—Have your doctor check out any growths that are larger than 6 millimeters, about the diameter of a pencil eraser. The mole shown at the right measures about 1 millimeter.

Table C.5 Barriers to Helmet Use			
Barrier	Parents	Children	Physician
Lack of perceived need	X	X	X
Lack of physician's recommendation	X		X
Do not think child will wear helmet	X		
Cost of helmet	X		
Peer pressure		X	
Lack of "coolness"		X	
Discomfort		X	

Table C.6 State-of-the-Art Care for Five Common Conditions		
Condition	Old Recommendation	New Recommendation
Lower back pain	Bed rest, stretching exercises	Continuation of normal activities; ibuprofen or acetaminophen
Early stage breast cancer	Mastectomy	Lumpectomy plus radiation therapy
Ulcers	Drugs to suppress stomach acid secretion	Antibiotics plus drugs to suppress stomach acid secretion
Simple ovarian cysts	Removal by surgery	Depending on age and family history, watchful waiting with periodic pelvic and ultrasound exams
Type II diabetes	Insulin or sulfonylureas	Diet and exercise; if not effective, insulin often combined with new oral drugs that prompt insulin secretion

Table C.7 World Population and Food Supply Production

Year	World Population (billions)	Wheat (millions of metric tons)	Rice (millions of metric tons)	Vegetables and melons (millions of metric tons)	Fruits (millions of metric tons)	Beef and pork (millions of metric tons)
1990	5.28	588	352	462	353	117
1995	5.69	538	371	565	411	118
2000	6.08	582	398	746	472	132
2003	6.30	549	391	842	480	139

Sources: U.S. Census Bureau, *Total Midyear Population for the World, 1950–2050*; and *Statistical Abstract of the United States: 2004–2005*, page 861, Table No. 1355, World Food Production by Commodity: 1990 to 2003.

Table C.8 Population Growth in Select Urban Areas

Year	Tokyo, Japan (millions)	São Paolo, Brazil (millions)	Mexico City, Mexico (millions)	New York City, United States (millions)	Shanghai, China (millions)
1975	19.8	10.3	10.7	15.9	11.4
2001	26.5	18.3	18.3	16.8	12.8
2015 (estimate)	27.2	21.2	20.4	17.9	13.6

Source: United Nations Population Division, *World Urbanization Prospects: The 2001 Revision.*

Glossary

A

Abnormal (ab nôr´ məl) Unusual or different from normal (p. 76)

Abnormality (ab nôr mal´ ə tē) A condition that is not usual (p. 286)

Abstain (ab stān´) Choose not to use or do something (p. 15)

Abstinence(ab´ stə nəns) The choice not to have a sexual relationship (p. 178)

Abuse (ə byüs´) Physical or emotional mistreatment; actions that harm someone (p. 189)

Acid rain (as´ id rān) Rain, snow, sleet, or hail that contains large amounts of sulfuric or nitric acids (p. 494)

Acne (ak´ nē) Clogged skin pores that cause pimples and blackheads (p. 130)

Acquire (ə kwīr´) To get after being born (p. 254)

Acquired immunodeficiency syndrome (AIDS) (ə kwīrd´ i myü nō di fish´ ən sē sin´ drōm) A disorder of the immune system (p. 270)

Added sugar (ad´ id shùg´ ər) Sugar that is added to a food (p. 211)

Addicted (ə dik´ tid) Unable to stop using alcohol or another drug (p. 80)

Additive (əd´ ə tiv) A substance added in small amounts to foods that changes them in some way (p. 241)

Adolescence (ad l es´ ns) The years between ages 13 and 19 (p. 151)

Adoptive family (ə dop´ tiv fam´ ə lē) Family that includes parents and an adopted child or children (p. 185)

Adrenal gland (ə drē´ nl gland) Part of the endocrine system that releases several hormones (p. 111)

Adrenaline (ə dren´ l ən) Hormone released into the bloodstream that causes the heart to beat faster and blood pressure to rise in an emergency (p. 111)

Advertise (ad´ vər tīz) Communicate to draw attention to a product (p. 233)

Advocacy group (ad´ və kə sē grüp) A prevention organization that helps specific groups get health services (p. 479)

Aerobic exercise (âr ō´ bik ek´ sər sīz) Activity that raises your heart rate (p. 135)

Affective disorder (ə fek´ tiv dis ôr´ dər) A mental problem in which a person has disturbed or uncontrolled emotions (p. 81)

Aggression (ə gresh´ ən) Any action that intends harm to someone (p. 39)

Alcohol (al´ kə hòl) A drug that slows down the central nervous system (p. 8)

Alcoholism (al´ kə hò liz əm) A dependence on alcohol and lack of control in drinking (p. 330)

Algae (al´ jē) A large group of plants that live in water (p. 496)

Allergy (al´ ər jē) A bad reaction of the body to a food or to something in the air (p. 129)

Alveolus (al vē´ ə ləs) Air sac with thin walls (plural is *alveoli*) (p. 115)

Amino acid (ə mē´ nō as´ id) A small chemical unit that makes up protein (p. 214)

Amphetamine (am fet´ ə mēn) A central nervous system stimulant (p. 333)

Anabolic steroid (an ə bol´ ik stâr´ oid) A human-made drug that is like the natural male sex hormone, testosterone (p. 340)

Anaerobic exercise (an ə rō´ bik ek´ sər sīz) Activity that quickly uses up oxygen in your body (p. 135)

Analgesic (an l jē´ zik) A medicine that eases or gets rid of pain (p. 319)

Anger (ang´ gər) Strong feeling of displeasure (p. 39)

Angina pectoris (an jī´ nə pek´ tər əs) Severe pain that happens when the heart does not receive enough blood (p. 289)

Antibiotic (an ti bī ot´ ik) Substance that can destroy the growth of certain germs (p. 256)

Antibody (an´ ti bod ē) A protein that kills a particular pathogen (p. 260)

Antiperspirant (an ti pėr´ spər ənt) A product that helps control perspiration by closing the pores (p. 130)

Anus (ā´ nəs) Opening through which solid waste leaves the body (p. 118)

Anxiety (ang zī´ ə tē) A feeling of uneasiness or fearful concern (p. 38)

Anxiety disorder (ang zī′ ə tē   dis ôr′ dər) A mental problem that makes normal life difficult because of intense anxiety (p. 80)

Arterial (är tir′ ē əl) Relating to the arteries (p. 286)

Arteriosclerosis (är tir ē ō sklə rō′ sis) Hardening of the arteries because of a buildup of fat (p. 287)

Artery (är′ tər ē) Vessel that carries blood away from the heart (p. 113)

Arthritis (är thrī′ tis) A group of diseases that causes swelling of the joints (p. 302)

Asbestos (as bes′ təs) A material used for building materials(p. 492)

Association (ə sō sē ā′ shən) Something that reminds a person of something else (p. 231)

Asthma (az′ mə) A respiratory disease that makes breathing difficult (p. 304)

Atherosclerosis (ath ər ō sklər ō′ sis) A form of arteriosclerosis in which the large and medium arteries become narrow from a fat buildup along their walls (p. 287)

Athlete's foot (ath′ lēts fut) Itching or cracked skin between the toes (p. 131)

Attachment (ə tach′ mənt) Emotional bond or tie to others (p. 30)

Auditory nerve (ȯ də tôr ē nėrv) Part of the ear that sends sound information to the brain (p. 108)

B

Bacteria (bak tir′ ē ə) Germs that cause disease (p. 121)

Barbiturate (bär bich′ ər it) A category of sedative-hypnotic drugs (p. 335)

Barrier (bar′ ē ər) Something that blocks passage (p. 259)

Behavior modification (bi hā′ vyər mod ə fə kā′ shən) Form of psychotherapy that teaches a person to replace a less effective behavior pattern with a more effective one (p. 85)

Benign (bi nīn′) Not harmful to health (p. 292)

Bile (bīl) Liquid in the liver that breaks down fats (p. 117)

Binge drink (binj dringk) To drink alcohol heavily, then stop for a time, then drink heavily again (p. 330)

Bipolar disorder (bī pō′ lər dis ôr′ dər) An affective disorder involving an uncontrolled shift from feeling too much energetic emotion to feeling very depressed (p. 81)

Birth defect (bėrth di fekt′) A deformity or an impaired function of the body that is present from birth (p. 472)

Blended family(blen′ dəd fam′ ə lē) Family made when parents live with children from an earlier marriage or marriages (p. 184)

Blizzard (bliz′ ərd) A violent snowstorm with winds above 35 miles per hour that lasts for at least 3 hours (p. 388)

Blood cholesterol (blud kə les′ tə rol) Cholesterol in the bloodstream (p. 213)

Blood pressure (blud presh′ ər) Force of blood on the walls of blood vessels (p. 113)

Body language (bod′ ē lang′ gwij) The way people move and hold their heads, arms, and legs that gives clues about what they think and feel (p. 28)

Brain stem (brān stem) The part of the brain that connects the cerebrum to the spinal cord (p. 105)

Bronchiole (brong′ kē ōl) A tube that branches off the bronchus (p. 114)

Bronchitis (brong kī′ tis) A lung disease that makes breathing hard and causes coughing (p. 490)

Bronchus (brong′ kəs) Breathing tube (plural is *bronchi*) (p. 114)

C

Calcium (kal′ sē əm) Mineral important for keeping bones and teeth strong (p. 217)

Calorie (kal′ ər ē) A unit that measures the amount of energy in food (p. 135)

Cancer (kan′ sər) A harmful growth that destroys healthy cells (p. 169)

Capillary (kap′ ə ler ē) Tiny blood vessel that connects arteries and veins (p. 113)

Carbohydrate (kär bō hī′ drāt) Chemical in foods that provides starches and sugars (p. 210)

a	hat	e	let	ī	ice	ȯ	order	u̇	put	sh	she	ə	a	in about
ā	age	ē	equal	o	hot	oi	oil	ü	rule	th	thin		e	in taken
ä	far	ėr	term	ō	open	ou	out	ch	child	ᴛʜ	then		i	in pencil
â	care	i	it	ȯ	saw	u	cup	ng	long	zh	measure		o	in lemon
													u	in circus

Carbon dioxide (kär´ bən dī ok´ sīd) A gas that is breathed out of the lungs (p. 112)

Carcinogen (kär sin´ ə jən) Material that causes cancer (p. 295)

Cardiac arrest (kär´ dē ak ə rest´) A condition in which the heart has stopped beating and there is no pulse (p. 404)

Cardiopulmonary resuscitation (CPR) (kär dē ō pul´ mə ner ē ri sus ə tā´ shən) A procedure for cardiovascular failure (p. 404)

Cardiovascular (kär dē ō vas´ kyə lər) Relating to the heart and blood vessels (p. 286)

Cartilage (kär´ tl ij) A cushion, or padding, in the joints (p. 302)

Cerebellum (ser ə bel´ əm) The part of the brain that controls balance and helps coordinate muscular activities (p. 105)

Cerebrum (sə rē´ brəm) The part of the brain that lets a person read, think, and remember (p. 104)

Cervix (sèr´ viks) Narrow outer end of the uterus (p. 165)

Cesarean childbirth (si zâr´ ē ən chīld´ bèrth) The delivery of a baby through a cut in the abdomen and uterus (p. 165)

Chancre (shang´ kər) A hard sore that is the first sign of syphilis (p. 276)

Chemotherapy (kē mō ther´ ə pē) A treatment that involves taking drugs to kill cancer cells (p. 295)

Chest cavity (chest kav´ ə tē) Part of the body that includes ribs and muscles that surround the heart and lungs (p. 115)

Chest compression (chest kəm presh´ ən) When doing CPR, the act of pressing against the chest over and over (p. 404)

Chlamydia (klə mid´ ē ə) A sexually transmitted disease (p. 276)

Cholesterol (kə les´ tə rol) A waxy, fatlike material in your body cells that helps with certain body functions (p. 213)

Chromosome (krō´ mə sōm) Tiny structure in cells that contains hereditary information (p. 167)

Chronic (kron´ ik) Lasting for a long time (p. 277)

Clinical depression (klin´ ə kəl di presh´ ən) An affective disorder involving long-lasting, intense sadness (p. 81)

Clotting (klot´ ing) Sticking together to form a plug and stop a wound from bleeding (p. 112)

Cocaine (kō kān´) A highly addictive illegal stimulant (p. 333)

Cognitive therapy (kog´ nə tiv ther´ ə pē) Form of psychotherapy that teaches a person to replace destructive thoughts with positive ones (p. 85)

Collaborative (kə lab´ ə rə tiv) Working together as a team (p. 180)

Coma (kō´ mə) A condition in which a person loses consciousness (p. 298)

Commitment (kə mit´ mənt) A promise (p. 178)

Communicable (kə myü´ nə kə bəl) Infectious (p. 254)

Complex carbohydrate (kom´ pleks kär bō hī´ drāt) Carbohydrate that contains fiber; the best source of dietary carbohydrates (p. 210)

Compromise (kom´ prə mīz) Agree by giving in a little (p. 57)

Conceive (kən sēv´) To become pregnant (p. 157)

Conflict (kon´ flikt) A difference of opinion between two or more people who have different ideas (p. 419)

Consequence (kon´ sə kwens) Something that happens as a result of something else (p. 183)

Consumer (kən sü´ mər) Someone who buys goods or services (p. 446)

Contact poisoning (kon´ takt poi´ zn ing) Poisoning that happens when harmful materials are absorbed through the skin (p. 408)

Contract (kən trakt´) Shorten (p. 101)

Cope (kōp) To deal with or overcome problems and difficulties (p. 41)

Cornea (kôr´ nē ə) Part of the eye that light passes through (p. 106)

Crack (krak) A form of cocaine that is smoked (p. 334)

Culture (kul´ chər) Beliefs, way of living, and language of a group of people (p. 13)

Custodial parent (ku stō´ dē əl pâr´ ənt) The parent who is responsible for a child after a divorce (p. 185)

Custody (kus´ tə dē) The legal right and responsibility to care for a child (p. 185)

D

Daily Values (DV) (dā´ lē val´ yüz) Section of a nutrition label that provides information about the percentage of nutrients in a product (p. 236)

Dandruff (dan´ drəf) Flaking from the scalp (p. 132)

Date rape (dāt rāp) Rape committed by someone the victim socializes with (p. 427)

Deductible (di duk′ tə bəl) The first part of each year's medical expenses before the insurance company makes payments (p. 457)

Defense mechanism (di fens′ mek′ ə niz əm) A mental device one uses to protect oneself (p. 77)

Deficiency (di fish′ ən sē) A lack of something (p. 223)

Deforestation (dē fôr əs tā′ shən) Cutting down and clearing trees (p. 499)

Deformity (di fôr mə tē) Abnormally formed body structure (p. 257)

Delusion (di lü′ zhən) A false belief (p. 82)

Denial (di nī′ əl) A refusal to believe or accept something negative or threatening (p. 77)

Deodorant (dē ō′ dər ənt) A product that covers body odor (p. 130)

Dependent (di pen′ dənt) Having developed a need for a medicine or drug (p. 321)

Depressant (di pres′ nt) A drug that slows down the central nervous system (p. 328)

Depression (di presh′ ən) A state of deep sadness (p. 40)

Dermis (dèr′ mis) Inner layer of skin made up of living cells (p. 120)

Designer drug (di zī′ nər drug) A drug with a slightly different chemical makeup from a legal drug (p. 339)

Deteriorate (di tir′ ē ə rāt) Wear away a little bit at a time (p. 15)

Detoxification (di tok sə fə kā′ shən) Removing addictive drugs from the body (p. 352)

Diabetes (dī ə bē′ tis) A disease caused by lack of insulin in the body or when the body cannot use insulin effectively (p. 298)

Diaphragm (dī′ ə fram) Band of muscle tissue beneath the respiratory organs (p. 115)

Dietary cholesterol (dī′ ə ter ē kə les′ tə rol) Cholesterol found in some foods (p. 213)

Digestion (dī jes′ chən) Breaking down food into smaller parts and changing it to a form that cells can use (p. 116)

Disadvantage (dis əd van′ tij) A condition or situation that makes reaching a goal harder (p. 58)

Discipline (dis′ ə plin) A fair and safe way to teach a child how to behave correctly (p. 183)

Discriminate (dis krim′ ə nāt) Treat differently on the basis of something other than individual worth (p. 67)

Disease (də zēz′) A condition that harms or stops the normal working of the body (p. 7)

Displacement (dis plās′ mənt) Shifting an emotion from its real object to a safer or more immediate one (p. 77)

Divorce (də vôrs′) The legal end of a marriage (p. 180)

Domestic violence (də mes′ tik vī′ ə ləns) Violence that happens mostly at home (p. 190)

Dominant (dom′ ə nənt) Having the most control (p. 168)

Dressing (dres′ ing) Layers of cloth and other materials that protect a wound (p. 398)

Drug (drug) A chemical substance other than food that changes the way the mind and body work (p. 8)

Dysfunctional (dis fungk′ shən əl) Harmed or unhealthy (p. 77)

E

Eardrum (ir′ drum) Thin piece of tissue stretched across the ear canal (p. 108)

Earthquake (èrth′ kwāk) The shaking caused when the major slabs of rock in the earth's crust shift and move (p. 387)

Eating disorder (ēt′ ing dis ôr′ dər) An attempt to cope with psychological problems through eating habits (p. 83)

Ecology (ē kol′ ə jē) The study of how living things and the environment work together (p. 489)

Ecstasy (ek′ stə sē) An illegal, psychoactive drug (p. 336)

Electrical shock (i lek′ trə kəl shok) A flow of electric current through the body (p. 373)

Embryo (em′ brē ō) Fertilized egg after implantation (p. 163)

Emotion (i mō′ shən) Feeling (p. 28)

Empathy (em′ pə thē) Recognition and understanding of other people's feelings (p. 68)

Emphysema (em fə sē′ mə) A serious respiratory disease that makes breathing difficult (p. 324)

a	hat	e	let	ī	ice	ô	order	ů	put	sh	she	⎧ a	in about
ā	age	ē	equal	o	hot	oi	oil	ü	rule	th	thin	e	in taken
ä	far	èr	term	ō	open	ou	out	ch	child	ℱℋ	then	ə ⎨ i	in pencil
â	care	i	it	ò	saw	u	cup	ng	long	zh	measure	⎩ o	in lemon
												u	in circus

Enabling (en ā´ bling) Actions of a friend or family member that help a person continue to use drugs (p. 349)

Endurance (en dür´ əns) The ability to stay with an activity for a long time (p. 134)

Enzyme (en´ zīm) Special chemical that breaks down food (p. 116)

Epidemic (ep ə dem´ ik) The rapid spread of a communicable disease that affects large populations at the same time (p. 468)

Epidermis (ep ə dėr´ mis) Outer layer of skin (p. 120)

Epilepsy (ep´ ə lep sē) A chronic disease that is caused by disordered brain activity and that causes seizures (p. 303)

Erection (i rek´ shən) Condition in which the penis becomes hard and larger (p. 159)

Esophagus (i sof´ ə gəs) Long tube that connects the mouth and the stomach (p. 117)

Essential amino acid (ə sen´ shəl ə mē´ nō as´ id) An amino acid the body cannot make by itself but that can be obtained from food (p. 214)

Essential nutrient (ə sen´ shəl nü´ trē ənt) Chemical in foods that the body cannot make (p. 206)

Esteem (e stēm´) Value or worth; how one sees oneself or others (p. 29)

Estrogen (es´ trə jən) Female sex hormone (p. 155)

Excretory system (ek´ skrə tôr ē sis´ təm) System that allows the body to eliminate liquid and solid waste (p. 118)

Exhale (els hāl´) Breathe out (p. 115)

Extended family (ek sten´ dəd fam´ ə lē) Family that includes parents, children, and other relatives (p. 185)

F

Fainting (fān´ ting) Short-term loss of consciousness caused by too little blood to the brain (p. 408)

Fallopian tube (fə lō´ pē ən tüb) Passage through which mature egg cells pass from the ovaries to the uterus (p. 157)

Family love (fam´ ə lē luv) Love based on attachment and support (p. 30)

Famine (fam´ ən) A time when there is not enough food for people (p. 499)

Fat (fat) Stored energy (p. 210)

Fatty acid (fat´ ē as´ id) Acid that includes saturated and unsaturated fats (p. 212)

Fear (fir) A strong feeling of fright; awareness of danger (p. 38)

Feces (fē´ sēz) Solid waste material remaining in the large intestine after digestion (p. 118)

Fertilize (fėr´ tl īz) An egg cell and a sperm join together (p. 159)

Fetal alcohol syndrome (fē´ tl al´ kə hòl sin´ drōm) A condition caused by drinking alcohol during pregnancy (p. 161)

Fetus (fē´ təs) Unborn baby from 8 weeks after fertilization until birth (p. 163)

Fiber (fī´ bər) The coarse material in fruits, vegetables, and grains that helps you digest your food (p. 211)

Fire extinguisher (fīr ek sting´ gwish ər) A portable device containing chemicals that put out small fires (p. 371)

First aid (fėrst ād) Immediate emergency care given to a sick or injured person before professional medical care arrives (p. 396)

Flashback (flash´ bak) Experiencing the effects of a drug without using it again (p. 336)

Flash flood (flash flud) A dangerous flood that occurs suddenly without warning because of heavy rains (p. 387)

Flexibility (flek sə bil´ ə tē) The ability to twist, turn, bend, and stretch easily (p. 134)

Flood (flud) A natural disaster that occurs when a body of water overflows and covers normally dry land (p. 387)

Food Guide Pyramid (füd gīd pir´ ə mid) A chart that helps you decide how much and what kinds of foods to eat (p. 204)

Fossil fuel (fos´ əl fyü´ əl) A material that is made from plant or animal remains that can be burned (p. 491)

Foster family (fo´ stėr fam´ ə lē) Family that cares for children who are in need of short-term parenting from people other than their birth parents (p. 185)

Fracture (frak´ chər) A broken bone (p. 409)

Fragile (fraj´ əl) Easily broken, destroyed, or damaged (p. 488)

Friendship (frend´ ship) Love based on choices (p. 30)

Frostbite (fròst´ bīt) A tissue injury caused by being in extreme cold (p. 411)

Fructose (fruk´ tōs) The natural sugar found in fruit (p. 211)

Frustrate (frus´ trāt) To block from something wanted (p. 13)

Fume (fyüm) Gas (p. 407)

Fungus (fung´ gəs) An organism that grows in damp places (p. 131)

Gallbladder (gȯl blad´ ər) Digestive organ attached to the liver that stores bile (p. 117)

Gender (jen´ dər) The condition of being male or female; sex (p. 167)

Gene (jēn) A tiny structure in chromosomes that controls the transfer of traits from parents to children (p. 167)

Genetic counselor (jə net´ ik koun´ sə lər) Health care professional who helps people determine the chance of passing inherited disorders to their children (p. 168)

Genetic disorder (jə net´ ik dis ȯr´ dər) A disease that is caused by abnormal genes or chromosomes (p. 168)

Genetics (jə net´ iks) The science that deals with heredity and inherited characteristics (p. 167)

Genital herpes (jen´ ə təl hėr´ pēz) A sexually transmitted disease (p. 277)

Genitals (jen´ ə təlz) Reproductive, or sex, organs (p. 154)

Genital warts (jen´ ə təl wôrts) Bumps caused by a virus spread through sexual contact (p. 278)

Gestation (je stā´ shən) The period of development in the uterus from the time the egg is fertilized until birth; pregnancy (p. 160)

Gingivitis (jin jə vī´ tis) First stage of gum disease (p. 132)

Gland (gland) A group of cells or an organ that produces a substance and sends it into the body (p. 110)

Glucose (glü´ kōs) The main sugar in blood; the major energy source for your body (p. 212)

Glycogen (glī´ kə jən) Glucose that is stored in your body (p. 212)

Gonorrhea (gon ə rē´ ə) A sexually transmitted disease (p. 275)

Good Samaritan laws (gu̇d sə mâr´ ə tən lȯz) Laws that protect people who help others in emergencies (p. 398)

Government regulation (guv´ ərn mənt reg yə lā´ shən) Rule that businesses must follow to protect public health (p. 476)

Grand mal seizure (grän mal´ sē´ zhər) A type of epileptic seizure in which a person passes out (p. 303)

Greenhouse effect (grēn´ hous ə fekt´) The warming of Earth's atmosphere (p. 493)

Grief (grēf) A feeling of sorrow; feelings after a loss (p. 40)

Guilt (gilt) A feeling of having done something wrong (p. 33)

Halfway house (haf´ wā hous) A place for recovering individuals to get help easing back into society (p. 354)

Hallucination (hə lü sn ā´ shən) A twisted idea about an unreal object or event (p. 82)

Hallucinogen (hə lü´ sn ə jən) A psychoactive drug that confuses the central nervous system and makes a person see, hear, feel, and experience things that are not real (p. 336)

Hazard (haz´ ərd) Something that is dangerous (p. 374)

Hazardous waste (haz´ ər dəs wāst) A material that can be harmful to the environment, human health, and other living things (p. 501)

Health (helth) A state of being well that has three parts physical, social, and emotional (p. 4)

Health care facility (helth kâr fə sil´ ə tē) A place where people go for medical, dental, and other care (p. 454)

Health insurance (helth in shu̇r´ əns) A plan that pays a major part of medical costs (p. 457)

Health literacy (helth lit´ ər ə sē) Gathering, understanding, and using information to improve health results (p. 18)

Health maintenance organization (HMO) (helth mān´ tə nəns ȯr gə nə zā´ shən) A form of managed care in which an organization controls how health care is delivered and its cost (p. 458)

a	hat	e	let	ī	ice	ȯ	order	u̇	put	sh	she	ə	a	in about
ā	age	ē	equal	o	hot	oi	oil	ü	rule	th	thin		e	in taken
ä	far	ėr	term	ō	open	ou	out	ch	child	ᴛʜ	then		i	in pencil
â	care	i	it	ȯ	saw	u	cup	ng	long	zh	measure		o	in lemon
													u	in circus

Health risk (helth risk) An action or a condition that contributes to injury or disease (p. 11)

Heart attack (härt ə tak´) A condition in which the blood supply and the nutrients to the heart are greatly reduced (p. 287)

Heat exhaustion (hēt´ eg zȯs´ chən) A condition that comes from hard physical work in a very hot place (p. 411)

Heatstroke (hēt´ strōk) A condition that comes from being in high heat too long (p. 411)

Heimlich maneuver (hīm´ lik mə nü´ vər) A way of giving firm upward thrusts below a person's rib cage to force out an object from the throat (p. 401)

Heredity (hə red´ ə tē) Passage of physical characteristics from parents to children (p. 11)

Heroin (her´ ō ən) An illegal narcotic made from morphine (p. 336)

Hierarchy (hī´ ə rär kē) Order from most to least important (p. 29)

Hodgkin's disease (hoj´ kinz də zēz´) A lymph gland cancer that often affects young adults (p. 295)

Hormone (hôr´ mōn) A chemical messenger that helps control how body parts do their jobs (p. 110)

Hospice (hos´ pis) A long-term care facility for people who are dying (p. 455)

Human immunodeficiency virus (HIV) (hyü´ mən i myü nō di fish´ ən sē vī´ rəs) A virus that infects body cells and severely damages the human immune system, causing AIDS (p. 270)

Hurricane (hėr´ ə kān) A severe tropical storm with heavy rains and winds above 74 miles per hour (p. 385)

Hygiene (hī´ jēn) Practices that promote cleanliness and good health (p. 128)

Hypertension (hī pər ten´ shən) High blood pressure (p. 286)

Hypothermia (hī pō thėr´ mē ə) A serious loss of body heat that comes from being in the cold too long (p. 411)

I

Immune system (i myün´ sis´ təm) Combination of body defenses that fight pathogens (p. 255)

Immunization (im yə nī zā´ shən) The process of making the body immune to a disease (p. 261)

Impair (im pâr´) Have a negative effect on (p. 15)

Implantation (im plan tā´ shən) Process during which the fertilized egg plants itself in the lining of the uterus (p. 162)

Impulse (im´ puls) The urge to react before taking time to think (p. 57)

Incubation period (ing kyə bā´ shən pir´ ē əd) Time it takes after a person is infected for symptoms of a disease to appear (p. 225)

Infection (in fek´ shən) A sickness caused by a germ in the body (p. 129)

Infectious (in fek´ shəs) Passed from a germ carrier to another living thing (p. 254)

Inferior (in fir´ ē ər) Not as good as others (p. 151)

Inflammation (in flə mā´ shən) Redness, soreness, and swelling after tissue damage (p. 260)

Influenza (in flü en´ zə) A common illness known as the flu (p. 254)

Inhalant (in hā´ lənt) A chemical that is breathed in (p. 339)

Inhalation poisoning (in hə lā´ shən poi´ zn ing) Poisoning caused by breathing in harmful fumes (p. 407)

Inhale (in hāl´) Breathe in (p. 115)

Inherit (in her´ it) To receive something passed down from parents (p. 254)

Inpatient (in´ pā shənt) Referring to someone receiving health care who stays overnight or longer (p. 455)

Insulin (in´ sə lən) Hormone produced in the pancreas that helps cells use sugar (p. 117)

Intimate (in´ tə mit) Very personal or private (p. 61)

Intoxication (in tok sə kā´ shən) Excitement or stimulation caused by use of a chemical material (p. 330)

Iris (ī´ ris) Colored part of the eye around the pupil (p. 107)

Isokinetic exercise (ī sə ki net´ ik ek´ sər sīz) Activity that builds muscle strength by using resistance (p. 135)

Isometric exercise (ī sə met´ rik ek´ sər sīz) Activity that builds muscle strength by using tension (p. 135)

Isotonic exercise (ī sə ton´ ik ek´ sər sīz) Activity that builds muscle strength by using weights and repeated movements (p. 135)

K

Kaposi's sarcoma (kä´ pə sēz sär kō´ mə) A rare type of cancer (p. 272)

Keratin (ker´ ə tin) A type of protein that makes nails hard (p. 121)

Kidney (kid´ nē) Organ in the excretory system where urine forms (p. 118)

L

Lactose (lak´ tōs) The natural sugar found in milk (p. 211)

Landfill (land´ fil) Low-lying ground where waste is buried between layers of dirt (p. 501)

Large intestine (lärj in tes´ tən) Tube connected to the small intestine (p. 117)

Latex (lā teks) A kind of rubber used to make thin gloves for health care professionals (p. 397)

Lens (lenz) The soft, clear tissue behind the pupil (p. 107)

Ligament (lig´ ə mənt) Tough band of stretchy tissue that holds joints together or keeps organs in place (p. 101)

Lightning (līt´ ning) An electrical discharge that commonly occurs during thunderstorms (p. 389)

Liver (liv´ ər) A large organ that produces bile (p. 117)

Look-alike drug (lůk´ ə lĭk drug) A drug made from legal chemicals to look like a common illegal drug (p. 339)

LSD (el es dē) A human-made hallucinogen (p. 337)

Lymph (limf) A colorless liquid that feeds tissue (p. 293)

M

Malignant (mə lig´ nənt) Harmful to health (p. 292)

Malnutrition (mal nü trish´ ən) Condition you get from a diet that lacks some or all nutrients (p. 222)

Managed care (man´ ijd kâr) A type of private health insurance in which an organization is a go-between for patients and doctors (p. 458)

Marijuana (mâr ə wä´ nə) A drug from the hemp plant, *Cannabis sativa* (p. 338)

Marriage counselor (mar´ ij koun´ sə lər) A person trained in helping couples work on their relationship with each other (p. 190)

Marrow (mar´ ō) The matter inside bones, which forms blood (p. 101)

Maximum heart rate (mak´ sə məm härt rāt) The number of heartbeats in a minute when one exercises as hard, fast, and long as possible (p. 136)

Media (mē´ dē ə) Ways people can communicate information; TV, Web sites, newspapers, radio, magazines, and so on (p. 233)

Mediator (mē´ dē ā tər) Someone who helps people find a solution to a conflict (p. 431)

Medicaid (med´ ə kād) Health insurance for people whose incomes are below a certain level (p. 459)

Medicare (med´ ə kâr) Health insurance for people age 65 or older and some people under age 65 with certain disabilities (p. 459)

Medicine (med´ ə sən) A drug that is used to relieve, cure, or keep a person from getting a disease or problem (p. 318)

Medulla (mi dul´ ə) The part of the brain that controls the body's automatic activities (p. 105)

Melanin (mel´ ə nən) Substance that gives skin its color (p. 121)

Menstrual cycle (men´ strü əl sī´ kəl) The monthly cycle of changes in a female's reproductive system (p. 158)

Menstruation (men strü ā´ shən) The process in females during which blood tissue leaves the lining of the uterus (p. 158)

Metabolism (mə tab´ ə liz əm) Rate at which cells produce energy (p. 110)

Methamphetamine (meth´ am fet ə mēn) A highly addictive, illegal amphetamine (p. 333)

Mineral (min´ ər əl) A natural material needed for fluid balance, digestion, and other bodily functions (p. 216)

Mouth-to-mouth resuscitation (mouth tü mouth ri sus ə tā´ shən) Rescue breathing (p. 403)

Mucous membrane (myü´ kəs mem´ brān) The moist lining of the mouth and other body passages (p. 259)

Mucus (myü´ kəs) The fluid that mucous membranes produce (p. 259)

Mutation (myü tā´ shən) Change (p. 296)

N

Narcotic (när kot´ ik) A pain-killing drug made from the opium poppy and in laboratories (p. 335)

Natural sugar (nach´ ər əl shůg´ ər) Sugar that exists in a food in nature (p. 211)

a	hat	e	let	ī	ice	ȯ	order	ů	put	sh	she
ā	age	ē	equal	o	hot	oi	oil	ü	rule	th	thin
ä	far	ėr	term	ō	open	ou	out	ch	child	ŦH	then
â	care	i	it	ȯ	saw	u	cup	ng	long	zh	measure

ə { a in about / e in taken / i in pencil / o in lemon / u in circus }

Neglect (ni glekt´) Failure to take care of a person's basic needs; regular lack of care (p. 189)

Negotiation (ni gō shē ā´ shən) Ability to help people reach a compromise (p. 431)

Nicotine (nik´ ə tēn) A chemical in tobacco to which a person can become addicted (p. 324)

Nonverbal (non vėr´ bəl) Unspoken (p. 13)

Nonverbal communication (non vėr´ bəl kə myü nə kā´ shən) Using one's body to send messages (p. 63)

Nuclear family (nü´ klē ər fam´ ə lē) Family made up of a mother, a father, and their children (p. 184)

Nurse practitioner (nėrs prak tish´ ə nər) A registered nurse with special training for providing primary health care (p. 453)

Nurture (nėr´ chər) Help someone or something grow or develop (p. 61)

Nutrient (nü´ trē ənt) A part of food that helps the body function and grow (p. 100)

Nutrient-dense (nü´ trē ənt dens) Having a good source of nutrients but being low in calories (p. 207)

Nutrition Facts (nü trish´ ən faks) Section of a food label that provides information about the product (p. 240)

O

Obesity (ō bē´ sə tē) Condition of being extremely overweight (p. 299)

Opportunistic pathogen (op ər tü nis´ tik path´ ə jən) Pathogen that the body would normally fight off but that takes advantage of a weakened immune system (p. 270)

Optic nerve (op´ tik nėrv) Part of the eye that sends information to the brain (p. 107)

Optimism (op´ tə miz əm) Tending to expect the best possible outcome (p. 56)

Oral poisoning (ôr´ əl poi´ zn ing) Poisoning that happens after a harmful material is swallowed (p. 407)

Organic food (ôr gan´ ik füd) Food raised without pesticides, unnatural fertilizers, antibiotics, or growth hormones (p. 234)

Osteoarthritis (os tē ō är thrī´ tis) A condition in which the cartilage in the joints wears away (p. 302)

Outpatient clinic (out´ pā shənt klin´ ik) A place where people receive health care without staying overnight (p. 454)

Outpatient treatment center (out´ pā shənt trēt´ mənt sen´ tər) A place where individuals go for drug-dependence treatment while living at home (p. 354)

Ovaries (ō´ vər ēz) Two organs in females that produce egg cells (p. 157)

Overdose (ō´ vər dōs) Too much of a drug (p. 334)

Over-the-counter (OTC) medicine (ō´ vər thə koun´ tər med´ ə sən) Medicine that can be bought without a prescription (p. 318)

Ovulation (ov yə lā´ shən) The release of a mature egg cell (p. 157)

Ozone layer (ō´ zōn lā´ ər) An area above Earth that guards and protects Earth from the sun's harmful rays (p. 493)

P

Pancreas (pan´ krē əs) A gland that produces insulin and enzymes (p. 117)

Panic attack (pan´ ik ə tak´) A feeling of terror that comes without warning and includes symptoms of chest pain, rapid heartbeat, sweating, shaking, or shortness of breath (p. 80)

Particulate (pär tik´ yə lit) Tiny piece of solid material (p. 491)

Pathogen (path´ ə jən) Germ that causes infectious diseases (p. 255)

PCP (pē sē pē) A human-made hallucinogen (p. 337)

Penis (pē´ nis) Male reproductive organ (p. 159)

Perinatal care (per ə nā´ tl kâr) Care of the baby around the time of birth and through the first month (p. 166)

Peripheral nervous system (pə rif´ ər əl nėr´ vəs sis´ təm) Network of peripheral nerves carrying messages between the brain and spinal cord and the rest of the body (p. 105)

Personality (pėr sə nal´ ə tē) All of one's behavioral, mental, and emotional characteristics (p. 50)

Perspiration (pėr spə rā´ shən) Sweat (p. 121)

Pessimism (pes´ ə miz əm) Tending to suspect the worst possible outcome (p. 56)

Pesticide (pes´ tə sīd) A chemical used to kill bugs (p. 488)

Petit mal seizure (pə tē´ mal´ sē´ zhər) A type of epileptic seizure in which a person does not pass out (p. 303)

Pharmacist (fär´ mə sist) Druggist (p. 318)

Phobia (fō´ bē ə) Excessive fear of an object or a specific situation (p. 81)

Phosphorus (fos´ fər əs) Mineral that works with calcium to keep bones and teeth strong (p. 217)

Photochemical smog (fō tō kem´ ə kəl smog) A form of air pollution (p. 490)

Physical environment (fiz´ ə kəl en vī´ rən mənt) The area around a person (p. 11)

Pimple (pim´ pəl) An inflamed swelling of the skin (p. 130)

Placenta (plə sen´ tə) An organ lining the uterus that surrounds the embryo or fetus (p. 163)

Platelet (plāt´ lit) Small part in the blood that helps with clotting (p. 112)

Pneumonia (nü mō´ nyə) A lung infection (p. 272)

Pollution (pə lü´ shən) Harmful materials in the soil, water, or air (p. 487)

Pore (pôr) Tiny opening in the epidermis (p. 121)

Postpartum (pōst pär´ təm) Following birth (p. 166)

Preferred provider organization (PPO) (pri fėrd´ prə vī´ dėr ôr gə nə zā´ shən) A form of managed care that has fewer rules and more choices of doctors than an HMO has (p. 458)

Pregnant (preg´ nənt) Carrying a developing baby in the female body (p. 159)

Prejudice (prej´ ə dis) Negative, or unfavorable, opinions formed about something or someone without enough experience or knowledge (p. 67)

Prenatal care (prē nā´ tl kâr) Health care during a pregnancy (p. 161)

Prescription (pri skrip´ shən) A written order from a doctor for a medicine (p. 318)

Preservative (pri zėr´ və tiv) A substance added to foods to prevent them from spoiling (p. 241)

Pressure point (presh´ ər point) A place on the body where an artery can be pressed against a bone to stop bleeding in an arm or a leg (p. 406)

Primary care physician (prī´ mer ē kâr fə zish´ ən) A doctor who treats people for usual problems (p. 453)

Product (prod´ əkt) Item for sale made by someone or something (p. 233)

Progesterone (prō jes´ tə rōn) Female sex hormone (p. 155)

Projection (prə jek´ shən) Assuming that another person has one's own attitudes, feelings, or purposes (p. 77)

Protein (prō´ tēn) A material in food needed for growth and repair of body tissues (p. 210)

Psychoactive (sī kō ak´ tiv) Affecting the mind or mental processes (p. 328)

Psychologist (sī kol´ ə jist) A person who studies mental and behavioral characteristics (p. 76)

Psychotherapy (sī kō ther´ ə pē) Psychological treatment for mental or emotional disorders (p. 85)

Puberty (pyü´ bər tē) Period at the beginning of adolescence when children begin to develop into adults and are able to have children (p. 152)

Public health (pub´ lik helth) The practice of protecting and improving the health of a community or a nation (p. 468)

Pulse (puls) Regular beat of the heart (p. 112)

Pupil (pyü´ pəl) Dark center part of the eye that adjusts to let in the correct amount of light (p. 106)

Q

Quackery (kwak´ ər ē) The promotion of medical products or services that are unproved or worthless (p. 448)

R

Rabies (rā´ bēz) A serious disease that affects the nervous system (p. 408)

Radiation (rā dē ā´ shən) A cancer treatment that involves sending energy in the form of waves (p. 295)

Radiation sickness (rā dē ā´ shən sik´ nis) Sickness caused by being around high levels of radiation (p. 502)

Radon (rā´ don) A gas with no smell or color that comes from the radioactive decay of radium underground (p. 492)

Rape (rāp) The unlawful act of forcing a person to have sex (p. 426)

Rational (rash´ ə nəl) Realistic or reasonable (p. 57)

Reaction (rē ak´ shən) Response (p. 28)

Realistic (rē ə lis´ tik) Practical or reasonable (p. 56)

a	hat	e	let	ī	ice	ô	order	u̇	put	sh	she	ə	a in about
ā	age	ē	equal	o	hot	oi	oil	ü	rule	th	thin		e in taken
ä	far	ėr	term	ō	open	ou	out	ch	child	ᴛʜ	then		i in pencil
â	care	i	it	ȯ	saw	u	cup	ng	long	zh	measure		o in lemon
													u in circus

Receptor cell (ri sep′ tər sel) Cell that receives information (p. 109)

Recessive (ri ses′ iv) Hidden (p. 168)

Rectum (rek′ təm) Lower part of the large intestine (p. 118)

Reflex (rē′ fleks) Automatic response (p. 106)

Rehabilitation (rē hə bil ə tā′ shən) Therapy needed to recover from surgery, illness, or an injury (p. 455)

Relief (ri lēf′) A light, pleasant feeling after something painful or distressing is gone (p. 40)

Repression (ri presh′ ən) A refusal to think about something that upsets you (p. 77)

Reproduction (rē prə duk′ shən) The process through which two human beings produce a child (p. 156)

Reproductive organ (rē prə duk′ tiv ôr′ gən) Organ in the body that allows humans to mature sexually and to have children (p. 154)

Rescue breathing (res′ kyü brē тнing) Putting oxygen from a rescuer's lungs into an unconscious person's lungs to help the person breathe (p. 403)

Residential treatment center (rez ə den′ shəl trēt′ mənt sen′ tər) A place where individuals live while being treated for drug dependence (p. 354)

Resilient (ri zil′ yənt) Able to bounce back from misfortune or hardship (p. 59)

Resistance (ri zis′ təns) The pushing back of something (p. 134)

Resistance skill (ri zis′ təns skil) A way to resist negative peer pressure (p. 356)

Respiration (res pə rā′ shən) Breathing in oxygen and breathing out carbon dioxide (p. 114)

Respiratory failure (res′ pər ə tôr ē fā′ lyər) A condition in which breathing has stopped (p. 402)

Retina (ret′ n ə) Part of the eye that sends information about light (p. 107)

Rheumatoid arthritis (rü′ mə toid är thrī′ tis) A condition in which the joints swell badly and become stiff and weak (p. 302)

Risk factor (risk fak′ tər) A habit or trait known to increase the chances of getting a disease (p. 290)

Role confusion (rōl kən fyü′ zhən) Being unsure about who one is and one's goals as an adult (p. 151)

Romantic love (rō man′ tik luv) Strong physical and emotional attraction between two people (p. 30)

S

Saliva (sə lī′ və) A liquid in the mouth (p. 116)

Sanitation (san ə tā shən) Measures related to cleanliness that protect public health (p. 474)

Saturated fat (sach′ ə rā təd fat) A material in food that comes from animal products and that can lead to health problems (p. 212)

Scoliosis (skō lē ō′ sis) A condition in which the spine is abnormally curved (p. 452)

Secondary sex characteristic (sek′ ən der ē seks kar ik tə ris′ tik) Feature that signals the beginning of adulthood (p. 154)

Secondhand smoke (sek′ ənd hand smōk) Smoke from a cigarette or cigar someone else is smoking (p. 15)

Sedative-hypnotic drug (sed′ ə tiv hip not′ ik drug) A prescribed depressant that lessens anxiety or helps a person sleep (p. 335)

Sedentary (sed′ n ter ē) Including little or no exercise (p. 14)

Seizure (sē′ zhər) A physical reaction to an instance of mixed-up brain activity (p. 303)

Self-actualization (self ak chü ə lī zā′ shən) Achieving one's possibilities (p. 32)

Self-awareness (self ə wâr′ nəs) Understanding oneself as an individual (p. 66)

Self-concept (self kon sept′) Ideas one has about oneself (p. 31)

Self-defeating behavior (self di fēt′ ing bi hā′ vyer) An action that blocks a person's efforts to reach goals (p. 76)

Self-esteem (self e stēm′) Self-respect; how one feels about oneself (p. 31)

Sensorineural deafness (sen sər ē nùr′ əl def′ nis) Hearing loss in which the tiny cells in the inner ear are destroyed (p. 501)

Separation (sep ə rā′ shən) A couple's agreement, or a court decision made for the couple, to stop living together (p. 187)

Sewage (sü′ ij) Liquid and solid waste from drains and toilets (p. 495)

Sex-linked (seks lingkd) Carried by a sex chromosome (p. 168)

Sexual abuse (sek′ shü əl ə byüs) Any sexual contact that is forced on a person, including unwanted talk and touching (p. 189)

Sexual assault (sek′ shü əl ə sòlt′) Forced sexual contact (p. 427)

Sexual exploitation (sek′ shü əl ek sploi tā′ shən) Using a person sexually to make money (p. 427)

Sexual harassment (sek´ shü əl har´ əs mənt) Making unwanted sexual comments or physical advances to another person (p. 426)

Sexual intercourse (sek´ shü əl in´ tər kôrs) Insertion of the penis into the vagina (p. 159)

Sexually transmitted disease (sek´ shü ə lē tranz mit´ əd də zēz) Any disease that is spread through sexual activity (p. 275)

Shock (shok) Failure of the circulatory system to provide enough blood to the body (p. 405)

Side effect (sīd ə fekt´) Reaction to a medicine other than what it is intended for (p. 318)

Simple carbohydrate (sim´ pəl kär bō hī´ drāt) A sugar the body uses for quick energy (p. 210)

Single-parent family (sing´ gəl pâr´ ənt fam´ ə lē) Family that includes a child or children and one adult (p. 184)

Small intestine (smòl in tes´ tən) A curled-up tube just below the stomach where most of the breakdown of food takes place (p. 117)

Smoke detector (smōk di tek´ tər) A device that sounds loudly when it senses smoke or high amounts of heat (p. 371)

Social comparison (sō´ shəl kəm par´ ə sən) Observing other people to determine how to behave (p. 66)

Social environment (sō shəl en vī´ rən mənt) Community resources such as access to doctors, hospitals, family counseling, and after-school programs (p. 12)

Social esteem (sō´ shəl e stēm´) How others value a person (p. 51)

Socializing (sō´ shə lī zing) Getting together with others during free time (p. 176)

Social support (sō´ shəl sə pôrt´) Help for those you care about (p. 69)

Sodium (sō´ dē əm) Mineral that controls fluids in the body (p. 218)

Soil erosion (soil i rō´ zhən) Soil moved by wind, water, or ice (p. 487)

Solid waste (sol´ id wāst) Garbage, trash (p. 500)

Specialist (spesh´ ə list) A doctor who works only in a certain branch of medicine (p. 453)

Sperm (spėrm) Male sex cells produced by the testes (p. 156)

Spinal column (spī´ nl kol´ əm) Series of small bones that surround and protect the spinal cord (p. 105)

Spinal cord (spī´ nl kôrd) Major pathway the brain uses to send messages to the body (p. 105)

Splint (splint) An unbendable object that keeps a broken arm, leg, or finger in place (p. 409)

Sprain (sprān) The tearing or stretching of tendons or ligaments that connect joints (p. 410)

Sterile (ster´ əl) Free from bacteria (p. 406)

Sterility (stə ril´ ə tē) Inability to produce a child (p. 276)

Stimulant (stim´ yə lənt) A drug that speeds up the central nervous system (p. 324)

Stress (stres) A state of physical or emotional pressure (p. 34)

Stress response (stres ri spons´) Automatic physical reactions to stress (p. 34)

Stroke (strōk) A cardiovascular disease that happens when the blood supply to the brain is suddenly stopped (p. 289)

Subcutaneous layer (sub kyü tā´ nē us lā´ ər) Deepest layer of skin (p. 121)

Substance abuse disorder (sub´ stəns ə byüs´ dis ôr´ dər) An unhealthy dependence on alcohol or other drugs (p. 80)

Sucrose (sü´ krōs) Table sugar (p. 211)

Suicide (sü´ ə sīd) The act of killing oneself (p. 81)

Surgery (sėr´ jər ē) Opening up the patient's body (p. 288)

Survival floating (sər vī´ vəl flō´ ting) A technique that can help prevent drowning (p. 378)

Symptom (simp´ təm) A bodily reaction that signals an illness or a physical problem (p. 59)

Syphilis (sif´ ə lis) A sexually transmitted disease (p. 276)

T

Taste bud (tāst bud) Receptor on the tongue that recognizes tastes (p. 109)

Temperament (tem´ pər ə mənt) A person's emotional makeup (p. 50)

Tendon (ten´ dən) A strong set of fibers joining muscle to bone or muscle to muscle (p. 102)

a	hat	e	let	ī	ice	ô	order	ù	put	sh	she
ā	age	ē	equal	o	hot	oi	oil	ü	rule	th	thin
ä	far	ėr	term	ō	open	ou	out	ch	child	ᴛʜ	then
â	care	i	it	ò	saw	u	cup	ng	long	zh	measure

ə { a in about / e in taken / i in pencil / o in lemon / u in circus }

Testes (tes´ tēz) Two glands in males that produce sperm cells (p. 156)

Testosterone (te stos´ tə rōn) Male sex hormone (p. 155)

THC (tē āch sē) The psychoactive chemical in marijuana (p. 338)

Thought disorder (thȯt dis ȯr´ dər) A mental problem in which a person has twisted or false ideas and beliefs (p. 82)

Tissue (tish´ ü) Material in the body that is made up of many cells that are somewhat alike in what they are and what they do (p. 287)

Tobacco (tə bak´ ō) Dried leaves from certain plants that are used for smoking or chewing (p. 14)

Tolerance (tol´ ər əns) The need for more of a drug to get the effect that once occurred with less of it (p. 334)

Tornado (tôr nā´ dō) A funnel-shaped column of wind with wind speeds up to 300 miles per hour (p. 385)

Toxic (tok´ sik) Harmful to human health or to the environment (p. 295)

Trachea (trā´ kē ə) A long tube running from the nose to the chest; windpipe (p. 114)

Trait (trāt) Quality (p. 167)

Tranquilizer (trang´ kwə lī zər) A category of sedative-hypnotic drugs (p. 335)

Trans fat (tranz fat) Type of fat from processed vegetable oil (p. 236)

Transfusion (tran sfyü´ zhən) Transfer of blood from one person to another (p. 272)

Trimester (trī mes´ tər) A period of 3 months (p. 163)

Tuberculosis (tü bėr kyə lō´ sis) A communicable lung disease (p. 471)

Tumor (tü´ mər) A mass of tissue made from the abnormal growth of cells (p. 292)

Type I diabetes (tīp wun dī ə bē´ tis) A condition in which insulin is needed to stay alive (p. 298)

Type II diabetes (tīp tü dī ə bē´ tis) A condition in which the pancreas makes insulin that the body cells cannot use correctly (p. 299)

U

Ultrasound (ul´ trə sound) The use of sound waves to show pictures of what is inside the body (p. 160)

Umbilical cord (um bil´ ə kəl kôrd) Structure that joins the embryo or fetus with the placenta (p. 163)

Universal distress signal (yü nə vėr´ səl dis tres´ sig´ nəl) A sign made by grabbing the throat with the hand or hands to show a person is choking (p. 401)

Universal precautions (yü nə vėr´ səl pri kȯ´ shəns) Methods of self-protection that prevent contact with a person's blood or body fluids (p. 398)

Unsaturated fat (un sach´ ə rā tid fat) Material in food from vegetable and fish oils that helps lower cholesterol (p. 213)

Ureter (yu̇ rē´ tər) Tube through which urine passes from a kidney to the urinary bladder (p. 119)

Urethra (yu̇ rē´ thrə) Tube through which urine passes out of the body (p. 119)

Urinary bladder (yu̇r´ ə nâr ē blad´ ər) Bag that stores urine (p. 119)

Urine (yu̇r´ ən) Liquid waste product formed in the kidneys (p. 119)

Uterus (yü´ tər əs) Female organ that holds a growing baby (p. 157)

V

Vaccination (vak sə nā´ shən) A means of getting dead or weakened pathogens into the body (p. 261)

Vagina (və jī´ nə) Canal connecting the uterus to the outside of a female's body (p. 157)

Vein (vān) Vessel that carries blood back to the heart (p. 113)

Victim (vik´ təm) A person who has had a crime committed against him or her (p. 418)

Villus (vil´ əs) Fingerlike bulge that absorbs food after it has been broken down into chemicals (plural is *villi*) (p. 117)

Violence (vī´ ə ləns) Actions or words that hurt people (p. 189)

Virus (vī´ rəs) Small germ that reproduces only inside the cells of living things (p. 255)

Vitamin (vī´ tə mən) A material needed in small amounts for growth and activity (p. 216)

W

Well-being (wel´ bē ing) State of being physically and emotionally healthy (p. 38)

Wellness (wel´ nis) An active state of health (p. 9)

Withdrawal (wiᴛʜ drȯ´ əl) A physical reaction to not having a drug in the body (p. 326)

Index

Federal Emergency Management Agency (FEMA), 389

Females, changes during puberty, 157–158

Fertility drugs, 182

Fertilization, 159

Fertilized egg, growth of, 162–163

Fetal alcohol syndrome (FAS), 161, 329

Fetus, 163

Fiber, 211, 212

Fights, staying out of, 431

Fire
    planning escape route for, 375
    reducing risk of, 370–371

Fire drills, 372, 377

Fire extinguishers, 16, 371–372

Fire safety devices, 371–372

First aid, 396, 408–412
    basic guidelines for, 396–397
    for cardiovascular failure, 403–404
    for choking, 401–402
    for poisoning, 407–408
    for respiratory failure, 402–403
    for serious bleeding, 405–406
    for shock, 405

First aid kit, putting together, 399

Fitness, importance of rest and sleep for, 140, 143

Fitness instructor, 143

Flashbacks, 336

Flash floods, 387

Flat bones, 100

Flexibility, 134
    exercises to improve, 138

Flood, preparing for, 387

Flu, 472

Fluoride, 461

Folic acid, need for, in pregnancy, 161

Food additives, 241

Food and Agriculture Organization (FAO), 478

Food and Drug Administration (FDA), 236, 239, 241 322, 459, 475, 476, 503

Food and Nutrition Board of the National Research Council, 239

Food choices
    effect of advertising on, 233–235
    effects on, 231–235

Food Guide Pyramid, 204–206, 207, 208, 221

Food label, information on, 239–241

Food poisoning, 373

Food safety, role of government, 239, 241

Fossil fuels, 491, 505

Foster family, 185

Fracture, 409

Fragile, 488

Freckles, 121

Freshwater, conservation of, 498

Friendships, 30, 53, 61

Frostbite, 411

Fructose, 211–212

Fruits, 212
    in Food Guide Pyramid, 206

Frustration, 13

FSH, 158

Fungus, 131, 255

G

Gallbladder, 117

Gang violence, 418, 425

Gender, determination of, 167

Generic drugs, 449, 460

Genes, 167, 257

Gene therapy, 352

Genetic disorders, 168, 256–257

Genetics, 167

Genital herpes, 277

Genitals, 154

Genital warts, 278

Geography, 82

Germs, avoiding, 219

Gestation, 160

Gingivitis, 132

Glands, 110

Global warming, 493, 499

Glucose, 212, 298

Glycogen, 212

Goals
    importance of, 56
    setting, 17–18

Gonads, 110

Gonorrhea, 275–276

Good Samaritan laws, 398

Government
    development of Food Guide Pyramid, 204
    role of, in food safety, 239, 241

Government health insurance, 459

Government regulations, 476

Grains, in Food Guide Pyramid, 206

Grand mal seizure, 303

Greenhouse effect, 493

Grief, 40

Groundwater, 495

Growth hormone, 110

Growth spurts, 152–153

Guilt, 33

Gun, keeping in the home, 374

Gynecologist, 453

H

Hair
  structure of, 121
  taking care of, 132
Halfway houses, 354
Hallucinations, 82
Hallucinogens, effects of, 336–337
Hammer, 108
Hate crimes, 425
Hazardous waste, 501
HDL cholesterol, 288
Health
  achieving good, 7
  defined, 4
  diet and, 204–224
  effect of environment on, 5, 486–489
  emotional, 4, 7, 55–60
  hygiene for good, 128–132
  overpopulation and, 196
  physical, 4, 7, 53
  setting goals for, 6
  social, 4, 7
  steps in maintaining, 8
  taking charge of, 17–20
  worldwide concerns, 473
Health assessment chart, 21
Health at Work
  adolescent counselor, 192
  conservation scientists, 508
  dietary aide, 238
  environmental protection specialist, 12
  fitness instructor, 143
  health unit coordinator, 264
  high school counselor, 69
  home health aide, 477
  industrial safety specialist, 376
  laboratory assistant, 274
  medical records technician, 462
  medical technologist, 155
  mental health specialist, 43
  911 operator, 400
  nutrition technician, 223
  pharmacy technician, 322
  resident assistant, 78
  substance abuse counselor, 355
  ultrasound technician, 305
  victim or witness advocate, 423
Health care, 8
  costs of, 470
  paying for, 457–461
Health care facilities, 454–455

Health care professionals, 453–454
  prevention of AIDS in, 273
Health costs, lowering, 460–461
Health habits, good, in adolescence, 153
Health insurance, 457
Health in the World, 92, 196, 246, 310, 362, 438, 512
Health in Your Life, 5, 44, 52, 86, 122, 133, 153, 191, 219, 235, 261, 280, 297, 327, 351, 375, 399, 422, 456, 476, 507
Health literacy, 18
Health maintenance organization (HMO), 458
Health Myths, 9, 17, 35, 36, 55, 86, 87, 101, 107, 131, 143, 159, 178, 181, 218, 222, 234, 236, 258, 260, 271, 273, 289, 294, 304, 326, 330, 348, 353, 374, 383, 410, 411, 424, 426, 449, 460, 470, 474, 494, 505
Health promotion, 461, 479
Health Resources and Services Administration (HRSA), 460
Health risk, 11
Health screenings, 452–453
Health services, 476
  getting, 471
  school, 452–453
Health unit coordinator, 264
Healthy eating patterns, 230–232
Healthy relationships, 61–65
Hearing
  noise and, 133
  sense of, 108
  taking care of, 129
Heart, 112, 115
Heart attacks, 232, 287–288
Heart disease, risk of, 135
Heart valves, 288
Heat, exposure to extreme, 411
Heat exhaustion, 411
Heatstroke, 411
Heimlich maneuver, 401–402
Helmets, 383, 384
Help, giving and accepting, 69
Hemophilia, 256
Hepatitis B, 256
  vaccine for, 261
Hepatitis C, 256
Heredity, 11, 167
  disease and, 11
  drug dependence and, 346
  as risk factor for cancer, 296
Heroin, 336, 347
Hierarchy, 29
Hierarchy of needs, Maslow's, 29, 31
High blood pressure, 286–287, 340
High school counselor, 69

Trans fat, 236
Transfusions, 272–273
Trimesters, 163
Tuberculosis, 471
Tumor, 292
Type I diabetes, 298
Type II diabetes, 299
Typhoid fever, 196

Photo and Illustration Credits

Cover photos: background, © Photodisc/Getty Images, Inc.; left inset, © SuperStock, Inc.; middle inset, right inset, © Digital Vision/Getty Images, Inc.; pp. x, 1, © Photonica/Getty Images, Inc.; pp. 7, 8, © David Young-Wolff/PhotoEdit; pp. 12, 31, © A. Ramey/PhotoEdit; p. 42, © David Young-Wolff/PhotoEdit; p. 43, © Tom Stewart/Corbis; p. 51, © David Young-Wolff/PhotoEdit; p. 52, Pearson Learning for AGS Publishing; p. 59, © John Kolesidis/Reuters/Corbis; p. 62, © Chuck Savage/Corbis; p. 68, © Tony Freeman/PhotoEdit; p. 69, © David Young-Wolff/PhotoEdit; p. 78, © Michael Pole/Corbis; p. 79, Pearson Learning for AGS Publishing; p. 86, © David Young-Wolff/PhotoEdit; p. 92, © Patrick Robert/Corbis; p. 96, Pearson Learning for AGS Publishing; p. 102, © Nancy Ney/Digital Vision/Getty Images, Inc.; p. 107, © Michael A. Keller/Zefa/Corbis; p. 122, © Pixland/Index Stock Imagery, Inc.; p. 133, © Charly Franklin/Taxi/Getty Images, Inc.; p. 138, © Michael Newman/PhotoEdit; p. 140, © David Young-Wolff/PhotoEdit; p. 142, © ThinkStock LLC/Index Stock Imagery, Inc.; p. 143, © Inti St Clair/Photodisc Red/Getty Images, Inc.; p. 153, © giantstepinc/Photonica/Getty Images, Inc.; p. 155, © Jacob Halaska/Index Stock Imagery, Inc.; p. 160, © Eurelios/Phototake; p. 177, Pearson Learning for AGS Publishing; p. 191, © Bruce Ayers/Stone/Getty Images, Inc.; p. 192, © Michelle D. Bridwell/PhotoEdit; p. 196, © Dinodia/The Image Works Inc.; p. 200, © Jenny Mills/PhotoLibrary.com; p. 219, © SW Productions/PhotoDisc, Inc.; p. 223, © Corbis Digital Stock; p. 231, © David Young-Wolff/PhotoEdit; p. 238, © Michael Heron/Prentice Hall; p. 246, © AP/Wide World Photo; p. 250, © David Arky/Corbis; p. 257, © Bill Losh/Taxi/Getty Images, Inc.; p. 261, © Stockbyte/Getty Images, Inc.; p. 262, © Blair M. Seltz/Creative Eye/Mira; p. 264, © Kim Steele/PhotoDisc, Inc.; p. 272, © PNC/Brand X Pictures/Getty Images, Inc.; p. 274, © Jay Freis/Image Bank/Getty Images, Inc.; p. 277, © Keith Brofsky/PhotoDisc, Inc.; p. 280, © Michael Newman/PhotoEdit; p. 297, © Phil Savoie/Index Stock Imagery, Inc.; p. 299, © Mark Harmel/Photographer's Choice/Getty Images, Inc.; p. 300, Pearson Learning for AGS Publishing; p. 304, © Michael P. Gadomski/Photo Researchers, Inc; p. 305, © Jeff Kaufman/Taxi/Getty Images, Inc.; p. 310, © AFP/Getty Images; p. 314, © John Wilkes/Taxi/Getty Images, Inc.; p. 322, © Jose Luis Pelaez, Inc./Corbis; p. 327, © Profimedia/SuperStock, Inc.; p. 332, © Royalty-Free/Corbis; p. 349, © SW Productions/Getty Images, Inc.; p. 351, © Bill Aron/PhotoEdit; p. 357, © Mary Kate Denny/PhotoEdit.; p. 358, Pearson Learning for AGS Publishing; p. 362, © Sandy Huffaker/Getty Images; p. 366, © Dennis O'Clair/Stone/Getty Images, Inc; p. 375, Pearson Learning for AGS Publishing; p. 376, © Jeff Greenberg/PhotoEdit; p. 382, © EyeWire Collection/Getty Images, Inc.; p. 386, © PhotoDisc, Inc.; p. 399, Pearson Learning for AGS Publishing; p. 400, © Lester Lefkowitz/Corbis; p. 401, © Keith/Custom Medical Stock Photo, Inc.; p. 410, © Dennis MacDonald/PhotoEdit; p. 423, © Creasource/Corbis; pp. 428, 431, © Pearson Learning for AGS Publishing; p. 438, © Jean-Marc Giboux/Getty Images; p. 442, © Color Day Production/Image Bank/Getty Images, Inc.; p. 446, © David Young-Wolff/PhotoEdit; p. 456, © Will & Deni McIntyre/Photo Researchers, Inc.; p. 462, © Myrleen Ferguson Cate/PhotoEdit; p. 470, © Jeff Greenberg/PhotoEdit; p. 472, © Larry Downing/Reuters/Corbis; p. 476, © David Young-Wolff/PhotoEdit; p. 486, © George Fray-Pool/Getty Images, Inc.; p. 496, © Andy Levin/Photo Researchers, Inc.; p. 507, © Bob Daemmrich/PhotoEdit; p. 508, © Annie Griffiths Belt/Corbis; p. 512, © V.C.L/Taxi/Getty Images, Inc.; Illustrations: John Edwards Illustration